D1717137

ROMAN COINS

From The Earliest Times

To The

Fall of the Western Empire

By

Harold Mattingly

SANFORD J. DURST
Numismatic Publications
New York, New York

PREFACE

IT is now more than sixty years since Mommsen, doing for numismatists what they would not do for themselves, published his great study of the Roman Coinage, and the time is certainly ripe for a new survey of the material in the light of later research. But the successor of Mommsen must be a bold man indeed not to feel the responsibility of the succession, for Mommsen's work bears the authentic stamp of his genius. The author of this book can only trust that however inferior in power, "ut viribus impar," to the great master, he has not entirely missed the inspiration of that devotion to truth which was Mommsen's most precious legacy to Roman scholarship.

The general plan of the book will appear at once from a glance at the table of contents. There are three main historical periods—Republic, early Empire, later Empire—and in each the material is grouped under three headings: the externals of the coinage, its content and meaning, its relation to the general life of the State. It is hoped that this arrangement will enable the student to find readily any subject he requires. A subject index has been added to facilitate the search, but the detail of the work defies thorough indexing. References to the plates have

been given in the text, but with some restraint, lest
they should prove too serious an interruption. An
independent study of the plates will probably contribute much to the understanding of the text. References to authorities have been sparingly given in
the text, but the names of the books most used appear
in the bibliography. It is only right here to acknow-
ledge my great and obvious debts to the work of many
colleagues in the study of Roman coins and history.
Particularly where results are generally accepted they
pass naturally and without special discussion into a
handbook of this kind.

Many branches of Roman numismatics still present
problems of great difficulty and obscurity: we may
instance the early history of coinage in Rome, the
reductions of the As, the interpretation of Republican
types, the money-systems of Aurelian, Diocletian and
Constantine. In all these cases the author has attempted to bring an independent judgment to bear on
the evidence; where his views are new or unorthodox,
he has tried to state the case fairly and to give good
grounds for the new view. On some subjects it would
be useless to write at all unless one were ready to face
the risk of making mistakes. He has chosen to take
that risk boldly. If this method does not always lead
direct to success, it may at least point the way to
future research.

Finally, I come to the pleasant task of thanking
all who have helped me in the writing of this book:
Dr. G. F. Hill, Keeper of Coins in the British Museum,
who has very kindly allowed the use of Museum coins
for the casts; Dr. A. B. Cook, the general editor of this
series, who, beside much kindly encouragement, has

given me a number of valuable suggestions in detail;
Mr. E. S. G. Robinson, my colleague, who has given
me the benefit of his valuable advice on many points
in the first book; Mr. F. S. Salisbury who, with great
generosity, has read the whole in proof and averted
many errors.

The writing of this book has been a great adventure, one in which no one can forecast success. I can
only hope that its imperfections will not prevent it
from opening up to the student the wealth of the
Roman Coinage and from encouraging others to make
these imperfections good.

H. M.

BRITISH MUSEUM
April, 1927

CONTENTS

CHAPTER IV

THE PROVINCIAL AND LOCAL COINAGE OF THE EARLY
EMPIRE

BOOK III

THE EMPIRE: DIOCLETIAN TO ROMULUS AUGUSTULUS

CHAPTER I

THE EXTERNAL HISTORY OF THE COINAGE: MINTS, MONEY-
SYSTEMS, ETC.

CHAPTER II

THE CONTENT OF THE LATER IMPERIAL COINAGE: TYPES AND LEGENDS

CHAPTER III

COINAGE IN THE GENERAL LIFE OF THE LATER EMPIRE

SELECT BIBLIOGRAPHY

GENERAL

E. Babelon. Traité des monnaies grecques et romaines. Part 1, tom. 1. Théorie et doctrine. Paris, 1901.

Jos. Eckhel. Doctrina numorum veterum. Vols. V.-VIII. Vienna, 1795-98.

Fr. Gnecchi. Roman Coins. Translated by Rev. A. W. Hands. 2nd edition. London, 1903.

G. F. Hill. Handbook of Greek and Roman Coins. London, 1897.

F. Lenormant. La Monnaie dans l'antiquité. 3 vols. Paris, 1878-79.

Th. Mommsen. Das römische Münzwesen. Leipzig, 1850. (French translation by the Duc de Blacas. Paris, 1865-75.)

S. W. Stevenson. Dictionary of Roman Coins. London, 1889.

BOOK I

E. Babelon. Description historique et chronologique des monnaies de la République romaine. 2 vols. Paris, 1885-86.

(Nachträge und Berichtigungen, by M. Bahrfeldt. Vienna, 1897, and also in *N.Z.*, 1918.)

M. Bahrfeldt. Die Münzen der Flotten-präfekten des Marcus Antonius. *N.Z.*, 1905, pp. 9 ff.

Die Römische Goldmünzen-prägung während der Republik, etc. Halle a S., 1923.

B. Borghesi. Oeuvres complètes. 4 vols. Paris, 1862-65.

British Museum Catalogue of Republican Coins (H. A. Grueber). 3 vols. London, 1910.

C. Cavedoni. Nuovi studi sopra le antiche monete consolari, etc. Modena.

Ragguaglio de' precipui ripostigli antichi di medaglie consolari. Modena, 1854.

D'Ailly. La monnaie romaine. Tom. 1, 2 ; 4 vols. Lyon, 1864-69.

E. J. Haeberlin. Aes Grave. 2 vols (text and plates). Frankfurt a. M., 1910.

Systematik des ältesten römischen Münzwesens. *Berl. Mzbl.* 1905.

G. F. Hill. Historical Roman Coins. London, 1909.

W. Kubitschek. Studien zu Münzen der römischen Republik. Vienna, 1911.

H. MATTINGLY. The Roman " Serrati." *Num. Chron.*, 1924, pp. 31 ff. The Romano-Campanian Coinage and the Pyrrhic War. *Num. Chron.*, 1924, pp. 181 ff.

SIR WILLIAM RIDGEWAY. The Origin of Metallic Currency and Weight Standards. Cambridge, 1892.

K. SAMWER and M. BAHRFELDT. Geschichte des älteren römischen Münzwesens, etc. Vienna, 1883.

PRINCE M. SOUTZO. Introduction à l'étude des monnaies de l'Italie antique. Mâcon, 1889.

E. A. SYDENHAM. Aes Grave. London, 1926. The Roman Monetary System (Pt. I). *Num. Chron.*, 1918, pp. 155 ff.

H. WILLERS. Geschichte der römischen Kupferprägung . . . bis auf Kaiser Claudius. Leipzig u. Berlin, 1909.

BOOK II

A. ALFÖLDY. Kleine Mittheilungen aus der Münzstätte Siscia. *Bl. f. Mzfr.*, 1923, pp. 9 ff., 314 ff.

M. BAHRFELDT. Contremarken Vespasians auf römischen Familien-münzen. *Z.f.N.*, 1876, pp. 354 ff.

M. BERNHART. Handbuch zur Münzkunde der römischen Kaiserzeit. Halle a. S., 1926.

A. BLANCHET. Les trésors de monnaies romaines, etc. Paris, 1900.

BRITISH MUSEUM CATALOGUE OF ROMAN MEDALLIONS (H. A. GRUEBER). London, 1874.

BRITISH MUSEUM CATALOGUE OF COINS OF THE ROMAN EMPIRE : Vol. I., AUGUSTUS TO VITELLIUS (H. MATTINGLY). London, 1923.

L. CESANO. Princeps iuventutis : studio numismatico-epigrafico. *Rass. Num.*, 1911, pp. 33 ff.

H. COHEN. Description historique des monnaies frappées sous l'empire romaine. 2nd edition. 8 vols. Paris, 1880-92.

J. DE WITTE. Empereurs des Gaules. Lyon, 1868.

C. H. DODD. The Cognomen of the Emperor Antoninus Pius. *Num. Chron.*, 1911, pp. 6 ff. Chronology of the Eastern Campaigns of . . . L. Verus. *Num. Chron.*, 1911, pp. 209 ff. Chronology of the Danubian Wars of . . . Marcus Aurelius. *Num. Chron.*, 1913, pp. 162 ff., 276 ff. On the Coinage of Commodus during the reign of Marcus. *Num. Chron.*, 1914, pp. 34 ff.

H. DRESSEL. Das Iseum Campense. *Sitzb. d. k. pr. Ak.*, 1909, pp. xv. ff. Der Matidia-Tempel auf einem Medaillon des Hadrians. *Corolla Numismatica*, pp. 16 ff. Oxford, 1906.

FR. GNECCHI. Appunti di Numismatica Romana. *Riv. It.*, 1890, ff. I Medaglioni Romani. Milan, 1912.

J. HAMMER. Der Feingehalt der griechischen und römischen Münzen. *Z.f.N.*, 1908, pp. 1 ff.

SELECT BIBLIOGRAPHY XV

L. Homo.   Essai sur le règne de l'empereur Aurélien.   Paris, 1904.

F. Kenner.   Moneta Augusti.   *N.Z.*, 1886, pp. 7 ff.

J. Kolb.   Die Legionsmünzen des Kaisers Gallienus.   *N.Z.*, 1873. pp. 53 ff.

W. Kubitschek.   Die Münzen der Ara Pacis.   *Oest. Jahreshefte*, 1902, pp. 153 ff.

Valerianus iunior und Saloninus.   *N.Z.*, 1908, pp. 102 ff.

L. Laffranchi.   La cronologia delle monete di Adriano.   *Riv. It.*, 1906, pp. 329 ff.

I diversi stili nella monetazione romana.   *Riv. It.*, 1907, ff.

Un centenario numismatico nell'antichità.   *Riv. It.*, 1911, pp. 427 ff.

La Monetazione d'Augusto.   *Riv. It.*, 1912, ff.

Sulla numismatica dei Flavii.   *Riv. It.*, 1915, pp. 139 ff.

E. Lepaulle.   Étude historique sur M. Aur. Probus.   Lyon, 1884.

A. Markl.   Die Reichsmünzstätten unter der Regierung Claudius II Gothicus.   *N.Z.*, 1884, pp. 375 ff.

H. Mattingly.   The Coinage of the Civil Wars of A.D. 68-69.   *Num. Chron.*, 1914, pp. 190 ff.

The Restored Coinage of Titus, Domitian, and Nerva.   *Num. Chron.*, 1920, pp. 177 ff.

The Mints of Vespasian.   *Num. Chron.*, 1921, pp. 187 ff.

Victoria Imperi Romani, and some posthumous issues of Galba.   *Num. Chron.*, 1922, pp. 186 ff.

The Restored Coins of Trajan.   *Num. Chron.*, 1926, pp. 232 ff.

H. Mattingly and E. A. Sydenham.   The Roman Imperial Coinage : Vol. I., Augustus to Vitellius ; Vol. II., Vespasian to Hadrian. In progress.   London, 1923 ff.

K. Menadier.   Die Münzen und das Münzwesen bei den Scriptores Historiae Augustae.   Berlin, 1913.

A. Merlin.   Les revers monétaires de l'empereur Nerva.   Paris, 1906.

A. Missong.   Gleichartig systemisirte Münzreihen unter Kaiser Probus.   *N.Z.*, 1873, pp. 102 ff.

Zur Münzreform unter . . . Aurelian und Diocletian.   *N.Z.*, 1869, pp. 105 ff.

R. Mowat.   Bronzes remarquables de Tibère, etc.   *R.N.*, 1911, pp. 335 ff., 423 ff.

Le bureau de l'Equité, etc.   *N.Z.*, 1909, pp. 87 ff.

Le monnayage de Clodius Macer, etc.   *Riv. It.*, 1902, pp. 165 ff.

Sir Charles Oman.   Coins of Severus and Gallienus commemorating the Roman Legions.   *Num. Chron.*, 1918, pp. 80 ff.

The Legionary Coins of Victorinus, Carausius and Allectus.   *Num. Chron.*, 1924, pp. 53 ff.

The Decline and Fall of the Denarius in the third century.   *Num. Chron.*, 1916, pp. 37 ff.

B. Pick.   Zur Titulatur der Flavier.   *Z.f.N.*, 1885, pp. 190 ff., 355 ff.

K. Regling.   Nochmals die Söhne des Gallienus.   *N.Z.*, 1908, pp. 115 ff.

Th. Rohde.   Die Münzen des Kaisers Aurelianus, etc.   Miskolcz, 1881.

F. S. SALISBURY and H. MATTINGLY. A Find of Roman Coins from Plevna in Bulgaria. *Num. Chron.*, 1924, pp. 210 ff.

O. SEECK. Sesterz und Follis. *N.Z.*, 1896, pp. 171 ff.

E. A. SYDENHAM. The Mint of Lugdunum. *Num. Chron.*, 1917, pp. 53 ff.

The Coinages of Augustus. *Num. Chron.*, 1920, pp. 17 ff.

Divus Augustus. *Num. Chron.*, 1917, pp. 258 ff.

The Coinage of Nero. London, 1920.

The Roman Monetary System (Pt. II). *Num. Chron.*, 1919, pp. 114 ff.

Historical References on Coins of the Roman Empire. London, 1917.

O. VOETTER. Die römischen Münzen des Kaisers Gordianus III, etc. *N.Z.*, 1894, pp. 385 ff.

Die Münzen des Kaisers Gallienus und seiner Familie. *N.Z.*, 1900, pp. 117 ff.; 1901, pp. 73 ff.

P. H. WEBB. The Reform of Aurelian. *Num. Chron.*, 1919, pp. 234 ff.

Third Century Roman Mints and Marks. *Num. Chron.*, 1921, pp. 226 ff.

The Reign and Coinage of Carausius. London, 1908.

The Coinage of Allectus. *Num. Chron.*, 1906, pp. 127 ff.

BOOK III

SIR ARTHUR EVANS. Notes on the Coinage and Silver Currency in Britain from Valentinian I to Constantius III. *Num. Chron.*, 1915, pp. 433.

H. GOODACRE. The Bronze Coinage of the late Roman Empire. London, 1922.

F. MADDEN. Christian Emblems on the Coins of Constantine I, etc. *Num. Chron.*, 1877, pp. 11 ff., 242 ff.; 1878, pp. 1 ff., 169 ff.

J. MAURICE. Numismatique Constantinienne. 3 vols. Paris, 1908-12.

O. SEECK. Die Münzpolitik Diocletians und seiner Nachfolger. *Z.f.N.*, 1890, pp. 36 ff., 113 ff.

E. A. SYDENHAM. The Roman Monetary System (Pt. II). *Num. Chron.*, 1919, pp. 114 ff.

O. VOETTER. The Coinage of Diocletian, etc. *N.Z.*, 1899, pp. 1 ff., 223 ff.; 1911, pp. 171 ff.; 1918, pp. 11 ff.; 1919, pp. 181 ff.; 1920, pp. 101 ff.

P. H. WEBB. The Coinage of the Reign of Julian the Philosopher. *Num. Chron.*, 1910, pp. 238 ff.

H. WILLERS. Römische Silberbarren mit Stempeln. *N.Z.*, 1898, pp. 211 ff.; 1899, pp. 35 ff.

A very complete bibliography of imperial coins is provided by MAX. BERNHART, "Münzkunde der römischen Kaiserzeit," Geneva, 1922. Further help will be found in L. CESANO's " Bibliografia Numismatica per gli anni, 1914-21," and in the B.M.C.[Empire (Vol. I), pp. lxxx. ff.

INTRODUCTION

TO trace the origin of Greek coinage we have to go back to the very edge of the historical period, to the twilight in which history and myth are blended in indistinguishable confusion. Roman coinage, on the contrary, is a late development—not far short of 400 years later than the first experiments of Greeks and Lydians. From prehistoric times Rome, in common with the other tribes of Italy, had been accustomed to the use of metal as a convenient instrument of payment. But gold and silver were as yet rare commodities, instruments of luxury and art rather than of commercial life, and bronze, the one metal in general use, circulated in the form of rough lumps (*Aes rude*), of varying weights, shapes, and sizes, and bore no stamp of official guarantee. It is probable, however, that the *As* or pound of bronze was known as a measure of value some time before it was actually cast as a coin. A more primitive method of reckoning, which has left its traces down to historical times, was that in sheep and oxen, the ox being valued at ten sheep.

We can hardly be wrong in deducing from these facts a very primitive condition of economic life. That an advanced civilization can exist without a coinage in the precious metals seems to be proved by the examples of early Babylon, Assyria, and Egypt. But in those early days coinage had not yet been invented. Rome, had she experienced any real need for a coinage, had not far to look to find a model. As long, then, as we find her contented with her cumbrous native methods of exchange we may reckon her as an undeveloped,—in Greek language, as a barbarian,—people.

We may reserve for chapter III of the first part the discussion of the relations of Roman coinage to other coinages of the West. All we need here is a general knowledge of the conditions prevailing at the time when Rome first adopted metallic currency. In Spain and Gaul the only earlier coinages are those of the Greek cities of Emporiae, Rhoda, and Massalia. In Italy, Etruria has a coinage of her own, going back to the fifth century B.C., based in its earliest stages on a silver unit of almost exactly the weight of two scruples, later of one scruple, and also on the Syracusan unit, the litra (13·5 gr.—0·87 gm.). In its latest development the coinage returns to a scruple standard (harmonized, it appears, with the litra standard), closely akin to the earliest Roman (Plate XXII, 9-14). Not till the third century can there be any possible question of Etruscan influence on Rome here. It appears that, in spite of their immediate proximity, the two States had no great commercial intercourse. In Campania and districts near it there is a cluster of Greek cities, chief among them Neapolis, issuing didrachms of Phocaic standard (Plate XXIII, 5-9). In the extreme South we find Tarentum with gold and silver staters, the former of full, the latter of something less than Attic weight, and Croton, Heraclea, Locri, Metapontum, Thurii, and Velia with the silver staters only. Rhegium prefers the tetradrachm and maintains it at full weight. In Sicily, Syracuse is the only power coining on a large scale (Plate XXII, 1-3). Under Agathocles we find gold drachms and silver tetradrachms of Attic standard, later under Hiero a silver coinage in many denominations based perhaps on the litra of 13·5 gr. (0·87 gm.). Carthage, at this period, was striking electrum pieces of about 146 gr. (9·46 gm.) and 73 gr. (4·73 gm.) and silver tetradrachms of Attic weight (Plate XXII, 4, 5). It was among these coinages that the Roman coinage grew and developed.

To sum up, we find Rome at first confined to a peculiar system, in which precious metal is hardly known and bronze in rough lumps is the one metal used for exchange. As there is no serious evidence in favour of an extensive early commerce in Rome, we accept this fact as proof of primitive economic conditions. The commercial treaties with Carthage, so far as we really know anything of them, do not very long precede the introduction of coinage at Rome. As soon as Rome, having begun to coin in bronze, felt the need of a more valuable medium of exchange, she had models to guide her choice near at hand.

ABBREVIATIONS

Æ	Silver.
A/	Gold.
Atti e M. Ist. It.	Atti e memorie dell' Istituto Italiano di Numismatica (Rome).
B.M.C.	British Museum Catalogue.
Berl. Mzbl.	Berliner Münzblätter (Berlin).
Bl. f. Mztr.	Blätter für Münzfreunde (Leipzig and Dresden).
Bull Soc. Num. Rom.	Bullettino della Società Numismatica Romana (Rome).
C.I.L.	Corpus Inscriptionum Latinarum.
Cl. R.	Classical Review (London).
Cod. Iustin.	Codex Iustinianus.
Cod. Theod.	Codex Theodosianus.
Gm.	Grammes.
Gr.	Grains.
J.R.S.	Journal of Roman Studies (London).
M.N.	Mélanges de Numismatique (Le Mans, Paris).
Mitth. f. Münzsammler.	Mittheilungen für Münzsammler (Frankfort a. M.).
N.d.S.	Notizie degli Scavi (Rome).
N.Z.	Numismatische Zeitschrift (Vienna).
Nat. Hist.	Pliny, *Naturalis Historia*.
Num. Chron.	Numismatic Chronicle (London).
R. It.	Rivista Italiana di Numismatica (Milan).
R.N. (Rev. Num.)	Revue Numismatique (Paris).
Rass. Num.	Rassegna Numismatica (Orbetello).
Revue Arch.	Revue Archéologique (Paris).
Sitzb. d. k. pr. Ak.	Sitzungsberichte der königlich-preussischan Akademie (Berlin).
Z.f.N.	Zeitschrift für Numismatik (Berlin).

BOOK I

THE ROMAN REPUBLIC

CHAPTER I

THE EXTERNAL HISTORY OF THE COINAGE : MONEY-SYSTEM, MINTS, ETC.

1. Historical Sketch—The primitive conditions which we have sketched in the Introduction could not continue indefinitely. Growing political power and trade relationships were bound to bring Rome within the circle of states using metallic currency ; and the advantages of silver over bronze were bound in the end to lead to the replacement of bronze by silver in the coinage. It is the story of this development that we have now to tell. We shall have to face many difficult problems, over which scholars have spent years of devoted labour. On some points we must still be content to suspend judgment ; but, thanks chiefly to the great advance that has been made in our knowledge of the coins themselves, we can hope to draw a complete and harmonious picture, in which the main features will stand out clearly, even if subsidiary details still remain in darkness.

The earliest Roman coins are, by general consent, the heavy cast pieces of the libral standard, comprising As, semis, triens, quadrans, sextans and uncia, with one constant reverse type, the prow of a ship, and, for obverses, the heads of various deities (Plates II, III, IV). The word As denotes a unit or whole,[1]— in this case, the unit of weight, the pound. We shall have to consider later what this original pound was ; for the existence of several distinct pounds in Italy is conclusively proved by a number of Italian series, parallel to the Roman, in which the As clearly represents a pound, but a pound of varying

---

[1] Or, perhaps, originally a bar (" assula "). See Ridgeway, *Origin of Metallic Currency*, pp. 351 ff.

magnitude.[1]　Of the origin of this coinage the Romans retained
no exact knowledge.　Some attributed it to the great reformer
Servius Tullius ; and even Mommsen so far paid tribute to
this tradition as to assign the new invention to the decemvirs.
But the coins themselves tell a clear story.　The general style
of both obverse and reverse is quite inconsistent with any date
earlier than the end of the fourth century B.C. and, if we work
back from the period when our knowledge becomes really
reliable (268 B.C.), we shall find it impossible to allow more
than forty or fifty years as a maximum for its earlier developments.　A study of the parallel Italian coinages absolutely
confirms this estimate.　Haeberlin fixed on the capture of
Antium by the Romans in 338 B.C. as the critical date ; Rome
now turns her eyes seaward and the prow of the reverse bears
witness to the new direction of her interests.　There are, however, serious objections to this view.　The capture of Antium
did not lead to any immediate development of the Roman
fleet.　The great Samnite Wars were fought on land and, not
till her power was firmly established ashore, could Rome devote
herself in earnest to naval expansion.　Further, the libral As,
as we shall shortly see, was still being cast as late as the Pyrrhic
War.　While it is impossible to determine with exactness the
duration of its issue from the development of style and fabric
in the coins themselves, there is evidence enough to justify an
approximate estimate ; and that estimate will lie in the region
of forty, rather than that of seventy years.　Again, the parallel
Italian series show very little independence of Rome : almost
without exception they seem to show the influence of the Roman
series.　Such a predominance of Roman initiative and influence

---

[1] These Italian issues can be conveniently studied in Haeberlin's great corpus
of *Aes Grave*.　The chief series are those of Apulia (Luceria, Venusia, etc.), Picenum
(Hatria, Firmum), Umbria (Ariminum, Iguvium, Tuder), and Etruria (Volaterrae
and uncertain cities).　Many coins have not yet been grouped in series or assigned
to their mints, but certainly belong for the most part to Central Italy.　There are,
further, five important series, described by Haeberlin as " Latin Aes Grave," which
bear definite marks of Roman influence and are closely related to the didrachms
discussed below on p. 6 ff.　Of the cities casting these pieces, Luceria, Venusia,
Hatria, Firmum, Ariminum, probably all issued them as Latin colonies of Rome.
Iguvium and Tuder issue independently.　The Etruscan *Aes Grave* cannot be dated
very early : its weight is low, and that is usually a sign of late date, and the style
points the same way.　Rome, then, did not borrow from Etruria, but Etruria from
Rome ; and such borrowing is only natural after Rome had established her supremacy in Italy.

is far easier to understand towards the close than at the beginning of the great Samnite Wars. The exclusive use of bronze
indicates that this coinage at present serves no other purpose
than the internal trade of the native Italian states. Contact
with the Greek South, as we shall see, brings silver coinage in
its train. The libral *Aes Grave* is only one step advanced from
the traditional bronze of Italy : the only change lies in the
replacement of rude lumps of varying weight by standard
pieces, bearing the mark of official guarantee.

If 338 B.C., then, is too early a date for the introduction
of the *Aes Grave*, can we suggest an alternative ? Appius
Claudius, the famous censor of 312 B.C., might well have been
capable of such an improvisation, and the appointment of
" duoviri navales," *circa* 311 B.C., and the renewal of the alliance
with Carthage in 306 B.C. speak eloquently of the growth of
interest in naval matters at Rome. It may well be that the
Aes Grave originated in this period. On the other hand,
Pomponius [1] seems to assign the institution of the mint officials,
the " tresviri aere argento auro flando feriundo," to about
289 B.C. ; and the institution of the office might naturally
follow closely on the coinage itself. We shall not be far wrong,
in any case, if we conclude that the first Roman coins were
cast a little before or after 300 B.C.

This first stage of Roman coinage was of no long duration.
Rome, now unchallenged on the Italian mainland, began to
aspire to a mastery of the Adriatic and came into conflict
with the already jealous Tarentum. Pyrrhus of Epirus was
called in to redress the balance in favour of the Greek South ;
but the moral strength and cohesion of the Roman state
proved too strong for that brilliant, but unsteadfast, adven-
turer and the victory brought the Greeks of Italy into complete
political dependence on Rome. The Pyrrhic War was no less
decisive in its effect on Roman coinage than on the general
direction of Roman policy. Rome ceased to be a state of
purely Italian interests and came into close relations with
communities long acquainted with silver as a medium of currency. The heavy bronze was ill adapted for dealings with
these states and during the course of the war itself Rome was
led to issue her first silver coinage, didrachms (Plate I, 1, 2)

[1] Digest 1, 2, 2, 30 (ed. Mommsen).

and rare subdivisions of the didrachm (litrae), struck at various
mints in South Italy, on the standard then prevailing in the
Campanian district (*c.* 112 gr.—7·25 gm. for the didrachm). Along
with this silver coinage were struck copper coins of small size,
undoubtedly representing more than their metal value (Plate I,
3-5). While still casting the *Aes Grave* for her trade with her
Italian neighbours, Rome borrowed, for her trade in the South,
the Greek use of copper as a subsidiary, or token, coinage.
Of the places of issue of these coins we shall have to speak
later : Suessa and Cales were probably among the number.
The coinage is primarily of a military character, serving the
purposes of the war : but it undoubtedly led on to increased
trade relationships.

This coinage,[1] which is traditionally known as the " Romano-
Campanian," has been assigned to the mint of Capua and to a
date from *c.* 335 B.C. down to the war with Pyrrhus. These
attributions must be unhesitatingly rejected.[2] The style of

[1] It comprises the following coins :—
    Didrachms—heavy. (*c.* 112 gr.—7·25 gm.)
        (*a*) obv. Head of Mars, l. : oak-branch. rev. Horse's head, r. : ear of
            corn. ROMANO.
        (*b*) obv. Head of Apollo, l. ROMANO. rev. Free horse, r. : star.
        (*c*) obv. Bust of Hercules, r. : club. rev. She-wolf and twins. ROMANO.
            (Pl. I, 1.)
    Didrachms—light. (*c.* 104 gr.—6·74 gm.)
        (*d*) obv. Head of Roma, r. : varying symbol. rev. Victory, r., crowning
            palm-branch. ROMANO. (Pl. I, 2.)
        (*e*) obv. Head of Mars, r. : club. rev. Free horse, r. : club. ROMA.
        (*f*) obv. Head of Mars, r. rev. Horse's head, r. : sickle. ROMA.
        (*g*) obv. Head of Apollo, r. rev. Free horse, l. : ROMA.
    Drachms of types (*f*) and (*g*).
    Litra. (10·1 gr.—0·65 gm.)
        obv. Head of Mars, r. rev. Horse's head, r. : ear of corn. ROMANO.
    Also copper of various denominations ; with the types :—
        obv. Head of Minerva, l. ROMANO. rev. Eagle on thunderbolt, l. :
            sword. ROMANO. K. (Pl. I, 5.)
        obv. Head of Minerva, l. rev. Horse's head, r. : ROMANO.
        obv. Head of Apollo, r. rev. Lion, r., with broken spear in jaws.
            ROMANO.
        obv. Head of Roma, r. rev. Dog, r. ROMA.
        obv. Head of Hercules, r. rev. Pegasus, r. : club. ROMA.
        obv. Head of Mars, r. : club. rev Free horse, r. : club. ROMA.
        obv. Head of Mars, r. : rev. Horse's head, r. : sickle. ROMA. (Pl.
            I, 3).
        obv. Head of Apollo, r. rev. Free horse, l. ROMA.
[2] Cp. here *Num. Chron.*, 1925, pp. 181 ff. " The Romano-Campanian Coinage and the Pyrrhic War."

the coins suggests not one mint, but several.   It is quite unlike
that of the later coins with Oscan legend which are known to
belong to Capua.   And, again, Capua as a community of Roman
citizens with the limited citizenship should, on constitutional
grounds, use Roman money and not issue in her own right.
The coins are clearly coins of the Roman state : it was only
considerations of military necessity and practical convenience
in finding suitable artists that led to their being struck in South
Italy, rather than in the capital.   As regards date, the case
against the traditional view is even stronger.   The whole
coinage is closely bound together by interlinking of types.   It
looks much more like the coinage of several mints over a limited
period than that of one mint over an extended one.   And, if
Rome knew the use of silver coinage as early as 338 B.C., what
can have induced her to postpone the introduction of her own
system of the denarius till as late as 268 B.C. ?   There are
positive indications, too, that force us to look to a later date.
Many of the types have Roman associations (e.g. she-wolf and
twins, eagle), others appear to belong to South Italy (e.g. the
head of Apollo, dog), etc. :   but prominent among the reverse
types are horse's head, free horse [1] and lion, all of which have
definite Carthaginian associations.   It is in vain that we try
to see a reference to the Campanian knights, for the types show
horse's head or horse only, not horse and rider as on the coins
of Tarentum.   What we have before us is, in one aspect at
least, a war coinage of Rome and Carthage, allied anew (279 B.C.)
against Pyrrhus.   The fighting is in the domain of Rome and
the coins therefore bear the Roman name.   But Carthage no
doubt helped to supply the bullion and is directly honoured by
the use of her distinctive reverse types.   Suidas has preserved
for us a curious statement,[2] that Rome, being in need of money
in the war against Pyrrhus, sought the advice of Juno and was
told that, if she waged war rightly, money would not fail her.
In thankfulness to the goddess for this good counsel, Rome
honoured her as " Moneta " and established a mint in her
temple on the Capitol.   Whether or no the word " moneta "
itself is of Carthaginian origin [3] we cannot doubt that the

[1] For a contrary view, see Ridgeway, *Cambridge University Reporter*, 24 Nov.,
1925, who applies the types to the festival of the *Equiria*.
[2] Suidas, s.v. *Moneta*.
[3] See Assman in *Klio.*, VI, pp. 477 ff. ; cp. *Num. Chron.*, 1910, pp. 1 ff.

introduction of silver coinage to Rome took place under Carthaginian auspices, and that it is no accident that the mint was
placed under the protection of the patron goddess of Carthage,
Juno. The fact that the coins of Cosa in Etruria, founded
after the Pyrrhic War, imitate these " Romano-Campanian "
issues is a strong confirmation of this theory : veterans of the
war, who would naturally figure largely in the colony, would
prefer the types with which they had become familiar. A
reduction of the weight of the didrachm from about 112 gr.
(7·25 gm.) to about 104 gr. (6·74 gm.), which takes place during
the issue of these " Romano-Campanian " coins, may be reasonably regarded as a war measure of inflation ; it is noteworthy
that a similar, but larger, reduction takes place at about the
same time at Tarentum.[1]

The issues of *Aes Grave* on the pound standard continued
unchanged throughout this period. There are, in fact, several
series, clearly Roman in character but distinct from the coinage
of the capital, which are most intimately connected with the
didrachms we have been discussing.[2] Roman coinage, it is
clear, now flows in two distinct channels. On the one side
we have the heavy bronze, cast, as before, for dealings with
Rome's Italian neighbours : on the other, silver and light
struck copper designed for trade with cities of the South.

Contemporary with the later *Aes Grave* of the pound standard are the oblong bars of about five pounds weight, bearing
types on both sides, which are traditionally known as *Aes
Signatum*. The exact meaning and use of these pieces still
remains a mystery. It is certain that they bear something of
a medallic character, possible that they served in some way as

[1] Cp. also Corinthian staters of reduced weight at Syracuse (Pl. XXIII, 4).
My friend, the Rev. E. A. Sydenham, while accepting this view in the main, would
prefer to attribute the introduction of *Aes Grave* and the striking of the earliest of
these didrachms, with Mars head, l., to the year of the alliance of Rome with Carthage
in 306 B.C As this one didrachm certainly appears slightly more archaic in style
than the others (cp. didrachms of Metapontum, *c.* 310 B.C., Pl. XXIII, 1), the suggestion has its attractions. It is a serious question, however, whether we can reasonably
give such wide limits to these issues of silver as 306 to 268 B.C. ; and the resemblance
of style between some of the heavy didrachms and the copper coin of Beneventum
(Pl. XXIII, 1, 2), that must be later than 268 B.C., is very striking.

[2] The " Latin Aes Grave " of Haeberlin, with the series of the Wheel, the
Roma head, the Janus Mercury, and the Apollo. For the connexions, partly of
type—head of Apollo, head of Roma, horse's head, free horse ; partly of symbol—
club, sickle—see Sydenham, *Aes Grave*, p. 54.

currency as well.[1]   The main point to be remembered is that they do not mark a distinct stage in the coinage, intermediate between the *Aes Rude* and the *Aes Grave* itself.

Let us pause for a moment and reflect on the meaning of the facts we have been investigating.   The growth of Roman power and interests, particularly in the direction of the sea—perhaps, too, the personal initiative of the great censor Appius Claudius—led to the adoption of the institution of coinage at Rome in the peculiar form of *Aes Grave*.   Bronze is, as before, the favourite medium of exchange, but it is now issued in pieces of fixed value, recognizable by marks of value and types. Under Roman influence, the new invention is widely imitated by the Italian tribes : in particular, the latest founded of the Latin colonies follow the lead of their mother city.   The necessities of the Pyrrhic War made the need of a silver currency felt, and Rome now issues coins of two distinct systems, destined for distinct areas of circulation.   In Latium and Campania the two systems exist side by side ; the question of their relation to another will require our consideration in a later section.   Etruria does not noticeably influence Rome in her adoption of silver money : it is the influence of Carthage that is clearly traceable beside that of the Greek cities.

After the defeat of Tarentum and the retreat of Pyrrhus from Italy, it remained only for Rome to gather in the fruits of victory.   The conflict, however, with Carthage over the fair island of Sicily, which Pyrrhus had predicted, drew on with a rapidity which no one could have expected ; and for the best part of a generation Rome was engaged in a struggle that strained her resources to the uttermost.   Obviously, in studying the development of Roman coinage, we must make due allowance for the special influence of this great war.   Soon after the successful termination of the Pyrrhic War, in the year 269 or 268 B.C.,[2] Rome, profiting by her war experience, introduced a silver coinage on a standard of her own. It consisted of the denarius, quinarius, and sestertius—the pieces of ten, of five, and of two and a half Asses respectively—each bearing its appropriate mark of value and all stamped

---

[1] See the discussion in Sydenham, *Aes Grave*, pp. 16 ff.

[2] Pliny, *Nat. Hist.*, XXXIII, 3, 13 ; Livy, *Epit.* XV : the measures taken may have extended over two years.

with the same obverse type, the head of Roma, and the same
reverse, the Dioscuri charging right (Plate II, 3-5). The
Roman coinage of South Italy was not discontinued ; didrachms
of reduced weight continued to be struck, but with the new
types, obverse, young Janus head, and reverse, Jupiter crowned
by Victory in a quadriga (Plate I, 6). The coinage of *Aes Grave*
underwent serious changes. There was first a sudden decline
from the libral standard to one of about five ounces ; this was
followed by a gradual falling away towards three ounces or less,
until finally a new stabilization was reached at a standard of
two ounces for the As—the sextantal standard. The As, semis
(Plate V, 2), triens and quadrans were still cast ; but the sextans
and uncia (Plate II, 13, 15), rarely also the semis, triens and
quadrans, were struck, as also were the subdivisions of the
ounce, the half and quarter (Plate II, 11, 12), now for the first
time introduced. Multiples of the As, the decussis, tripondius
or tressis and dupondius (Plate V, 1) (10, 3 and 2 Asses respectively) were also cast in small numbers.[1] At the same time,
in connexion, it appears, with the South Italian didrachms,
heavy pieces of the weights of triens, quadrans, sextans, uncia
and semuncia were issued (Plates I, 10-12 ; II, 1, 2), with special
types distinct from the Roman for each denomination.

Questions of mint may safely be reserved for a later section ;
all we need to know for the moment is that silver was definitely
introduced into the Roman home system and was struck at
Rome itself. Questions of date are vital to an understanding
of the whole matter and must be faced at once. Fortunately
the year of the introduction of the denarius is established by
certain evidences. The early denarii, quinarii and sestertii are
all relatively rare. It is only with the introduction of mint
letters and symbols, which certainly do not become frequent
before the second Punic War, that they become at all common.
The " quadrigati," the didrachms with the reverse of Jupiter
in quadriga, are clearly contemporary with the earlier denarii ;
as only one symbol, the ear of corn, appears on them, we must
assume that they were struck mainly before about 217 B.C. at
the latest. So far, all is plain sailing. With the *Aes* difficulties arise. Our authorities, it is true, tell us plainly that the
libral As continued to be issued to the time of the first Punic

---

[1] Only in the later stages of this issue.

War, and that it was under the stress of that war that the standard was reduced to two ounces.[1] This view of the case involves us in serious difficulties when we come to consider the relation of silver to bronze in the coinage, and modern scholars have been disposed to reject it. Haeberlin, for example, has placed the first reduction, to about five ounces, in 286 B.C., the reduction to two ounces in 268 B.C. The traditional view must, however, be retained, with this one alteration, that the As issued from the introduction of the denarius onwards, though nominally of libral standard,[2] was in actual fact the piece of five ounces which we have just mentioned. Under the strain of the war the weight gradually fell, until finally, at a date probably near 245 B.C., the standard of two ounces was reached and held. With the reduction to the sextantal standard, the process of casting was entirely abandoned, and all denominations from As to half ounce (the quarter ounce was omitted) were now struck. With the difficulties herein involved we must deal later : for the moment we have only to establish the fact. In the first place, our literary evidence is sufficiently inspiring of confidence. From 268 B.C. on Pliny the Elder, in particular, is remarkably well informed about the history of the coinage. In the second place, the coins themselves bear out this view. The struck pieces of the five ounce standard are clearly contemporary with the heavy bronze attached to the " quadrigate " didrachms, the date of which, as we have just seen, can be determined within narrow limits, as from *circa* 270 B.C. onwards. The ten As piece, which belongs to the same system of *Aes Grave*, is most naturally taken to be the expression in bronze of the new silver denarius. Further, we find the libral As still issued during the Pyrrhic War. The Latin colony of Ariminum, founded in 268 B.C., probably only issues *Aes Grave* after its foundation as a colony and yet issues it on the libral standard. The colony of Brundisium, founded in 244 B.C., begins with issues of a three ounce standard. The traditional account, then, must be accepted with the slight modification above mentioned, and we must face its difficulties, instead of trying to prove that they do not exist.

[1] Pliny, *Nat. Hist.*, XXXIII, 3, 13; Festus, *De Verb. Sig.*, s.v. *Grave* and *Sextantarii ;* Festus puts the second, for the first Punic War, obviously in error.

[2] Probably the silver was deliberately over-tariffed in terms of bronze. while the bronze coinage was itself inflated by the reduction of the As.

Leaving points of detail for later discussion, let us ask what policy underlies the facts of coinage just enunciated. Rome found herself after the Pyrrhic War with a dual money system— *Aes Grave* for Rome and Central Italy, silver for the South. Her first endeavour lay naturally in the direction of co-ordinating these two branches of coinage. Into her system of *Aes Grave* she introduces the denarius, into her system of silver heavy bronze, expressing real value, as subdivisions of the As. The silver in the system of *Aes Grave* does not yet play a dominant part ; it was in all probability the " quadrigatus," struck on a standard long familiar in South Italy, on which Rome mainly fought the first Punic War. How far the " quadrigatus " was already ousting the independent coinages of other Italian states is a difficult question, which will receive consideration in a later chapter. There were, however, two disturbing factors in the problem—the difficulty of establishing satisfactory relations between the two metals, bronze and silver, and the need for inflation of the currency to meet the demands of the war. These two together led to the breakdown of the system of 268 B.C. and to the establishment of the new As of two ounces, in place of the nominal As of semi-libral weight.[1]

---

[1] The Italian *Aes Grave* is mainly of the libral standard. A number of reduced series, however, are known :—

Luceria (independent)—As of about three ounces.
Luceria (as subsidiary mint of Rome)—As of about three ounces.
Asculum—As of about four ounces.
Venusia—As of four to five ounces.
Tuder—As of about three ounces.
Umbria (oval coins)—As of five to six ounces.
Etruria—As of five to six ounces.
Uncertain series of Central Italy (Velecha, MEL, retrograde, etc.)—As of about five ounces. Later As of about three ounces.
Brundisium—As of about three ounces.

It is probable that the reduction of the As began at Rome and that these reduced series are mostly subsequent to the first Punic War. The series of Velecha and " Mel " probably belong to the Hannibalic period : the rebels who issued them began with an As of about five ounces and later dropped away towards two. In the Apulian district we find a denomination, the quincunx, which Haeberlin assumes to be the half of an As of ten ounces : it is possible, however, that the As was here as elsewhere one of twelve ounces, and that there were special reasons for issuing the five-twelfths piece.

The silver coins of Populonia, with marks of value XX, X, V, IIV, and weights corresponding approximately to two denarii, one denarius, a quinarius and a sestertius respectively, must be related to the Roman system. As with the *Aes Grave*, it is probably Etruria that borrows from Rome, not *vice versa*.

The next period, from the close of the first to the outbreak of the second Punic War, sees only one important change. The denarius was still struck on the original standard, though in practice the weight tended to fall away. The quinarius and sestertius were rarely struck. The heavy bronze of the South Italian system ceased to be issued, but the As and its parts of the sextantal standard continued to hold the field, though here, too, we notice a gradual decline in weight. The one important change was the institution, beside the issue of " quadrigate " didrachms, of a drachma [1] of the same system named after its reverse type the " victoriatus " or Victory coin (Plate II, 6), and equal in value to three-quarters of a denarius.[2] A double and a half victoriate were struck but rarely. Pliny tells us that the victoriate was " ex Illyrico advectus," and his evidence certainly puts us on the right track. There was known from ancient times in Illyria and Thessaly a silver unit of the " victoriate " weight, and it was undoubtedly the wars in the Adriatic and Rome's increasing interest in the western shores of Greece that led her to strike the new coin. What Pliny does not tell us, though the coins enable us easily to fill the gap, is that Rome grafted the new piece on to her already existing South Italian coinage, by treating it as a drachm of the system, in which the " quadrigatus " was the didrachm. The existence of rare drachms of " quadrigatus " type and of excessively rare " victoriates " of " quadrigatus " weight absolutely confirms this view. So, too, does the undoubted fact that victoriates were struck largely in South Italian mints. Pliny further tells us—and we have no grounds for questioning his statement—that the victoriate " loco mercis habebatur," was treated as a commodity, not as a coin. The importance of this fact to our knowledge is immense ; for, as what was true of the victoriate was presumably true also of the " quadrigatus," a flood of light is thrown on the early coinage policy of Rome. Only the *Aes Grave* and the denarius and its parts were Roman coins proper. The coins issued for South Italy and later for the Adriatic region were commodities intended solely to facilitate trade abroad. The explanation of Rome's dual system is seen to lie

[1] Very rarely struck with the " quadrigatus " reverse ; cp. Pl. I, 7.
[2] Pliny, *Nat. Hist.*, XXXIII, 3, 13 ; cp. Maecianus, *Distributio*, 45.

in the fact that the coinage of the Roman system was predominant, that of the foreign market a mere appendage of it,
valuable for trade purposes but without official standing in
Rome's own domains.   The next stage to be expected was the
elimination of the subsidiary system and the establishment of the
denarius and As as the Roman coinage both at home and abroad.
This stage is only reached during the course of the second Punic
War.   But the fact that already in this period denarii, victoriates and Asses were sometimes issued from the same mints,
shows that it was already in view.   Of special issues for the
new provinces won from Carthage,—Sicily, Sardinia and Corsica
—we know little in detail ; it is probable that they were held
to belong to the area of the victoriate rather than to that of the
denarius.

The second Punic War, the struggle for life and death with
Hannibal in Italy, left a deep mark on the coinage.   Rome had
to place and maintain on a war footing for a long series of years
an unprecedentedly large army, and the effort, as we know
from Livy, was almost beyond her strength.   As it was, for a
term of years there was a sort of moratorium for state debts,
and the armies are said to have consented to renounce their
pay.[1]   In these circumstances we expect to find inflation ; and
inflation we certainly find in a variety of forms.   The weight
of the denarius was definitely reduced to $3\frac{1}{2}$ scruples, and that
of the victoriate in due proportion.   The As was reduced to
one ounce (Plate II, 14), but a change in its tariff from ten to
sixteen to the denarius preserved very nearly the old relationship of the metals in currency.   Moreover, Rome for the first
time issued a gold coinage and, what is more, tariffed it very
high in terms of silver.   In spite of all these measures she was
unable, as we have seen, to meet all her liabilities in ready
money.   The result seems to have been that, after very heavy
initial issues, the coinage was partially suspended during the
middle years of the war and was only resumed more freely after
the " crowning mercy " of the Metaurus in 207 B.C.   The reduction of the As is placed by Pliny the Elder [2] in the dictator-
ship of Q. Fabius Maximus, i.e. in 217 B.C.   It is often

[1] Cp. Livy, XXIV, 18 ; XXVI, 35.
[2] Pliny, *Nat. Hist.*, XXXIII, 3, 13.   The measure, by which it was made, was
known as the " Lex Flaminia minus solvendi," Festus, *De Verb. Sig.*, s v. *Sestertii*.

assumed, but on no certain evidence, that the reduction of weight of the denarius was carried out under the same law. It is reasonable, at any rate, to assign it to much the same date. The gold issues are of two kinds. The first, with obverse, head of Mars, and reverse, eagle on thunderbolt, was struck in three denominations, weighing 3, 2 and 1 scruple and marked 60, 40 and 20 respectively (Plate II, 8-10); Pliny tells us that it was issued fifty-one years later than the first denarius, i.e. in 217 B.C., and that it was tariffed in sestertii.[1] Attempts have been made to find a different occasion for this coinage—the end of the first Punic War or even earlier. But Pliny's statement is admirably clear and self-consistent and the arguments, drawn from style and use of symbols, which have been urged against it, are inconclusive. The second series, with obverse, head of youthful Janus, and reverse, warriors swearing an oath over the body of a pig, is struck in two denominations, weighing 6 and 3 scruples respectively (Plate I, 8, 9). A third denomination, weighing four scruples and marked XXX, has been thought to be represented only by modern forgeries.[2] We have no certain literary evidence for the date of this issue, but general considerations lead us to assign it to the same period as the first. The obverse type clearly connects it with the silver quadrigatus and this coin was certainly still current in Southern Italy as late as the battle of Cannae.[3] Willers[4] has adduced very ingenious arguments for placing the issue in the year 209 B.C., and his suggestion holds the field as the best made up to date. It seems clear, however, that this second series of gold belongs to the foreign coinage of Rome, i.e. the system of the victoriate, which does not rank as actual state coinage. The pieces with the head of Mars, on the other hand, by being tariffed in sestertii, are proved to belong to the system of the capital.

This issue of the victoriate [5] does not extend below about

---

[1] Pliny, *Nat. Hist.*, XXXIII, 3, 13.   [2] But see below, p. 25.

[3] Livy, XXII, 52, 54, 58.

[4] In *Corolla Numismatica*, pp. 310 ff.: a very able paper, though one needing to be read critically. The occasion would be that described in Livy, XXVII, 10, 11, 13, the withdrawal of the "aurum vicensimarium" from the reserve for war purposes.

[5] For references to the victoriate in literature, cp. Cato, *De Agri Cultura*, XV and CXLV; it is also mentioned in the judgment given by the Minucii to the people of Genoa, late second century B.C. (*C.I.L.*, I, 199).

212 B.C. The distinction between the home and foreign areas of coinage was obliterated in a war in which Roman arms were carried so far and wide abroad. Henceforward the Roman coin " loco mercis " ceases to exist ; the denarius enters on its career as a world currency. There was an end, too, of practically all Italian currency independent of Rome.[1] Hannibal and the Italian states that joined him have left coinage in electrum, in silver, in *Aes Grave* and in struck bronze. Capua, in particular, issues an imposing series of bronze pieces, with her name defiantly set out in native Oscan. With the victory of Rome these coinages one and all ceased, and all that is carried over into the following century is a small range of bronze coinages at South Italian towns, all on Roman models, in low denominations and at a lower standard of weight than the Roman.

A stage of Roman coinage here reaches its close. The *Aes Grave* has given place to a struck bronze of much reduced weight, more or less dependent on a coinage of silver. The emergency coinages of gold pass with the crisis that gave them birth. The issues of silver for foreign trade are merged in the Roman issues of the denarius. The mints of this first period will require discussion in a separate section. Rome was always the chief mint for the *Aes Grave* and perhaps for the denarius too. But the quadrigatus and victoriate were probably issued mainly at other mints, and As and denarius too figure among the local issues. These local mints have only been very imperfectly determined as yet : they lie, as far as we can see, in the coast towns of South Italy, on the Adriatic coast, possibly in Sicily and certainly, from the second Punic War onwards, in Spain.

---

[1] Coinage of the second Punic War on the side opposed to Rome comprises :—

    (a) Electrum issued by Hannibal at Capua, c. 215 B.C. (?), with obverse, Female Janus head, and rev. Jupiter in quadriga.

    (b) Silver issues of Tarentum in revolt against Rome.

    (c) Gold, silver (?) and bronze issued by Capua (Pl. XXIV, 1, 3), and bronze issued by Atella, in revolt against Rome.

    (d) Cast *Aes Grave* of Velecha and " Mel."

    (e) Bronze issues of such towns as Salapia and Arpi, during Hannibalic occupation. A coin of Canusium (Pl. XXIV, 2) shows a head on obverse remarkably like one on Carthaginian silver struck in Spain.

After the war we find nothing but small bronze coinage at such places as Brundisium and Paestum.

After the rapid and eventful changes which we have been describing, Roman coinage enters on a long period of quiet and orderly movement, with little of external change to mark it. The denarius continued to be struck at the same weight until the close of the Republic. During the war against the Cimbri and Teutoni, 113 to 101 B.C., the half-piece, the old quinarius, was re-introduced. It was, however, struck with the reverse type of the old victoriate [1] and, in future, bears its name (Plate VI, 9). Its issues were, however, sporadic ; they belong to the period of the Cimbrian War, to the years 90 to 85 B.C. (Plate VI, 10), and to the rule of Caesar in Rome, 49 to 44 B.C. ; on the last two occasions, the sestertius was also struck (Plate VI, 11). The bronze remained at the uncial standard for well over a century, though, in the later years, only the denominations from semis to uncia were struck (Plate VI, 4, 5). In 89 B.C., during the great Social War, the standard was reduced to half an ounce and the As was again struck (Plate VI, 8). Mommsen believed that the reduction was primarily due to the fact that the South Italian issues, which had already been struck on the reduced standard, were now taken up into the Roman. The new coinage, in any case, did not give satisfaction and was suspended in or about the year 86 B.C. The only later issues in bronze of the Roman Republic were due to generals in the provinces and follow varying standards.[2] The general tendency was to reduce the standard even further. The " Fleet " coinage of Antony, struck after his participation in the campaign against Sextus Pompey in Sicily in 36 B.C., seems to follow the standard of a quarter of an ounce : it consists of sestertius, tressis, dupondius, As

---

[1] The victoriate had been a popular coin in the north-east of Italy and this fact may help to explain the revival of its type now. Cp. Livy, XLI, 13, booty from Istria and Liguria. It was now struck under a *Lex Clodia.*

[2] The chief of these are : The Asses of Julius Caesar, struck by C. Clovius and Q. Oppius (Pl. VI, 14), *c.* 45, 44 B.C.—mint uncertain, perhaps Italian ; weight, ½ ounce (Clovius) or a little less (Oppius). The Asses of Sextus Pompey, struck in Spain, 45-44 B.C. ; weight ranges from just under ½ ounce to nearly an ounce. The Asses of Octavian, struck in Gaul, *c.* 38 B.C. ; weight ranges round about ¾ ounce. The issues of L. Bibulus and the other prefects of the fleet for M. Antonius, struck in the East, *c.* 35 B.C. The denominations are marked ΔHS (4 Asses—sestertius), Γ (3 Asses), B (2 Asses), A (As), s (semis). The weights are very irregular, but follow two standards : (1) a heavier with an As of about ¼ ounce ; (2) a lighter with an As of about half that weight.

and semis, all struck in bronze or, more strictly speaking, in the new metal, orichalcum, which was coming into favour. The issues of gold were resumed by Sulla in his Eastern command (Plate VI, 12). Julius Caesar brought the gold coinage with him to Rome, but entrusted it to special officials (Plate VI, 13). On his death, the Senate gave it to the ordinary moneyers, but the coinage of the capital was soon suspended and the provincial issues of the triumvirs and their subordinates took its place. Gold, however, had come to stay, and the Empire of Augustus, from the first, gave that metal a place beside, or even above, the silver.

During the second century B.C. the denarius, following the Roman arms, began its conquest of the world. In the Western Mediterranean, it reigned with few rivals. It was certainly struck in Spain, later, in Africa and Greece as well, and circulated freely in all those countries. In the East the case was different. Rome fought her Eastern wars with the currency of the countries in which she campaigned; the wars with Macedon and Syria did more to familiarize Rome with the gold Philippus and the silver tetradrachm of Athens and of Asia than to familiarize Greece and Asia Minor with the denarius.[1] In the closing years of the Republic, provincial issues, Eastern as well as Western, became more and more predominant; but the contrast between the East, with its abundance of home coinage, and the West, with its almost unlimited demand for the denarius, lasts on into Imperial times. The bronze coinage becomes more and more subsidiary and is mainly limited to Rome and Italy.

2. **Money Systems—Denominations, Metals, etc.**—After this historical survey, the way is now clear for a closer discussion of the treatment of the metals in the successive Roman systems, of the denominations and their weights and their values in terms of one another.[2]

---

[1] Cp. Livy, XXXIV, 52, 5; XXXVII, 46, 3, 58, 4, 59, 3, etc. (booty brought from East).

[2] Apart from names of special coins, a few general words for " money " demand consideration. *Pecunia*, derived from *pecus*, looks back to the primitive times, when cattle and sheep were measures of wealth. *Aes* means primarily bronze coin, then by extension coin of any kind. *Nummus* strictly means " sestertius," then any coin of gold or silver, finally any coin at all. *Nomisma* in verse equals *nummus*, in prose denotes the coin as a curio, not as an article of use. *Moneta*, originally said to be an epithet of Juno, denotes first mint, then at a later stage, money.

In the first period of coinage at Rome, *c.* 312 (?)-280 B.C., bronze was the standard metal, the unit of coinage was the As of a pound weight and the denominations issued were the As (Plate III, 1) and its parts, the semis—a half (Plate IV, 1), the triens—a third (Plate IV, 2), the quadrans—a fourth (Plate IV, 3), the sextans—a sixth, the uncia—a twelfth. The marks of value I, S, ..., . . ., . ., ., leave no possible doubt as to the different denominations. We have spoken of an As of a pound weight : but, as a matter of fact, the average weight of the coin does not exceed about ten ounces of the later Roman pound of 5057 gr. (327·45 gm.). We have either to assume with Mommsen that the nominal standard was from the first inter- preted freely, or, to say with Haeberlin, that Rome originally used a lighter pound, the Oscan (4210 gr.—272·87 gm.), that was only five-sixths of the latter. The Italian pounds of a standard other than the Roman [1] could not conveniently be exchanged against it ; but, as they belonged to local systems and probably served only local purposes, the difficulty would not so frequently arise ; when necessary, Asses of different weight were presumably traded against one another as com- modities, not coins.

In the second period, *c.* 280-268 B.C., the As and its parts were issued as before, but a coinage of silver was added for the purposes of the war in South Italy. The chief coin was the didrachm, weighing first about six and a half, later six scruples (Plate I, 1-2) ; very rarely, the tenth was struck in silver, possibly under the name of " litra." The bronze coins of the series are struck at very variable weights and certainly re- present values above their metal. It is possible that we have pieces of two and one litra, and also the half and quarter (Plate I, 3-5). The South Italian silver was probably only struck for foreign trade and formed no part of the regular Roman currency. The question of its value in terms of the As does not therefore arise, but we shall come again in a moment to the question of the relation of silver to bronze in this period. In the series of " Latin Aes Grave " we find the " Oscan " pound predominant ; but two series, the Apollo and the Janus-Mercury, are also struck on heavy standards, with pounds of 5267 gr. (341·1 gm.) and 5057 gr. (327·45 gm.)

---

[1] See Haeberlin, *Aes Grave*, pp. 37 ff., 179 ff., 202 ff., 214 ff., 241 ff., etc.

respectively. The pound of 341·1 gr. is probably characteristic of Apulia ; the pound of 327·45 gr. is the later Roman
pound. The transition, then, from Oscan to Roman pound,
or from ten to twelve ounce standard, falls at the end of the
Pyrrhic War, perhaps just before the introduction of the
denarius.

With the introduction of silver into the Roman system in
the third period (268 B.C. to c. 242 B.C.), we are face to face
with the problem of the relations of silver and bronze. It is
essential to grip at once the main questions involved. Do the
successive reductions of the bronze at Rome reflect simply
variations in the relation of bronze to silver in the market or
rather do they represent also different methods of treating the
two metals in the coinage—a transition, in fact, from a system
of bronze coinage, through a bi-metallic system of bronze and
silver, to one in which silver is predominant ? The first alternative has often been preferred, but cannot possibly be accepted :
the variations in the relative values of the two metals which it
would imply are past all belief. Soutzo,[1] who will not admit
that Rome ever used bronze as token money at all, is driven
at last, when he comes to the standard of half an ounce for the
As, to suppose that forty, and not sixteen, of these Asses went
to the denarius—a supposition for which there is no real evidence and which is contradicted by positive testimonies. It
is on the other theory then that we must mainly depend. Now
for the facts of the coinage. The denarius was first struck at
the weight of four scruples, the quinarius of two, the sestertius
of one (Plate II, 3-5). The As and its parts down to the uncia,
with the half and quarter ounce added, were now issued at a
standard of about five ounces for the As, falling away by
almost imperceptible degrees to under three ounces (Plate V,
2 ; II, 11, 12, 13, 15). The pieces of ten, three and two
Asses (Plate V, 1) were only issued during the later years of
the series. Now our authorities tell us plainly that the denarius was equal to ten libral Asses, the quinarius to five, the
sestertius to two and a half.[2] The marks of value on the
coins, X, V and IIS, obviously refer to a unit, which can only
be the As. The As contemporary with the first denarii weighed,

---

[1] Cp. Soutzo, *Rev. Num.*, 1910, pp. 443 ff.
[2] Cp. Pliny, *Nat. Hist.*, XXXIII, 3, 13.

as we have seen, a diminishing five ounces. What are we to make of these facts of coinage and the literary evidence just quoted ? The ratio of silver to bronze implied in the equation, 1 denarius = 10 libral Asses, of 1 to 720 has appeared so incredible, that the equation has been almost universally rejected. An escape from the difficulty has been sought either in making a lighter As, the sextantal,[1] the contemporary of the earliest denarius, or in treating the As of five ounces as a new value worth only half the libral and tariffing the denarius in terms of it. The first solution is ruled out by the facts of the coinage : the second is credible, but involves a rejection of the literary evidence and an assumption of a standard for the As not recorded by our authorities. Is it possible to find a solution that will avoid all these drawbacks ? The Pyrrhic War undoubtedly led to a great inflation of the coinage, which was met for the moment by the issue of silver for South Italy, as well as by an increase in the mass of *Aes Grave*. The tendency towards inflation outlasted the war and permanent means were required to cope with it. The unit of account, the As of pound weight, was not changed, but the actual volume of currency was doubled by the issue of Asses, of actual five ounces weight, but of nominal pound value. At the same time, the silver, which was so convenient a method of representing higher money value, was introduced at an abnormally high tariff. It was only issued in relatively small quantities and, like the five-ounce As, may have been exchangeable, theoretically, for the appropriate number of Asses of full weight. The older *Aes Grave* would naturally continue in circulation ; since its nominal value was still equal to its metal, there would be no temptation to withdraw it. For the South, meanwhile, a didrachm of six scruples (Plate I, 6) continued to be struck, worth, as silver, one and a half denarii, but not an actual part of the Roman money system. The bronze of the Southern system, triens, quadrans, sextans, uncia and semuncia, can only have represented small fractions of the didrachm (1/45th, 1/60th, 1/90th, 1/180th, 1/360th), if the same treatment was applied here to bronze and silver as in the Roman system. But it is quite

[1] See here Samwer-Bahrfeldt, *Geschichte des älteren römischen Münzwesens*, pp. 9 ff., etc.—a work of very great value. The view of the coinage there given rests on careful and thorough research, but the literary evidence is unduly neglected.

possible that in this distinct system, higher values were assigned to the bronze.[1]

This new coinage had scarcely been well established before the first Punic War broke out, bringing with it inevitably a new and greater inflation of the coinage. This was effected, partly by an increased employment of the over-tariffed silver, partly by a further actual reduction in the weight of the As. Finally, matters came to a desperate pitch and the State became bankrupt. The unit of reckoning was reduced from the As of one pound to the As of two ounces, and the silver was reckoned in terms of the new As ; this gives a relation of 1 : 120, which was perhaps not very far removed from the actual market values of the metals.[2] The inconvenience and loss caused to individuals must have been most serious ; but the experience of recent years in Europe shows that the infliction of such inconvenience and loss may easily be tolerated in times of national necessity. On this occasion we might suggest a possible hypothesis which would imply a very considerable mitigation of the loss involved. It has been noted that Livy, in his reckoning, often treats the later sestertius as identical with the libral As.[3] Such a change of reckoning must naturally be attributed to the time of a change of standard, and, as the later uncial reduction hardly affected the relative values of bronze and silver in the coinage, it might seem that only the sextantal reduction enters into the question. It would follow, then, that on the occasion of that reduction, the sestertius replaced the As as the unit of account, and that it was equated to the old libral As. To take an example, the creditor for 100 of the old libral Asses (about 1000 ounces of bronze) would still be paid 500 ounces (100 × 5 ounces, the new bronze equivalent of the sestertius), not 200 (100 × 2 ounces, the bronze weight of the new As). The loss would therefore be one in two, not four in five. Attractive as this hypothesis is, it must be rejected, as the reforms of 217 B.C. are meaningless,

---

[1] Haeberlin, *Aes Grave*, pp. 134 ff., regards these pieces as pieces of 4, 3, 2, 1 and ½ *libellae*, the *libella* being equal to one-tenth of a silver scruple.

[2] About the relative values of silver and bronze in the market, much has been written but very little is known. For Sicily a relation of 1 to 250 has been considered probable.

[3] Cp., for example, Livy, XXII, 10, with the parallel passage in Plutarch, *Fabius Maximus*, IV.

unless the As was still the unit of reckoning then. After the inevitable disturbances wrought by the change, the new bi-metallic system promised greater stability for the future ; the need of inflation was now met by an increasing use of silver coin ; inasmuch, however, as the unit of account was still a bronze coin, the As, silver does not yet rank as the chief metal in the currency.

At about the beginning of the period we find the new Roman pound of 5057 gr.—-327·45 gm. as the basis of the bronze coin-age. Haeberlin has maintained that the As of the dimin-ishing five-ounce standard was divided decimally, and not duodecimally, i.e. into ten, not into twelve ounces.[1] But the arguments on which he rests, drawn from the weights of the smaller denominations, do not count for much, in a system in which the weight was continually dropping, nor does his theory fully explain the difficulties. Decisive against his view is the fact that the half-piece, the semis, is marked S as before, not ‘. . . . ., as it certainly should be under a decimal division of the As. It is not even likely that the analogy of the Apulian bronze, on which he relies, will hold : for there it is quite reasonable to maintain that the As contained twelve ounces, and that the pieces of ten-twelfths (dextans) and five-twelfths (quincunx) were issued to meet special local needs.

In the fourth period (c. 242-217 B.C.), the denarius and the As maintained their theoretical standards but suffered a pro-gressive decrease in actual weight. The quinarius and sester-tius were seldom struck and, in the sextantal system of Aes, the quarter-ounce disappeared. In the foreign coinage of Rome, beside the " quadrigatus " didrachm (Plate I, 6) was struck the drachm of three scruples, named the victoriate (Plate II, 6), which shared in the gradual loss of weight of the denarius. In the coinage issued locally by Rome in the Apulian district, the dextans and quincunx (Plate VI, 1, 2) are sometimes struck : the existence of the semis in the series in which they appear is strong evidence against the existence of an As of ten ounces in those regions.

We reach the fifth period (217-202 B.C.), with the far-reaching changes involved by the second Punic War. In or about 217 B.C. the weight of the denarius was reduced to

[1] Haeberlin, *Aes Grave*, pp. 103 ff.

$3\frac{1}{2}$ scruples, and that of the victoriate proportionately. In 217 B.C. the As was reduced to a standard of one ounce (Plate II, 14; VI, 3), but was at the same time retariffed at the rate of 16, instead of 10 to the denarius. The relation of silver to bronze under the sextantal standard was 1 : 120 ($1/72$nd pound, a denarius $= 10 \times \frac{1}{6}$ pound of bronze—an As). The new relation under the uncial standard was 1 : 112 ($1/84$th pound—a denarius $= 16 \times 1/12$th pound of bronze—an As). No serious change of relationship between the two metals, then, is involved. The reduction of weight of the silver clearly represents a very moderate degree of inflation—as high a one, perhaps, as Rome thought advisable where the interests of other States as well as her own were involved. The reduction of weight of the As and the accompanying change of standard are hard to explain ; they suggest a slight readjustment of the relation of silver to bronze, carrying with it no further consequences. This cannot be the whole truth. The unit of reckoning must still have been the As and Rome must have proposed to pay debts incurred in sextantal Asses in uncial, a drastic measure, but possible in Rome's own domain. The denarius circulated abroad too and could not be reduced to the same extent. This fact involved a new expression of the As in terms of denarii. In the soldiers' pay the old relation of As to denarius was retained, i.e. the As was treated as if still sextantal : it was considered too dangerous to cut down the pay of the troops. The silver now became the predominant metal and the sestertius came to replace the As as unit of reckoning. It is noteworthy that Rome is said to have resorted at this crisis to the expedient of debasing her silver. The gold coins of 3, 2 and 1 scruples (Plate II, 8-10) were tariffed at 60, 40 and 20 sestertii respectively. If, as seems probable, this coinage was subsequent to the reduction of the weight of the silver, gold was tariffed to silver as 1 : $17\frac{1}{2}$ [1] (3 scruples N. $= 60 \times \frac{7}{8}$ scruple R., the reduced sestertius). The rate is very high, but this is only to be expected with an emergency issue. To the issues of 6 and 3 scruples we should naturally assign values

---

[1] A relation of gold to silver as 1 to 10 was common from the time of Alexander the Great. In 189 B.C. the ratio was apparently 1 : 10 at Rome (cp. Livy, XXXVIII, 11 ; Polybius, XXII, 15, 8). At the end of the Republic it was 1 : 11·9.

of 120 and 60 sestertii respectively. The pieces of 4 scruples, marked XXX, if genuine (and its similarity in style to some quadrigati makes this at least a possibility), can hardly be tariffed in anything but victoriates. If this piece, then, equalled 30 victoriates, or 90 sestertii, the pieces of 6 and 3 scruples must have equalled 45 victoriates (135 sestertii) and $22\frac{1}{2}$ victoriates ($67\frac{1}{2}$ sestertii) respectively.

The sixth period, 202 B.C. to *c.* 105 B.C., brings no change in denominations or standards. The issue of the victoriate had been suspended before the end of the last period and it was not restored. The new " victoriate " was simply the old quinarius (Plate VI, 9). The uncial standard prevailed for the bronze, but the As was seldom struck in the second half of the period and the lower denominations began to be struck at light weights (Plate VI, 4, 5). The dodrans (nine ounces, S . . .) and the bes (eight ounces, S . .) were occasionally struck (Plate VI, 6, 7).

Our final period, the seventh, extends from *c.* 105 B.C. to the end of the Republic. In the silver coinage the chief event was the striking of the quinarius (Plate VI, 9), with the reverse type and name of the " victoriate." [1] The sestertius, too, was again issued (Plate VI, 11), but both denominations were only struck at intervals and in small quantities. The gold coins (aurei), struck by generals from Sulla (Plate VI, 12) [2] onwards in the provinces, were issued on varying standards. It is probable that at first they were not tariffed at so many denarii, but were bought and sold at market prices. The aureus of Julius Caesar of 1/40th pound (Plate VI, 13) is the direct predecessor of the imperial aureus of Augustus, which was tariffed at 25 denarii. Julius Caesar's campaigns in Gaul brought great quantities of fresh gold into the market and led to a drop in price : the pound of gold was for the time sold for 3000 sestertii. [3] We have already seen how the bronze coinage was reduced to a standard of half an ounce for the As by the " Lex Plautia Papiria de Aere Publico " of 89 B.C., [4] how coinage on this standard ceased by about 86 B.C., and how, for the rest of the

---

[1] By the Lex Clodia, Pliny, *Nat. Hist.*, XXXIII, 3, 13.
[2] Sulla's aureus weighed 1/30th pound.　　　[3] Suetonius, *Divus Iulius*, 54.
[4] It was under this same law that the sestertius was re-issued : cp. *E.L.P.* (*ex lege Papiria*) on sestertii of L. Piso.

Republican period, bronze was issued only outside Rome and at varying standards. We must pause to consider a little further this last reduction of the bronze. As it, like the sextantal and uncial reductions, was effected in a time of war and financial strain, we are disposed to see in it an attempt at inflation of the coinage. The sestertius, the unit of reckoning, was equal to four Asses and the reduction of the As to one half of its value implied a corresponding reduction of that unit. The sestertius, however, was represented by a silver coin, and, as its standard remained unchanged, how could this reduction have been affected ? For there is no evidence for the view that the sestertius was retariffed in terms of Asses. The explanation is probably to be found in the condition of the silver coinage. The issue of plated coins had been reintroduced in mass and the coinage had reached such a pitch of debasement, that no man knew what he was really worth. To pay debts incurred in uncial Asses the Government issued either base silver or light bronze and, as it aimed at making much the same profit in both cases, allowed the same relation to continue between them that had existed between the pure silver and the heavier bronze. This was already a form of bankruptcy, but worse was still to come. The " Lex Valeria de aere alieno " (86 B.C.) provided that debts should be paid at the rate of quadrans for As,[1] i.e. allowed a repudiation of three-fourths of the principal. It was not feasible to inflate the coinage further by debasement and reduction of weight, and recourse was had to an open bankruptcy, in which only 5s. was paid in the pound. The private debtor, no doubt, took full advantage of the relief thus afforded, but it is unlikely that the State, in sanctioning the relief, had any interests other than its own in view. The expenses of an intensive campaign, which did not actually bring in bullion in mass as spoils, could only be met under the Roman Republican system by some form of evasion. The only alternative—the funding of a debt and the provision for its repayment over a long term of years—seems to have been unknown to the financiers of Rome. After the immediate crisis

---

[1] Mommsen assumes that what the law did was to substitute for the sestertius of reckoning (one-fourth of the denarius—equal to the libral As) a new As of reckoning equal to the sixteenth of the denarius. This interpretation is not given by our authorities and seems to be inconsistent with the facts of the semuncial reduction.

was over [1] the striking of the reduced bronze was not resumed, and the debasement of the denarius seems to have been kept within limits. But the unit of reckoning was no longer as stable as it had been and Rome was certainly exposed to variation and, in the main, to a sharp rise in prices.

The cistophoric tetradrachm (= 3 denarii) of Mark Antony was an Asiatic denomination (Plate VI, 15).

The bronze of the Republic was an alloy of copper and tin, with a slight admixture of lead. Brass, or orichalcum, as the Romans called it, an alloy of about four parts of copper to one of zinc, was first used in the issues of Clovius and Oppius (Plate VI, 14) for Julius Caesar and of the prefects of the fleet of Mark Antony. Gold was struck very true to weight and very pure. Silver was struck pure, except on particular occasions of debasement. It is probable that debasement usually took the form not of alloy of all the metal, but of the issue of a certain proportion of plated pieces, with silver envelope and heart of bronze. The standards of weight were only observed with some degree of freedom.

Let us recapitulate our results to see the use made of the different metals in the Roman system. The bronze coinage was paramount from the beginnings down to *c.* 245 B.C. ; from 245 to 217 B.C. silver played an equally important part and, from 217 B.C. on, dominated the coinage. Gold was never a regular part of the currency. The original unit of currency was the bronze As of a pound weight, replaced in 245 B.C. by a reduced As of two ounces. Even after the sestertius replaced the As as unit of reckoning (probably soon after the reform of 217 B.C.), the As remained at the base of the system ; for the sestertius was thought of rather as four Asses than as one-fourth of the denarius. The proof of this is seen in the fact that, as late as 89 B.C., when the State wishes to inflate, it is the As that is attacked. It will be seen that we are admitting that the Roman Republic never reached the point of making its As a mere token coin : that final step was left for the Roman Empire. But we are not committing ourselves to the view that the coinage only reflects varying market relations of bronze and silver. There is no good reason for supposing that these fluctuated very widely. Silver was at first vastly

---

[1] One of Sulla's first acts was the repeal of the " Lex Valeria."

over-valued in terms of bronze—partly perhaps by accident, but also by intention. Under the sextantal standard a ratio of 1 : 120 was arrived at, which, though not necessarily exactly the market value, proved satisfactory [1] : at any rate, a ratio only slightly different, 1 : 112, was deliberately maintained after the uncial reduction. The semuncial reduction, had it lasted, would undoubtedly have converted the As into a token coin, or, alternatively, have led to its retariffing in denarii. Bimetallism was at last breaking down, but, rather than avow the abandonment of the use of bronze as true value money, the Romans preferred to suspend its issue and shelve the problem.

Here, for the time, we leave the Roman reductions of the As. It is unlikely, in our present stage of knowledge, that any one statement of the case will command general assent. But we shall come nearer an agreement as to the truth if we keep firm grip of one vital fact : all three reductions were war measures of emergency and must be interpreted as such. Many interpretations are at once ruled out of court, because they neglect this obvious point of view. Our account probably comes somewhat near the truth, just because it considers it throughout.

3. **Financial Administration, Mint Officials, etc.**—The next question that confronts us is that of the financial administration and the control of the mint. The Senate, as we know from our general history, was in practice responsible for the handling of all finance, while particular functions were reserved for the censors and quaestors. Coinage was certainly no exception to this general rule. The earlier issues tell us little on the subject, but the " S.C." and " Ex. S.C. " which appear on special issues from a date near 100 B.C. leave no doubt as to the authority which controlled them. When there was any question, however, of change of system, the latent rights of the sovereign people came into play : all the changes of which we have any detailed knowledge were sanctioned by definite laws (the " Lex Flaminia," " Lex Clodia," " Lex Plautia Papiria," etc.). The only function that is likely to have fallen to the censors is the letting out on contract of particular duties, such as the supply of metal for the coinage. It was the custom of the Roman State to invite the aid of private enterprise in

---

[1] The market value of bronze in terms of silver set a limit to the possible depreciation of the As.

such cases and it is probable that contracts of this kind were made under the direction of the censors. The quaestors, as we shall see, took some part in the actual issue of coins in the later period, both at Rome and in the provinces. The urban quaestors, moreover, had at all times the control of the State chest, the " aerarium Saturni," and, in virtue of this control, had some kind of supervision over the coinage.

In general, however, the actual issue of coins was under the direction of special magistrates, the " tresviri aere argento auro flando feriundo."[1] The mention of all three metals and the reference to " casting " as well as to " striking " indicates that their duties extended beyond the actual issue of coin to the control of the State supplies of metal in bar form. The office is said to have been instituted c. 289 B.C.[2] It formed one of those minor offices, making up the " vigintisexvirate," which were held by young senators at the outset of their career. At the close of the Republic it came before the quaestorship, but instances are known in which it succeeded it. The office lasted for one year and it was probably filled annually : re-election to it was probably abnormal. Not all " tresviri " struck coins ; we have not nearly enough names to fill the office even for the last century of the Republic, where the coins are most fully signed, and we know from literature of moneyers, whose names are unknown to the coinage.[3] The earliest age at which it could be held was apparently 27. We can now turn to the coins and see how they correspond with these evidences. On one point we must be clear at starting, as erroneous statements on it are wildly prevalent. In the late Republic we undoubtedly find the coinage divided practically into two branches : (a) coinage of the capital ; (b) coinage of the provinces. The latter coinage is largely divorced from the control of the Senate and

---

[1] This is the more usual form : in Cic. *Ep. ad Fam.*, VII, 13, the order of metals is " auro, aere, argento."

[2] The first mention of the office in an inscription is in the " elogium " of C. Claudius Pulcher, consul 92 B.C. (*C.I.L.*, I, p. 279). In spite of the evidence of Pomponius (*Digest*, I, 2, 2, 30), Mommsen does not believe that the office was more than an exceptional commission till about 90 B.C. He notes that it is not mentioned in the inscription of Bantia or in the " lex repetundarum " of C. Gracchus (*C.I.L.*, I, 197 and 198). It is mentioned in Cicero's survey of the Constitution (*De Legibus*, III, 3, 7). Mommsen's scepticism seems to be extreme here.

[3] E.g. the Vettienus, with whom Cicero quarrelled : cp. Cic. *Ep. ad. Att.*, X, 11.

follows laws of its own.   For the period after Sulla this system
is certain : the trouble is that many scholars have attempted
to trace it as far back as the third century B.C.[1]   This involves
a very serious error.   The growth of a semi-independent provincial coinage is simply one of many symptoms of that drifting
loose of the provinces from senatorial control, which was one
of the chief causes of the fall of the Republic.   There is no
evidence, either in literature or in the coins themselves, of any
such independence earlier.   An occasional governor, like Cn.
Manlius Vulso in Galatia, might act high-handedly, with scant
regard for instructions from home : but it is precisely because
such conduct was unusual that we find it so carefully recorded.
Both in the third and second century B.C. coins were issued at
other mints than Rome.   The probabilities are that, whenever
a mint was at all permanent, it was controlled by the Senate
on the analogy of the mint of the Capital.   When the mint
struck for a short time only, the arrangements may have been
more provisional.   But, in all cases, we shall do well to assume,
pending definite evidence to the contrary, that all issues,
whether at Rome or in the provinces were under the central
control of the Senate.   Issues outside Italy may have been
directed by the provincial quaestors, instead of by the "tresviri"
of Rome : the vital point is that the instructions of the Senate
were binding in both cases.   We can now approach the evidence
of the coins.   The earliest coins in all metals (Plate II, 3-5, etc.)
bear no magistrates' signatures.   Certain symbols, however,
appear both on silver (Plate I, 2) and on *Aes Grave* of the
Pyrrhic War and, from about 245 B.C. on, form a regular
feature of the Roman coin (Plates II, 7 ; IX, 2, 3, 6, 7).   While
a few of these symbols certainly indicate plan of mintage, and
others may mark special issues, the majority are probably the
identifying marks of moneyers—perhaps the designs selected
by them for their signet-rings.   Early in the second Punic War,
abbreviated forms of names appear (Plate VII, 1), and from the
end of that war onwards more complete signatures are regular.
The simplest and most probable view is that these are the
signatures of those regular " tresviri" of the mint, whom we

[1] Cp. especially Lenormant, *L'Histoire de la Monnaie dans l'Antiquité*, II,
pp. 272 ff.   It is very doubtful whether the signatures Q and MP stand for
" quaestor " and " imperator."

have been discussing. Whenever the Senate decided on an issue of coins, it would commission one of these magistrates to take the necessary steps, and his signature appears as a mark of responsibility. The three " tresviri " strike singly and not as a body. It is precisely in those cases where more than one name occurs on a coin that we are disposed to look for exceptional moneyers. The actual mention of the title " III vir " occurs rarely, and only in the later period (Plates VII, 12, 16 ; VIII, 15 ; X, 13, 14, etc.) ; the reason for its sporadic appearance is quite uncertain. Probably it was only used when there was something irregular about the issue, when a moneyer was striking outside his ordinary routine, outside Rome, for example, or for some exceptional purpose in the Capital. As a general rule, the signature on a Roman coin may be taken as that of a triumvir, when there is no evidence to the contrary. In 44 B.C. Caesar, increasing the number of the minor magistrates, substituted " quattuorviri " for " tresviri." [1] The new title appears on coins and L. Flaminius Chilo expressly notes that "he was the first quattuorvir to cast" (*IIII VIR PRI. FL.* (Plate VII, 15)). Under Augustus we find the triumvirate again restored. The discussion of the occasions on which coins were issued will be left to a later chapter.

It has been customary to describe Roman Republican coins under the two names of " consular " and " family." The " consular " are the early unsigned coins, tentatively assigned to the jurisdiction of the consuls. The signed coins of the moneyers are called " family " coins because the names and badges of the great families occur on them and because reference to family history is written large on the later types. Both names are pardonable as convenient shorthand terms, as long as their true significance is not forgotten : unfortunately, the use of them has obscured the obvious truth that one and all are primarily issues of the Roman State, and many collectors of Roman coins have probably spent their days under a hazy impression that the great Roman families had some sort of private right to utter coinage in the name of Rome.

So far we have been discussing the ordinary moneyers, to whom the issue of coins usually fell. Many other officers,

---

[1] The denarius of T. Carisius with obv. MONETA may refer to this mint change (Pl. VII, 13).

however, struck coins on occasion. For a long time we have no
indications that enable us to distinguish coinages that may
have been exceptional from the ordinary ones. The gold
stater of Ti.Q. (the great Flamininus) was struck in Greece on
a Greek standard, and is not strictly a Roman coin at all.
After about 130 B.C. we find on coins of non-Roman mintage
the names of several moneyers combined, e.g. M. Calidius,
Q. Metellus and Cn. Foulvius on one denarius (Plate VII, 3),
C.F.L.R.Q.M. on another (Plate X, 3), Q. Curtius and M. Silanus on a third (Plate VII, 4) : there is also a series of bronze
from semis to uncia with the names of Q. Curtius and M. Silanus on the reverse and that of Cn. Domitius on the obverse.
The triumvirs of the mint, as we have seen, struck individually :
we seem then to have other magistrates to deal with here.
Perhaps the most likely explanation is that all these coins were
struck for new colonies, and that the signatures are those of
the commissioners who founded the colonies, or, more probably, of special subordinates assigned to them. Even before
these issues there is some reason to think that coins for new
colonies had been struck. But, as in no single case do the
names on the coins coincide with the names of the commissioners of colonies given us in Livy, we can only attribute
them to minor officials.[1] One issue of great importance, which
has now been assigned with great probability to the foundation
of Narbo Martius, 118 B.C.,[2] deserves special attention. The
obverse of all the coins is signed by two officers, L. Licinius
and Cn. Domitius : these were the commissioners for the new
colony. The reverses are signed by no fewer than five different
men, M. Aurelius Scaurus and L. Porcius Licinius, who issue
denarii, with the mark of value, $\ast$; L. Cosconius, L. Pomponius
and C. Malleolus, who issue denarii with the mark X (Plates
VII, 2 ; VIII, 11). It is possible that the first two of these
were the urban quaestors, the last three the " triumvirs of the
mint." The issue must have been a very heavy one, which
may account for the special arrangement made to issue it :
the serration of the edge may have been intended primarily
for circulation in Gaul. Another issue bearing three names,
those of A. Albinus, C. Malleolus and L. Metellus (Plate VII, 6),

[1] See a fuller discussion in Chapter III.
[2] See *Num. Chron.*, 1924, pp. 31 ff., especially 45 ff.

seems also to have been destined for a colony—in this case
Eporedia, founded by Marius at the close of the great Cimbrian
War. Apart from these joint issues, we find evidence from
about 120 B.C. of officials other than triumvirs issuing coins.
M. Sergius Silus and L. Torquatus strike denarii in Spain or
Gaul as quaestors (Q) (Plate VII, 5)—since their coinage is not
in the capital, probably as quaestors of provinces. In Rome
itself, the urban quaestors, Piso and Caepio, issue denarii in
100 B.C. " for the purchase of corn" (*AD. FRV. EMV. EX. S.C.*)
clearly in connexion with the corn-law of L. Saturninus.
M. Fannius and L. Critonius, as plebeian aediles (Plate VII, 8),
issue denarii in connexion with a distribution of corn about
87 B.C. More common are the issues of the curule aediles.
To these magistrates fell the charge of many of the great
Roman games, and to them was entrusted the issue of special
coinage in honour of such occasions. Among moneyers of this
rank are P. Fourius Crassipes, P. Galba (Plate VII, 10), M.
Plaetorius (Plate VII, 11) and Cn. Plancius (Plate VIII, 19), and
M. Scaurus and P. Hypsaeus (a joint coinage), all of the period
from just before 80 B.C. to 50 B.C. Quite exceptional is the
issue of Q. Antonius Balbus as praetor of Sardinia in 82 B.C.
(Plate VII, 9). Apart from this the major magistrates only
take part in coinage in the confusion of the great civil wars of
Caesar and Pompey : to the beginning of this struggle belong
the coinages of L. Lentulus and C. Marcellus as consuls, with
Cn. Nerius as urban quaestor, and of C. Coponius as praetor
with the triumvir Q. Sicinius (Plate VII, 16). Julius Caesar
entrusted the issue of aurei in Rome to special " praefecti
urbi," A. Hirtius and L. Plancus (Plate VII, 14). Whether
L. Cestius and C. Norbanus, who struck aurei just after Caesar's
death, were " praefecti urbi " or praetors is matter of dispute.
In general, it is clear that the delegation of the power of coining
to other magistrates than the *tresviri* in Rome was a feature of
the last century of the Republic and that such coinage was
designed for special purposes falling within the competence of
those other magistrates.

So far we have been discussing either the coinage of the
capital or that earlier period of provincial coinage in which
the Senate's right of control was still effective. We come now
to the provincial coinage of the late Republic, which is,

3

practically speaking, independent of Rome and is struck by the proconsul or the " imperator " in virtue of his " imperium." This coinage is quite exempt from the ordinary rules applying to the city coinage. Often it bears the name of the governor or general for whom it is struck, with the name of the subordinate who superintends the striking for him. Thus we have coins of C. Valerius Flaccus " imperator " in Gaul (*c.* 84 B.C., Plate VII, 7), and of C. Annius, proconsul in Spain (*c.* 81 B.C., Plate X, 12). Antony and Lepidus strike as " consuls " and " imperators " in Gaul (*c.* 43 B.C., Plate VII, 18). Sometimes the name of the general, sometimes the name of the subordinate is omitted. The coinage of Octavian, Antony and Lepidus as *IIIViri reipublicae constituendae* is almost imperial in form, except that there are three supreme rulers instead of one (Plate VII, 18). Among the generals who strike thus are L. Sulla (Plate X, 9), Julius Caesar, Cn. Pompeius, Q. Metellus Pius Scipio (Plate X, 15), Cn. Pompey the Younger, Sextus Pompey (Plate X, 16), Cn. Domitius Ahenobarbus, L. Murcus, Brutus and Cassius (Plate X, 18) : we shall see more of the detail of this coinage when we consider, in Chapter II, the coins relating to contemporary history. Octavian struck, probably in camp in Italy, as " imperator " during the year 43 B.C. (Plate VII, 20). Among the subordinate officials are quaestors (A. Manlius for Sulla, C. Sosius for Antony), proquaestors (L. Manlius for Sulla (Plate X, 9), Cn. Piso and Varro for Pompey, L. Sestius for Brutus), propraetors (Balbus for Octavian), *legati pro praetore* (C. Flavius Hemicellius for Brutus, Crassusiun. for Q. Metellus Scipio, Plate VII, 17), or *legati* (Eppius for Scipio, Costa for Brutus), quaestors *pro praetore* [1] (M. Barbatius and L. Gellius for Antony), *praefecti classis* (M. Oppius Capito for M. Antony). More remarkable are the issues of M. Agrippa and C. Sosius as consuls designate for Octavian and Antony respectively and of C. Sosius as consul for Antony. There are further coinages of " imperatores," not striking independently (as Cn. Domitius Ahenobarbus) but for the triumvirs (the same man and P. Ventidius Bassus for Antony). L. Antonius strikes as consul during the Perusine War and we have proconsular coins of Cn. Pompey the Great in Spain, A. Allienus

---

[1] This is the usual interpretation of the signature " Q.P."

in Sicily, Brutus in the East, C. Antonius in Macedon (Plate X, 17), and L. Plancus in the East.   To look for order and precedent in a coinage, where immediate necessity or convenience are the controlling influences, would obviously be absurd. This provincial coinage was, in its essence, an irregular development and no fixed norm had been established before the Republic fell and the whole coinage was re-modelled on new lines by Augustus.

It is only during the last century of the Republic that the formulae S.C. and EX S.C. appear on coins.   The difference between the two is a slight one, if, indeed, a difference exists—the difference, perhaps, between an issue expressly ordered and an issue involved in a " senatus consultum " relating to some other matter.   These formulae seem to be used on two distinct classes of coins : (1) for special issues of the capital, entrusted by the Senate to extraordinary moneyers, and (2) for issues in the provinces.   Of the first class we have already had many examples : it is, in fact, a normal thing for the extraordinary moneyer to refer to the authority of the Senate, in virtue of which he strikes.   Thus Piso and Caepio strike coins for the purchase of corn *EX S.C.*, in 100 B.C. L. and C. Memmius, who strike *c.* 87 B.C., *EX S.C.*, with obverse, head of Saturn, were probably urban quaestors in charge of the " aerarium Saturni."   Occasionally the *EX S.C.* suffices by itself as a signature, as on the denarius of the Sullan age, with obverse, head of Venus, reverse, cornucopiae.   The formula is very rare on bronze.   The form S.C. is used, with little appreciable difference : it is particularly common on a group struck between 80 and 70 B.C., probably largely in Spain. After that period it seems to be almost restricted to Rome. On provincial issues the reference to the Senate is found on a few issues, chiefly of the time of Sulla, but not later.   The chief of these issues are : M. Sergius Silus and L. Torquatus, quaestors in Gaul or Spain, *c.* 125 B.C., *EX S.C.* (Plate VII, 5) ; C. Valerius Flaccus, " imperator," probably in Gaul, *c.* 84 B.C., *EX S.C.* (Plate VII, 7) ; C. Annius, proconsul in Spain, 82-80 B.C., by his quaestors, L. Fabius Hispaniensis (Plate X, 12), and C. Tarquitius, *EX S.C.* ; Cn. Lentulus, quaestor and also " curator denariis flandis," in Spain (?), *c.* 75 B.C., *EX S.C.*

Sulla on his Eastern coins makes no reference to the Senate :

but that was only natural, when the Senate was in the hands of his enemies. It is clear that in the first stage of the new provincial coinage the authority of the Senate was still respected, at least up to the point of lip-service ; afterwards it ceased to be regarded at all. Another set of formulae, often found in connexion with the *S.C.* and *EX S.C.*, refers to the source from which the bullion for the coinage is drawn. We find *publice* (*P., PV.*, Plate VIII, 4), *publice ex S.C.* (Plate VIII, 1), *de thesauro* (*D.T.*, Plate VIII, 5), *argento publico* (*ARG. PVB., EX A.P. EX A. PV.*, Plate VIII, 3). The use of the stocks of bullion in the treasury for the issue of coinage is obviously a measure of emergency : all our examples come from the days of the Cimbrian and Social Wars. In the ordinary course, bullion was evidently provided from the general market and was simply issued in the form of çoin by the State. The formulae *E.L.P.* and *L.P. D.A.P.* (Plate VIII, 2) mark the coinage—sestertii and bronze—that was issued under the provision of the " Lex Plautia Papiria de Aere Publico."

All the officials of the mint whom we discussed in a recent section were of the administrative grade : that is to say, they arranged issues and took the responsibility for them, but were presumably not concerned in the technical details of the coinage. If we say less about the internal organization of the mint it is not because our interest but because our knowledge fails. The little that we know about the ways of a Roman mint will be found below in the first chapter on the Early Empire. For the Republic we can only say that something not dissimilar was probably the rule then. With the exception of the *Aes Grave* before the sextantal reduction, all Republican coins were struck ; but the blanks were always produced by casting. The plating of silver coins (much more rarely of gold coins) was a practice of the mint, not exclusively at any rate of the forger. The precise method by which the close envelope of precious metal was fastened down over the base core is still a secret. The serration or cutting of the edge of the denarii, the ostensible object of which was to show the most casual observer that the metal was silver all through, was apparently produced by a succession of cuts with a chisel before the coin was struck. The cuts are so irregular in every way— in depth, in angle, in distance from one another—that it seems impossible to attribute them to any mechanical device. The labour involved in making them by hand is immense ; but, as slave labour was undoubtedly employed at the mint, it is perhaps possible that this may have been the actual method employed.

We have a large material for the study of the inner workings of the mint in the various marks—numbers, fractions, letters and symbols, which appear freely on coins of the period from *c.* 125 B.C. to 66 B.C. [1] (Plate VIII, 6-10, 12-14, etc.). They are common on silver, very rare on any other metal. A close special study of these marks would probably yield us very valuable results. For the present, we must content ourselves with a few general observations. The general purpose implied in them was certainly the effective control of the mint by the definite identification of the work of particular artists and officinae. Some of the marks clearly denote dies—i.e. all coins with the same mark are from the same die. This, however, is not always the case, and we must look for other explanations. The marks may denote periods of time—the work produced in a particular month or even perhaps on a particular day. Where we have a symbol accompanied by a further mark, such as a number or a letter, the symbol may be the signature of a foreman in charge, the letter or number the mark of a workman under his control. It is much to be hoped that some scholar will find time to devote to this very fascinating problem, which promises to throw a flood of fresh light on Republican coinage.

It is an interesting subject of speculation, what part of the work of the mint was directly performed under State management and what part was left to private enterprise. On general analogies it is probable that the task of supplying bullion was let out on contract. A private company would undertake to furnish a given amount of gold, silver or bronze at a rate fixed by tender. The contracting out of such duties would naturally fall to the censor. The preparation of the dies and the striking of the coins were probably done by a staff of public slaves, with freemen in charge—the whole staff being answerable to the masters of the mint.

[1] The earliest moneyer to show them is N. Fabius Pictor, the latest C. Piso Frugi.

The cutting of the dies was the work of trained workmen, who will often have been of Greek origin. The number of these workmen will never have been very large and the style of a mint is often so uniform over a period of years that we may recognize the individual work of an artist or his school. By " art " or " style " in coins we generally denote this individual quality, and in it we have an important criterion for questions of mintage. By " fabric " we denote rather the subordinate features of the make of a coin—the particular method of striking, the size of the flan and die ; and with " fabric " rather than with " art " we may class such details as particular forms of lettering, which depend less on individual gift and more on the local customs of a mint. Fabric is an even better criterion than art for mintage ; an individual artist may easily move from mint to mint—local peculiarities of fabric tend to change but slowly. On art and fabric considered together we have to rely for the first step of our determination of mints— the dividing off of different series of coins. A few examples must suffice here. The earliest *Aes Grave* is clearly distinct in style and fabric from the five-ounce series that follows it. The didrachms of the Pyrrhic War are closely related to some of the earliest denarii and to the struck pieces of the five-ounce standard. The local issues of the third century B.C., distinguished by mint letters or symbols, show a great variety of distinct styles. The main series of denarii, which we may assume to be of Roman mintage, shows a development of artistic treatment which helps us to fix the dates. The treatment of the helmet of Roma, of her hair, of her ear-ring varies, the Dioscuri on horseback on the reverse are rendered in a variety of styles. A little later, when we have no longer mint signatures to help us, style and fabric enable us to separate off series of denarii, so unlike the ordinary Roman, that we may safely attribute them to foreign mintage, in such provinces as Spain, Africa and Gaul. One set of denarii, struck round about 120 B.C., is distinguished by a very peculiar fabric, small dies and very neat and small figures. In the last century of the Republic the art reaches a very high level, particularly on the denarii of L. Torquatus (Plate X, 13), M. Piso (Plate VIII, 18) and M. Lepidus. It seems certain that Lucullus and Pompey brought back with them from the East Greek artists who made a permanent mark on the style of the Roman mint. The serration of the edge is a striking point of fabric which enables us to draw important conclusions about date and mintage (Plate VIII, 11-15).

Roman art, we know, was at no stage of its development free from Greek tradition, and the inspiration of the finest products of the Roman mint is undoubtedly Greek. We find, however, elements that must be put down to other sources. The hard, dry and precise style which is seen on many denarii of the late Republic seems to be peculiarly Italian, and peculiarities noted on coins of Spanish mintage may reasonably be attributed to local influence. In the main, the influence of Rome and her provinces is seen more in the direction given to art, for instance in the choice of portraits and actual events for illustration, than in the art itself.

Questions of epigraphy are chiefly interesting in their bearing on dates and will be reserved for the section that deals with them. The discussion of the occasions on which coinage was issued will find its natural place, when we consider the part played by coinage in the life of the Roman State.

4. Chronology and Mints—As long as coins of the Roman Republic are classed under the name of the magistrates who issue them and arranged in alphabetical order of names, a serious study of the coinage is impossible. Dates and mints must be considered. With the most important form of scientific classification, dating, much progress has been made and the main outlines have been approximately drawn ; much still remains to be done in the way of correcting and rendering more precise current attributions. The question of mints was fully treated for the first time in Grueber's *Catalogue of the Coins of the Roman Republic in the British Museum :* but much still remains to be done. We will first review in succession the main criteria which bear on the date of a Roman coin, then give some examples of the methods of classification by mints.

We begin with the tests of date :—

(1) *Weights*—The bronze coins can invariably be assigned to their approximate period by their weight alone. In the case of the silver the denarii of the four-scruple standard are all early, the denarii that are definitely of the $3\frac{1}{2}$-scruple standard are in no case earlier than the second Punic War.

(2) *Types*—We shall see in Chapter II that Roman types develop according to certain ascertainable laws. In the presence or absence of the head of Roma on the obverse or of the Dioscuri or chariot type on the reverse we have always valuable evidence of period.

(3) *Symbols, etc.*—The symbol as the sole signature on a coin belongs mainly to the period from *c.* 245 B.C. to 212 B.C. The symbol as a subsidiary signature, in addition to moneyers' names, is common in the second century B.C. The elaborate series of symbols, letters and numbers as die or series-marks characterizes the period from *c.* 125 B.C. to 66 B.C.

(4) *Mark of value*—On the bronze, marks of values for the different denominations are normal throughout. On the denarius, the original mark, X, is found on all coins for many years after 217 B.C., when its tariff in Asses was raised to sixteen. The mark XVI occurs on a small group struck round about 150-145 B.C. The mark X̵ (X differentiated by a bar as a mark of value) follows, but the old mark X continues to appear —though probably not on coins of the Roman mint. After about 110 B.C. marks of value are usually absent from the silver. On the bronze the mark is normally on both sides, on the silver on the obverse only.

(5) *Epigraphy and other details*—The word *ROMA* appears first on the reverse of the denarius. It is usually in a sort of oblong cartouche and, in the early issues, is sometimes almost incuse, i.e. the letters are not raised, but are sunk below the surface of the coin. For the detailed study of form of letters and numbers we must refer to the particulars given in a good catalogue. The form Λ for A and Ʌ for L are decidedly archaic. Γ, with the square top, is earlier than Γ: the closed P is quite abnormal. Other curious features, such as the use of K for C before A (cp. Kalenus) of EI for long I (cp. *PREIVERNVM*), of XS for X (cp. *MAXSVMVS*), of V for Greek Υ (cp. *SIBVLLA*), the dropping of the double consonant (cp. *CINA, PILIPVS*), or of the aspirate (cp. *PILIPVS, CETEGUS*) are of interest, but throw no special light on chronology. Among numerals, we may note the forms for 50, ↓ early and also, chiefly in a modified form ⊥, later, ⊥ from about 88 B.C. on.

(6) *Name of moneyers*—In general, the most abbreviated

forms, with initial letters or monograms or a curtailed form of one name only, are the oldest. The full form, with three names, only dates from a little after 200 B.C.

(7) *Careers of moneyers*—The moneyer could not hold office before the age of 27, and a period of years, more or less fixed by custom, must intervene before he could reach the highest offices of the State. When, therefore, we can find reason for identifying a moneyer with a praetor or consul of known date, we can reckon back to within a little his actual year of office as moneyer. Unfortunately, certain identifications are not very easy to find. A particular case will help to make the point clear. A certain C. Pulcher strikes denarii, which, on general grounds, must be assigned to a date near 100 B.C. We have an inscription (*C.I.L.*, I², p. 200) of a C. Claudius Pulcher, who was consul in 92 B.C., after having previously held the offices of quaestor, triumvir of the mint, curule aedile in 99 B.C., and praetor in 95 B.C. Evidently the two men are the same : the year of the coins must be a little before 100 B.C., not 91, the date to which Grueber (*B.M.C. Rep.*, I, p. 198 f.) assigns them.

(8) *Style and fabric*—These criteria are always of the first importance, and must be studied in every case of doubt.

(9) *Definite reference to contemporary historical events*—For illustration of this we must refer to Chapter II. Here we need only say that such references are far commoner than has been supposed and will often determine the date of a coin beyond question.

(10) *The use of a number of these criteria in combination*—This, of course, is the way in which they should ordinarily be used, but a single set of examples will make the point clearer. A certain C. Curiatius Trigeminus strikes coins with mark of value X, reverse type, Juno in quadriga. Another man of the same name, who adds to his name the letter F, was clearly his son. He strikes with the same mark of value X and the same reverse type. Contemporary with this second Curiatius is a C. Augurinus, who strikes with mark of value X and reverse type, a memorial to an ancestor in Rome. His son, Ti. Minucius Augurinus, repeats this reverse, with mark of value X, in a style appreciably later. The date of the second Augurinus can be fixed on grounds of style and association with other moneyers to the period *c.* 123 B.C. We can then reckon back

something like a generation to the earlier Augurinus and the second Curiatius, and again another generation to the first Curiatius. By fixing approximate dates for this string of moneyers, we obtain at once a most valuable control of our dating for the period from about 155 B.C. to 125 B.C. ; for round each moneyer are spread issues of other moneyers, which can be determined roughly by relation to him.

(11) *Hoards.*—We come to the most objective, and, there-fore, the most valuable of all evidences of date, that of hoards. In ancient times, when no highly developed system of banking existed, the concealment of money in the earth was a normal feature in life. But naturally the practice was very much commoner in times of danger than in times of peace ; and, as only a very small proportion of ancient hoards actually come to our knowledge, times of profound peace hardly figure in our records of finds. The Republican hoards that have come down to us are mainly of silver : for the dating of the bronze prac-tically no evidence of this kind is available. Often denarii only occur, occasionally quinarii or victoriates are intermixed with them. The great value of a hoard as evidence is just this, that, when once we have determined the date of burial, we have a limiting date for all issues contained in it : all must obviously have been prior to the burial. In practice, of course, the case is not always quite simple. Records of the find may never have been complete or may have been lost. " Stragglers " may have intruded—that is to say, coins of a date certainly later than the main hoard, but confounded with the hoard either by sheer accident or by the carelessness of some un-trained observer. And, again, there is never any certainty that a hoard gives us a complete picture of the coinage up to its burial : even among the latest issues there are likely to be chance omissions. But, when a number of hoards of the same period are available for study, we can more or less eliminate these sources of error and place our chronology on a sure founda-tion.

Unfortunately, the evidence of finds is scarcely available before about 122 B.C. In the third century B.C. silver was still a rare metal in Roman coinage and denarii were certainly not hoarded in mass : otherwise more hoards must have come down to us to-day. After the Hannibalic War, Italy was free from campaigns for nearly a hundred years ; the only province in which hoards are likely to have been frequent is Spain, and none of the early second century happen to have come down to us. The last period of the Republic was never free from wars or rumours of wars and hoards are correspondingly plentiful. For the years after 120 B.C., then, our chronology has one new basis, which it lacked before then. For the study of hoards the list in Grueber, *B.M.C. Rep.*, Vol. III, pp. 2 ff., will be found invaluable : [1] it has only one serious blemish—the issues of *L. LIC. CN. DOM.* are erroneously assigned to 92 B.C. (the year in which those two men were censors) and the chronology of the period has been warped to correspond. Let us cast a rapid glance over the material there collected. Three finds seem to be closely connected with the revolt of Fregellae in 125 B.C., though a little later than that date. This is intelligible enough, for the discontents of the Italians and the reaction on the part of the Romans lasted on beyond that year. Then follows a large group of finds, associated with different periods of the great

---

[1] It seems to be only right to add a supplementary list of finds, mainly published since Grueber's work appeared :—

Finds of *Aes* (seldom sufficiently well reported to be of much value) : Arpino (*Notizie degli Scavi*, 1913, pp. 448 ff.) ; Avola (*Rivista Italiana*, 1911, pp. 283 ff.) ; Feniglia and Ansedonia (*Atti e Mem. Ist Ital.*, II, pp. 181 ff.) ; Giulia Nova (*N.d.S.*, 1900, p. 7) ; Orbetello (*Berliner Münzblätter*, 1916, pp. 605 ff.) ; Ostia (*R. It.*, 1911, pp. 275 ff.) ; Pietrabbondante (*N.d.S.*, 1900, pp. 645 ff.) ; San Giorgio di Nogaro (*N.d.S.*, 1917, pp. 235 ff.) ; Solmona in Samnium (*Berl. Mzbl.*, 1916, p. 605) ; Via Prenestina (L. Cesano, *La stipe di uno antico sacrario*).

Finds of silver (in chronological order) : Aldone in Sicily, third century B.C., victoriates (*N.d.S.*, 1915, p. 134) ; Orzivecchi, third century B.C., denarii and victoriates (*N.d.S.*, 1921, p. 297 ; *R. It.*, 1921, pp. 67 ff.) ; Calatia, *c.* 118 B.C. (*N.d.S.*, 1914, pp. 172 ff.) ; Maddalona, denarii and victoriates, *c.* 115 B.C. (*N.d.S.*, 1914, pp. 172 ff.) ; Sierra Morena, *c.* 102 B.C. (*Num. Chron.*, 1921. pp. 179 ff.) ; Centenillo, *c.* 102 B.C. (*Num. Chron.*, 1912, pp. 63 ff.) ; Imola, *c.* 100 B.C., denarii and victoriates (*N.d.S.*, 1916, pp. 159 ff.) ; Crognaletto, denarii and quinarii, *c.* 93 B.C. (*N.d.S.*, 1900, p. 43) ; Peiraeus, *c.* 86 B.C., denarii (MS. description in British Museum) ; Berchidda in Sardinia, *c.* 82 B.C. (*N.d.S.*, 1918, pp. 155 ff.) ; Alba di Massa, *c.* 81 B.C. (*R. It.*, 1913, pp. 23 ff.) ; Rio Marina, *c.* 79 B.C. (*Atti e Mem. Ist It.*, I, pp. 196 ff.) ; Fragagnana, *c.* 74 B.C. (*N.d.S.*, 1907, pp. 95 ff.) ; Broni, denarii and quinarii, *c.* 55 B.C. (*N.d.S.*, 1902, pp. 475 ff.) ; Caraleone, denarii and quinarii, *c.* 54 B.C. (*N.d.S.*, 1908, pp. 91 ff.) ; Mornico Losana, *c.* 38 B.C. (*R. It.*, 1919, pp. 205 ff. ; *N.d.S.*, 1921, pp. 298 ff.) ; Terni, denarii and bronze, *c.* 38 B.C. (*R. It.*, 1915, pp. 1 ff.) ; Cerriolo, *c.* 29 B.C. (*Atti e Mem. Ist It.*, II, pp. 199 ff.) ; Villatte. denarii and Gallic silver, *c.* 25 B.C. (*Rev. Num.*, 1921, p. xxxi) ; Sante Stefano Roero, denarii, half-victoriates, quinarii, *c.* 18 B.C. (*N.d.S.*, 1914, pp. 86 ff.) ; Fornacette, denarii and quinarii, *c.* A.D. 5 (*Blätter für Münzfreunde*, 1923, pp. 433 ff.) ; Vico Pisano, denarii and quinarii, *c.* A.D. 5 (*N.d.S.*, 1920, pp. 240 ff.).

Cimbrian War. Nearly all Republican finds of which we have knowledge are Italian, but here appears a group of finds from Spain : they form a definite historical evidence of the great invasion of that province by the Cimbri in 103 B.C. A short interval and the Social War in Italy produces a fresh batch of hoards, followed by hoards closely connected with the wars of the Sullan and Marian factions and the Slave War of Spartacus. After the crushing of Spartacus, Italy had peace for nearly a generation : the short crisis of the Catilinarian conspiracy appears to have left no such numismatic record. With the great Civil War of Caesar and Pompey our hoards recommence, and from about 50 B.C. to the end of the Republic hardly a year but is represented by some piece of such evidence.

A glance at a single find will give a good idea of the use that can be made of this class of evidence. The *Monte Codruzzo* hoard consisted of some 5000 pieces, and as many as 4734 of them were examined by Borghesi and described by Cavedoni (*Ripostigli*, p. 19 f.). It represents, then, an extensive piece of evidence, reported by highly competent observers. The presence of a number of coins in mint condition enables us to detect the latest issues included in it. Among these are thirteen coins of Q. Antonius Balbus, appointed praetor of Sardinia by the Marians in 82 B.C. There are also coins of C. Annius, who was sent by Sulla to Spain to oppose Sertorius in the same year. These are the latest issues that we can trace, and we may date the hoard with high probability to the end of 82 B.C. As a very high percentage of all earlier Republican denarii were included in this hoard, its evidence for dating is obviously very great.

Finally, we come to the question of mintage—the determination of the places at which Roman Republican coins were struck. The importance of this study must not be exaggerated, for all Roman Republican coins, wherever struck, were coins of the Roman State and, from some points of view, the exact place of striking is an irrelevant detail. The study of mints, however, possesses an importance of its own, and it is to be feared that the prevalent neglect of it is due rather to its inherent difficulties than to a real conviction of its uselessness. For one thing, it helps greatly to clear up difficulties in chronology. As long as we try to arrange in chronological sequence coins that are really contemporary issues of several mints, we fall into hopeless confusion. A good example of this is seen in the silver of the Pyrrhic War, which, instead of being assigned to several mints over a short period, has been spread out over a long term of years. Again, the exact significance of some types is completely missed until we can determine their place of origin. There are denarii struck for Sertorius by his moneyers in Spain, on which definite historical references to his career have till recently been overlooked, just because their place of mintage was unknown. Add to this the natural interest that the specialist has in the right arrangement and grouping of his material and it becomes apparent that mints deserve the most careful study. Few students of the coinage have failed to contribute something to the subject, but the one work yet published in which mints have been considered in their true importance is Grueber's *Catalogue of the Republican Coins in the British Museum.* It is based on the pioneer work of Count de Salis, in the sixties of last century, and represents a decided advance on anything previously attempted. The technical skill shown in classing issues by style and fabric is very high. In the interpretation of the results obtained by numismatic study, there are some more questionable points. In particular, Count de Salis attributed to two Italian mints, a Central and a Southern, a number of issues of the second century B.C., which, though certainly not of Rome, are far more likely to belong to the Western provinces than to secondary Italian mints. Actual mint marks in the form of initial letters, abbreviated town names or symbols, are hardly met with except in the third century B.C. In the first century B.C. the circumstances of many issues, the officials signing them, the types, etc., prove provincial origin. But a large number of cases remains, in which closer study is needed to resolve the question ; and on the principles that govern this study a few words may be needed. The chief criteria are :—

(*a*) *Style and fabric*—It is unnecessary to repeat here what has already been said above. But we must insist on the fact that these tests alone are often quite sufficient to prove that an issue is of exceptional mintage, i.e. not struck at the main mint of the capital. They cannot, as a rule, help us much to determine the exact place of issue.

(b) *Allusions of types*—We have to walk warily here, for a local reference does not necessarily imply local mintage. There are, however, cases in which types help to confirm an attribution made probable on other grounds.

(c) *Names of moneyers*—A most important evidence for the later period but seldom of use earlier, when we cannot identify the moneyer with sufficient accuracy.

(d) *Mark of value*—In the period from the introduction of the mark of value X̶ to its disappearance from the coinage, this form of evidence is important. We saw above that the old form X still persists after the introduction of X̶. It is a fairly safe inference that the Roman mint did not continue for long to use old and new mark indifferently side by side. We are driven, then, to attribute all later occurrences of the mark X to mints outside Rome, or, if to Rome, to special issues for provincial circulation. The coinage of *L. LIC. CN. DOM.* is most instructive in this context. Two moneyers strike the denarius with mark of value X̶ (Plate VII, 2) ; the other three have mark of value X (Plate VIII, 11). Evidently the two sets of coins were designed for different areas of circulation.

(e) *The General Evidence of History*—This will be mainly useful in helping us to interpret numismatic differences. We shall look for issues, where history indicates likely occasions for them. A study of the third to fifth decades of Livy is highly instructive. From the wars in the East, against Macedon and Syria, the Roman generals bring home Eastern coins, —Attic and " cistophoric " tetradrachms and gold *Philippi*,— from Spain and North Italy they bring, along with native silver, Roman denarii. Any provincial issues of the period are, therefore, to be attributed to the West : Rome fought her first wars in the East with the coinage of the country.

Some conception of the problem of Roman mints may be drawn from Plates IX and X. We have first a variety of styles of the period, 268-220 B.C. (Plate IX, 1-7), mainly Italian : on Plate IX, 2, we probably see the earliest style of Rome. Plate IX, 8-10, show non-Roman styles of the beginning of the second Punic War : the letters D and GR (Plate IX, 8, 9) are perhaps mint initials. On Plate IX, 11-16, we see various styles of the period from 230 B.C. onwards : Croton (Plate IX,

11), Hatria (?) (Plate IX, 12), Vibo (Plate IX, 16).   The early style of Spanish mintage is probably seen in Plate IX, 17-20. A non-Roman issue of *c.* 145 B.C. is seen in the denarius of P. Calp. (Plate X, 1).   Coins of Spanish and Gallic mintage of the period of the war with Viriathus, Numantia and the Arverni next appear (Plate X, 2-5).   There follow a coin struck for the Jugurthine War in Africa (?) (Plate IX, 6), North Italian issues of the Cimbrian War and after (Plate X, 7-8), an Eastern and two Italian (?) issues of Sulla (Plate X, 9-11), and a Spanish issue of C. Annius (Plate X, 12).   The beautiful denarius of L. Torquatus was either struck in the East or in Rome from a die made by an Eastern artist (Plate X, 13). Moving on to the period of the Civil Wars we have an Eastern issue of Q. Sicinius for Pompey (Plate X, 14), a coin of Scipio struck for the campaign of Thapsus (Plate X, 15), issues of C. Antonius at Apollonia (?) (Plate X, 17), and of Sextus Pompey in Sicily (Plate X, 16) ; finally an Eastern aureus of C. Cassius (Plate X, 18), a Gallic denarius of Octavian (Plate X, 19), and an Eastern denarius of Mark Antony (Plate X, 20). A full edition of illustrations, such as is to be found in the British Museum catalogue, is needed for a serious study of mint questions.

CHAPTER II

THE CONTENT OF THE REPUBLICAN COINAGE— TYPES AND LEGENDS [1]

1. General Principles—We have been looking, up to the present, at what may be called the externals of Republican coinage ; it is time to turn to its content, to its types and legends and the information that they give us. Coins may be said, with hardly a suggestion of metaphor, to have a language of their own ; but it is a language that is only partially expressed in words and depends more on pictures to convey its meanings. The pictorial part of this language needs much study and something of imagination, too, before it can be understood. We have to learn the symbolism of an age other than our own, and, although much is revealed to the first serious glance, the impression gains on the student that a lifetime of study must leave much still unknown.

With the origin of coin-types we have, fortunately, not to deal. Rome begins with the system in vogue in Greek states in the third century B.C., a system in which types of a general character, mainly religious, relating to the life and traditions of the community, predominate. For some hundred and fifty years Rome does not move far outside the circle of this tradition. After that time, however, an extraordinary prominence is given to the ancient history of the State, chiefly in connexion with the families of the moneyers. It is not until the Empire that the Roman coin assumes the rôle of the modern medal and offers a full commentary on contemporary events. But,

[1] It has seemed impossible in this chapter, without overburdening the text, to give full references for all the types quoted, or to note every case in which a coin discussed in the text is shown in the plates. The student who wishes to go fully into the subject is advised to turn to the *British Museum Catalogue of Republican Coins*, or to one of the other general works noted in the Bibliography. The Key to the plates, with its general references to the text, will help to remedy any deficiencies here.

even under the Republic, the strong taste of the Roman for actuality did not lack expression in coinage and comment on events of the day, under certain conventional disguises, became common.

2. Types of the Aes—It will be convenient to begin with a discussion of the types of the bronze, which throughout follow laws of their own, then to consider the types of the silver and of the much rarer gold issues in their chronological development.

The regular reverse type of the Republican bronze is the prow of a ship, turned usually to the right, far less frequently to the left (Plates II, 11-15, III, IV, V). Pliny has a mysterious statement to the effect that the reverse of the triens and quadrans was a ship (*ratis*) and not a prow. This is unquestionably a mistake. He seems to have misinterpreted the description " ratitus " applied by Festus to the two denominations : what possible meaning may lurk in that gloss we cannot say.[1] The type obviously originated in a time when Rome's interests were turning towards the sea—probably, as we have seen, in the generation before the Pyrrhic War. The tradition of later days, when Rome ranked as the great land power, but sadly neglected her fleet, has little understanding for these earlier interests. The coins suggest that, if we had fuller knowledge of the years preceding the first struggle with Carthage, we might find the miracle of the building of the great Roman fleets something less than miraculous after all. The obverse type varies with the denomination, but is in every case the head of a deity—Janus on the As (Plate III), Jupiter on the semis (Plate IV, 1), Minerva on the triens (Plate IV, 2), Hercules on the quadrans (Plate IV, 3), Mercury on the sextans (Plate II, 13), Bellona on the uncia (Plate II, 15) ; Mercury appears again on the half-ounce (Plate II, 11), Bellona on the quarter-ounce (Plate II, 12). Of the larger denominations, the decussis and tripondius have Roma, the dupondius has Minerva on the obverse (Plate V, 1). On the bronze struck at Italian mints, variations occur : in particular, the two denominations, unknown at Rome, dextans and quincunx, bear

---

[1] Pliny, *Nat Hist.*, XXXIII, 3, 44 ; Festus, in extract, p. 275 : " quadrans ratitus " is found in Lucilius. The word may date from the coinage of P. Calpurnius, whose small denominations actually show a ship on the reverse.

4

heads of Ceres and Apollo respectively (Plate VI, 1, 2). For
the series marked Ⱶ-T, Minerva appears on the sextans, Roma
on the uncia, the Dioscuri on the half-ounce. In this selection
of divine types, some points are clear enough. The choice of
Janus,[1] god of beginnings, for the unit needs no comment :
Jupiter, the king of the gods, naturally follows him. Mercury,
as god of trade, must have a place, and Hercules, too, figures
rather as a god of gain than of physical strength. The warrior-
goddess who appears on several denominations has been variously described as Minerva, Roma and Bellona.[2] Roma is
clearly distinguished by a special Phrygian helmet from Minerva, with her Corinthian crest. The goddess of the uncia
and quarter-ounce, in her Athenian helmet, is not quite like
either model and may, perhaps, represent the female counterpart of Mars, Bellona. Minerva was, by tradition, a great
goddess of city life, and Roma is little more than a special
version of her. The presence of the two here, then, is not surprising. The omissions are harder to explain. Vesta, it is
true, was not personified at an early date. But why should
Juno and Mars be missing ? Evidently the exact choice of
these types depended on particular circumstances of the time,
which we cannot fully appreciate to-day. Marks of value, we
have seen, were normal on both sides of the coins. The name
ROMA, as a mark of sovereignty, occurs for the first time on
the struck pieces of the five-ounce series and remains as an
integral part of the coin. Signatures of mints occur from
about 245 B.C., and symbols or initials of magistrates from much
the same date, later still fuller signatures ; but, as the same
laws seem to apply here as on the silver, we will leave the discussion of them till a later section.

The types of the South-Italian bronze,[3] which were prob-

---

[1] If Janus is really an older Jupiter, as A. B. Cook in *Zeus*, Vol. II, pp. 331 ff.,
suggests, his priority is easier still to explain.

[2] See also below, p. 55.

[3] A note seems the right place for a short discussion of the types of the " Latin
Aes Grave " and the " Aes Signatum," which are a little off our main line, but cannot
be entirely omitted.

In the " Latin Aes Grave " we note three main points :—

      (1) There is unmistakable reference to Rome : cp. the Roma head, the
           Janus head, the Mars head ; perhaps, too, the Dioscuri.

      (2) There is a very close relationship to the silver didrachms, signed

ably not Roman coins, but only coins issued on local standards for Rome's account, follow different rules. The horse's head and free horse (Plate I, 3) refer to Carthage, Rome's ally against Pyrrhus. When associated with the obverse, head of Mars (Plate XIV, 1), they may perhaps have suggested the "Equiria," the great festival of horse-racing held in honour of the god on March the 14th;[1] but the Carthaginian allusion is primary. The heads of Mars and Minerva and the eagle (Plate I, 5), belong to the Roman sphere of interest. The lion has, again, an African reference, the dog (Plate I, 4) perhaps a local reference to South Italy.[2] The later bronze, of heavy weight, struck for the South, is very obscure in its allusions. The she-wolf and twins of Roman legend appear on the sextans (Plate I, 12), and a towered head of Roma (?) on the half-ounce (Plate II, 2). The bull of the quadrans (Plate I, 11) is certainly the emblem of Italia (Viteliu-Vitulus). But the goddess[3] and the Hercules and Centaur of the triens (Plate I, 10), the Hercules (?) of the quadrans (Plate I, 11), the bird holding flower of the sextans[4]

ROMANO, ROMA, of South Italian mintage: cp. the horse's head, the head of Apollo, the dog, etc.

(3) There is close interlinking of some of the various series: cp. the obverses of triens, quadrans, sextans, uncia and half-ounce common to the "Roma head" and "Janus-Mercury" series.

The wheel suggests a road, perhaps the extension of the "Via Appia" from Beneventum to Brundusium. Other types,—bull, dog, tortoise, mussel, acorn, dolphin, boar,—suggest local references, probably to South Italy, and perhaps stand in connexion with the road-building.

The "Aes Signatum" is connected by Haeberlin with the "Latin Aes Grave." There is no proof of this, but the date is certainly about the same.

The Eagle-Pegasus bar (*ROMANOM*) belongs to the same order of references. The shield and sword and sheath bars are too general in character to attribute. The corn-ear, tripod and anchor-tripod bars may be associated with the Apollo types of the "Latin Aes Grave" and the trident-caduceus bar with the "Janus-Mercury" series. The feeding hen, rostra and dolphin bar might suggest favourable auspices prior to the Roman sea victories (Mylae, for example, but not Drepana!). The bull-bull bar certainly suggests the bull of Italy and might refer to the subjection of Samnium (so Haeberlin). The elephant-sow bar presumably refers to the story of the rout of Pyrrhus's elephants by the grunting of swine.

[1] I am indebted for this suggestion to the late Professor Sir William Ridgeway. I cannot agree with him in pressing this point to the exclusion of the Carthaginian reference.

[2] It occurs as reverse type on quadrans of the "Wheel" series of "Latin Aes Grave."

[3] Juno Moneta (?).   [4] Cp. a rather similar reverse on bronze of Laus.

(Plate I, 12), the horseman of the half-ounce (Plate II, 2) [1] have not been convincingly explained. The sun and crescent and stars of the uncia (Plate II, 1) suggest the thought of auspicious influences : but we cannot give the suggestion any precision. On the earlier of these issues we find the signature *ROMANO*, on the later *ROMA*.

We return to the coinage of the capital. On the bronze of the sextantal and uncial standards conservatism reigned supreme : no attempt was made to change any of the main types. The rare denominations, dextans and quincunx, have obverse types of their own, Ceres and Apollo (Plate VI, 1, 2). At most, some subordinate detail was occasionally introduced on the reverse, as for instance, a flying Victory (Plate XII, 1) : but this should perhaps be regarded as no more than a symbol. Not till late in the second century B.C. do more marked changes appear. The rare denominations, dodrans and bes, have distinctive obverses, heads of Vulcan and Bacchus (Liber) respectively (Plate VI, 6, 7). Vulcan, the god of smiths, may be the patron god of the mint. Bacchus, the god of wine, suggests a possible " congiarium " of wine, in connexion with which the coin may have been struck. Both denominations are very rare and seem to be connected with the supply of corn or wine to the people at specially reduced prices. L. Opeimius has a club as reverse to the Hercules of his quadrans (Plate XII, 3). Quite outside the ordinary tradition are the issues of Cn. Domitius, M. Silanus and Q. Curtius, with heads of Saturn, Minerva, Hercules, Mercury and Apollo on obverses of semis to uncia, and divine emblems, harpa, aegis, club, bow and arrow (Plate VII, 4), caduceus and lyre on reverses. So, too, is the reverse of the quadrans of Ti. Veturius, strigil and oil-jar. Both these coinages were issued outside Rome and the types presumably refer to the unknown occasions of their issue. Other local issues show unusual types, such as the Victory erecting trophy on the As of Cn. Blasio (Plate XII, 2), the Mars in quadriga of the uncia of C. Fonteius, the rudder on the quadrans of M. Cipius and the Saturn head and dog (or lion ?) on the uncia of L. Philippus. In general, it is the lack of variety that challenges attention here. The bronze coinage of

[1] A Campanian knight (?).

Rome was the original coinage of the land : it always served the
home market and played little part in Rome's expansion abroad :
it is perhaps not surprising, then, that it resisted change more
persistently than the world currency of the denarius.

The bronze of the semuncial standard, in its short course,
showed itself more open to the changes which were re-modelling
the Roman coinage. L. Piso has a Victory on prow on his
reverse (Plate XII, 4). A head of Apollo appears on the
quadrans of L. Piso (Plate XII, 7), sometimes an anchor and
rudder crossed on its reverse. Entirely new are the semis,
triens and quadrans of Q. Titius, with head of Apollo and
Minerva in quadriga, mask of Pan and Ceres with torches,
mask of Pan and mask of Silenus. C. Pansa has a triple prow
on the reverse of his As (Plate XII, 6), C. Censorinus busts of
Ancus Marcius and Numa Pompilius on his obverse, and prow
before two arches on the reverse (Plate XII, 5). So, too,
L. Rubrius Dossenus has a Janus head of Hercules and Mercury
on obverse, a prow behind a temple on reverse of his As. In
this series, too, we occasionally find such formulae as *EX S.C.*,
D.S.S. (" de Senatus sententia ") on the bronze. The
L.P.D.A.P. refers to the " lex Papiria de aere publico." Had
the coinage continued the bronze might have swung entirely
into the lines on which the silver coinage was developing.

The remaining bronze issues of the Republic belong chiefly
to the provincial coinage and follow no fixed laws of types.
C. Clovius has, for obverse, a bust of Victory, for reverse,
Minerva advancing, l. ; Q. Oppius a head of Venus and a Victory
on reverse. The Asses of Gnaeus Pompey the Younger and
Sextus Pompey, struck in Spain, have the weight and types
of the uncial As ; but the Janus head shows curiously realistic
features. Octavian's Gallic coins celebrate his deified father.
The " fleet " coinage of Mark Antony is original in types, as
in other details. The obverses are given up to portraits
of Antony, Octavia and Octavian : the reverse types are
adapted to the denomination—a quadriga of hippocamps for
the sestertius, three galleys for the tripondius, two for dupondius, one for the As. The bronze of Canidius Crassus, struck
in Egypt *c.* 31 B.C., has as types crocodile and rostrum, and
head of Apollo and fasces (Plate XII, 8, 9).

The types of Republican bronze, then, only teach us a

very moderate amount about the history. With the silver and gold coinage we reach a far more fruitful field of study. Only in the early periods can we satisfactorily deal with the types in one rapid survey. In the last century of the Republic, after a preliminary review, we shall have to consider the context of the coinage under a number of subject headings—archæological, historical and the rest. The little that has to be said about legends will be worked into the discussion of the types.

3. **Types of early Gold and Silver**—The didrachms of the Pyrrhic War and later lie outside the main Roman series and its development. The types at first refer partly to places, partly to contemporary history. The heads of Roma and Mars (Plate XIV, 1) and the she-wolf and twins suggest Rome herself, the horse's head, the free horse and the lion her ally, Carthage. The head of Apollo is also found at Arpi and other South Italian towns. The Victory crowning palm is borrowed from the coinage of Agathocles and applied to the circumstances of the war. The " quadrigatus," which is more or less contemporary with the earliest denarii, has fixed types, which do not vary in any important detail. The Janus of the obverse is clearly borrowed from the Roman deity : why the head should here be young and beardless, we do not know.[1] The Jupiter crowned by Victory in the quadriga of the reverse is an apt emblem of victorious Rome. The same motif is carried on in the victoriate : but Jupiter is now given place of honour on the obverse (Plate XIII, 16), while Victory, crowning a trophy, fills the reverse. To complete the survey, we will take in the gold coins of a rather later date. The scene of the reverse, two warriors swearing to a treaty over the body of a pig,[2] is certainly a symbol of the union of Rome and her allies against Hannibal. The electrum coins attributed to Hannibal in South Italy have a Janiform head with distinctly feminine features on the obverse, and the " quadrigatus " type on the reverse. The signature of Rome on her South Italian issues has at first the form, *ROMANO*, perhaps equal to *ROMANOM*, an old genitive plural ; later, the more usual *ROMA* takes its place.

The way is now clear for the study of the main Roman

---

[1] Is it a Janiform Apollo ?

[2] Cp. Vergil, *Aeneid*, VIII, 638 f., the kings " caesa iungebant foedera porca."

coinage. The original obverse of all Roman silver—denarius, quinarius and sestertius—is the head of the city-goddess, Roma, in a winged helmet, adorned with a griffin crest. The earlier type, with Phrygian helmet, only occurs at rare intervals on the silver. The conception of Roma as a tutelary goddess of the city has much in common with that of Minerva (Athene), as seen on coins of Athens and of other cities, such as Rhegium. It is not surprising, then, that the type of Roma is near to that of Minerva and can sometimes hardly be distinguished from it. The Phrygian helmet suggests an Amazon—a representation of Roma which we shall meet later on Imperial reverses. The exact reason for the choice of wing and griffin crest as distinguishing features is unknown.[1] The representation of the city goddess on obverse was felt to be so natural that it passed into a settled tradition : not till about 112 B.C. do we find any variation in the obverse of the denarius (for various styles, cp. Plates XIV, 13-16 ; XVII, 19). The type of the reverse was at first the Dioscuri, with stars above their heads, charging right with spears in rest. It is the epiphany of " the great twin brethren who fought so well for Rome " at Lake Regillus that is portrayed (Plate XI, 1-2, 4, 10, etc.). The Dioscuri, too, were the special patrons of the Roman knights. The first change in the reverse can be dated to the early years of the second Punic War. The Diana in biga who now appears is presumably the Diana of Aricia, the goddess of the Latin League ;[2] the type was better fitted than that of the Dioscuri for the Roman League in war with the invader (Plate XI, 3). Whether there is any suggestion of Luna and questions of the calendar is very doubtful.[3] After no long interval, a new biga type, with Victory in place of Diana, appears (Plate XI, 5, 6, 11, 18)—very probably in direct celebration of the victory over Antiochus, 189 B.C. This type, with that of the Dioscuri, which never goes entirely out of use, is dominant till about 150 B.C. The gold coinage, marked LX, XXXX, XX, has as obverse, head of Mars, as reverse, eagle on thunderbolt : it is a war coinage under the protection of the supreme god, Jupiter, and the god of war, Mars.

[1] Cp. Haeberlin, " Der Roma-typus," in *Corolla Numismatica*, pp. 135 ff.
[2] Cp. Livy, I, 45.
[3] Cp. Hill, *Roman Historical Coins*, pp. 58 f.

The legend *ROMA* appears regularly on the reverse, as evidence, that is to say, of the authority coining, not as description of the obverse type, and is at first the only legend. Symbols to mark a mint or a moneyer are common from about 245 B.C. We find, for example, a Victory crowning the Dioscuri (Plate XI, 1), or a Victory crowning Rome (Plate XI, 4). Mint signatures occur at about the same time and also names of moneyers, at first in a very abbreviated form, later in greater detail. The earliest forms show abbreviated praenomen and nomen or cognomen,—sometimes one of the two latter only.[1] The conjunction of nomen and cognomen (as *AV* (relius) *RVF* (us)) is rare. From about 202 B.C. three names often occur, sometimes divided between obverse and reverse. Further descriptions, such as *C.F.* (Gaii filius), also occur. *F.* is very occasionally used to distinguish a son from a father of like name. Extra names (*agnomina*), such as " Asiagenus," are not uncommon. The tribe is very seldom given—*A. MANLI Q.F. SER.* (*Sergia*)—*c.* 130 B.C.—is one of the few cases known.[2] One moneyer, L. Atilius (*c.* 149 B.C.), places the letters *NOM.* in the place usually taken by the name *ROMA.* There can be no question of an engraver's error as all specimens plainly show the letters *NOM.*; but the interpretation " Nomentanus," as surname of the moneyer, carries no conviction, as the name is not known in connexion with the Atilian gens. The true explanation still awaits discovery. The mark of value, X, appears regularly behind the head of Roma on the obverse, as do the corresponding V and IIS on the quinarius and sestertius.

About 150 B.C. the traditions of the reverse type suffer further change. The Secular Games, which were due for celebration in 149 B.C. and were actually celebrated in 146 B.C., had probably some influence. Quadrigae, as well as bigae, now appear and are driven by new charioteers. We find Juno in a biga of goats (C. Renius—Plate XI, 7), Diana in a biga of stags (no moneyer), Hercules in a biga of centaurs (M. Aurelius Cotta—Plate XI, 9) ; Venus crowned by Cupid in biga (Plate XI, 17), Pax in biga (Plate XI, 19). Quadrigae of horses are

---

[1] Cp. Grueber, *B.M. C. Republic*, I, p. lxxxi f.

[2] Cp. also *L. MEMMI GAL.* (*Galeria*), *C. MARIVS C. F. TRO.* (*Tromentina*).

driven by Apollo (Cn. Baebius Tampilus—Plate XI, 13), Sol
(M. Aburius Geminus—Plate XI, 16), Juno (C. Curiatius Trigeminus—Plate XI, 8, 14), Mars and Nerio (?) (Cn. Gellius),
Libertas (C. Cassius). The Diana above-mentioned is identified
as moon-goddess by the torch in her hand and the crescent
in field. Particularly common is the type of Jupiter in quadriga (Plate XI, 15)—so common, in fact, that the name " quadrigatus," originally appropriated to the didrachm, came to be
transferred in later use to the denarius. Chariot types are
common in so many series of ancient coins that we come to
accept them without further explanation. There is, however,
something peculiarly Roman in the representation of particular
deities as charioteers. The explanation probably lies in the
Roman passion for circus races, which formed a main part of
the celebration of festivals of the gods. It is probably these
festivals which give us the Roman chariot types ; the particular deity in whose honour the festival is given is represented
as charioteer and, occasionally, the team is varied, to suit the
character of the deity, from horses to goats for Juno (Plate
XI, 7), stags for Diana, or centaurs for Hercules (Plate XI, 9).

Variation in the reverse beyond this narrow range is still
uncommon. The earliest examples seem to be the shepherd,
she-wolf and twins on the reverse of Sex. Pompeius Fostlus and
the bronze monument erected to L. Minucius Augurinus, prefect
of the corn market in 439 B.C., on the reverse of C. Augurinus
(Plate XI, 12, cp. 20). In both cases there is obvious allusion
to the family history of the moneyers—probably also some contemporary reference which cannot now be recovered. Certain
contemporary allusions may be found in the coinage of the age
of the Gracchi. C. Serveilius uses as reverse, a warrior on horseback, with shield inscribed M, spearing another warrior who
flees before him. Under cover of a reference to an ancestor,
the famous C. Servilius Structus Ahala, who slew Spurius
Maelius, the man who, by supplying cheap corn to the Roman
people, affected the crown, C. Serveilius applauds the murder
of the second Maelius, Ti. Gracchus. Coins of a slightly later
date hint, as definitely, at the activities of the younger Gracchus
—M. Marcius, with the ears of corn that accompany the Victory
in biga of his reverse, M. Porcius Laeca with Libertas in
quadriga crowned by Victory, C. Cassius with a similar type.

References to family history are, no doubt, present in each case : but, as we shall often see below, this was the conventional form in which comment on current events was introduced on the Republican coin. But we are now reaching a time when a more detailed and systematic study of types will be needed. The reverse is given up more and more to types of the new kind,—reflecting on topical events, whether connected with the moneyer or with the history of the State or with both. When the obverse, too, is released from the old tradition and various divine heads replace the head of Roma, the old conservatism is finally defeated and the coinage enters on its fullest and freest development. We can hardly be wrong if we associate these changes with the stirring events of foreign history and the increasing ferment in political life that began with the age of the Gracchi. The tradition broke down on two sides, on that of the conservatives and the democratic party. The conservatives themselves surrender to the new movement to the extent of allowing free play to the personal ambitions of individuals ; to the democrats more particularly we may attribute the new desire to make the coinage reflect more faithfully the active and changing life of the State.

In the use of legends no great changes are to be noted. The signature *ROMA* is still normal on the reverse : the crowded reverse type of C. Augurinus causes it to be transferred to the obverse and there it occasionally reappears. It begins to be omitted from about 112 B.C. on and after a time only appears very rarely and then as description of type rather than as signature. Further legends, helping to identify the types, occur sporadically from about the same date. They become more and more common and more and more explicit, until at last we get such full legends as " Sex. Nonius pr(aetor) l(udos) V(ictoriae) p(rimus) f(ecit)" or "C. Vpsae(us) cos (consul) cepit Priv(ernum)." Of the various symbols, letters and numbers that distinguish so many denarii of the period from 125 to 66 B.C. we have spoken above. The mark of value, X, is replaced by XVI about 150 B.C., and later by $\bar{X}$, though X persists on certain issues. It disappears altogether as a normal feature of the coin at about the same time as the signature of *ROMA*. Of the forms of moneyers' names little remains to be said except that they tend to become fuller and more explicit, often with all three names given in full and with name of father and even of grandfather added.   A not uncommon feature is the genitive case of possession in place of the more obvious nominative.

4. **Types of the later Republic**—We have now to review the coinage in its days of full development and draw from it what lessons we can for history and archæology.   It is hardly possible to find any classification that is complete and that does not involve a certain amount of overlapping.

The following will serve our purpose :—

(*a*) Religious types.
(*b*) Personal types.
(*c*) Historical types.
(*d*) Animate and inanimate objects.
(*e*) Architecture, art, etc.

(*a*) *Religious Types* (Plates XIII, XIV)—The religious element is always prominent in the Republican coinage.   In the early period most of the stock types are more or less definitely religious.   This feature is not peculiar to Rome ; it is one that she shares with the majority of Greek States.   The theory of the religious origin of coin types is now generally abandoned, but the facts on which it seemed to rest remain.   Religion was an integral part of the national life of Greece and Rome, and coinage, reflecting the life of the community, naturally acquires a religious tinge.   The earlier religious types of Rome seem to be of a purely religious character : they honour a divinity simply as a permanent part of the religious life of the State. In the later period, which we have now to discuss, this kind of general reference seems, indeed, to occur often enough, but references to the history of the State or the moneyer's family are sometimes involved ; if our knowledge were wider, we should probably have few types of the more general character left.   A complete treatment of the subject is, of course, impossible here ; all we can hope to do is to discover, as we survey the Roman Pantheon on the coins, to what sorts of uses it might be put.

Jupiter, as the chief god of the State, naturally appears freely on the coinage.   L. Rubrius Dossenus, with his obverses of Jupiter, Juno (Plate XIII, 12), Minerva and Neptune and triumphal chariots or Victory on the reverse, refers to thanks-giving to the gods for the victory in the Social War. The coinage of Q. Antonius Balbus (c. 82 B.C.) was struck from temple treasures, and the reference of his obverse to Jupiter may imply that the god's blessing was invoked on the measure. L. Scipio Asiagenus, both of whose types refer to Jupiter, seems to invoke his blessing on the Roman arms against the Cimbri (c. 103 B.C.). A youthful Jupiter, armed with the thunderbolt, seems to represent the god as armed against the national enemy : we meet him on coins of L. Caesius (c. 109 B.C.), L. Licinius Macer and M. Fonteius (c. 88 B.C.) and Gar. Ocul. Ver. (c. 87 B.C.—Plate XIII, 20). L. Volteius Strabo (c. 80 B.C.) associates Jupiter with the myth of Europa and L. Procilius (c. 82 B.C.) refers to him in company with Juno Sospita (Plate XIII, 17).

The long series of divine types of M. Volteius have been well explained as referring to the five chief agonistic festivals of the Roman—the " ludi Romani " (Jupiter), the " ludi plebeii " (Hercules), the " ludi Cereales " (Ceres, Liber and Libera), the " ludi megalenses " (Cybele) and the " ludi Apollinares " (Apollo). The Jupiter of the denarii of L. Lentulus and C. Marcellus (consuls, 49 B.C.), is, perhaps, the " Ζεὺς Ἐλευθέριος " of Syracuse (cp. Plate XIX, 5). The Capitoline tripod, Jupiter, Juno and Minerva, appear on the reverse of Cn. Blasio (Plate XVI, 1). Q. Pomponius Rufus, with his head of Jupiter and eagle, may be referring to his ancestor Numa, the great traditional founder of Roman rites and ceremonies (Plate XIII, 18). Petillius Capitolinus (c. 45 B.C.) seems to have had a family connexion with the worship of Jupiter Capitolinus, whom he honours on his coins (cp. also Plate XXI, 15). C. Vibius Pansa (c. 48 B.C.) alludes to the special cult of Jupiter at Anxur,—which may have been the home of his family. A special Spanish and African cult of Jupiter is, it appears, celebrated on the Spanish coins of Varro (c. 49 B.C.), and the African of Q. Metellus Pius Scipio (c. 47-46 B.C.). The Jupitor with ram's horn of Q. Cornuficius (c. 44-42 B.C.) and Scarpus (c. 31 B.C.) is, of course, the famous Jupiter Ammon. On the denarius of Cn. Cornelius Sisenna (Spain (?), c. 130 B.C.), Jupiter in his quadriga hurls a thunderbolt at an anguipede giant. The same giant is seen in the pediment of a temple on the reverse of M. Plaetorius Cestianus and on the reverse of

L. Valerius Acisculus, with obverse, head of Jupiter (Plate XIII, 19). The myth of the war of gods and giants is, of course, familiar, but there is some special Roman application of it involved here. It is conceivable that we have a giant Valens, connected in myth with the hidden name of Rome, Valentia.[1]

Saturn is distinguished by his emblem, the " harpa," and is honoured as the guardian of the State treasury, the " aerarium Saturni." Piso and Caepio (100 B.C.), who strike as quaestors of the city, place him on their obverses, as does Cn. Nerius in 49 B.C. The issues of L. Memmius (c. 103 B.C.), L. C. Memies, L.F. (c. 87 B.C.), and Sufenas (c. 60 B.C.), all with this obverse, may have been specially provided for out of the " aerarium."

The Janus heads of M. Fourius Philus (c. 115 B.C.—Plate XVIII, 6) and C. Fonteius (c. 110 B.C.) have no special meaning for us, unless in the second case the head is that of Fons or Fontus, son of Janus and ancestor of the Fonteian gens. The heads of Dioscuri on coins of M. Fonteius (Plate XIII, 10) and C. Sulpicius (Plate XVII, 17) are perhaps meant to represent the " Dei Penates Publici " of Rome : can there be a reference to the returning of the troops to their homes after the end of the wars ? The cult of the Dioscuri at Tusculum is certainly the occasion of the appearance of the gods on the obverse of L. Servius Rufus (Plate XVII, 8) and perhaps on that of M. Cordius Rufus too (Plate XIII, 11). Pan and Silenus appear, in virtue of the sound of their names, on coins of D. Silanus (c. 90 B.C.—Plate XIII, 9) and the two men named C. Vibius Pansa (c. 88 and 49 B.C.—Plate XIII, 10, 11). Why Pan and panther should appear on the sestertius of T. Carisius (c. 43 B.C.), we cannot say. Mercury, on the coins of C. Mamilius Limetanus (c. 83 B.C.—Plate XVI, 18), is the ancestor of Ulysses, whose grand-daughter Mamilia was the ancestress of the Mamilian family ; to such extremes did Roman genealogists run. The terminal bust of Mercury on coins of M. Piso Cn. f. Frugi has been interpreted as that of the " guardian of the streets," and the issue has been supposed to be that of a curule aedile. Mercury and his lyre on the sestertius of L. Papius Celsus is unexplained.

Mars, as the god of war, is a natural type for any issue in time of battle. We find him on coins of Q. Lutatius Cerco

[1] *Rev. Num.*, 1849, pp. 325 ff.

(Jugurthan War), Q. Thermus M. f. and C. Malleolus (Cimbrian War), Cn. Lentulus (Civil War, 87 B.C.—Plate XIV, 2), P. Satrienus (Plate XIV, 3), L. Axsius Naso (Plate XIV, 4), L. Rustius (Sertorian War), Albinus Bruti f. (Great Civil War —Plate XIV, 5), and L. Mussidius Longus and P. Clodius M. f. (war of second triumvirs against the "Liberators"). The last two types are standing types of the reverse, not busts of the obverse—far less common, but extending in use towards the close of the Republic.

Neptune, as god of the sea, has for attribute the trident ; he is naturally invoked on occasion of wars at sea. The denarii of L. Lucretius Trio, with his head on obverse, belong to the Sertorian War (Plate XIV, 8), when the alliance of Sertorius with the pirates lent a naval aspect to the campaign : the coins of Q. Crepereius Rocus, of about the same date, are full of references to the sea :—Amphitrite on obverse, Neptune drawn by hippocamps on reverse, sea-creatures as symbols in the field (Plate XVIII, 20). Brutus honours Neptune for his sea victory off the Lycian coast (denarii of Casca Longus, c. 43-42 B.C.) ; Murcus expresses, by the use of his portrait, the fact that he was "praefectus classis" (Asia, c. 43-42 B.C.— Plate XIX, 19). P. Hypsaeus traced his descent from Leu-conoe, daughter of Neptune, and places both heads on his coins (c. 61 B.C.). Sextus Pompey, during his time of power in Sicily, struck coins full of reference to the sea-god who gave him his power : the proud title *NEPTVNI*, "Son of Neptune" (cp. denarius of Q. Nasidius) was actually claimed by him after a victory over Octavian.

Bacchus or Liber, the god of wine, appears, in connexion with the Lampsacene Priapus, on coins of Q. Titius (c. 87 B.C. —Plate XIV, 12), in connexion with Pan on coins of C. Vibius Pansa (c. 49 B.C.). As "Liber" the god was regarded as patron of "Libertas" and this certainly leads to his appearance on coins of the two Cato's (c. 100 B.C. and 47-46 B.C.) and, perhaps, also of L. Cassius (c. 78 B.C.—Plate XIII, 3) : in this latter case his female counterpart, Libera, is associated with him.

Apollo, the god of poetry and music, and, in another aspect, the god of the sun, appears in several distinct capacities. On the coinage of Q. Pomponius Musa (c. 67 B.C.) he, with Hercules Musagetes, is associated with the nine Muses. As sun-god he

appears on denarii of M'. Aquillius (XIV, 18), L. Lucretius
Trio,[1] M. Cordius Rufus and L. Valerius Asisculus.   Again, on
coins of P. Clodius M. f. (c. 42 B.C.—Plate XXI, 7) and coins
of Antony struck in the East (Plate XX, 3), in most, if not all
these cases, he symbolizes the " Rising Sun " (Oriens).   It is
as the patron of Apollonia that he appears on coins of the
consuls L. Lentulus and C. Marcellus, struck at that town in
49 B.C., perhaps also on coins of Brutus.   As god of prophecy
and the Sibylline books he may find his place on the issues of
C. Malleolus and his colleagues which are probably connected
with the founding of Eporedia (Plate VII, 6).   The Apollo of
the coins of L. Piso Frugi, C. Vibius Pansa, C. Marcius Censorinus, P. Crepusius, L. Censorinus (c. 90-87 B.C.) and M.
Metellus Q.F. (c. 81 B.C.—Plate XIII, 2), may refer to the
" templum Apollinis " outside the pomoerium in which the
Senate conferred with generals in the field.   The same reason
might account for the Apollo head on quinarii of c. 104 B.C.
and on the denarii of C. Piso, probably struck for the campaign
of Pompey against the pirates (Plate XIII, 1).   The Apollo
of Ser. Sulpicius is possibly the god of Delos, the great slave-
mart (Plate XIX, 1).   The Sibyl, the mythical authoress of
the Sibylline books which Rome used to consult in time of need
under the direction of Apollo, is represented on coins of L. Torquatus, T. Carisius and L. Valerius Asisculus.   In the first
case, the consultation of the books on the question of Egypt
may be referred to, in the second two the prophecy that Parthia
could only be conquered by a king and that Julius Caesar must
therefore assume the royal title.   The young god of the obverse
of L. Iulius Bursio combines attributes of more than one
divinity (Plate VIII, 10).

The young laureate head suggests Apollo, the wing Mercury, a trident in the field Neptune.   No satisfactory explanation of the type has yet been suggested.   Such syncretism
became common in the third century A.D., but was quite
unusual under the Republic.

Hercules, on the obverse of " Lentulus Marcelli filius "
(c. 99 B.C.) is a thin disguise for Marius returning in triumph

---

[1] If the worship of the sun-god was hereditary in the " gens Lucretia," we should
find a special reference in such passages of the poet Lucretius as II, vv. 59 ff. ; III,
vv. 91 ff. ; VII, vv. 39 ff.

from the Cimbrian War. The legend of Hercules and the Nemean lion forms the reverse of C. Poblicius (Plate XIV, 16). The Spanish Hercules of Osca appears on coins of P. Lentulus P.f.L.N. and of Domitius, both struck in Spain, *c.* 76 B.C. and 38 B.C. respectively, the African Hercules (Melcarth) on denarii of Q. Metellus Scipio (struck in Africa, *c.* 47-46 B.C.). The same allusion is, perhaps, to be seen on the issue of Ti. Q., struck during the Jugurthine War. The Hercules of L. Livineius Regulus may refer to the claim of M. Antony to descent from Anteon, the son of the hero.

Vulcan, as the god of smiths, is patron also of the mint, and as such appears on denarii of L. Cotta (*c.* 102 B.C.).

Juno, the queen of the gods, is honoured under two main forms, as Juno Sospita and as Juno Moneta. As Sospita, she was the special goddess of Lanuvium, wearing goatskin head-dress and armed with spear and shield. Her great function is the protection of men in the grip of danger, as of war. Her earliest appearance is on coins of L. Thorius Balbus [1] (Plate XIII, 13), later we find her on coins of L. Procilius, L. Papius and L. Roscius Fabatus (Plate XIII, 14). The last three moneyers were probably all adherents of the popular party, which seems to have had a special devotion to this goddess. The clearest testimony to the character of the goddess is found on the African denarius of Q. Cornuficius. Cornuficius had been a devoted Caesarian, but, after Caesar's death, espoused the cause of the Senate and, in his province of Africa, gave asylum to fugitives from the proscriptions. His reverse shows him receiving a crown as reward from Juno Sospita, whose work he has been doing (Plate XX, 4). L. Papius Celss places as reverse to the portrait of Juno Sospita a curious type of eagle and wolf, relating to the foundation of Lavinium which is confused with Lanuvium. Juno Moneta (the " Adviser " in Roman etymology) is the goddess of the mint, which stood in her temple ; her origin, perhaps Carthaginian,[2] was certainly forgotten at a later date. We meet her under the name *MONETA* on coins of L. Plaetorius (Plate XIII, 15) and T. Carisius : perhaps we should also attribute to her some unnamed busts, as, for instance, those of the obverses of C. Naevius

[1] With legend I.S.M.R., " Juno Sospita Mater Regina."
[2] This point is still much debated.

Balbus, L. Flaminius Chilo, and L. Mussidius Longus. The coins of L. Plaetorius were struck by him as quaestor by decree of the Senate: it is possible that he opened a new mint. T. Carisius places on his reverse implements of minting and refers undoubtedly to the reform of the mint by Julius Caesar.

Minerva, the goddess of wisdom, of city-life, of war, is a rarer type than one might have expected: no doubt her place is often taken by Roma. Her bust, distinguished by aegis, is seen on obverses of P. Servilius Rullus, C. Considius Paetus, and C. Vibius Varus. She drives a quadriga on the reverse of C. Vibius Pansa (Plate XIV, 7). Rome herself appears but seldom after about 100 B.C. Most interesting is the reverse of Kalenus and Cordous, which shows the concord of Roma and Italia, after the final settlement of the great war for the citizenship. A later rendering of the " Roma " head is seen in the aureus of C. Vibius Varus (Plate XIV, 17).

Diana of the Aventine, we have seen, played a notable part in the earlier history of Roman types. Sertorius in Spain worshipped Diana the huntress with exceptional devotion and imposed on the credulous natives as her protégé: to this fact we may attribute the frequent appearance of the goddess both on coins of the Sertorians (A. Postumius A. f. S. n. Albinus, Ti. Claudius Ti. f. Ap. n., Plates XIII, 7 ; XVIII, 18), and of their opponents (C. Postumius Tatius—Plate XIII, 8, and L. Axsius L. f. Naso). C. Hosidius Geta refers to her in connexion with the Calydonian boar (Plate XIII, 9). As patroness of the great Sulla she is honoured by his son Faustus in 61 B.C. (Plate XVI, 3). P. Clodius M. f. has a reverse type of Diana Lucifera, in connexion with obverses of Apollo and Sol. The Diana of Ephesus, on the reverse of the consuls L. Lentulus and C. Marcellus, may point to the place of minting of the issue.

Ceres, the goddess of the earth, is naturally associated with distributions of corn, as on the issues of M. Fannius and L. Critonius, the plebeian aediles, and of L. Furius Brocchus. She appears to be connected with the foundations of colonies on coins of L. Cassius Caeicianus (Plate XIII, 4) and C. Marius C. f. Capito ; on other issues, such as those of C. Memmius C. f., L. Sestius proquaestor, L. Mussidius Longus, and P. Clodius M. f., we are less sure of the occasion. On issues of Julius

5

Caesar and Q. Cornuficius—struck in Africa—she represents the great grain-producing province.

Nemesis, the goddess of the divine Anger, appears on the reverse of C. Vibius Varus (Plate XIV, 17).

Venus, as the divine ancestress of the Julian " gens," figures on coins of L. Iulius L. f. Caesar, and more prominently on coins of the moneyers of Julius Caesar, M. Cordius Rufus, C. Considius Paetus, M. Mettius, and L. Aemilius Buca ; also on Spanish issues of the dictator and on the Sicilian issue of A. Allienus. Venus Victrix was the watchword of the Caesarians at Pharsalia. The reason for her appearance on coins of L. Censorinus and his colleagues (Plate XIV, 19) is uncertain. Sulla, too, claimed to be under the special protection of the goddess (" Epaphroditus ") : she appears on the coins of L. Sulla " Imperator iterum," and on the anonymous aureus with reverse, double cornucopiae. The Memmian " gens," too, had a special cult of Venus, to which we owe the magnificent address to the goddess in the first book of Lucretius, who thus honoured his patron. C. Considius Nonianus honours the Venus of Eryx and places her temple on his reverse (Plate XXI, 17). Venus Verticordia appears on the reverse of M. Cordius Rufus (Plate XIII, 11). The Venus and Cupid on coins of Cn. Egnatius Maxsumus still await their explanation.

The Cybele of M. Volteius, M. Plaetorius Cestianus (Plate VII, 11) and A. Plautius is probably in the first place the goddess of the " ludi Megalenses." [1] Whether the towered goddess of C. Fabius C.f. (Plate XIII, 5) and P. Fourius Crassipes is a Cybele or a towered Roma is open to question. Cybele appears in a chariot drawn by lions on the aureus of C. Norbanus and L. Cestius (Plate XIII, 6).

A veiled Vesta appears on coins of P. Galba as curule aedile (Plate VII, 10) and of Q. Cassius (Plate XIV, 20) and Longinus. In the last two cases a reference to the trial of the Vestal Virgins in 113 B.C. for unchastity is probable.

C. Serveilius C.f., alluding to the first celebration of the games of Flora, places her head on his obverse ; and a similar reference to her games is probably implied on the coins of C. Clodius C.f. Vestalis.

---

[1] Perhaps compare also Pl. XIX, 3.

It will have become abundantly clear from this short survey that the religious life of the Roman State in the last century of the Republic found a full record in the coinage and that allusions drawn from it were made to serve a great variety of purposes. At the same time it is not unfair to speak of a decline in true religious feeling. In the older types, religion was dominant and was considered for its own sake. In these latter days, it often serves no higher purpose than the gratification of family pride or the conveyance of an allusion to the events of the day. Of mythological references we have already had occasion to speak in passing ; we shall review them in a little more detail, as a preparation for the study of the early history of Rome. Of genuine belief there can be little question ; mythology is little more than a picturesque appendage to the history of the great families.

From the divine world we pass to the semi-divine sphere of those minor powers or virtues, who played such a prominent part in Roman religious belief (Plate XV). The Roman tended to see divine activity in every happening of life, however trivial. In course of time whole chains of happenings came to be associated with the powers of the major deities of the State—war with Mars, agriculture with Ceres. But there was still room enough left for the activity of minor powers, conceived of as persons with more or less clearly defined functions and attributes. Thus the great unknown power that turns the wheel of human fate was worshipped as " Fortuna." Peace had no presiding major deity, but was placed under the guardianship of the minor goddess Pax. Over the harmonious relationships of public and private life Concordia presided, Pietas over the various manifestations of the peculiarly Roman virtue of " Loyalty." The ideal of political freedom is committed to the charge of Libertas, that of honourable dealing to Fides. In the military sphere we meet the two soldier virtues, Virtus and Honos, and above all others the Victory that accompanies step by step the march of Rome. Finally, the Genius or spirit that presides over every person or place is invoked in particular contexts. Under the Empire we shall be astonished at the extent to which these minor cults develop. Under the Republic their place is a restricted one. How old the belief in their powers was may be learned from a cursory reading of such an

author as Plautus.   But their rôle was chiefly played in private
life, and it is only towards the close of the Republic that they,
with so much else of individual interest, make serious en-
croachments on the coinage of the State.

Concordia appears first on issues of Paullus Lepidus,
c. 55 B.C., as a woman veiled and diademed.   We meet her later
on coins of P. Fonteius Capito, L. Vinicius, and L. Mussidius
Longus (Plate XV, 2).   In all cases the thought of harmony
in the State is prominent ; the shadow of the Civil Wars hangs
over the coinage.   Later, Concordia is a sign of the harmonious
co-operation of the triumvirs : she appears on a quinarius of
M. Antony and Octavian with another expression of the same
idea, the clasped hands, on reverse.   A personification of Fides
appears, once only, on the denarius of A. Licinius Nerva
(Plate XV, 6) ; as the reverse shows a horseman dragging a
captive, the allusion seems to be the military devotion of some
member of Caesar's forces.

The Fortuna of the people of Rome is very appropriately
placed on the obverse of the Pompeian moneyer Q. Sicinius at
the outbreak of the great Civil Wars.   The same Fortuna is
invoked by M. Arrius Secundus in the days of the siege of
Mutina.   The Fortuna standing with rudder and cornucopiae
on the reverse of P. Sepullius Macer will be rather the fortune
of Julius Caesar himself, and the same figure is used for Octavian
by Ti. Sempronius Graccus (Plate XV, 7).

The Genius of the Roman people appears on the denarius
of Cn. Lentulus (Plate XV, 4) and the tutelary Genius of Africa,
under the form of the Egyptian goddess Sekhet, on the denarius
of P. Crassus iun. struck for Q. Metellus Scipio in Africa.

Libertas, the spirit of the Republican constitution, is one
of the commonest of personifications.   On the reverses of M.
Porcius Laeca and C. Cassius she is seen driving a quadriga.
There are probably double references in each case, to popular
measures carried by ancestors of the moneyers and to the
present activities of the " populares," led by C. Gracchus.   A
large place is assigned to Libertas in the coinage of C. Egnatius
Maxsumus,—a bust of the goddess on one obverse, the goddess
in a biga on one reverse, and a second reverse of a temple of
Jupiter and Libertas.   Uncertain as are the exact circumstances of this issue, it seems to be beyond doubt that Libertas

here means the newly-won rights of the Italian peoples. On denarii of Brutus (Plate XVII, 7) and Q. Cassius (Plate XV, 5) Libertas represents the constitution, endangered by the ambition of the first triumvirate. On the denarius of Palikanus she suggests the loyalty of Julius Caesar to the constitution (Plate XIX, 19). In the coinage of the Liberators Brutus and Cassius the goddess naturally plays a leading part.

The Pax in a biga on the reverse of the denarii with symbol, an elephant's head, may refer to the foundation of Junonia on the site of Carthage—a final peace now sealing the long series of African wars. The obverse of the quinarius of L. Aemilius Buca (Plate XV, 10) celebrates the final triumph of Julius Caesar. The kindred goddess, Felicitas, appears on the obverse of the quinarius of Palikanus (Plate XV, 3) and on the reverse of the denarius of L. Flaminius Chilo. She represents the happiness and prosperity which Peace brings in her train.

The Pietas of M. Herennius (Plate XV, 11) is explained by the type of the reverse, the Catanian brothers,[1] as an allusion to family affection—probably in reference to the family of the moneyer. On the obverse of Q. Caecilius Metellus Pius she is identified by her bird, the stork ; Metellus won the epithet " Pius " by the filial devotion which led him to strive to secure the return of his father from exile. The Pietas of the obverse of A. Hirtius, if indeed it is rightly described, denotes " Piety " in a religious sense and alludes to the chief priesthood of Julius Caesar. On the reverse of denarii of Mark Antony of the Perusine wars, the reference is to L. Antonius, the consul, brother of the triumvir, who took the title " Pietas " in token of his devotion to his brother's interests (Plate XX, 8).

Salus on denarii of D. Silanus (Plate XV, 12) looks to the safety of the State, endangered by the outbreak of the great Social War. On the denarius of M. Acilius the two personifications, Salus and Valetudo, look back to the first medical practitioner of Rome, a certain Archagathus, who, in 219 B.C., was given a shop at the public expense in the street Acilia.[2]

Victory is the commonest of all personifications and is a familiar feature of the coinage at all times. She represents

---

[1] See below, p. 75.

[2] A secondary allusion to the critical illness of Cn. Pompeius in 50 B.C. is probable.

the overcoming power of the Roman arms in general rather than any particular triumph. At first standing figure or figures in chariots are the rule : she is seldom without her attributes wreath and palm, and is always winged. The seated Victory of the reverse of M. Cato bears the simple epithet " Victrix " (Plate XV, 14). Later in the Republic a winged bust appears as, for instance, on coins of L. Valerius Flaccus (Plate XV, 15), Q. Titius, L. Papius Celsus, T. Carisius, L. Plancus praefectus urbi (Plate XV, 16), Q. Oppius and C. Numonius Vaala (Plate XV, 17).[1] We have no space here to describe the variety of ways in which Victory is represented : she crowns a trophy, crowns the drivers of quadrigae, flies with a shield in her arms, or is shown standing or seated with her wreath and palm. The triteness of the conception tends to make us oblivious of the true splendour of this visible expression of the power of the Roman State in action.

Virtus, the personification of martial valour, is represented by a helmeted head on denarii of M'. Aquillius M'. f. M'. N. ; it is the valour of his grandfather, the conqueror of the slaves in Sicily in 101 B.C. (Plate XVII, 13). Conjoined with Honos, Virtus appears, too, on the denarius of Kalenus and Cordius (Plate XV, 8). Both coins were probably struck by Caesar as governor of Gaul : hence the military allusions are doubly appropriate. Honos on the denarius of Palikanus is probably the type of public office (Plate XV, 9). The spirit of the Triumph is personified on the denarius of L. Papius Celsus (Plate XV, 13), celebrating the triumph of Julius Caesar in 46 B.C.

One last class of personifications remains to be considered —personifications of towns or provinces. With the figure of Roma herself we are already familiar. The rebel Italians of 91-89 B.C. substituted for Rome the figure of Italia, similarly conceived as an armed goddess. Hispania on the denarius of A. Postumius Albinus celebrates the province to which the Sertorians were looking to retrieve their fallen fortunes (Plate XVIII, 19). It is doubtful here, whether the long falling hair is an evidence of mourning : if it is, the province is represented as mourning till her deliverers come to save her. The denarius

[1] Cp. also Pl. VII, 7 ; X, 20 ; XX, 20.

of Kalenus and Cordius shows on the reverse the reconciliation of Rome and Italy (Plate XV, 8). The Gallic man [1] and woman on the obverses of L. Hostilius Saserna certainly represent the Gallic nation, subdued by Caesar : but, inasmuch as the conquered province is now allied to Caesar against his domestic enemies, the allusion is not an unfriendly one. Of the tutelary genius of Africa we have already spoken. A head of Africa, in her distinctive head-dress of an elephant's trunk and skin, is seen on the rare aureus of Pompey the Great and on the denarius of Eppius, struck for Q. Metellus Scipio, and again on the denarius of Q. Cornuficius. A towered female head on denarii of Crassus jun. probably represents the town of Utica. C. Antonius, as pro-consul of Macedon, places on his obverse the spirit of his province, wearing the national broad-brimmed hat (Plate X, 17). Asia is seen on the reverse of L. Murcus, as a kneeling figure waiting to be raised to her feet by the Roman general. On denarii of the younger Cn. Pompey, struck in Spain, figures representing Hispania and Baetica welcome the Roman as their deliverer.

(b) *Personal Types* (Plate XVI)—The reference to the family history of moneyers runs through the whole Republican series and will confront us again and again under almost every section. To avoid needless repetitions, we will make no attempt to give a full list of such allusions here. Rather we will content ourselves with a short survey of the various forms that such allusions take at different periods, enforcing our points by a few characteristic examples. To this survey we may aptly append a discussion of the use of portraiture under the Republic and of the emergence of the personal element, as the dominant feature, at the close of its coinage.

The earliest moneyers were content to mark their coins with a badge or device, such as may well have been used for a signet-ring, and these badges continued in use even after signatures by name had become general. Thus the staff (*scipio*) may represent the famous " Scipio " branch of the Cornelian gens. The elephant's head of the Metellan family was derived from the famous victory of L. Caecilius Metellus at Agrigentum in 251 B.C., when the war elephants of Carthage

---

[1] The identification as Vercingetorix is attractive.

were captured. Another family glory of the " gens Metella "
was the Macedonian victory of 146 B.C. (Plate XVI, 13, 15). An
apex and hammer (*tudes*) may stand for an Apicius Tuditanus,
a dog for a member of the Antestian gens (Plate XVI, 11), an
ass's head for one of the Silani. Later, allusions to family
history assume larger proportions. They may be of various
kinds—references to the history of the Republic (cp. Fostlus
and the legend of Roma, Plate XVI, 12), or to the mythical
history of the Greek world in the misty background, or to the
old Roman mythology—Mars and Nerio (Plate XVI, 14), Acca
Larentia (Plate XVI, 19). When the Trojan origin of Rome
had come to be accepted as an article of faith, it became fashion-
able for the great Roman houses to develop " stemmata " running back into the divine and heroic past of Greece. It became
a sort of patent of nobility, much like " coming over with
William the Conqueror " here. There was a wide field for
misinterpretation of genuine tradition, for embroidery and
for plain inventions. Greek hangers-on were no doubt largely
responsible for supplying the necessary myths, but the Romans
themselves must bear a full responsibility for their fatuous
indulgence in this childish form of self-glorification. In the
last century of the Republic the abuse, for such it must be
called, had gone so far that the glorification of the family
almost overlaid the true national character of the coinage.
But an emphatic warning must be registered here. It would
be a grave mistake to assume that the most obvious references
are the only, or even the dominant, ones. The convention did,
indeed, become well established that the moneyer should select
his types with an eye to the past glories of his own family.
But the Roman world at large must obviously have been more
interested in the events of the day than in these mythical
splendours ; and its interests were so far consulted, that topical
allusions were interwoven, often with considerable ingenuity,
in the web of family legend. Research on Roman coin-types
has aimed mainly at elucidating the history of the " gentes,"
and with such success that further explanation has hardly
been sought. We must remember that this is but half the
case : if few moneyers brought themselves to renounce the
right to belaud their ancestors, few were entirely oblivious of
the current events of the day.

A few examples will illustrate the forms that family allusions may take. The Mamilian " gens " celebrates its descent from Mamilia, the grand-daughter of Ulysses (Plate XVI, 18), the Hypsaean " gens " its descent from Leuconoe, daughter of Neptune. We are all familiar with the Trojan pedigree of the Julian " gens " ; but this special familiarity is simply due to the prominence which Julius Caesar gave to his house and its family legend (Plate XVI, 20). The flatterers of the Empire wanted to provide Vespasian with an ancestry from Hercules, but the Emperor himself laughed the project down. Other houses based their nobility on the Roman kingship. N. Fabius Pictor claims association with Quirinus (Plate XVI, 17). The " gens Marcia " claimed to derive from Ancus Marcius (Plate XII, 5), the " gens Calpurnia " from Calpus, son of Numa Pompilius, the " gens Pomponia " from Pompus, another son of the pious king. More than one family of Sabini boasted descent from the old Sabine king, Titius Tatius. The family of the Pompeii Fostli claimed as ancestor the shepherd Fostlus, who found Romulus and Remus with the she-wolf. Other moneyers boast of great Republican ancestors—Brutus, the murderer of Caesar, of Brutus the first consul, C. Serveilius of the Ahala, who put to death Sp. Maelius ; the Metelli had a particularly honourable place in the " Fasti,"—they could boast of the victory of Agrigentum and the victory in the third Macedonian War. The Aquillian gens could point to the conqueror of Aristonicus and the pacifier of Sicily, the Aemilian gens to L. Aemilius Paullus, conqueror of Perseus (Plate XVI, 16) ; M. Aemilius Lepidus, the later triumvir, has a gallery of family honours on his coinage—the Aemilius Lepidus who slew a foeman in battle at the age of fifteen, the Lepidus who was guardian to Ptolemy V, the vestal Aemilia, for whom the goddess miraculously re-kindled the sacred fire, which had been suffered to go out, the Aemilius who restored the " Basilica Aemilia " in 78 B.C. Faustus Sulla, son of the dictator, uses for reverse his father's signet-ring, showing the surrender of Jugurtha by Bocchus (Plate XVII, 14). M. Aemilius Buca, striking in 44 B.C., depicts on one of his reverses the dream of Sulla, who thought that he saw the goddess Bellona, whom the Romans sometimes identified with the moon, standing by him and putting thunder in his hand, with which to destroy his enemies.

The sons of the great Pompey naturally write large on their coinage the honours of their father. Other heroes of the coinage were decidedly stars of the second or third magnitude —the Sex. Nonius Sufenas, who first celebrated the games of Victory, the Coelii Caldi of the coinage of Caldus, the C. Plautius Venno Hypsaeus who took Privernum in 341 B.C., the Restio of the coins of C. Antius Restio.

One particular kind of reference is that of the punning or canting badge—Pan for Pansa (Plate XIV, 10), Silenus for Silanus, the Septemtriones for Trio, the jackdaw for Gragulus, the wren for Todillus. Badges of this character were evidently common, and were freely used for coin-types : but it is doubtful whether all the explanations offered of this description can be seriously accepted.

The question of portraiture demands a word to itself. Tradition at first forbade any portrait other than that of a god. The earliest infringements of the rule date from about 110 B.C. Cn. Blasio portrays the famous Scipio Africanus the Elder (Plate XVI, 1), and L. Philippus the Philip of Macedon who was defeated at Cynoscephalae (Plate XVI, 2). The helmet with goat's horns and the letter ϕ on obverse leave no doubt of the identity of this person. It has been thought strange that an enemy of Rome should figure on his coinage ; but we must remember that the coin is two generations later than the king, that the king is represented as the friend of the Philippan family, and that after all he died as an ally of Rome. On the analogy of this coin, the diademed head on the obverse of Faustus Sulla (Plate XVI, 3) has been interpreted as Jugurtha. So, too, we may perhaps recognize in the Gaul on the obverse of L. Hostilius Saserna a portrait of Vercingetorix himself. From about 90 B.C., we meet portraits of early great men of Rome—Numa Pompilius, Titius Tatius, Ancus Marcius, Brutus the first consul (Plates XVI, 5 ; XVII, 6), Ahala (Plate XVI, 5), the tribune Ser. Sulpicius Rufus, the consul M. Claudius Marcellus (Plate XVI, 6). Then come later personages, Aemilia Lepida the Vestal, the consul C. Coelius Caldus (Plate XVI, 4), the consul Q. Pompeius Rufus, the consul A. Postumius Albinus, the tribune Antius Restio, the praetor L. Regulus (Plate XVI, 10).

The representation of the living man only begins in the year

44 B.C. with the portrait of Julius Caesar, which the Senate ordered to be placed on the coin (Plate XIX, 9, cp. 15). Before that date, allusion to the living had always been subsidiary and indirect, as in the case of Marius, Sulla and Pompey the Great.[1] But the times were ripe for the change. The example of Julius Caesar was readily followed, not only by his successors, the second triumvirs (Plates XIX, 14 ; XX, 1, 2, etc.), but by the Liberators, Brutus and Cassius themselves (Plate XIX, 18) ; henceforth every man who has confidence in his destiny does not hesitate to place his portrait on the coins.[2] Cn. Pompey jun. strikes with his father's portrait (Plate XVI, 9). Sextus Pompey associates with his own portrait those of his father and brother (Plate XVI, 8 ; cp. XIX, 11, 12). The way was, in fact, open to the full Imperial coinage. Augustus had not to educate the public to accept the appearance of personal types : all he had to do was to concentrate attention on his own person by eliminating rivals.

(c) *Historical Types, etc.* (Plates XVII-XX)—In passing over to our third section, that of mythology and history, we are not wandering far from family history, for, even where we cannot now trace it, family allusion is always to be suspected in reference to the past. Among the Greek myths represented on Republican coins are the story of Medusa, of Bellerophon and Pegasus, the hunt of the Calydonian boar (Plate VIII, 15), the rape of Europa (Plate VIII, 14), Hercules and the Nemean lion, the flaying of Marsyas, the home-return of Ulysses, Apollo and the Muses, Attis and Cybele, Scylla and Charybdis, and Trinacrus, the legendary hero of Sicily. The legend of the Catanaean brothers, Amphinomus and Anapias, who carried their aged parents on their shoulders from an eruption of Etna, is used as a type of " Pietas " by M. Herennius (Plate XV, 11) and Sex. Pompeius. In a similar way the more famous story of Aeneas and Anchises figures on coins of Julius Caesar. Among Roman legends we may cite the rape of Nerio by Mars,

---

[1] The famous gold stater of Flamininus, the Liberator of Greece, was a Greek, not a Roman coin. The placing of a portrait of a living Roman on the coin of another State was no direct concern of Rome.

[2] The heads on coins of M. Arrius Secundus and C. Numonius Vaala (Pl. XVI, 7) perhaps represent living men, as does possibly that on the coin of L. Servius Rufus. Later, even women are allowed to appear : apart from the very doubtful cases of Fulvia and Scribonia, we have certain portraits of Octavia and Cleopatra.

the story of the shepherd Fostulus and his wife Acca Larentia, who cared for the infants, Romulus and Remus, and Anna Perenna, the sister of Dido (Plate X, 12). The anguipede giant on coins of Cn. Cornelius Sisenna, M. Plaetorius Cestianus and L. Valerius Acisculus may represent a mythical deity of Valentia, the oldest name of Rome,—conceived of sometimes as a destructive, sometimes as a beneficent and healing power. A further set of allusions to the mythology of the Valerian gens has been very ingeniously traced on coins of L. Valerius Acisculus by Ch. Lenormant : but the types are, in fact, very obscure, and all we can safely say is that some of Lenormant's suggestions are ingenious enough to be true.

From mythology we pass, with little change, to the history, so closely interwoven with mythology, of early Rome. The coins supply us with a pictorial history of much of the tradition of the kingdom and Republic—the foundation legend (Plate XVII, 1), the kings, Romulus (Plate XVII, 2), Numa Pompilius (Plate XVIII, 4, 5), Ancus Marcius (Plate XVII, 3), Titius Tatius, the rape of the Sabine women (Plate XVI, 6, 7), the death of the traitress Tarpeia, Brutus the first consul, the battle of Lake Regillus, the treaty with Gabii, Ahala, the slayer of Sp. Maelius, the relief of the siege of Tusculum (Plate XVII, 8), the capture of Privernum, the exploits of the Metelli, of Scipio Africanus and M. Claudius Marcellus (Plate XVI, 6), the Lepidus who was guardian of Ptolemy (Plate XVII, 9), the young hero, M. Lepidus, who killed a foeman at the age of fifteen (Plate XVII, 11), the conquest of Perseus (Plate XVII, 10), the sack of Corinth, the victories of the Aquillii in Asia and Sicily (Plate XVII, 13), the trial of the Vestal Virgins, the surrender of Jugurtha by Bocchus to Sulla (Plate XVII, 14), the triumphs of Pompey (Plate XVII, 15). The motive for such allusions is partly family pride, partly antiquarian interest, intensified by the desire to see the present parallel to the past event. More peaceful events, such as the foundation of the games of Ceres and Flora (Plate XVII, 2, 12) and Victory (Plate XVII, 16) are also recorded. Interesting references to Roman customs are seen in the oath sworn over the body of a pig (Plate XVII, 17), the appeal of a soldier against sentence (Plate XVII, 18), the voting scene (Plate XVII, 19), and the seated Vestal Virgin (Plate XVII, 20)

More interesting, if harder to detect, are the references to contemporary history. Before about 135 B.C. such references as have yet been discovered are few indeed. The horse's head and free horse of the Pyrrhic War point to the alliance with Carthage. The introduction of the Diana in biga on reverse suggests the Latin League united with Rome against Hannibal, the Victory in biga may come in with the victory over Antiochus. An occasional symbol seems to have topical point, e.g. Victory flying over the Dioscuri may mark the end of the first Punic War—Victory crowning Rome the end of the second Macedonian War : the shield and dragon-trumpet suggests the wars against the Gauls of North Italy in the years just before 220 B.C. Behind the introduction of new types in the period after 150 B.C. some historical allusions may lurk : the types of Sex. Pompeius Fostlus and C. Augurinus, in particular, depart so far from the beaten track that we are forced to suspect a very special occasion for the coinage. It is just possible that there is some reference to the fall of Carthage—the dates would about fit. The fall of Rome's great rival might give point to grateful remembrance of Rome's own foundation [1] (cp. the reverse of Fostlus) and the addition of a great corn-producing province to the Empire may have suggested the monument of the Augurini, who tried to provide the people with cheap corn.

A little later we find ourselves on surer ground. The three moneyers M. Metellus Q.F., Q. Maximus and C. Serveilius struck coins after the murder of Ti. Gracchus. Serveilius with his reverse of Ahala slaying Sp. Maelius, expresses the belief, sanctioned by the Senate, that Gracchus had aimed at the kingdom as Maelius had done (Plate XVIII, 1). Some fifty years later, when Sulla restored the power of the Senate after the rule of the Marians in Rome, these three coinages were restored (Plate XVIII, 2), a head of Apollo replacing that of Roma on the obverse. The Senate, safely arrived, as it fondly hoped, at the end of the Civil Wars, looks back to the first blow struck on its side.

Indirect allusions to the legislation of C. Gracchus are seen

---

[1] The Secular Games, celebrated in 149 or 146 B.C. may possibly have had some influence.

in the Libertas in quadriga on the reverse of M. Porcius Lacca
and C. Cassius and in the ears of corn on the reverse of M.
Marcius. Here, too, belongs the revival of the reverse type of
Augurinus by his son Tiberius. The anonymous denarius with
reverse Pax in biga and symbol, elephant's head (emblematic
of Africa), may suggest the foundation of Junonia on the site
of Carthage.

There are coins of Spanish mintage which appear to belong
to the war of Numantia and the foundation of Valentia and
Segobriga in Spain. The great Gallic Wars, culminating in the
foundation of Narbo Martius, have left their record in coinage.
The man attacking a dog on the reverse of Cn. Domitius
reminds us of the huge dogs of war kept by the Arvernian
king Bituitus (Plate XVIII, 3).[1] The reverse of C. Metellus,
Jupiter in biga of elephants, makes us think of the victorious
general Cn. Domitius, who rode through the province of Narbonensis in a similar car (Plate XVIII, 4). The warrior in
biga on the reverse of the L. Licinius-Cn. Domitius issues is
certainly a Gaul and relates to the war with Bituitus, whether
or no we identify him with the king himself. The issue was
certainly struck on the occasion of the foundation of Narbo
Martius. Victories in Illyria are perhaps commemorated by
M. Fourius Philus (Plate XVIII, 6). A little later we find
allusions to the Cimbrian War, the Dioscuri riding right and
left (C. Serveilius—Plate XVIII, 5), the Roman and barbarian
fighting (M. Servilius) and the similar type of Q. Thermus
(Plate XVIII, 8). The " Roma " types of M. Cato undoubtedly
celebrate the triumphal end of the war. Allusion to the
Jugurthine War may be seen in the galley types of C. and M.
Fonteius, in the Scipio Africanus of Cn. Blasio, perhaps also
in the Hercules of T.Q.

C. Fundanius shows on his reverse Marius triumphing over
the Cimbri and Teutoni, and Lentulus Marcelli f. honours the
same general by the Hercules of his obverse and by the armed
figure crowned by the Genius of the Roman people on his
reverse (Plate XVIII, 9). When Saturninus, in 100 B.C., proposed his famous corn-law, Q. Caepio, the urban quaestor, informed the Senate that the treasury could not bear the financial

---

[1] Perhaps compare also coins of L. Torquatus (Pl. XVIII, 7).

burden. But the law went through and we have actual coins of Caepio and his colleague Piso struck for the occasion. The foundation of Eporedia after the war is perhaps glanced at on the reverse of L. Cassius Caeicianus. A special coinage, that of C. Malleolus, A. Albinus, L. Metellus, and L. Pomponius Molo was struck for the occasion. The Roma crowned by Victory marks the conclusion of the war ; the Dioscuri, while associated with the family history of A. Albinus (A. Postumius Albus was dictator at Lake Regillus), suggests the colony rich in horses ; the Apollo of the obverse may be the god of colonies, or, perhaps, rather of the Sibylline books which ordered the foundation. The Social War has left a full record of both sides, Roman and rebel. On the Roman side, we note the " Salus " type of D. Silanus, the galloping horseman (a despatch-rider) of L. Piso (Plate XVIII, 13),[1] the rape of the Sabines of L. Titurius Sabinus (a reference to a previous war of Rome with her close kindred), the chariots of the great gods (thanksgiving services) of L. Rubrius Dossenus. Corn distributions are celebrated by P. Fourius Crassipes (Plate XVIII, 14), and M. Fannius and L. Critonius (Plate VII, 8). On the Italian side, we find the head of Italia in place of Roma, the swearing of alliance over the body of a pig, Italia crowned by Victory, the bull of Italy trampling the she-wolf of Rome, the visit of envoys of the Italians to King Mithradates. The inscriptions are part Latin, part Oscan, and the names of various generals, among them Q. Silo, C. Papius Mutilus and Numerius Lucilius appear (cp. Plate XVIII, 10-12). Many of the types are adopted from Roman coins of the period of the Cimbrian Wars. The brotherhood in arms of that war had undoubtedly done much to revive the hope of citizenship in the allies, the more so as Marius himself had shown a very liberal attitude towards the question. It is naturally to that brotherhood that the rebels now chose to appeal. The great war of the Sullan and Marian factions is illuminated for us by a curious accident of coinage. The Marians adopted as part of their programme the cry of pure silver and the issue of serrate denarii as a guarantee of purity. The Sullans would have none of the device. We have here a most valuable criterion for distinguishing the coinage of

---

[1] He bears either a torch (a " fiery cross " (?)) or a palm, as sign of victory.

the two factions, from about 86 B.C. when the Marians adopted
the serration to the fall of the Sertorians in Spain. On the
Sullan side, we have Sulla's own coinage, struck in the East or
in South Italy on his return. The coinage issued by L. Lucullus
on Sulla's orders from the 20,000 talents levied on the cities of
Asia Minor is probably represented by the aurei and denarii,
with obverse, Venus and Cupid, and reverse, jug and lituus
between trophies. Other coins show us Sulla in his triumphal
chariot (Plate VI, 12) and an equestrian statue raised in his
honour. The Sullan restoration was celebrated, as we have
seen, by a re-issue of types of the days of Ti. Gracchus. There
are also coins of C. Annius, the Sullan governor of Spain, 82-80
B.C., of Q. Metellus Pius, who waged a long and doubtful war
with Sertorius, and of C. Valerius Flaccus in Gaul. The triumphal banquet of Metellus,[1] when he was crowned at the feast
by a Victory, is shown on the reverse of P. Lentulus P.f.L.n.
(Plate XX, 11). Other coins of Roman mintage were probably struck for the war with Sertorius, with such types as
Mars, Diana and Neptune.

The coinage of the Marians is more eloquent. Their relations with the Italians are portrayed on a number of types
(Plate XVIII, 15-17). C. Mamilius Limetanus, with his
reverse of the home-returning Ulysses, suggests the return of
the Marians from their wanderings. The coins of Q. Antonius
Balbus may represent the products of the robbing of the
temples in 82 B.C. The transference of the war to Spain by
Sertorius is clearly expressed on the coins of A. Postumius
Albinus, with his obverse of Hispania, and his reverses, a sacrifice of a bull on a hill, and a togate figure standing between
fasces and standard (Plate XVIII, 18, 19) : it is a clear picture
of the inauguration of civil and military government in Spain
by Sertorius. The bust of Diana, the patron-goddess of Sertorius, is several times represented. The coinage of Q. Crepereius Rocus, which is full of references to the sea, certainly
alludes to the naval war and Sertorius's allies, the pirates
(Plate XVIII, 20). The somewhat obscure reference to
Libertas, Venus and the sea (oars) on the issues of C. Egnatius
Maxsumus seem at least to be closely identified with the

---

[1] Described by Plutarch, *Sertorius* (Chapter XXII).

alliance of the Italians with the Marians in the closing stages of the struggle in Italy.

The period from 70 to 50 B.C. yields us several striking examples of contemporary allusions and would undoubtedly yield more if we understood more of its detail. A very rare aureus celebrates the triumph of Pompey the Great on his return from the East ; the obverse shows the head of Africa, the scene of his earliest triumphs, the reverse the hero in his chariot accompanied by his son on one of the horses. Definite allusions to Pompey's exploits against the pirates [1] and against Mithradates, as also to those of his predecessor, Lucullus, are lacking, so far as we know : but several issues, notably those of L. Torquatus, M. Plaetorius Cestianus, M. Piso Frugi, seem to be connected with these Eastern campaigns. M. Aemilius Scaurus, who had served under Pompey in Syria, celebrates the surrender of the Nabathaean king Aretas : the coin was struck in 58 B.C. when Scaurus was curule aedile (Plate XIX, 2). A similar type of A. Plautius showing the submission of " Bacchius Judaeus," obviously refers to some episode of the Eastern Wars (Plate XIX, 3). There seems to be no authority for identifying this Bacchius with the Jewish prince, Aristobulus, tempting as the suggestion appears, and we are left to suppose that it was some minor prince, whose surrender is here recorded.

The coinage of Brutus, with types of Libertas, Brutus the first consul, and Ahala, is proved by finds to belong to this period, not, as one would have imagined, to the period after Caesar's death. But appropriate to the day it certainly was : it was issued as a piece of Republican propaganda against the first triumvirate. Caesar, Pompey and Crassus were denounced as " reges," and men called for a second Brutus or Ahala to deal with them. The coinage of P. Crassus, son of the triumvir, was issued by special permission of the Senate, probably in connexion with the raising of a troop of Gallic horse for the Parthian War in 55 B.C. The consulship of Messalla (53 B.C.) is celebrated on the coinage of his son (Plate XIX, 4). A coinage of Julius Caesar, struck probably in Cisalpine Gaul for circulation there and beyond the Alps, has recently been

[1] But perhaps compare the denarius of Ser. Sulp. (Pl. XIX, 1).

6

found in the issues of Kalenus and Cordius, M'. Aquillius
M'.f.M'.n., T. Vettius Sabinus, L. Roscius Fabatus, Libo,
Paullus Lepidus, and others. The reverse of Kalenus and
Cordius, Roma and Italia clasping hands, refers to Caesar's
policy of treating the Transpadanes as Roman citizens. The
"Concordia" and "Bonus Eventus" of Paullus Lepidus and
Libo seem to relate to the Conference of Luca.

The outbreak of the great civil war leads to a great enliven-
ment of the coinage, which now provides a running comment
on the course of events. On the side of the Pompeians, we
have the emergency issues of Q. Sicinius, with the head of the
"Fortune of the Roman people," and of L. Lentulus and
Q. Marcellus, the consuls, with the ominous reverse, eagle and
standards. The scene now shifts to the provinces. In Spain
we have coins issued for Pompey by Cn. Piso and Varro, a
second issue of the two consuls in South Italy, a third in Sicily,
a fourth at Ephesus, with the reverse of "Diana of the Ephesians" (Plate XIX, 5). After Pharsalia we have the issues of
the Pompeians for the campaign of Thapsus, with definite
allusions to Africa. Most interesting is the coinage of M. Cato,
struck at Utica, the town that witnessed his death and gave
him a name (Plate XIX, 8). In Spain the sons of the great
Pompey, Gnaeus and Sextus, strike for the campaign of Munda,
with types celebrating their hearty welcome by the provinces
(Plate XIX, 11, 12).

On the side of Caesar, we have the denarius with the elephant and the implements of the priesthood, perhaps struck
a little before 49 B.C., and the aurei and denarii, with the remarkable legend II.L (52) apparently giving the age of Caesar
himself (Plate XIX, 6).[1] References to Gaul are seen in the
Gallic arms of the reverse of Albinus Bruti f., and, above all,
in the Gallic warrior and Gallic woman on the obverses of
L. Hostilius Saserna. A. Licinius Nerva refers to the devotion of Caesar's troops, Palikanus to his regard for the constitution, L. Papius Celsus to his triumph, T. Carisius to his reforms
of the mint, L. Valerius Acisculus to the Sibylline prophecy
that only a king could conquer the Parthians. Other types
probably have topical allusions, Ceres and Bacchus to dis-

---

[1] Cp. *Revue Arch.*, 1866, p. 20 : article of Count de Salis.

tributions of corn and wine, Venus to the legendary history of
the Julian gens.   Finally a group of moneyers strike with the
portrait of Caesar.[1]   Other issues seem to belong to the provinces, either in the name of Caesar only or of a legate, like
A. Allienus, proconsul of Sicily in 48 B.C.   It is noteworthy
that Eastern issues on both sides are still rare : the Eastern
campaigns are fought mainly with Eastern currencies.

Finally, with the last period of the Republic, we find a
coinage that wanders further and further from the Republican
traditions and, were it not for the number of competing poten-
tates, might almost be called imperial.   At Rome, the Senatorial restoration is represented by a group of moneyers who
coin on the old lines.   L. Servius Rufus, referring to the relief
of Tusculum by an ancestor in 374 B.C., hints at the attempts
made by Octavian and the consuls, Hirtius and Pansa, to raise
the siege of Mutina.   The types of M. Arrius Secundus and
C. Numonius Vaala seem to bear on the same campaign.   Then
comes the second triumvirate and, on the next coinage, the
portraits of the triumvirs and references to their family history
are interspersed among pure Republican types (Plate XIX,
14, 15).   The " Liberators " and their friends meanwhile struck
freely in the East (Plate XIX, 17-19).   There is one reference,
in the most perfect taste, to the battle of Philippi—the coin of
L. Mussidius Longus, with, obverse, head of Concordia and,
reverse, statues of Venus Cloacina on a platform (Plate XIX,
16).   The Romans and Sabines in early days had purified
themselves after their combat on the spot where statues of the
goddess were afterwards erected ; and, with this reference, the
moneyer passes skilfully over a terrible episode of civil war,
which must have brought as much sorrow as joy to dwellers in
Rome.   The coins of Q. Voconius Vitulus and Ti. Sempronius
Gracchus, which show Octavian only, to the exclusion of his
colleagues, certainly belong to the days of the Perusine War.
The reverse of Gracchus, standard, plough and sceptre, points
directly to the allotments of land to veterans which were the
immediate occasion of the breach.

Here the Republican coinage of the capital closes : the
triumvirs agreed for the future to supply their needs of money

---

[1] For coins of Caesar, see Pl. XIX, 7, 9, 10.

from provincial mints. In Spain we have a single issue from
the mint of Osca by Cn. Domitius Calvinus, *c.* 39-37 B.C. In
Gaul we have joint issues of Antony and Lepidus at Lugdunum,
followed by coinage in the name of all three triumvirs and by
coins of Antony, including the interesting quinarii that give
his age on two successive birthdays (XL and XLI) (Plate XX, 1).
The mint then passes to Octavian, for whom Balbus, Q. Salvius,
and the famous M. Agrippa issue coins (Plate XX, 9). Several
issues of Octavian appear to belong to irregular mints (" Moneta
castrensis ") of the days when he levied an army in his own
name to combat Antony (Plate XX, 2). The side of Antony
in the Perusine War is represented by coinage in his name
issued by his brother, who alludes to himself by his self-chosen
name of " Pietas " (Plate XX, 8), and by P. Ventidius Bassus,
the later victor over Parthia (Plate XX, 5). In Sicily we have
the coinage of Sextus Pompeius, bearing the title " praefectus
classis et orae maritimae," which he extorted from his unwilling rivals. The proud title " son of Neptune " on the coinage
of Q. Nasidius refers to Sextus's initial success over Octavian's fleets in the decisive campaign (Plate XX, 10). In Africa,
Q. Cornuficius, governor 44-42 B.C., celebrates the refuge that
he gave to fugitives from the proscriptions (Plate XX, 4).
And in the same province, or perhaps in Sicily, we have coinage
of Lepidus and, after him, of Octavian, struck, no doubt, for
the campaign against Sextus Pompey, the sequel to which was
Lepidus' bid for supreme power and dismissal into private life.

In the East, there is first an ample coinage of the " Liberators," Brutus and Cassius, boasting of their fight for " Libertas,"
of the famous ancestors of Brutus, of their victories in Lycia
and over Rhodes (Plate XIX, 17, 18). Murcus, the admiral,
who joined their cause, celebrates with a denarius his arrival
in Asia (Plate XIX, 19). Cn. Domitius Ahenobarbus, another
admiral of the " Liberators," struck in his own name after his
victory over the fleet of Octavian off Brundisium on the day
of Philippi, but soon joined Antony and struck for him. A
special place of dishonour must be reserved for Q. Labienus,
son of the Labienus who deserted Caesar : joining the Parthians
to invade Syria, he has the effrontery to boast of himself as
" Parthicus Imperator " (Plate XIX, 20). Finally we come to
the extensive coinage of Antony himself. We see his alliance

with Octavian (Plate XX, 3, 6), the temporary estrangement over Perusia (Plate XX, 7), his marriage alliance with Octavia (Plate XX, 12), last of all his capitulation to the influence of Cleopatra, " the queen of kings and of kings who are her sons " (Plate XX, 16). His ill-fated son, Antyllus, shared the honour of a portrait with him (Plate XX, 15). There is the remarkable bronze issue celebrating the naval help sent to Octavian against Sextus Pompey and the reference to the conquest of Armenia, notably on the denarius of Cleopatra (Plate XX, 13, 14, 16). Lastly, for the campaign of Actium, Antony struck his famous series, with types complimentary to his army and fleet, proudly setting out by name the full number of his legions (Plate XX, 17-19). To the same occasion belongs the coinage of Scarpus in Cyrenaica (?) in the name of the eighth legion, with which he held Egypt against attack from the West (Plate XX, 20).

Here we may leave the study of Republican times. The war of claimants for the supreme power has forced itself into the foreground and the way is open to the development of a purely imperial coinage.

(d) *Animate and Inanimate Objects* (Plate XXI, 1-14)—The use of various animate and inanimate types to express ideas is an important branch of the language of coins. A few typical examples must suffice us here. The symbolism, we shall see, is sometimes direct and obvious, sometimes, to our minds at least, far from obvious. Firstly, there are types related to the worship of the gods—for Jupiter the eagle and thunderbolt (Plates XIII, 18 ; XXI, 20), for Juno Sospita the serpent and the griffin (?) (Plate VIII, 13), for Juno Moneta the implements of coinage, for Neptune the dolphin, for Apollo the tripod and patera (Plate VIII, 18), for Diana the stag or hunting dog (Plate XIII, 8), for Hercules the club, bow and arrow and lion-skin, for Mars the wolf (Plate XIV, 3), for Minerva the aegis and helmet, for Mercury the caduceus and the tortoise, for Ceres the modius and corn-ears, for Vesta the priestly vessels. Secondly, there are types relating to moneyers : the calf for Q. Voconius Vitulus, the ram (?) for L. Rustius, the elephant for Q. Metellus Pius (cp. Plate X, 15), the Macedonian shield for M. Metellus. The sphinx of T. Carisius represents the signet-ring of Julius Caesar. Thirdly, there are types relating to places—the triskelis for Sicily, the lion for Lugdunum, the winged horse for Lampsacus (Plate XIV, 12), the horse for Parthia, the tiara for Armenia. Finally, there remains a mass of types of general symbolic significance.[1] The eagle and standards represent the army (Plate VII, 7), the ship or prow the fleet, trophy and captives stand for victories. The clasped hands denote concord (Plate XXI, 9, 13), the caduceus trade, the palm and wreath victory, the globe world-power, the cornucopiae general prosperity, the fasces the constitution, priestly vessels the sacred offices (Plate XXI, 4, 14), curule chairs curule office (Plate XXI, 5, 6, 10), the sceptre dignity and power, the rudder, government. The statue of Marsyas seems to represent the forum as the centre of Roman institutions (Plate XXI, 2). The star over a prow suggests good fortune to the fleet (Plate XX, 12). The pileus and daggers of Brutus hardly need the legend *EID MAR* to call to our minds the bloody deed by which Roman liberty was vindicated. Crescent and stars or stars (Plate XXI, 7) represent the heavens, the star by itself may be a symbol of consecration.

(*e*) *Architecture, Art, etc.* (Plate XXI, 15-20)—The Roman passion for building is not unfairly represented on the coins. The representations are often sketchy and inadequate, but, in the absence of better records, have an importance of their own. Apart from temples—the Capitol (Plate XXI, 15, 20), the temple of Neptune, the temple of Vesta (Plate XIV, 20), the temple of Venus Erycina (Plate XXI, 17), the temple of the deified Caesar, the temple of the Clemency of Caesar and a temple of the Sun, and another of Jupiter and Libertas,—we have views of the rostra (Plate XXI, 19), the platform from which tribunes addressed the people, of the Villa Publica, the state guest-house in the Campus Martius (Plate XXI, 18), the " Basilica Aemilia " restored by M. Aemilius Lepidus in 78 B.C. (Plate XXI, 16), and the Aqua Marcia, the famous aqueduct brought to Rome in 144 B.C. by Q. Marcius Rex. Other objects of topographical interest are the corn-memorial of the Augurini by the Porta Trigemina, the statue of Marsyas in the

---

[1] See Pl. XXI, 1, 3, 8, 11 ; VII, 13, 14, 16, 17, 18 ; X, 10, 11, 14, 16, 17, 18 ; XII, 7, 8, 9 ; XIII, 9, 15 ; XIV, 5 ; XV, 1, 2, 4, 9, 16 ; XV, 10, 13, 14.

Forum, and the " puteal," or well-head of Libo, also in the Forum, the resort of money-lenders.

A few special features of Roman life are illustrated on exceptional issues.   Piso and Caepio and M. Fannius and L. Critonius show public distributions of corn, C. Serveilius C.f. show two gladiators measuring swords, L. Regulus a fight between men and wild beasts in the arena (Plate XVI, 10).   Caldus offers a view of a " lectisternium " (Plate XVI, 4), the religious banquet to the gods, when their statues were brought out and exhibited on the sacred couches.   The " Sors " type of M. Plaetorius Cestianus alludes to the lots of the " Fortuna " of Praeneste, whether we interpret the youthful figure leaning on the balcony as a personification of the spirit of the lot or as a young attendant.   A voting scene appears on the reverse of the denarius of P. Nerva and, in less elaborate form, on that of Longinus.   The reverse of P. Laeca shows a soldier appealing against the sentence of his general, represented by his lictor, to a togate figure, representing the Roman people.   In this case, a contemporary reference to the demand of the allies to a share in the right of " provocatio " seems to be implied.

The relation of the art of the Roman die-sinker to other contemporary forms of art can only be glanced at here.[1]   The portraits on coins probably derive largely from the " imagines " or waxen masks, kept as part of the family heir-looms of all the great houses.   Only in the last period, for contemporary portraiture, is a copying from statues probable.   We suspect originals in statuary for a number of divine types, for the Muses of Q. Pomponius Musa, for the Catanaean brothers of Sex. Pompey, the Perseus group of Paullus Lepidus, the group of Marcus Lepidus and Ptolemy V as his ward, the Aeneas and Anchises of Caesar.[2]   The surrender of Jugurtha by Bocchus to Sulla was, we know, the subject of a signet-ring of the dictator Sulla.   The most interesting, because the most certain, example of the copying of a major work of art is seen on the reverse of L. Plautius Plancus.   Pliny [3] tells us that L. Munatius Plancus placed in the Capitol a picture by Nicomachus,

---

[1] For types of special interest or beauty cp. Pl. VIII, 16-20 ; X, 13.

[2] The reverse type of Eppius seems to show a representation (or caricature ?) of the Hercules of Lysippus.

[3] *Nat. Hist.*, XXXV, 10, 36.

showing " Victoria quadrigam in sublime rapiens." This description so perfectly describes the reverse of the coin that we cannot doubt the identification (Plate VIII, 20).

Here we must leave a subject, which by its wealth of allusion and detail as well as by the obscurity of many of its references, appears to defy a summary treatment. Even the brief sketch here given will have served a useful purpose if it leads Roman students to exploit the material already available and to provide, by research into outstanding difficulties, further material for the next generation to exploit.

COINAGE IN THE GENERAL LIFE OF THE ROMAN REPUBLIC

FOR this, our third chapter, we have reserved some aspects of coinage which bear on the general political life of the State. Our inquiry will lead us over ground already, in part, covered, and will confront us with some problems of great difficulty and obscurity ; it will, however, reward us with some light on questions that are as interesting in their present bearings as in their place in the past. We will consider first the general part played by the coinage in the economic life of the Republic ; secondly, emergency measures affecting the coinage ; thirdly, coinage in relation to foreign policy, that is to say, in relation to Italy, the provinces and foreign powers.

1. **Occasions of Issues**—Coinage in ancient times was issued far less regularly and uniformly than it is to-day. A few great commercial States—Athens, Corinth, the Roman Empire— maintained an almost continuous flow of coinage over long periods of time. Most of the ancient world, however, coined only at intervals, as particular necessities dictated. Out of this phase, the Roman Republic, despite the extent of its foreign conquests, never entirely passed. Granted, then, that the issue of money is to be left to the dictation of circumstances, it becomes obvious that war will play a decisive part in decid- ing when and where money shall be issued. War, for the ancient State, was a normal condition of life,—not an excep- tional emergency. For a State like Rome, a general peace was a happy ideal seldom realized. The requirements of war, then, were the main deciding factor for the coinage : during the great wars it flowed in a full stream, during the intervals of more or less complete peace its volume diminished. All the great wars of the West, the Pyrrhic War, the first and

second Punic Wars, the wars in North Italy and Spain, the war
with Jugurtha, the war with the Cimbrians and Teutons, the
series of civil wars—one and all are represented by great addi-
tions to the coinage.   The wars in the East bore a somewhat
different character.   Rome, still relatively a poor country, found
herself fighting in lands where masses of coinage had been ac-
cumulating for centuries.   She allowed herself to be led by
circumstances here and, instead of turning fresh masses of
bullion into coin, used her victories to transfer vast quantities
of coined money from the defeated countries to herself.   The
gold Philippus, the Attic and the cistophoric tetradrachm
flooded the Roman market and supplemented the deficiencies
of the somewhat meagre native system.   Only in the last
century of the Republic do we find Rome issuing her own
denominations in the East.

Roman coins, then, were issued largely to meet the requirements of wars.   What more can we add to our knowledge
of the occasions of coinage ?   Regular issues for purposes of
trade can hardly be proved.   Even the " quadrigati " and
victoriates of the third century, which were certainly struck
for foreign trade, must often have been issued for immediate
occasions of war.   The foundation of new colonies was certainly accompanied at times by special coinages : we are
certain of the fact in the case of Narbo Martius and may consider it as highly probable both for foundations in Spain
(Valentia, Segobriga, 140-130 B.C.) and for Eporedia in North
Italy (99 B.C.).   Similar issues probably occur earlier, but
cannot yet be identified with certainty, as they are not signed
by the founders of the colonies, many of whose names are preserved for us by Livy, but only perhaps by subordinate officials,
either the ordinary moneyers or officials specially appointed
for the occasion.   It was, however, only natural that the
colony, often an outpost of Rome in a district as yet remote
from her power, should be started in life with a supply of
Roman coinage.   In the later Republic, we can place our
finger on other occasions of a special character—the distributions of cheap corn to the populace or the celebration of games,
notably those of the curule aediles in Rome.   In the case of the
distributions the expense was normally borne by the State.
In the case of the shows, the burden fell on the magistrates,

who received special permission from the Senate to commemorate their magnificence by special coinage. Probably, if we
could trace the occasions of all Republican issues, we should
find that the vast majority fall under one or other of these
headings. By the time of Cicero, we have evidence of bullion
being brought to the mint by private individuals to be stamped
as money.[1] We may well doubt whether any serious proportion of Republican coinage was thus issued. In time of emergency, the reserves of precious metal in the " aerarium Saturni "
could be drawn upon. In earlier times, the State probably
depended for its supply of bullion partly on the spoils of war,
partly on the existing stocks of metal, struck or unstruck,
in the home market ; the task of finding the metal for particular issues was, to judge from analogies, let out on tender
to private companies. The general tendency throughout the
Republic was for the volume of currency especially in the
precious metals to increase. As the wealth of the world was
drawn more and more steadily towards Rome, money became
an ever commoner commodity and prices rose in a steadily
soaring curve. Rome experienced, in full measure, the consequences, good and bad, of this economic development : with
it we may connect a fact of such political import as the rise of
the capitalist class, the " equites," to power from the days of
Gaius Gracchus.

2. **General Financial Policy and Theory**—Such was the
general trend of Roman economic policy. Economic theory is
little understood to-day and we can hardly credit the Roman
financiers with even our limited knowledge. The immediate
need was always their guide. They took such measures as it
dictated and had to bear the consequences as best they might.
We have now to consider some occasions of special urgency,
where reforms of the coinage were definitely used to extricate
the State from her financial straits. The great Eastern Wars,
we have seen, more than paid for their cost and brought to
Rome reserves of coin and bullion. Even the campaigns
against Spaniards and Ligurians were not barren of spoils,
and Carthage had to pay heavily the price of defeat. But
what of the great wars that strained the financial resources of

---

[1] Cp. Cic., *Ad. Att.*, VIII. 7, 3.

the State and yet brought no immediate reward ? We arrive at once at an astonishing conclusion. The Romans never learned how to accept the fact of a permanent war-debt, to be funded and repaid over a long period of time.[1] They preferred the alternative, disastrous to individuals but not without its conveniences for the State—that of partial repudiation of debt. That this repudiation was not nakedly announced, but was covered under the show of a reform of the coinage, alters nothing of the essence of the case.

The debt of the Pyrrhic War was met by a reduction of the As, the unit of account, from ten to five ounces and by the introduction of silver at a rate above its normal market value. In this case our authorities do not report any alteration in the unit of currency, and it is possible that, in theory, both the denarius and the reduced As could theoretically be exchanged for ten and one libral Asses respectively. In the long run, a large proportion of the debt was probably lost by the creditors. In the first Punic War, Rome was brought to the very edge of financial ruin. This time there was less attempt at disguise. The As was reduced to a sixth of its original value—in other words, five-sixths [2] of the national debt was repudiated. The effects on individuals were naturally various. Debtors escaped lightly, while many creditors were ruined. But neither the loss of the one or the gain of the other class was anything but incidental to the measure. The State owed what it could not pay and the Roman statesmen cut the Gordian knot by " reforming " the coinage.[3]

The second Punic War led to a repetition of the same device. As early as 217 B.C. financial difficulties were becoming serious. The As was accordingly reduced to half of its previous value, and the State paid only 10s. in the pound. The denarius, however, retained seven-eighths of its metal value and was re-tariffed at 16, instead of 10, Asses, to maintain without serious alteration the relation of the two metals. At the same time,

[1] But the *tributum* was conceived of as a forced loan, to be paid back as occasion offered.

[2] Assuming, that is to say, that the As had not been already formally reduced by a half. See above, pp. 11.

[3] We should naturally expect—but do not find—a re-tariffing of the denarius in terms of the reduced Asses. The explanation, perhaps, is that the early denarius was a rare coin and was not really worth the ten semi-libral Asses to which it was equated : only with the sextantal reduction did the denarius, now really worth the ten Asses at which it was valued, begin to play a large part in currency.

however, recourse was taken to the dangerous practice of debasement. For the pay of the troops, the As continued to be reckoned as one-tenth of the denarius. Gold, too, was issued at a tariff considerably too high for its normal market value.

Let us stop for a moment to consider this curiously complicated reform. The reduction of the As leaves no doubt as to the general fact of repudiation of debts. The man who was creditor for 100 sextantal Asses only received 100 uncial Asses in payment ; if he was paid in silver, he received in place of 10 denarii of 4 scruples each $6\frac{1}{4}$ denarii of $3\frac{3}{4}$ scruples. But there was the Italian market as well as the home market to be considered. Here Rome could not proceed so boldly in repudiation. All she ventured to do was to strike off one-eighth of the weight and to make an extra unavowed and perhaps undetected profit by means of debasement. The army was treated on the same lines as the foreign, not as the home creditor. The army pay was reckoned in Asses and a strict application of the reform would have reduced the soldier's pay by about half. This was evidently considered too dangerous. The fiction of a sextantal As was still maintained and the reduction in pay was restricted to that involved in the reduced weight and debasement of the silver.[1] Even these drastic measures proved insufficient. Rome was driven to resort to a moratorium, postponing the payment of her debts till the end of the war. The final victory and the war indemnity from Carthage set her in a position to clear a large part of these debts : it is probable that a large part owing to individuals was lost account of and never repaid.

The debasement of the silver appears to have taken the form of the issue of a certain proportion of " plated " denarii,

---

[1] The original pay of the troops was 1200 Asses (120 denarii, or, according to the later reckoning, 75 denarii, 3 aurei). Under Tiberius we find the legionary drawing 3600 Asses (225 denarii) per year, but claiming to be paid a denarius per day, instead of ten Asses. Evidently the reckoning of a denarius as equal to ten Asses has been discarded, but not forgotten. All that we hear for certain between the time of Polybius and that of Augustus is that Caesar doubled the pay. The fact that the mark X persists on the denarius long after 217 B.C. seems to be connected with the use of the old reckoning. Evidently we have lost part of the history. Julius Caesar may have raised the pay to 2400 Asses (= 240 denarii) ; Augustus may, while adding a third stipendium (1200 × 3 = 3600 Asses), have actually reduced the pay to 225 denarii by tariffing the Asses at sixteen to the denarius. Cp. *B.M.C. Empire*, I, p. xlviii, n. 2, for further discussion and suggestions.

i.e. coins with a thin envelope of pure silver enclosing a heart
of base metal. The serration or cutting of the edge of the
denarius is met with on a single issue of the period *c.* 220 B.C.,[1]
and looks like a protest against such fraudulent coins.   As we
shall later find the democratic party in favour of pure silver,
it is tempting to attribute this protest to the democrats under
C. Flaminius.

After the victory over Carthage Rome entered on a period
of rapid political and commercial growth.   She had departed
once and for all from the simple conditions of the Italian city-
State ; she was on the road to becoming a world power and
must expand her coinage to answer to her new position.   The
indemnity from Carthage and the spoils of defeated enemies
in East and West relieved her of any difficulty about supplies
of bullion.   Inflation of the coinage. was inevitable, but it
was inflation of the better kind, the issue of ever-increasing
amounts of good money.   There was no need for the debasement of the silver or for reduction of the standard.   Money,
however, became ever cheaper in relation to other articles
and there was a steady rise both in prices and in wages.   As
usual, however, the rise in prices was more automatic and
inevitable than the rise in pay.   Let us take the case of the
soldier as an example.   In the time of Marius he still drew
only the 120 denarii which he had been drawing in the second
Punic War.   We can see that there must have been justifiable
discontent among the troops and a demand for a raising of the
pay.[2]   It is probable that the just grievance of the soldiers
was never fully satisfied, but that temporary relief was afforded
by handsome donations after victories.   The general result of the
increase of money must have been an increasing inequality in
possession.   The accumulation of capital began and the class of
" equites " came to rank next to the Senate as an aristocracy of
money.   The causes of the new conditions may not have been
very clearly understood, but the conflict of interests was

[1] If this date is correct, the issue of base coins probably actually preceded the
second Punic War.

[2] The appearance of the mark of value, XVI, on the denarius, might seem to
imply the abolition of the old reckoning of ten Asses to the denarius and a consequent
reassessment of the soldier's pay ; but it is possible that that mark has a quite
different history.

obscurely felt and began to find political expression. The moneyed classes came to stand for pure money and a check to inflation. The impoverished could see no objection to measures which diminished the power of the capitalist ; and the Senate, which was an aristocracy of land, not of money, was not always indisposed to foster their interests.

We come to the age of the Gracchi, when so many latent conflicts of the preceding years came at last to an open clash. The policy of the democrats was in no sense a single one. The Gracchi attempted to unite around them many different classes of malcontents and had to try, as best they could, to harmonize interests not always at one. There was first of all the policy of helping the poorer citizens—on the land by restoring agriculture, in the city by cheap doles of corn, abroad by citizen colonies. For all these purposes large issues of coinage were essential.[1] C. Gracchus included in his alliance against the Senate the capitalist class, the knights. They were willing to accept the democratic proposals of Gracchus, but insisted that there must be no tampering with the coinage : the State must pay for its new expenditure either out of its reserves in the treasury or from the new revenues of Asia. The Senate found itself opposed to this demand ; the new expenses must be met by inflation of the coinage, i.e. the burden must be shifted on to the shoulders of the moneyed classes. This is evidently the meaning of the enactment of M. Livius Drusus, who, in his tribunate, " mixed an eighth part of bronze with the silver." Our authorities do not tell us which Drusus brought in this measure, but the probabilities are in favour of the elder.[2] A protest was not slow in coming. The foundation of Narbo Martius, itself a triumph for the democratic party, was accompanied by a large issue of serrate denarii : the cutting of the edge was designed to give palpable evidence that the new coinage was of pure silver. The great wars that followed against the Northern barbarians and Jugurtha led to a renewal of the practice of plating ; but the return of the democrats to power with C. Marius in 105 B.C. is accompanied by a

[1] In the period from 135 to 122 B.C. we appear to have a double series of coins at Rome, part perhaps issued by the Gracchi, part by the Senate.
[2] The measure has usually been attributed to the younger Drusus, tribune in 91 B.C.

return to a serrate coinage. After the decisive victory, however, the democratic party suffered a second catastrophe; the extremists lost touch with the moderates and Marius was forced to take the leading part in suppressing his former allies, Saturninus and Glaucia. The serrate coinage was abandoned and, with the outbreak of the Social War, the need for plated coins became more and more acute. The silver was debased to such an extent that no one knew what he possessed [1] and, to make matters worse, the monetary standard, still based on the As, was again tampered with. The As was reduced to half its weight and 50 per cent. of the State debt was repudiated. Had the silver still been pure a re-tariffing of the As in denarii would have been inevitable. As it was, the reduced As and the debased denarius could be left at the old ratio. Even so, the enormous expenses of the unprofitable war could not be covered.[2] The State and the individual were on the verge of bankruptcy and the cry arose for " novae tabulae "—a clean sheet, with a cancelling of all existing debts. Something very like this was actually decided on, when the Lex Valeria [3] provided that debts should be paid at the rate of quadrans for As,—5s. in the pound. This last measure, though not operative for any long time, no doubt wiped out most of the remaining State debt. But the position was intolerable in the long run,

---

[1] Cp. Plautus, *Casina*, Prologue and V, 9 ; *Mostellaria*, IV, Sc. 2 : the references probably belong to this time. Cp. also Pliny, *N.H.*, XXXIII, 3, 46 ; XXXIV, 6, 27 ; 9, 132 ; Cicero, *De Officiis*, III, 20, 80.

[2] The loss of Asia to Mithradates was, of course, a contributory cause.

[3] The " Lex Valeria " was a measure of the democratic party. They found themselves on the horns of an awkward dilemma, for, while they stood for a pure currency, they had to face an impossible burden of State debt. They thought no more than did the *optimates* of funding it. The " Lex Valeria," then, was passed as an emergency measure of repudiation to satisfy malcontents and to extricate the State from its immediate difficulty. The debt once disposed of, coinage was for the future to be pure and trustworthy. Definite repudiation of debt was preferred to indirect repudiation by debasement. The passage in the manifesto of the rebel leader, C. Manlius, in Sallust (Catiline, Ch. XXXIII, 3) : " novissime memoria nostra propter magnitudinem aeris alieni volentibus omnibus bonis argentum aere solutum est," might seem to refer to the Lex Valeria, but what then does " argentum aere solutum est " mean, and did all " boni " approve that law ? A reference to the compulsory circulation of base denarii seems more probable. Mommsen, *Röm. Münzwesen*, pp. 383, 384, applies the passage to the Lex Valeria : he thinks that that law substituted for the old libral As, equal to a sestertius, the As of the coinage only worth a quarter of that amount. For criticism of Mommsen's general view, see *Proceedings of the Cambridge Philological Society*, 1925, pp. 21 ff.

and the return of the Marians to power enabled the financial interests to make their voice heard.   The cancelling of a large portion of existing debt was a necessary evil that must be endured.   But for the future the coinage must be re-established on a firm basis.   The As was not restored to its old value, but its issue on the lower standard was suspended [1] and the silver, which now had to bear the chief part in currency, was purified. M. Marius Gratidianus the praetor " invented [2] the art of distinguishing pure money."   The serration of the denarius was resumed and the issue of base denarii ceased.   Sulla, on his return, repealed the Lex Valeria, but reimposed the compulsory currency of base coin.   The State was to be allowed to inflate the coinage to just such an extent as seemed advisable, [3] and, fortified with this power, could dispense with the extreme measure of cancelling debts.   The serration of the denarius is now found only on denarii of the Marian faction in Spain : on the coinage of Rome it disappears.   The savage vengeance wreaked on M. Marius Gratidianus by the Sullans proves that his measures had had far-reaching consequences.   He had evidently touched the *optimates* in the tenderest of all spots— the pocket.

The victory in the long conflict rested with the Senate. The Marian faction split into conflicting sections.   The "equites" came to be afraid of the extreme " populares " and, encountering a more accommodating spirit in the Senate, moved towards that " concordia ordinum," which Cicero set before him as his ideal.   Minor differences of policy between possessors of different kinds sank into insignificance before the essential conflict between the " haves " and the " have nots."   The demand for " novae tabulae " was steadily resisted.   The serrate denarius was not reintroduced—it had been discredited by the later issues of the Marians in Spain, who had been driven by financial necessity to stultify their own policy and issue plated serrati.   The plating of denarii was not abandoned, but, in deference to the knights, the Senate used its powers with some discretion.   The awkward question of the bronze was left unsolved.   It was not reintroduced at Rome either on

---

[1] There are no issues of semuncial standard from the Marian moneyers.

[2] The earlier serrate issues prove that " invented " is not quite the right word.

[3] Cp. *Digest*, XX, 109.

7

the uncial or on the semuncial standard. A return to the uncial standard would have meant a going back on a previous policy. A continuation of semuncial coinage would have led to a difficult question in tariffing the bronze in terms of silver. That the old Marian policy was not forgotten is proved by the serrate issues of Julius Caesar in Cisalpine Gaul : [1] but the fact that they are interspersed with non-serrate issues seems to show that the policy was only in part restored and that the issues of plated coin were only designed for circulation among the tribes of the North, which had a natural preference for pure silver. The victory of Julius Caesar which led on to the Empire was, of course, a victory for the democratic party, and we expect to find its financial policy triumphant. We shall discuss later the question of debasement under the Empire. Here we must only say that the early Emperors appear to have been true to the democratic policy of pure money. The temptations of an easy inflation, however, soon made themselves felt, and later Emperors were drawn into the same baleful courses as the Senate of the Republic.

3. **Coinage and Foreign Policy**—Finally we have to consider the coinage in its relation to foreign policy, first in Italy, then in the provinces and abroad. We shall have to consider how far other than economic considerations entered into the account, whether Rome used her coinage as a means of advertising her name in the world and whether she used her military power to secure herself unfair advantages.

We begin with Italy. We must distinguish at once between the various kinds of states in relationship to Rome. On the one hand, there is Rome herself, the colonies of Roman citizens, whether with the full or with the restricted citizenship, the smaller communities of citizens lacking urban organization. For all these Roman coinage is naturally valid : it would be against all constitutional law for a burgess colony to strike in any name than that of Rome. Next come the various allies of Rome, bound to her by treaties of a more or less favourable complexion—prominent among them the great class of Latin colonies, enjoying a privileged position and able to aspire, under given conditions, to the citizenship. For all these,

---

[1] See *Num. Chron.*, 1924, pp. 41 ff., 50 ff.

independent coinage is theoretically possible. Finally, we have States bound by no fixed ties to Rome—who would obviously decide for themselves whether to coin or not.

Let us now consult the evidence of the coins. In the period down to the end of the Pyrrhic War, we find coinage in silver and bronze at a number of independent Greek States and in Etruria, and also at such Latin colonies as Cales (Plate XXIII, 6), Suessa (Plate XXIII, 9), Arpi (Plate XXIII, 5), Signia, Alba Fucentia. The coinage of the Bruttii in gold, silver and bronze begins in the Pyrrhic War (Plate XXIII, 2, 3) : but the silver and bronze continues for some time after it. *Aes Grave* is issued by Latin colonies such as Hatria, Ariminum, Luceria and Venusia and by independent communities such as Volaterrae, Iguvium and Tuder. Rome is simply one of many States issuing coins ; her own allies coin freely in their own name, sometimes, as in the case of the *Aes Grave* of Hatria, on local standards distinct from the Roman. In the *Aes Grave* Rome certainly took the initiative in inaugurating her issues ; and it is quite doubtful whether any of the silver issues of Latin colonies are earlier than the Pyrrhic War. There are no coins attributable to burgess colonies. Mommsen thought that he must make an exception in favour of Capua, but, as we have already seen, the " Romano-Campanian " issues, attributed by him to that city, are purely Roman issues, struck for the needs of the Pyrrhic War at several South Italian mints.

In the period from the end of the Pyrrhic to the second Punic War, Roman coinage assumes a predominance proportionate to the political importance of the Roman State. The issue of silver by the Latin colonies ceases, but bronze is still struck and *Aes Grave* continues to be cast at Luceria and Venusia. The coinage of the Greek cities of the South declines but it is probable that such cities as Tarentum (Plate XXIII, 10, 11, 13) and Naples (Plate XXIII, 7) may have continued to issue down to the second Punic War. We still find *Aes Grave* in Etruria and Umbria. The Roman "quadrigatus" and, later, the victoriate certainly tend to replace the local issues,—but probably not to the point of entire suppression. The second Punic War marks a decisive period of change. The rebel States have their own coinage—we can trace it at Capua, Atella, Tarentum (Plate XXIII, 13), and one or two other cities. The conclusion of the war leaves Rome supreme. Henceforth there is no silver current in Italy except the Roman, and even issues of bronze are restricted to a few communities of the South, such as Brundisium and Paestum, issuing the lower denominations of the Roman system of the As, on a lower system of weights. The victoriate, the coin for foreign trade, gives place to the denarius. Rome clearly made it a principle to claim the monopoly of coinage and only allowed exceptions within a very limited range. Our results correspond admirably with the political history. The Pyrrhic War lays the foundation of Roman supremacy, the second Punic War crowns the edifice.

Even before Rome's supremacy in Italy was finally reached she had acquired her first transmarine provinces and had to face the problem of how to provide coinage for them. She came further into close contact with foreign powers and had to decide on what principles to treat their currencies and how to relate them to her own. It will be necessary to treat this question in detail, province by province, but a few introductory comments will help to clear the ground. Rome does not attempt to enforce any one uniform policy—she allows herself to be influenced strongly by local circumstances. She does not to any great extent issue coinage as a means of flying the flag abroad. If in the West she gradually assumes something like a monopoly, it is practical convenience rather than principle that guides ; for in the East, where local money was readily available, she shows no disposition to enforce her own money system and only a very moderate anxiety to coin in her own name.

In Sicily the local coinage was almost restricted to Syracuse (Plate XXII, 1-3) when the Romans first set foot in the island. When, after the death of Rome's faithful ally, Hiero, Syracuse revolted and was re-conquered, Rome stopped the Syracusan issues of silver (cp. Plate XXIII, 14), but allowed small coinage in bronze both at Syracuse (Plate XXIV, 4) and a few other towns. She herself issued bronze, signed by Roman officials, at Panormus (Plate XXIV, 5), and perhaps at other mints. Her treatment of Sicily, in fact, followed the same lines as her treatment of Italy. The Roman silver—first the victoriate and then the denarius—filled the gap, but we cannot point with confidence to issues from Sicilian mints till the great civil war (49 B.C. onwards). The silver litra seems to have been reckoned as one-fifth of the denarius.

Sardinia and Corsica depended from the first on Rome for coinage. The one bronze issue of Sardinia, with obverse of " Sardus Pater," signed by M. Atius Balbus, is not earlier than the time of Julius Caesar (Plate XXIV, 9).

In Spain Rome found provincial silver coinage of the Carthaginians and silver issues of the Greek cities of Emporiae and Rhoda (Plate XXII, 7, 8),—the latter continuing into the second century.[1] From an early date Rome struck denarii for the use of her armies in Spain.[2] We can trace Spanish issues, at intervals, from the second Punic War till after the Numantine War and later in the war with Sertorius and the civil war of Caesar and Pompey. Beside this Roman coinage, we find a native silver, the " argentum Oscense," so named from one of the chief mints, Osca (Plate XXIV, 6), with names of towns or tribes in Celtiberian and such types as obverse, head of Hercules, reverse, horseman. The standard is that of the denarius. A lighter coin of victoriate weight is found early in the series. This coinage has been variously dated—to the period before the fall of Numantia, or to the Sertorian War. Livy attests the existence of the " Oscan silver " soon after the second Punic War and, as pieces in mint condition have been found with Republican coins of about 100 B.C., it must have been issued at any rate near the latter date. We must therefore allow it a range of nearly a century, 200 to 100 B.C., and perhaps longer.[3] The lack of development in style and types might lead us to assign it a shorter term, e.g. from the pacification of Spain after the fall of Numantia : but the testimony of Livy is too definite in favour of an earlier beginning for us to disregard it. In the existence of this native silver, certainly tolerated if not actually instigated by Rome, we have clear evidence of a liberal policy, aiming at making the province of the silver mines self-supporting. The bronze coinage is of less importance. We

---

[1] The later drachms are of denarius weight.

[2] The early Roman didrachms are rarely found in Spain, " quadrigati " and victoriates more commonly.

[3] The denarius of Cn. Domitius, c. 37 B.C., imitates the obv. of the Oscan silver.

find issues with Latin legend and types of Roman pattern at Saguntum (Plate XXIV, 8), Segobriga and Valentia (Plate XXIV, 7) in the years following the overthrow of Viriathus. The coinage with Celtiberian types and legends seem to belong mainly to the last century B.C., perhaps after the cessation of the issue of "Oscan silver."

In Africa, Carthage, the conquered enemy, and Numidia, the favoured ally of Rome, issue money during the second century. The Carthaginian coinage, of course, ceases with the fall of the city, the Numidian continues to the time of Juba the First, the ally of the Pompeians.[1] The denarius clearly supplied the needs of the Roman province, though we cannot be certain of issues from African mints before the great civil war. The special coinage for the Jugurthine War may have been issued from a South Italian mint.

In Gaul, Massalia was the one community issuing coins during the early second century (Plate XXII, 6). To harmonize her coinage with the Roman, she replaced her drachm by a lighter coin, corresponding to the Roman victoriate (Plate XXIV, 10).[2] But this was probably the act of enlightened self-interest, rather than of compulsion. Denarii were struck for Narbo Martius, perhaps also for the war preceding its foundation, again in the Cimbrian Wars, then under C. Valerius Flaccus, c. 84 B.C., again by Julius Caesar as governor, and then by the second triumvirate. The native Gallic coinage is difficult to date. The silver, struck on the standard of the half-denarius (the later victoriate) is all late, and the same is true of much of the bronze, which clearly betrays Roman influence. It evidently belongs to the period of Romanization from Julius Caesar to Augustus. The bulk of the gold and part of the coinage in base silver and bronze is earlier in date but certainly not nearly so early as has been suggested. The establishment of the Roman province of Narbonensis may well have been the decisive event. The gold, as is well known, is largely dependent for types on the aureus of Philip of Macedon. But this coin, as we shall see, was well established in circulation at Rome and may well have come to Gaul by way of Rome and Massalia.

---

[1] In the later of these issues, the standard of the denarius prevails.
[2] The date of this change is uncertain, probably not far from 200 B.C.

Late in the Republic we find the beginnings of a provincial coinage in silver and copper in the town issues of Lugdunum (Plate XXIV, 12), Vienna, Cabellio (Plate XXIV, 11), and Nemausus (Plate XXIV, 13). We shall later find Gaul playing a decisive part in the establishment of the imperial coinage.

Britain hardly concerns us as yet. Suffice it to say, that our island follows, at a little distance, a development similar to the Gallic. The purely native coinage, mainly in gold and uninscribed, may date roughly from 100-50 B.C., the later inscribed coinage shows traces of Roman influence and is later than Julius Caesar.

In the Adriatic district—Illyricum, Epirus, Acarnania— the Roman victoriate, which corresponded to a local unit of weight long familiar there, played an important part from about 235 B.C.[1] But it did not oust the local coinage : we continue to find silver issues of the same standard at Apollonia (Plate XXIV, 14), Dyrrhacium, Corcyra and other mints.

Turning from West to East, we find a different policy prevailing. There are no certain issues of coins of Roman standard before the coinage of Lucullus for Sulla. Even after his time, such issues are rare—not till the days of Mark Antony can the Roman aureus and denarius have been really familiar coins. The great Macedonian and Syrian Wars served rather to bring the money of the East to Rome than that of Rome to the East (cp. Plate XXV, 1, 2, 4). When Rome, establishing her provinces, is led to take a part in the coinage, she maintains the local standards. To the end of the Republic silver was struck freely at many Eastern mints and even the Emperors followed the policy of maintaining local standards. Issues by Rome herself are few and far between,—the silver tetradrachms of Aesillas (Plate XXV, 3) and Sura for Macedon, the silver tetradrachm of Metellus for Crete, the cistophori of Asia with the names of the Roman governors (Plate XXV, 6).[2] Far from enforcing her own coinage, Rome is chary of any

---

[1] We also find multiples of the victoriate (2 and 4) and coins of denarius weight (e.g. at Corcyra, Pl. XXIV, 15). The introduction of the later victoriate (= a quinarius) at Rome may have led to the reduction here of double victoriates to denarii.

[2] On Pl. XXV, 5, is shown a rare copper coin, perhaps struck by Brutus in Macedon.

interference with local coinage.   Here, as elsewhere, she follows
that wise policy of "laissez aller," which was perhaps the
mixed product of a wise self-restraint and embarrassment in
face of a very complicated problem.   It has been maintained
that coinage in gold was considered from the time of Alexander to be a prerogative of the Empire, not of the king or
city State, and that Rome showed herself jealous of this prerogative.   The comparative scarcity of gold coinage, however,
is probably attributable rather to the well-known preference
of the Greeks for silver.   It is doubtful whether Roman jealousy
has much to do with the matter.

One problem, however, Rome could not entirely evade—
the intricate problem of co-ordinating the masses of gold and
silver in her Eastern provinces both with one another and with
her own denarius.   No better evidence of the question is yet
available than the powerful sections of Mommsen's great work,[1]
to which we must refer the reader who seeks further detail.
It is necessary, however, to add the warning that the evidence
to be drawn from metrological writers is very obscure and uncertain of interpretation.[2]   The first main fact to be grasped
is, that the Roman denarius, at first a little heavier, later a
little lighter than the Attic drachm, was normally equated to
it : this equation was still maintained, even after the reduction
of Nero.   The tetradrachms of Athens herself (Plate XXV, 9),
then, and all other pieces of Attic weight were reckoned as
equal to four denarii.[3]   The Rhodian drachm (Plate XXV,
10) was equated to the old victoriate, $\frac{3}{4}$ths of the denarius ;
the "cistophorus" (Plate XXV, 6), a tetradrachm of the
Rhodian system, was therefore equal to three denarii.   In

---

[1] *Geschichte des Römischen Münzwesens*, pp. 661 ff.

[2] We may instance the statements of Festus and Pollux about the different
kinds of talents.   The Attic equals 6000 drachms or denarii ; the cistophoric accordingly equals 4500.   So far so good.   But what of the Alexandrian, which
equals 12 denarii, the Neapolitan which equals 6, the Rhegine which equals $\frac{3}{4}$ths ?
The unit of these later talents is obviously a copper, not a silver drachm, and in
some cases a reduced drachm at that.   We find ourselves at once floundering in a
morass of conjecture about relations of silver and copper and reductions of standard.
Until scholars have straightened out these problems, there is no choice but to disregard them in a handbook.

[3] Livy, XXXIV, 52, says " equal to three in weight "—possibly a mere error ;
but Mommsen argues from this passage that this rate was actually applied to Attic
tetradrachms in the province of Asia.

Syria the tetradrachms of Attic weight (Plate XXV, 7) were equated to four denarii, and Mommsen thinks that the same rate was applied to the lighter Tyrian tetradrachms (Plate XXV, 8) : such an over-tariffing of foreign money is, however, improbable, and Mommsen's arguments are not strong. So far as the Aeginetan standard still survived (e.g. in Crete and Cilicia), it is probable that the Romans treated the Aeginetan didrachms as equivalent to the cistophoric tetradrachm, i.e. as three denarii.   The Attic and the cistophoric were almost the only two Greek standards with which Rome had much to do and we may assume, as a sound working principle, that Rome treated all Greek drachms as equal either to denarii or to victoriates.   Of any deliberate attempt to favour the Roman coin unduly we have barely a trace.   Bruno Keil [1] has shown some reason to think that the substitution of the new victoriate ($\frac{1}{2}$ denarius) for the old ($\frac{3}{4}$ths denarius) may have been fraudulently used to depress the value of Greek currencies equated to the victoriate, but it is best to suspend judgment pending the discovery of decisive evidence.   For gold and silver Rome seems to have accepted the standard of 1 to 10, and at that rate would tariff the aureus of Philip at about 20 denarii.

To sum up our results : at home, Roman coinage was always intimately bound up with the political life of the State—its flow was determined by the requirements of war, by the expenditure on corn-distributions and shows, even more than by the more normal requirements of trade.   In the absence of a developed banking system, it was probably not easy to put money on the market for general trade purposes : the nearest we get to such commercial issues are probably those issues which were destined for the use of new colonies.   In time of emergency the State availed itself of the dangerous right of " reforming " the coinage to reduce the national debt.   The false theory that the State can lower the standard and debase the currency was, indeed, contested, and sometimes defeated,— but only to come up again.   But it was particularly a theory of the Senate and, when the Senate fell, the Empire started with good chances of building on a sound basis.   Abroad,

---

[1] *Z.f.N.*, 1920, pp. 47 ff.

Rome does not use her right of coinage in any very aggressive or avaricious spirit. There is clearly something of political choice in her partial monopoly of coinage in the West. In the East, where economic considerations were strongly in favour of another policy, those considerations in the main seem to triumph over the political. Autonomy in coinage is one of the last elements of autonomy to disappear in the Eastern provinces and was, in fact, preserved largely intact into the Empire.

BOOK II

THE EMPIRE. AUGUSTUS TO DIOCLETIAN

CHAPTER I

THE EXTERNAL HISTORY OF THE COINAGE. AUTHORITIES, MINTS, MONEY-SYSTEMS, ETC.

1. **Historical Survey**—Not the least troublesome of the problems which Augustus had to face was that of the coinage. Out of the storms of the Civil Wars, which had wrecked the old system, had, indeed, emerged a new one in its place ; but it was not one which had any claim to permanence. The Senate, in losing control of its governors and generals in the provinces, had lost control of the coinage : the mint of Rome was closed and gold and silver were being struck only on a military basis for military needs. With the bronze there was the additional difficulty that the standard was now quite uncertain ; since the failure and cessation of the semuncial issues of Rome, no one could say with authority what coin a Roman As ought to be. There were the needs of the provinces as well as Rome to be considered ; nor must any serious attempt at reform fail to take account of the great rise in prices that had accompanied the development of Imperial power. The position of Rome as mistress of the world seemed to demand for her the primacy in coinage ; at the same time, the urgent needs of the armies in the provinces must receive due consideration. What policy was Augustus to follow ? Was he to reinstate the Senate in its old position of control ? That would mean a vexatious hampering of his powers as " Imperator." Was he to share with the Senate the direction of the Roman mint ? That solution had already been tried by Julius Caesar and by Augustus himself, as triumvir with his colleagues, and had been abandoned as unsuccessful. Either the share of the Senate would be a real one and might embarrass the Emperor, or it would be a mere pretence and would simply create bitterness. The Senate could not be expected to abdicate as readily

as it abdicated later in the case of the corn-supply and the city-police. Nor, as a third choice, could the existing system be allowed to continue without reform. It was on that system, however, that Augustus decided to build. As paymaster of the armies, he must keep in his own hands the issue of the precious metals; the coins in which the troops received their pay must bear his image and superscription. This was the more necessary as the Imperial gold at least was to be a coinage of the Empire; and in the provinces there must be no question as to who was the real master of the Roman world. Augustus decided, however, to avoid the direct challenge to the Senate that the establishment of an Imperial mint in Rome would have implied. Grafting his new coinage on to the coinage of the generals in the provinces, he issued his gold and silver at provincial mints in his capacity of " Imperator." At the same time, he was able to gratify the Senate by a concession, which complimented them without unduly embarrassing him. The bronze coinage of Rome was at first designed for circulation in Rome and Italy only and it was to be subsidiary to that in the precious metals. He could therefore safely separate it from the Imperial and place it under the control of the Senate,—a control which would supply a necessary guarantee against possible abuses of a token coinage. It is probable that this solution was only reached gradually, after a period of experiment, as our following survey of the measures taken by Augustus will show.

After Actium Augustus struck gold and silver (Plate XXX, 6, 7) in the East for his troops, in direct continuation of his coinage as triumvir. In 27 B.C., when he laid down his exceptional powers and received the first grant of those that went to make up the principate, this military coinage was suspended, but provision was made for the needs of Asia by a provincial coinage in silver and bronze. The future of the Imperial coinage was left undecided—a clear indication of the thorny problems involved therein. The re-organization of the Imperial powers in 23 B.C. on the dual basis of the " imperium " abroad and the " tribunicia potestas " at home advanced the problem a long stage further. The foundation of the military colony of Emerita in Lusitania gave Augustus occasion to issue silver at that mint through the agency of his legate,

P. Carisius (Plate XXX, 2).   At the same time, the Roman
State resumed its issues of " Aes." [1]   After a very brief initial
experiment, the Emperor renounced sole rights here and gave
the initiative to the Senate,—an initiative marked by the
almost invariable signature S.C. (" Senatus consulto ").   He
himself shares in the coinage, as representative of the Roman
people in virtue of his tribunician power : the coinage is
definitely that of the " Senatus populusque Romanus."   The
issues of P. Carisius were followed by other issues, with no
name but that of Augustus, at Emerita (Plate XXX, 3) and
other Spanish mints (Plate XXX, 4, 5), and Augustus's visit
to the East, 21-19 B.C., was accompanied by similar coinage
there (Plate XXX, 8).   The final solution was now in sight,
but there were still doubts and hesitations.   When Augustus
returned to Rome in 19 B.C., he consented to a coinage of gold
(Plate XXX, 1) and silver in the capital, in which he and the
Senate shared responsibility.   Here, as on the bronze, the
signatures of the moneyers appear, but the distinctive mark,
S.C., is absent as a normal feature and the portrait of the
Emperor is prominent from the first ; on the " Aes " it was
restricted to one denomination, the As.   This coinage lasts
till 12 B.C., but during Augustus's absence in Gaul, 15-14 B.C.,
it was suspended, and the Imperial element in it steadily en-
croached on the Republican.   The Senate had clearly not yet
resigned all interest in the coinage in gold and silver and could
influence Augustus to respect its wishes.   But Augustus had
by now arrived at a decision.   Lugdunum, the capital of the
great Imperial province of Gaul, was a natural centre of coinage for the great wars on the German frontiers that were now
in prospect : it lay in a region rich in gold and the Emperor
could coin there as general, without having to choose between
insulting the Senate or submitting to its interference.   In
15 B.C. Augustus opened Lugdunum as his Imperial mint and
there struck gold and silver for the rest of his reign. [2]   Soon
after his return to Rome in 12 B.C. he closed the Roman mint ;
the death of his colleague Agrippa, whose influence on Augustus

---

[1] This is a convenient description for the coinage in base metal, which consisted
partly of brass, partly of copper.
[2] For his famous " Altar " series in *Aes*, cp. Pl. XXXIV, 1.

was certainly conservative, may have made it easier for him
to take the decisive step. The coinage of Rome in " Aes "
ran with only slight intermissions from 23 B.C. to about 4 B.C. ;
the moneyers' names appeared throughout and on the smallest
denominations, the quadrans, the Emperor was not even mentioned (Plate XXXIII, 13). A break followed, lasting till
A.D. 11—perhaps due to some question of right, more probably to the absence of need for further coinage. When coinage was resumed in A.D. 11, the moneyers' names no longer
appear ; the privilege of the great families was finally abolished,
but the authority of the Senate witnessed by the mark S.C.
persists.

Of the money system of Augustus and of his arrangements
for the provinces, which belong to a later chapter, we need
only say here, that he made permanent a bimetallic system,
based on the aureus and denarius, that he reduced the " Aes "
to the status of token money, and that, while giving the aureus
and denarius free currency over the whole Empire, he provided provincial currencies of " Aes " for Gaul, Asia, Syria
and Egypt and encouraged local issues of small change over
almost the whole of the Empire. The solution of the problem
had been sought and found in a truly Imperial spirit.

Tiberius [1] followed faithfully in the footsteps of Augustus.
The one important innovation of his reign—the severe restric-
tion of local coinage in the West—was probably forced on him
by the nationalist movements under Sacrovir in Gaul and
Tacfarinas in Africa. There was some justification for mis-
trust of anything that fostered separatist tendencies in those
provinces. The special Gallic issues, the " Altar " coins of
Lugdunum, were suspended ; but the Imperial gold and silver
continued to be struck at that mint till the end of the reign.
The nationalist revolt just referred to and the end of the great
German wars might well have led Tiberius to close the Lugdunum mint. But if that mint were closed, another must be
opened in Rome or in some province ; so the cautious and conservative Tiberius preferred to let well alone and leave it to
his successors to make a change. That Tiberius's conservatism was not shared by the Imperial ministers of finances is

---

[1] For an issue for Commagene, revived by Vespasian, see Pl. XXXIV, 3, 6.

proved by the fact that the change came in the very first year of his successor.   The mint of Lugdunum was closed and the Imperial mint of Rome opened (Plate XXX, 9, 10).   This was no mere piece of autocracy on the part of the young Caligula— he began his reign, we hear, with fair promises of constitutional government.   But the Empire was now firmly established, the practical advantages of a mint in Rome were obvious, and the particular claims of Lugdunum had ceased to count.   The scruples which had hindered Augustus no longer carried the same weight ; the Senate had learned by experience to submit to the Emperor's will and seems to have made no serious protest.   In the Western provinces the policy of Tiberius was carried to its logical conclusion and local issues practically came to an end.   The short reign of Caligula, then, marks an important development of policy, based on sound considera- tions of expediency ; the megalomania of the Emperor's later years has hardly left a trace on the coinage.   The financial policy of the mad nephew was carried on unchanged by the pedantic uncle who succeeded him ; we can trace a continuity which must lie in the financial advisers of the Emperor, not- ably in the great chancellor, the " a rationibus," Pallas.   The one serious fault in the system was the lack of supplies of " Aes " for the West, which led to extensive imitation of the S.C. issues of Rome.[1]

The minority of the young Nero, under the guardianship of Seneca and Burrhus, led to a revival of the Senate which became the more marked when Agrippina and her protégé, Pallas, were forced out of public life.   On almost all the gold and silver of Rome of Nero's early years the formula *EX S.C.* appears (Plate XXX, 11).   In the first place, it may have referred to the oak-wreath, which formed the type of the reverse ; but when we find it still present on the later reverse types of Ceres, Roma and Virtus, we must accept it as applying to the coinage itself.   The Senate does not, indeed, go so far as to resume its rights of coinage ; the gold and silver is not struck *S.C.*, simply in pursuance of a decree of the Senate. But the right of authorization, expressed by *EX S.C.*, is definitely claimed ; the Senate will at least share in the

---

[1] For a Western imitation of Claudius, cp. Pl. XXXIV, 2.

responsibility. This partial return to the old Republican system did not outlast the years of Nero's tutelage. The reform of the coinage of A.D. 64 marks a return to the system of Claudius. The *EX S.C.* disappears from the gold and silver and the Emperor again monopolizes the coinage in those metals. At the same time, the issues of "Aes," though still left to the Senate, are conformed more closely to the Imperial coinage. In A.D. 59 the control of the " aerarium Saturni " was transferred from the quaestors to " praefecti " nominated by the Emperor. Some measure of Imperial control was henceforward assured and this is no doubt the reason why we now find the mint of Lugdunum reopened to supply the needs of the West in " Aes " (Plate XXXIII, 14). The Senate, as an independent authority, had no place in the Imperial province of Gaul ; but the Emperor, who could now exercise a real authority over the " Aes " issues of the capital, need not trouble about an infringement of his rights which was hardly more than nominal.

The great civil wars of A.D. 68 and 69, which revealed the secret that an Emperor could be made away from Rome, interrupted the even development of the Roman mint. Coinage was necessary for the rebels both for the pay of the troops and for the public proclamation of their programmes. Vindex and Galba issued coins of a general Republican character in Spain and Gaul (Plate XXX, 13, 14), laying stress on the Senate and people of Rome ; in the case of Vindex, some hint of a nationalist character in the movement can be detected. Galba, accepted after Nero's death as Emperor, struck in his own name in Spain and Gaul (Plate XXX, 16, 17) ; the fact that he also issued " Aes " with the formula *S.C.* suggests that the Senate's control over this coinage hardly went beyond the complimentary form. Clodius Macer tried to dignify his ill-considered rising in Africa by striking as a propraetor by authority of the Senate (Plate XXX, 12). The mutinous legions of Germany began late in A.D. 68 to issue coins without the head of an Emperor and with types magnifying rather the army and the people than the Senate of Rome. These gave way in A.D. 69 to the imperial issues of Vitellius himself. The mints of all these coins are far from certain. Galba probably struck at Tarraco in Spain and the mint soon passed with the province to Vitellius (Plates XXX, 18; XXXIV, 4). In Gaul Lugdunum had stood loyal to Nero and may have struck one siege issue in his name. Galba, in revenge, closed the mint and chose to strike at another centre, perhaps Narbo. Vitellius reopened the mint of Lugdunum and restored the city to the honours it had lost under Galba. And throughout the whole turmoil the mint of Rome continued to strike for its masters—Galba, Otho and Vitellius succeed one another on its issues. The notorious absence of " Aes " issues of Otho is certainly to be explained by the distaste of the Senate for the murderer of Galba. Pretexts for delay were easily invented and, before the Senate could be forced to declare itself definitely, Vitellius had won the day at Bedriacum.

The armies of Spain and Gaul and the praetorian guard at Rome had all tried their hands at Emperor-making, with indifferent success. It was left to the legions of the East to fulfil the prophecy that " a ruler of the world should come from Judaea " and to give to the Empire in Vespasian a man who could restore to it the stability and rest which it so sorely needed. Vespasian, like his predecessors in Gaul and Spain, could not wait for the possession of the Roman mint before he coined. We have his imperial coinage at Antioch (Plate XXXI, 6, 7), Alexandria, Ephesus (Plate XXXI, 4), Byzantium and other Eastern mints (Plate XXXI, 5), then, as his cause triumphed, at Tarraco, Lugdunum (Plates XXXI, 1, 2; XXXIV, 5, 7) and Rome itself. One small issue is certainly to be attributed to the armies of Illyricum, which won Italy for their candidate. The mint is uncertain : Poetovio has been suggested—the seat of the council of war—but Aquileia is, perhaps, a more probable site (Plate XXXI, 3). Vespasian, however, soon showed that he had no intention of standardizing the chaotic conditions of the civil wars and dividing imperial coinage over a number of local mints. One by one the local mints close [1]—Antioch in A.D. 72, Ephesus in A.D. 74, Tarraco in A.D. 72 or 73, Lugdunum at about the same date. When Lugdunum struck again towards the close of the reign,

[1] A single exception, seen in the issues of an Eastern mint in silver which signs with the letter O under the bust, is perhaps to be explained as an inaugurative coinage for the new province of Lycia : the O might then stand for the town of Olympus (Pl. XXXI, 8).

it was only, as under Nero, as a subsidiary mint for " Aes." Vespasian, then, at a time when the course of events rather suggested the creation of provincial mints, deliberately chose to centralize coinage at Rome. There was obviously an immediate wisdom in this policy. The Civil Wars had shaken the Empire to its foundation, the revolt of Civilis and the Empire of the Gauls, which had issued a small treasonable coinage of its own, had shown how imminent was the danger of a cleavage in the Imperial structure. Vespasian's whole endeavour was to repress the dangerous local movements and to do everything possible to restore Rome to her position of power and honour. But, in shunning the more immediate danger, Vespasian steered direct towards a danger, less obviously threatening, but calculated in the long run to defeat the best hopes that the Empire offered. Centralization of government at Rome meant stability and efficiency for the time ; but it also meant a severe strain on the resources of government and a discouragement of all that was alive and vigorous in local life. The more liberal and hopeful policy of the best of the later democrats and of Julius Caesar received a fatal set-back. The provinces lost all chance of a timely sharing in privilege and power : when, in the inevitable course of development, the prestige of Rome and Italy became obsolete, there was no longer freedom, but only servitude, to be shared.

The centralizing policy of Vespasian held the field for over a hundred years after his death. Provincial issues are few and far between—a few " Aes " coins of Titus and Domitian from the Lugdunum mint (Plate XXXIV, 8), a small issue of bronze of Trajan from a mint in Cyprus, rare silver issues of Trajan [1] and Hadrian (Plate XXXI, 10, 11) from Eastern mints. These can only be regarded as exceptions that prove the rule. Had there not been a very firm principle that Rome was the proper place of issue for Imperial coins, the wars of Domitian and Trajan on Rhine and Danube and the Empire-wide wanderings of Hadrian would naturally have called local mints into being. The burden that now fell on the two mints, Imperial and Senatorial, of the capital was an extremely heavy one, and we may conjecture, with much probability, that both

---

[1] Compare an Eastern (?) aureus of Trajan (Pl. XXXI, 9).

were enlarged and subdivided, in order to deal more efficiently with their task.   But, although it may have seemed advisable to divide the mints into sections or " officinae " and to allot to each a special part of the coinage, those " officinae " were kept within the capital itself ; Rome did not send out branch mints into the provinces.   If central control was the aim, it could be most efficiently exercised at a single centre.   Trajan even seems to have made an attempt to centralize many of the provincial silver coinages of the East at the mint of Caesarea in Cappadocia ; but the experiment was abandoned after his death.   The regularity of the succession in this period and the scarcity of pretenders in the provinces made it easier to maintain the monopoly of coinage for Rome.   Avidius Cassius, who rebelled against Marcus Aurelius in the East, has left no coinage. His rebellion was, indeed, nipped in the bud, but had he had close at hand a mint already issuing imperial coins, we might expect him to have struck at the very beginning of his usurpation.

The great civil wars that followed the death of Commodus bear a remarkable similarity to the wars that followed the death of Nero.   Again the emergence of rival emperors in the provinces led to issues from local mints.   Pescennius Niger struck gold and silver at Antioch (Plate XXXI, 13), Septimius Severus struck in Illyricum, in Asia Minor and in Syria (Plate XXXI, 14). Albinus, when after his brief period of Caesarship he disputed the Empire with Severus, struck at Lugdunum (Plate XXXI, 16)   The fact that the provincial issues of Pescennius and Albinus show no sort of similarity in style to the Roman is clear enough proof that no branch mints were working at the time at Antioch and Lugdunum ; had they been, there must have been traces of the normal style on the first issues of the pretenders.   On this occasion it was Septimius Severus, the Emperor who held the capital, that won the day.   But Septimius, unlike Vespasian, did not return immediately to the policy of centralization.   Himself a provincial, he had a full understanding of the point of view of the provinces ; and, after the struggle with Albinus, he found himself out of sympathy with the leading classes of Rome, who had inclined dangerously to favour his rival.   He had no objection then to opening an important branch mint in Syria for the supply of his armies in his great Parthian War (Plate XXXI, 16), and, although he suspended these issues in A.D. 202 and did not open a mint in Britain for his British War,[1] he had established a precedent which was not to be forgotten.   The period from Severus to Valerian is one of transition from the system of Vespasian to that of Diocletian.   Rome was still the only mint that struck regularly and continuously.   But the mint of Antioch was never closed for long at a time.   It was revived by Elagabalus in revolt against Macrinus (Plate XXXI, 17), it struck for Alexander Severus, and later for Gordian III and Philip I (Plate XXXII, 1) on their Eastern campaigns.[2]   There are issues of Trajan Decius and Trebonianus Gallus, which, if possibly not of Antioch, are yet unmistakably Eastern ; the mint might be rather sought near the shores of the Propontis (Plate XXXII, 4).   The troubles on the Danube under Gordian III and Philip I, which were the prelude to the great Gothic Wars, led to the opening of a mint at Viminacium, which, along with local " Aes," issued imperial Antoniniani (Plate XXXI, 18, 19). This mint fell into the hands of the pretender Pacatian in A.D. 248 (Plate XXXII, 2), and, after his fall, issued only a few denarii under Valerian : the plan of striking locally for the needs of the Balkan armies was, however, never again abandoned.

With the reign of Valerian we pass into a period of transition, in which the principles that had governed the early Empire one by one decay and the first experiments are made which led on to the new organization of the Empire by Diocletian.   Our knowledge of the period is too imperfect to admit of very confident judgments ; but we may suspect that, if we knew its details better, we might regard it rather as the preface to the new order than as the last chapter of the old.   Decentralization in coinage assumed larger and larger proportions. To the demand of the provinces for equality with Italy, which found its full expression in the emergence of the Gallic Empire, were now added decisive considerations of practical convenience.   With the collapse of the Imperial coinage under Gal-

---

[1] There is some evidence for local British issues of a semi-barbarous character at Chester, cp. finds in the Deanery Field, Chester.   Report, Liverpool, 1924, by Professor R. Newstead.

[2] For a Syrian (?) issue of Iotapianus, cp. Pl. XXXII, 3.

lienus, the local coinage of the cities began to totter to its fall. On the imperial mints must now fall the burden of supplying the entire needs of the Empire and for such a burden no one mint could possibly suffice. With the multiplication of mints that inevitably ensued went an increasingly severe control of the coinage, by means of signatures identifying mint, officina and issue. The temptations to abuse were now unusually acute, owing to the debasement of the silver, and easier and readier means of control were sought than those which may have sufficed, when only the one mint of Rome demanded supervision.[1]

Antioch strikes, with little interruption, except for the Palmyrene occupation, from Valerian to Diocletian (Plates XXXII, 16; XXXIII, 6). A second mint in Syria, that of Tripolis, was opened by Aurelian. Cyzicus struck from the reign of Gallienus or Claudius to that of Diocletian (Plates XXXII, 9, 16; XXXIII, 8), and Serdica opened not later than Aurelian (Plate XXXIII, 2), perhaps already under Claudius. Viminacium struck for Valerian and Gallienus; then, towards the end of the reign of the latter, Siscia took its place (Plate XXXIII, 5, 7). The great Gallic war of Gallienus led to the reopening of the mint of Lugdunum (Plate XXXI, 5). The Gallic Emperors struck at Lugdunum, Cologne and Mogontiacum (?) (Plate XXXII, 12-15). When Gaul was brought back to its allegiance by Aurelian, Lugdunum resumed its place as a great Imperial mint (Plate XXXIII, 9) : possibly under Tacitus its place was taken by the neighbouring Arelate. When Gallienus lost Gaul he still felt the need of a local centre of coinage for armies in the North of Italy. He accordingly opened the mint of Mediolanum (Plate XXXII, 7), which henceforward ranked as second in importance only to Rome. The mint seems for a short time to have fallen into the hands of Postumus—Aureolus, who held Mediolanum against Gallienus, may have been in league with Postumus and have struck in his name.[2] Its seat was transferred by Aurelian to Ticinum ; it signs with letter T, or TI under Tacitus and Florian (Plate XXXIII, 1, 3). Africa and Spain, both provinces which

---

[1] For issues of Rome, cp. Pl. XXXII, 8 ; XXXIII, 4.

[2] This view is being expanded and demonstrated in a paper by my friend, Professor A. Alföldy, in a coming number of the *Zeitschrift für Numismatik*,

played little part in the military history of the period, have no mints of their own. The attempt has been made, and is not yet finally abandoned, to attribute the coins above assigned to Ticinum to Tarraco. The arguments against Tarraco are, however, absolutely decisive :—

1. We have the signature M under Aurelian, giving place to T and TI.
2. The mint is mainly in the hands of Gallienus, only for a moment in those of Postumus. This is not what we should expect if it were situated in Spain.
3. Coins of the mint are admitted to be especially common in North Italian finds.
4. The style of the mint is allied to that of Rome and Siscia, not to that of Lugdunum.

We have only to realize that the military unimportance of Spain is a full explanation for the absence of a Spanish mint, and we can say good-bye once and for all to an unfortunate misattribution. It goes without saying that, in this age of provincial mints, local pretenders found it easy to issue coins in their own name away from Rome. Quietus (Plate XXXII, 10) and Macrianus II strike in the East, Regalian at an uncertain Balkan mint, in a style that is almost barbarous (Plate XXXII, 11), Saturninus at Tripolis (?), Carausius at Rotomagus, Londinum and Camulodunum (Plate XXXIII, 10-12), and Allectus at the two latter mints.

Diocletian, then, when he grasped the reins of power, found a system of provincial coinage already in full swing. Even before his reform he opened two new mints, at Heraclea Thracica (the old Perinthus) and at Treveri in Gaul. In A.D. 296 he made permanent and regular the new order for all time. Coinage was distributed over a large number of mints, each serving the needs of a limited district, all normally signing their issues with a distinctive mint-mark. Rome was simply one mint among many, no longer even " prima inter pares." But, as we have already suggested, this breaking down of the Italian monopoly came too late to foster the independent growth of the provinces. It was still one powerful central Government that held firmly the reins of power ; if that Government spread itself over a number of local centres it was only to tighten its grip, not to give play to local interests and traditions. The mechanical unity of the Government was still strong enough to hold the Empire together ; but the invisible links that go to build up an organic unity were being seriously loosened. Let the Government once give way and there was no spirit living in the Empire to find expression in a new constitution.

2. **The Money System in its various Stages**—The way is now clear for the discussion of the money system of the Empire in its various developments.[1] Augustus, accepting the facts of the existing system, very cleverly adapted it to his needs. During the last period of the Republic gold had been freely struck at a standard of 40 to the pound. Augustus standardized the aureus[2] (Plate XXVI, 1) at 42 to the pound and fixed its value at 25 denarii ; the denarius he continued to strike at the later Republican standard of 84 to the pound (Plate XXVI, 4). Half pieces in both metals were struck, in gold fairly frequently, in silver but rarely and, till Vespasian, only at the Eastern mints (Plate XXVI, 2, 3).[3] A gold coinage was clearly necessary for the Empire, both for the sake of prestige and for the practical necessity of dealing with expanding trade and rising prices. The sequel will show how wisely Augustus acted in maintaining the quality of the silver. But his system could not escape the weakness of all bimetallic systems—the establishment of a fixed relation in coinage of two metals which are naturally liable to fluctuations in the open market. In the base metals, there was more room for innovation. Since the collapse of the half-ounce

---

[1] We must here mention some few monetiform pieces, which, not being strictly coins, will not concern us here :—

  (a) Tesserae of brass and lead, used for distributions of corn, for shows, for various private purposes. Among these are the " spinthriae," tesserae showing " curious " subjects, perhaps to be explained as the " lasciva nomismata " of Martial, VIII, 78, 9.

  (b) " Medallions " of *Aes*, used for distribution on special occasions,—not struck on any fixed standard. The " medallions " of gold and silver, though perhaps used for similar purposes, are normally multiples of the aureus and denarius.

  (c) Imitations of coins used as ornaments, such as bracts, or thin one-sided pieces of gold.

[2] Aureus is an abbreviation for " aureus denarius." For gold, silver and billon multiple pieces, " medallions," see Pl. XXVII, 9-11 ; XXIX, 6.

[3] The silver piece was regularly named " victoriate " from the normal reverse type, Victory ; a similar use for the gold would be natural enough, but it is not definitely attested.

standard the Republic had had no fixed rules here and Augustus had to create an entirely new system. Instead of one metal, bronze, he made use of two, brass or orichalcum and pure copper —the former for the sestertius and dupondius, the latter for the As and quadrans [1] (Plate XXVIII, 1, 3, 4). There are several points of interest to be noted here : (1) the sestertius is no longer struck in silver ; (2) the two metals, brass and copper, are based on different standards—the sestertius, weighing 1 oz.,[2] presumes a theoretical As of brass weighing $\frac{1}{4}$th oz. whereas the actual *As* of copper weighs $\frac{2}{5}$ths oz. ; (3) the only division of the *As* now struck is the quadrans—triens, sextans and uncia disappear. The fact that the sestertius, which still remained the unit of account, was struck in brass has led to the suggestion that Augustus's system was really a trimetallic one—that brass in the coinage bore something like its true market value. This is, on the whole, improbable ; the ratio of the metals suggest that all the base coinage was now in some degree token money. But why, then, did Augustus trouble to use two metals, brass and copper, instead of choosing one of them for the whole of the base currency ? The answer seems to lie in the survival of the tradition of an As, of $\frac{1}{10}$th, not $\frac{1}{16}$th, of the denarius in the soldiers' pay. The copper As stands to the theoretical *As* of brass in the exact proportion of 16 to 10 and may be held to represent the old As of the soldiers' pay. It is possible that Augustus, when he inaugurated his reform, had some intention of replacing the As on its old standard for the army : the mutinous legions of Pannonia and Germany on his death demanded an increase of pay to just this extent—a denarius, instead of 10 asses, per day. If so, the project was never realized ; the increased weight of the As made it a more considerable coin and paid homage to the old tradition, but it did not affect its value in the market. The copper of which the As was struck was subordinated in value to the brass of the orichalcum. The use of two metals, however, was desirable, in order to make some distinction

---

[1] The closest parallel in the Republic is to be found in the " fleet " coinage of Mark Antony. The " Triumphal " issues of Augustus in *Aes*, *c.* 7 B.C., were apparently of two denominations, dupondius (Pl. XXVIII, 2) and As.

[2] The dupondius normally weighs $\frac{1}{2}$ ounce, but, in the Early Empire, was sometimes struck at a rather heavier weight.

between the dupondius and the As. Both were struck carelessly and actually overlapped in weight, so that confusion would have been inevitable, had there not been distinction of metallic colour to keep them apart. As it was, some further distinction, such as the use of radiate crown on dupondius and laureate crown on As, was at times found desirable. The rise in prices made the use of many subdivisions of the As unnecessary :—

We have then the following system :—

1 aureus (122·9 gr., 7·96 gm.) = 25 denarii = 100 sestertii = 400 Asses.
1 gold quinarius (61·45 gr., 3·98 gm.) = 12½ denarii = 50 sestertii = 200 Asses.
1 denarius (61·46 gr., 3·99 gm.) = 4 sestertii = 16 Asses.
1 silver quinarius (30·73 gr., 1·995 gm.) = 2 sestertii = 8 Asses.
1 sestertius (1 oz., brass) = 4 Asses.
1 dupondius (½ oz., brass) = 2 Asses.
1 As ($\frac{2}{5}$ths oz., copper) = ¼ sestertius.
1 quadrans ($\frac{1}{10}$th oz., copper) = ¼ As.

The relations of the metals in coinage are :—

Gold is to silver as 1 : 12½.
Silver is to brass as 1 : 28.
Silver is to copper as 1 : 45.
Brass is to copper as 28 : 45 (5 : 8 nearly).

Gold and silver are both struck almost pure and very true to standard weight. Brass and copper are struck much more carelessly—*a marco*, not *a pezzo*—i.e. not on a carefully adjusted weight for each piece, but at so many to the pound. The quadrans was often struck at a little above its normal weight. The brass contains almost exactly 80 per cent. of copper to 20 per cent. of zinc ; it seems to have been a natural alloy, obtained first from the Bergomate territory in Germany, later from the Mons Marianus in Spain.[1] The copper was struck almost pure

The period from Augustus to Nero saw no change of system. The weight of the aureus was gradually reduced,—but only in practice, not by legislative act ; a drop in the denarius accompanied it. The weight of the dupondius rose under Caligula and Claudius to nearly $\frac{5}{8}$ths of an oz. and that of the sestertius to about 1 oz. and $\frac{1}{10}$th. We conjecture a drop in

[1] Pliny, *Nat. Hist.*, 34, 2.

the market price of brass as the cause : but, as the change is definitely greater in proportion for the dupondius than the sestertius, we may see also an attempt to make a better distinction between dupondius and As.

The reform of Nero has three main features, two permanent and of lasting importance, one of experimental interest only : (1) The aureus and denarius were permanently reduced in weight, the former to $\frac{1}{45}$th, the latter to $\frac{1}{96}$th of a pound—their relations in coinage remaining unchanged (Plate XXVI, 5, 6) ; (2) The silver began to be alloyed to the extent of about 10 per cent. ; (3) An orichalcum coinage of sestertius, dupondius, As, semis and quadrans (Plate XXVIII, 5, 7, 8), based on an As of $\frac{1}{4}$ oz. was introduced, but was abandoned after a short trial in favour of the old system. The semis was also struck in copper at the weight of half the copper As (Plate XXVIII, 6). The last reform had no permanence : on its merits it deserved to succeed, but it was unpopular, because it reduced the As to a purely subsidiary position, and was therefore abandoned. The other two reforms had far-reaching results. The reduction of weight, though it brought a certain temporary gain to the exchequer must not be condemned as the short-sighted act of an embarrassed Government. During the first century of the Empire, the depreciation of money values and the rise of prices reached and passed its zenith. Gold and silver were steadily lost to the money market, both through foreign trade, notably with the Far East, and through being immobilized in articles of luxury. The reduction in weight of the standard pieces tended to restore the balance and stabilize prices again. There can be no question of any attempt to secure a better relation of Roman coinage to Eastern currencies, for the provincial silver of the East undergoes a corresponding change of weight. The debasement of the silver was a more serious innovation. For the moment it may have helped to re-establish in the coinage the market relation of gold and silver. In the long run it meant the unavowed abandonment of the bimetallic system and the opening up of a dangerous means of saving to any embarrassed Government.

The system of Nero then is :—

> 1 aureus (114·10 gr., 7·39 gm.) = 25 denarii.
> 1 denarius (52·68 gr., 3·41 gm.) = 4 sestertii.

The relations of the metals now are :—

Gold is to silver as 1 : 11·73 (nearly), or, allowing for the debasement, about
    1 : 13.
Silver is to brass as 1 : 32.
Silver is to copper as 1 : 51.

The relations of brass to copper remained unchanged.

For nearly a century and a half no further change of system is to be recorded.[1] The old heavier aureus was again struck sporadically in the civil wars and regularly from about the second year of Domitian to the second year of Trajan. At the same time a slight increase in the weight of the denarius is to be noted. Debasement of the silver was steadily on the increase,—about 15 per cent. under Trajan, 25 per cent. under Marcus Aurelius, nearly 40 per cent. under Septimus Severus. The danger lay in the fact that the change of standard was not openly avowed : the silver was still issued as a value, not as a token currency, and debasement was definitely used as a means of easy but unsound inflation. The expenses of Government were steadily increasing out of proportion to any increase in receipts and the State was moving slowly in the direction of bankruptcy. The old heavier coinage steadily went to the melting pot. Finds seldom show any pieces earlier than Nero ; and Trajan, in A.D. 107, actually withdrew from circulation such Republican denarii as were still current.[2] Under Trajan we find the semis struck at an Eastern mint, under Hadrian a tiny coin, perhaps the uncia, issued at Rome (?). Small coins (quadrantes) were issued in the second century for limited circulation within the precincts of the mines. Quadrantes without the head of Emperor, but with the signature of the Senate, *S.C.*, were probably issued as coins by the Senate on special occasions in the capital.

Caracalla, in A.D. 215, introduced definite reforms in the monetary system. He reduced the weight of the aureus to $\frac{1}{50}$th of a pound (Plate XXVI, 9) [3] and struck, beside the denarius, a new piece distinguished by its larger module and the radiate head of the Emperor, weighing about 80 grains

---

[1] The silver quinarius was again struck by Vespasian (Pl. XXVI, 7).
[2] Cp. *Num. Chron.*, 1926, on restored coins of Trajan.
[3] For a double aureus, see Pl. XXVI, 8.

(5·18 gm.). This coin, which is known to us from the Augustan history as the "Antoninianus" (Plate XXVI, 10), has been variously interpreted as the equivalent of 2, $1\frac{1}{2}$, or $1\frac{1}{4}$ denarii. There can be little doubt that 2 is the right figure. The Government was evidently concerned to increase the volume of the coinage ; the expenses of the State were steadily mounting and the loss of gold and silver in foreign trade and in articles of luxury was still felt. The debasement of the silver had already attained dangerous proportions. The only alternative was to reduce the weight and the Government preferred to make the reduction on a new coin rather than on the one in common use. The denarius was still worth more as a coin than as metal and was thereby saved from the melting pot ; but the double denarius brought the Government a larger profit. The sequel confirms this ·view. The two coins, denarius and "Antoninianus," were not accurately adjusted to one another ; they did not, therefore, settle down into general use side by side. Severus Alexander early in his reign ceased to strike "Antoniniani." Balbinus and Pupienus, driven to issue coin rapidly and in quantity for the war against Maximin, recommenced the issue (Plate XXVI, 11), and from that time on the "Antoninianus" gradually replaces the denarius as the main silver coin : after the reign of Gordian III (Plate XXVI, 12), the denarius and its half, the quinarius, were hardly struck at all.[1] The weight and fineness of the "Antoninianus" steadily declined, until finally, at the crisis of the reign of Gallienus, when Valerian fell into Persian captivity and Postumus seceded in the West, the Government took the final plunge and flooded the market with masses of base silver (billon) scarcely distinguishable from copper.[2] It was little less than absolute bankruptcy. Business must have been terribly hampered and the losses of private individuals must have been heart-breaking. The mischief would have been less serious had the gold coinage remained stable. But this prop, too, gave way. The weight of the aureus had been reduced by slow degrees to about 90 gr. (5·83 gm.) under Alexander Severus, falling to about 70 gr. (4·54 gm.) under

---

[1] For a quinarius of Trajan Decius, see Pl. XXVI, 15.
[2] For "Antoniniani" of Gallienus, see Pl. XXVII, 1, 2.

Philip I and Trajan Decius (Plate XXVI, 13). Serious variations of weight occur in individual specimens and even the metal itself was occasionally debased. A division of the aureus into three became common : under Trebonianus Gallus we find a whole of c. 84 gr. (5·44 gm.), and a two-thirds piece of c. 56 gr. (3·63 gm.). Under Valerian and Gallienus we find the third, the " triens," commonly called by the Augustan historians the " triens of Saloninus " (Plate XXVI, 14). In the confusion of the reign of Gallienus the standard is almost completely lost ; gold pieces of almost every weight occur and can hardly have passed in commerce except by weight. So far as a standard can be traced, it seems to have been one of about 78 gr. (5·05 gm.) for the whole piece, with subdivisions of one and two-thirds and multiples running up to as many as ten aurei at the least. The Gallic Emperors attempted to maintain a better standard of about 90 gr. (5·83 gm.) (Plate XXVII, 3), but it, too, fell away under Victorinus and Tetricus I to about 70 gr. (4·54 gm.). Our literary tradition cannot be trusted in details, but it records two facts, which are inherently probable : (1) that coins were now frequently named after the Emperor issuing them, so that one could tell exactly what signed piece of metal was intended in each case ; and (2) that the Government tried to collect taxes, not in its own unsatisfactory coin, but in gold and silver bullion.

We presume, without certainty, that the aureus, as long as it was a clearly defined denomination, equalled 25 denarii as before, and therefore 12½ Antoniniani. In the period of utter chaos the relations of coins to one another were probably only determined in the market. The coinage in base metal appears to have been issued in the same denominations as before,—sestertius,[1] dupondius, As. Trajan Decius introduced a double sestertius and re-issued the semis (Plates XXIX, 1 ; XXVIII, 9). Orichalcum almost went out of use, the dupondius and As were struck so carelessly that their weights constantly overlapped, and only the radiate crown of the dupondius remained to distinguish it from the As (Plate XXIX, 3). The debasement of the denarius led to a reduction of weight in the base metal, which did not, however, keep pace with it ;

---

[1] For a sestertius of Postumus, see Pl. XXIX, 5.

the Senatorial coinage began to be relatively valuable and was hoarded.   The final crash under Gallienus deprived it of its *raison d'être* and it practically ceased to be issued.   Again we presume, without certainty, that as before, the denarius contained 4 sestertii, 8 dupondii or 16 Asses.

Aurelian, the restorer of the Roman world, made a gallant attempt to reform the coinage and give his Empire the foundation necessary for an orderly commercial life.   In gold he struck coins of a rather heavier standard than Gallienus, but so irregular in weight, that we cannot attribute to them any fixed tariff (Plate XXVII, 4).   He struck no true silver money, but he replaced the utterly debased billon of Gallienus and Claudius II by pieces of rather higher weight and quality and of decidedly better workmanship.   A process was invented whereby a coin, containing perhaps only 4 per cent. of silver, received a thin coating of silver, which might enable it to rank as more or less a true silver coin.   Copper he struck only sparingly—in his own name, without the co-operation of the Senate.

Numismatists have taxed their ingenuity in vain to find a satisfactory explanation of Aurelian's reform.   Certainty is as yet unattainable ; but, if we first look carefully at the actual coinage of the period, A.D. 270-296, and then consider its problems in the light of what went before and after, we may hope at least to strike the correct path.

For gold we cannot be sure of a fixed standard, until Diocletian issues his pieces of $\frac{1}{70}$th of the gold pound, marked with the Greek numeral o (Plate XXVII, 8).   Pure silver was struck only by the British Emperor Carausius at a standard of about 50 gr. (3·24 gm.), and, even here, plated coins are not uncommon.   The main coinage is of base billon, containing about 4 per cent. of silver.   The only piece that is at all common has the radiate crown and the module of the " Antoninianus " and weighs about 60 gr. (3·89 gm.).   It is frequently marked *XX, XX.I, XXI, KA, K.A*, and it may now be taken as almost certain that all these varied marks have but one meaning : the coin is a unit containing twenty smaller units.[1]   A smaller billon coin, occasionally marked *VSV* in exergue under Aurelian

---

[1] XXI can conceivably mean " twenty units—one unit " ; but XX.I could hardly mean " twenty-one units."   Missong first made this point clear in *N.Z.*, 1869, pp. 105 and especially 112 ff.

and Severina, weighs about 38 gr. (2·46 gm.), and one smaller still, struck by Aurelian's successors, weighs about 25 gr. (1·62 gm.).   Copper is struck in three or four denominations—about 300 gr. (?) (19·44 gm.), about 230 gr. (14·9 gm.), about 120 gr. (7·77 gm.), falling to about 90 gr. (5·83 gm.), and about 30 gr. (1·94 gm.).

So much for the coins.   The problem that faced Aurelian was the restoration of the coinage from the degradation into which it had sunk under Gallienus.   That he honestly attacked it is certain : what is doubtful is, whether he attempted a complete restoration by making his " Antoninianus " of bad billon pass as the old " Antoninianus " of Caracalla or whether he was content to assign to it a value, well below its original value but also well in advance of the low value to which it must have fallen in its worst period.   We know that the reckoning in sestertii was still in force as late as c. A.D. 295 ; but the mark of value, *XX*, on Aurelian's " Antoniniani " shows us that we have now to deal with a decimal system, in place of the division of the denarius into 16 Asses.   When we come to Diocletian's reform of A.D. 296, we find that he issues a new coin of about 150 gr. (9·72 gm.) to represent twenty of his units of account, the " denarii communes," which represent about $\frac{1}{50000}$th parts of the pound of gold, but incorporates the " Antoninianus " of Aurelian in his system as a subdivision of the larger coin.   The " twenty " piece of Aurelian is no longer the " twenty " piece under Diocletian, but something smaller : either the value of the coin or the unit of reckoning has been changed.   We might have been tempted to select the latter alternative, but the evidence of a papyrus compels us to prefer the former.[1]   It probably belongs to the end of the third century and records a reduction of the " Italian coinage " to the half of a " νοῦμμος."   This, if our date be correct, is definite evidence for a reduction of the value of the piece of Aurelian ; if, as seems natural, " νοῦμμος " here means " sestertius," it records a reduction to a fourth of its value.[2]

We can now attempt to reconstruct the system of Aurelian. The reckoning in sestertii was still in vogue, but the value

[1] Cp. article due to appear in *Num. Chron.*, 1927.   " Sestertius and Denarius under Aurelian."

[2] See below, p. 130.

9

of the denarius,[1] owing to its association with the debased " Antoninianus " (the double denarius), had fallen far below its nominal tariff. Aurelian wished to restore a coinage that would express real value, but lacked the necessary silver for a sound coinage. He therefore abandoned the denarius alto-gether and put in its place the sestertius ; his " Antoninianus " is, in fact, a piece of two sestertii (Plate XXVII, 5), and represents in value the $\frac{1}{2500}$th part of a gold pound.[2] Thus the sestertius of Aurelian is the $\frac{1}{5000}$th part of the gold pound —a very probable valuation, if we remember that under Caracalla it had already fallen to that value and that no official change of system had taken place since him. The second billon coin of Aurelian will be this sestertius itself (Plate XXVII, 6), and the letters VSV will probably stand for " Usualis " and mark the piece as the " normal " coin or unit of account.[3] The sestertius was always divided decimally into ten libellae, and we now see why Aurelian divides his XX piece into these twenty parts : they are nothing more nor less than libellae of his new sestertius. Traces of a similar decimal reckoning are to be found in the late Greek copper of Southern Asia Minor, with marks of value IB (12), IA or I (10 Assaria, 10). We are in transition here from the old reckoning in Asses to the new in libellae ; it is not surprising to find the name " Assaria " carried forward to the new unit, for which no exact Greek equivalent was available.

We arrive, then, at the following system for Aurelian :—

1 lb. A/ = 2500 double sestertii (XX pieces) = 5,000 sestertii (VSV pieces) = 10,000 smallest billon (Plate XXVII, 7) = 50,000 libellae.

The value of the copper cannot be determined with certainty. If, as seems probable, the smallest piece is the libella or quad-rans (Plate XXVIII, 11), the other denominations will represent four, eight and ten libellae respectively : the largest piece of

---

[1] The base billon tetradrachm of Alexandria had been equal to a denarius and may have still retained its original value. It is quite probable that the denarius and the tetradrachm were now regarded essentially as copper and not silver coins, and were rated at only $\frac{1}{4}$th of the original value ($\frac{1}{50000}$th in place of $\frac{1}{12500}$th pound A/, the value under Caracalla).

[2] This idea was first suggested to the author by an article of Seeck in *N.Z.*, 1896, pp. 171 ff., *Sesterz und Follis*, but Seeck handles the subject in quite a different way.

[3] Cp. Babelon, *Note sur quelques Exagia Solidi*, etc., Paris, 1918.

Aurelian will be actually, what we should naturally term it, a sestertius,[1] his second piece a dupondius (Plate XXIX, 2), his third an As [2] : with the decimal division of the sestertius, the old value of the As as $\frac{2}{5}$ths, not $\frac{1}{4}$th of the sestertius, returns.

Under Tacitus, Carus and Carinus we find on pieces more or less closely resembling the normal XX piece, the marks of value *I.A*, *X.I*, *X.I.I*, *X.ET.I*. These are probably anticipations of the reform of Diocletian : the value of the piece is to be reduced to just a half of its tariff under Aurelian.[3] What value Carausius assigned to his silver coins is unknown, but it must have been something like the $\frac{1}{1000}$th part of the gold pound. Diocletian's aurei of $\frac{1}{70}$th of a gold pound will not fit exactly into the system we have proposed.   It is possible that, by a slight readjustment,

1 gold lb. $=$ 70 aurei $=$ 2520 XX pieces $=$ 5040 sestertii (VSV pieces) $=$ 10,080 smallest billon $=$ 50,400 libellae.

The view of Aurelian's reform here presented has no claim to finality, but it is unlikely that it is seriously at fault. Aurelian did not attempt the impossible,—to restore a coinage of silver value without the necessary metal.   He accepted the fact of the immense decline in money value and operated with a smaller unit, the double sestertius, in place of the double denarius. Diocletian, when he restored with the good silver the old value of the denarius, was able to incorporate the system of Aurelian into his own.   Once again we see that the reform of Diocletian, imposing as it is at first sight, does not really represent any very decisive change : it is only the completion of the work of the great restoring Emperors who had preceded him.

3. Mint Authorities.   Emperor and Senate.   Organization of the Mint—The issue of coins, we have seen, was divided between Emperor and Senate, the Emperor striking gold and silver, the Senate " Aes."   The Emperor, however, could on occasion issue " Aes " without the mark of Senatorial control (*S.C.*) [4] and, after Gallienus, actually took over this branch of the coinage.   The *S.C.* coinage was originally struck only for Rome and Italy. Under Nero its circulation became general in the West ; whether

[1] For a sestertius of the " Interregnum " after the death of Aurelian, see Pl. XXIX, 4.

[2] For an As of Probus, cp. Pl. XXVIII, 10.

[3] The counter-marking of copper of Southern Asia Minor of the size of the I (10) piece with the mark ϵ (5) would be an exact parallel.

[4] Cp. for example Caligula's sestertii with the reverse type " Adlocutio."

it was ever current, in any real sense, over the whole Empire
is not quite certain—it occurs but rarely in Eastern finds. In
the early Empire the Senate may have exercised a genuine
control, but from the time of Nero onwards the Emperor seems
to have had a decisive say in the administration.

The mint of the Emperor was under the general control of
the chief financial minister, the " a rationibus." A special
procurator of the mint is first met with under Trajan. The
provincial mints probably fell to the charge of the provincial
procurators : special procurators of the mint in the provinces
only appear in the third century.[1] The Senatorial mint must
have been under the general oversight of the heads of the
Senatorial treasury, the " aerarium Saturni "—from Nero on,
" praefecti aerarii," nominated by the Emperor. The " III viri
a.a.a.f.f. " [2] are proved by inscriptions to have existed as late
as the early third century, and were presumably still employed
on the Senatorial—but not on the Imperial—coinage ; their
names, however, do not appear on gold and silver after 12 B.C.
or on " Aes " after c. 4 B.C.   The Senatorial mint of the Republic
had been housed in the temple of Juno Moneta on the Capitol ;
the Imperial mint in the reign of Trajan was in the fifth region,
near the Baths of Trajan.   Beyond this we are left to conjecture.   It is best to assume for the time that the Senatorial
mint remained under the same roof as before and that the
Imperial mint was from the first in the fifth region.   It has
been suggested, on slight evidence, that Domitian housed the
two mints in the same building.[3]   The coinage of Nero, Vespasian, Titus and Domitian, considered in relation to the Great
Fires of Rome, may help to throw light on the matter.   The
decline in the " Aes " coinage of Nero in the later years of his
reign, though not directly due to the great fire of A.D. 64, may
be connected with a subsequent reorganization of the mint ;
the gold and silver is not affected.   The destruction of the
Capitol by fire in December, A.D. 69, must have affected the
Senatorial mint, if it was still in the temple of Juno Moneta.
As a matter of fact, " Aes " of the first year of Vespasian is very
rare at Rome, whereas gold and silver are plentiful enough.

[1] Cp. for Treveri, *C.I.L.*, VI, 1641.
[2] The retention of the old title was probably a mere piece of conservatism.
[3] Mowat in *N.Z.*, 1909, pp. 87 and especially 95 ff.

The great fire of A.D. 80 under Titus seems to have affected both mints—at any rate there is little or no coinage at Rome in any metal during the last year of the reign.   Domitian, in A.D. 81, strikes in all metals, but suspends his " Aes " issues in A.D. 82, and commences in A.D. 83 with a new selection of reverse types, including the new type *Moneta Aug.*   It looks as if Domitian first restored the Imperial mint to working order and temporarily had " Aes " issued from it, then, after an interval of a year, reopened the Senatorial mint in a building of its own.   The evidence of the coins cannot be considered decisive, but it certainly suggests that the two mints were still separate.

For the internal organization of the mints we depend on a few scattered inscriptions, mainly relating to the Imperial mint under Trajan, and on the evidence of the coins themselves. The Imperial mint was staffed with freedmen and slaves, was organized on military lines, and was under the superintendence of an " optio et exactor auri argenti et aeris ; " this title seems to indicate that the supply of all metals was in the same hands.   The workmen fell into four main classes :—

1. The skilled artists, " scalptores," who engraved the dies.

2. The " officinatores," the unskilled workers, including the " flaturarii " (casters), the " aequatores " (trimmers), the " malleatores " (strikers) and the " suppostores," who held the dies in position under the hammer.   From an early date in the Empire, die-position is regular, and we must assume that the adjustment of the dies to one another could be accurately determined.   The " signator " was an important official, connected with the actual striking : he probably superintended operations and may have been responsible for affixing some mark, which would identify the issue to which any coin belonged.

3. The " nummularii "—probably State bankers, whose duties it was to bring the new money on to the market.   Their duties would include the receipt of obsolete coin or bullion and the issue of new money in its place.

4. The " dispensatores," or accountants, who kept the books.

Exaggerated ideas of the numbers of men employed have been founded on the account of the war of the moneyers under Aurelian, which is said to have cost thousands of lives.   In point of fact it is doubtful whether more than a couple of hundred men at the outside were employed.   It must be remembered that, according to the ancient practice, only a part of the work was directly run by the State.   Part was let out on private tender—as, for example, the casting of the blanks for the coinage.[1]   General analogies lead us to suppose that direct State management came more and more into force in the second and third centuries.   The information we have been considering applies mainly to the Imperial mint under Trajan ;   it is unlikely, however, that procedure varied very much, either at different periods or in the Senatorial mint.

It was clearly a matter of great importance to establish a firm control over the workers and to ensure that the responsibility for the issue of coin should be brought home to the right quarter.   A division of the mints into " shops " or " officinae " is certain for the second to third centuries and is inherently probable for the first.   Mint-marks of any kind are rare in the first two centuries ;   they begin to be common under Gallienus and mark not only the mint, but the " officina " and the particular issue to which each coin belongs.   Curiously enough, the gold is less regularly and fully marked than the billon. That the authorities, however, had at all times means of fixing responsibility is made probable (1) by general considerations and analogies, (2) by the existence of a separate officer styled " signator."   We can hardly resist the conclusion that coins at all times bore certain " privy marks," which would identify their issues, and that all that was done in the third century was to make this control apparent to the general public, particularly in the case of the billon, where abuses were most to be feared.   Such abuses might take two forms : (1) coins of irregular weight or alloy might be issued from the mint ; (2) coins might be issued by the regular moneyers outside the official premises.   Both forms of abuse were evidently rampant in the time of Aurelian and the second form, which might involve many who were not regular mint officials, may account for the huge dimensions assured by the " war of the moneyers " under the dishonest finance minister, Felicissimus.

The temptation to the mint officials to tamper with the weight and title of the coin obviously became acute only when the State itself set the evil example.   Debasement of the gold

---

[1] Cp. *B.M.C. Emp.*, I, p. lx, and n. 2.

was never common, that of the silver began, we have seen, under Nero, and went to desperate extremes in the third century.   But even the Early Empire has not escaped suspicion of dishonesty ; the existence of masses of plated coins of the Emperors, from Augustus to Nero, has led to the belief that these formed part of the regular issues, that the Government, in fact, was not true to the standards it had itself set up.   The evidence is conflicting and hard to sum up.   The plated coins are often irregular in style and in details of type and legend, and thus betray their unofficial origin ; often, again, they might pass for official money.   We have also to remember that the melting down of pre-Neronian gold and silver would naturally not extend to plated pieces.   We shall not be far wrong if we conclude that the plated coins are mainly forgeries, that Augustus and Tiberius did not countenance their official issue, but that Caligula and Claudius, under whom they are particularly common, relaxed their diligence here.   After Nero, when the State avowedly debased its silver, we do not expect to find it resorting further to plating ; and, as a matter of fact, most plated coins are now obviously forgeries and often combine obverses and reverses that could never occur together on regular issues.

Of the different meanings usually attached to the words "style" and "fabric," and of the use of the two as criteria of date and mintage we have already spoken in our first book.   It is remarkable, in view of the immense volume of the Imperial coinage, how uniform the style of a mint can be over considerable periods ; we can often trace the individual work of particular artists or schools of artists, almost as clearly as in the case of larger works of art.   Good examples may be found in the coinage of Augustus, of Nero, of Hadrian, of Septimius Severus, and of the Emperors from Tacitus to Diocletian in Gaul.   The explanation, no doubt, is that a single fine model might be very closely copied by pupils or even multiplied mechanically by the process of " hubbing." [1]   The most striking feature is the care bestowed on the obverse.   It is hardly too much to say that all the best ability of the time went to the rendering of the features of the Emperor ; the reverses

---

[1] That is, by the production of a number of identical dies in incuse from one original in relief.

were treated with much less care, and are hardly ever of much
artistic value, however interesting their subject-matter may be.
But even here there is some advance in conception, if not in
execution ; the large field of the sestertius, in particular, lent
itself to elaborate compositions, which occasionally, as in the
" Annona Augusti Ceres " group of Nero, achieve real distinction. The nationality of Imperial art was undoubtedly mainly
Greek ; the best work follows the Greek tradition, and is most
probably due to Greek artists, drawn to Rome by the prospects
of advancement. What Rome contributes is mainly the new
direction given to artistic impulse—the concentration on portraiture and the interest in matters of immediate interest rather
than in general types and abstractions. The local art of the
West, as seen, for example, in the coinages of Gaul, Spain and
Africa in the years after A.D. 68, and in the Lugdunum coinage
of Albinus, is technically weak, though not wanting in ambitious
design. The best coinage of the Gallic Empire reaches a very
high level, but we are less certain here of the local character of
the art. The coinages of the Illyrican district are frequently
rough and uncouth. In the East itself we find occasional work
of exceptional beauty, as, for example, on the gold of Augustus,
and on the Ephesus coins of Vespasian. In general, the coins
bear out the view that the best of Greek artists worked at Rome
itself. Fabric is usually fairly uniform for any given period
at any one mint and is a very valuable aid to classification.
Even where the art ranges from high to low levels, uniformity
in lettering, in size of flan, in the exact method of striking,
often enables us to determine the issues of a mint.

We have just spoken of the uniformity of style in the different mints. There are, however, variations within the same
mint from " officina " to " officina," which show differing ren-
derings of the same general model. A recent large find of coins
of the reign of Trajan Decius was very instructive in this respect.[1]
It was possible to distinguish varieties of portraiture, which
almost certainly correspond to the different " officinae " of the
mint. The lessons of this find were most promising for future
work ; they suggest the possibility of gradually extending our
knowledge of the Imperial coinages into details, so that we may

[1] Cp. *Num. Chron.*, 1924, pp. 210 ff.

be able to state with confidence, not only at what mint, but at what period of the mint and in what sections coins were struck.

4. Chronology and Mints—Questions of chronology bulk less large here than in the Republican coinage, inasmuch as the reign is usually given by the obverse portrait, while the details of the Imperial title often give an exact date to a year or part of a year. A few cases remain where expert knowledge must be called in to our aid.

(*a*) There are certain coins of the Empire that bear no Imperial portrait. Most of these belong to the Civil Wars of A.D. 68-69. The attribution is determined by weight, style and similarity to contemporary issues of Galba and Vitellius. An anonymous sestertius of the late third century, with obverse, *GENIVS P.R.*, probably belongs to the interregnum, before the elevation of Tacitus.

(*b*) Issues struck in honour of members of the Imperial family. These are frequently commemorative in character, and have to be dated on grounds of style and historical probability. The *As* of Agrippa was certainly struck long after his death,—possibly by Tiberius, more probably by Caligula. The memory of Augustus was kept in honour long after his death,— by Tiberius, Caligula, Claudius, Galba, Titus and Nerva. The sestertius of Britannicus may not have been issued till the reign of Titus, who had been his intimate friend in boyhood. The dated coinage of Alexandria is often most valuable in supplying probable dates for undated Roman issues.

(*c*) Issues struck in honour of Emperors after their death. The deserving Emperor was in the normal course consecrated, and bears the title " divus " on his posthumous coinage. The bad Emperor suffered " damnatio memoriae." A number of cases remain in which Emperors, though not consecrated, were honoured after their death with coinage bearing the titles of their lifetime. Caligula struck a coin that might represent the deified Tiberius ; but he added no identifying legend and, finally yielding to the opposition of the Senate, substituted the portrait of the divine Augustus.[1] Coins of Spain under Galba show Augustus, with his lifetime titles, as well as " divus." Galba himself received back his honours from Vespasian, among

[1] Cp. *J.R.S.*, 1920, p. 37.

them the honour of a posthumous coinage.[1] A large issue of
Hadrian seems to have been struck by Antoninus Pius during
the months when he was extorting his consecration from a
reluctant Senate.[2] Other such issues,—perhaps for Trajan
Decius under Trebonianus Gallus,—may still await discovery.
We must not be misled by a false calculation of probabilities
here. Wherever we have a case of doubt as to whether an
Emperor was definitely consecrated or condemned the possibility of posthumous coinage, without the title " divus," must
be carefully considered.

(d) Issues struck in honour of the deified Emperors and
Empresses and their kindred. Such coins are normally issued
by the immediate successor and can readily be dated. But
here, too, exceptions occur. " Divus Augustus " is honoured
by Caligula, Claudius, Galba, Titus, Domitian and Nerva,
" Diva Augusta " (Livia) by Claudius and Galba. Trajan has
a gallery of his divine predecessors, in which Tiberius, though
not a god, is allowed a place. A series of coins of the " divi "
of about the middle of the third century, long attributed to
Philip I or Gallienus, may now be assigned with confidence to
Trajan Decius and may be regarded as a part of the religious
policy which involved the first general persecution of the
Christians.

Even these few examples will show that, even in the Empire,
the scientific study of chronological detail cannot safely be
neglected.

The evidence of finds has already been used at various
points of the argument, but there may be room for a summary
of it here. Pre-Neronian gold and silver very rarely occur
after the reform of Nero ; Republican denarii are occasionally
found, but very seldom after this same date. The one exception consists in the legionary coinage of Mark Antony, which, by
its very baseness, escaped the melting-pot, and occurs in hoards
as late as the middle of the third century. With hoards of the
very early Empire Gallic coins are occasionally interspersed,
and, later, provincial or local silver, as of Lycia or Amisus, is
not infrequently found with the Imperial. From Nero to Gallienus the silver is hoarded as a single series—coins of Domitian

---

[1] Cp. *Num. Chron.*, 1922, pp. 186 ff.   [2] Cp. *J.R.S.*, 1925, pp. 209 ff.

and Nerva, which seem to have represented an improvement
on the Neronian standard, are seldom found.   Denarii and
" Antoniniani " are often found in quantity in the same hoards.
Finds of gold often cover considerable periods of time and
show progressive degrees of wear : they do not, on the whole,
bear out Mommsen's view that gold went out of circulation
very rapidly.   The aurei of Domitian and Nerva, which revert to
something like the pre-Neronian standard, are absent.   " Aes "
was not very much hoarded until the third century, when the
debasement of the silver enhanced its relative value.   The
debased billon of Gallienus and his successors is, on the whole,
clearly separated in hoards, both from the earlier silver and
from the later " reformed " billon of Aurelian.   The debased
billon of the Gallic Empire is often associated with masses of
similar Roman coins in Gallic hoards ; the two currencies,
being of about equal badness, ran side by side, but Gallic money
was apparently not very willingly accepted by the Empire.
The reformed coins of Aurelian and his successors are usually
found by themselves with only slight admixtures from earlier
times.

The general question of classification by mints was fully
treated in the first chapter of Book I ; we have here to consider it in its special application to the Empire.   Is classification by mints really desirable here, or should the chronological
order have the supremacy throughout and should attributions
to mints be relegated to the notes ?   To this question we must
return an emphatic answer in the negative.   The mints of
the Empire are, in the great majority of cases, not simply
subordinate branches of the central mint of Rome, but independent organizations with traditions of their own.   If the
issues of provincial mints are scattered over the mass of the
coinage, we gain no true conception of these smaller bodies ;
all that happens is that our picture of the mint of Rome becomes
somewhat blurred or distorted.   It is only with the closer attribution to mints that the coinage of Augustus has become
intelligible.   The issues of the Civil Wars of A.D. 68 to 69 are
partly meaningless, partly misleading, until we can distribute
them locally.   The determination of the mints of Vespasian
illustrates the political history and throws light on his general
policy.   In the period after Severus, the tracing of the issues

of Antioch and Viminacium throws a flood of light on the direction in which coinage was moving.   Unless we are content to remain in permanent ignorance of many facts of historical value and to run the risk of drawing entirely erroneous conclusions from details of types, it is essential that we should determine not only when, but where each coin was struck.

But, granting the necessity of such a classification, how are we to arrive at it ?   There is no short cut to success ; long practice in distinguishing differences of style and fabric and discovering which of these are characteristic of different mints is essential ;   only in this way can the various local groups be separated off.   History, then, comes to our assistance.   In the early Empire we are led first by a consideration of the conditions prevailing at the end of the Republic and by the general policy of Augustus.   Later, after Nero, we have to study the history of the movements in the provinces that led to the elevation of new Emperors.   Later again, after Septimius Severus, when provincial coinage had come to stay, we have to follow the trend of the campaigns, trace the movements and consider the needs of the armies.   The study of types is valuable as a confirmation of our results, and comparison with local issues in copper will often supply useful clues.   But here a word of warning is needed.   Similarity of style to local issues does not prove local striking ;   at the most it suggests the probability that the area of circulation was the same.   The evidence of types again can be positively misleading.   The central mint of Rome must obviously often have had occasion to celebrate events of particular local interest in the provinces, and, conversely, the provincial mints cannot be entirely indifferent to the course of events in the capital.   Some critics have absolutely refused to countenance the attribution of a large series of coins of Augustus to Spain on the one ground that reference to events in the capital is writ large on them.   The objection is really irrelevant.   Augustus had definite reasons for issuing his coins in the provinces, but he had no reason for eliminating from them the reference to the seat of his Empire.   The Spanish origin of the coins is adequately attested by general considerations, as well as by style, and should not be doubted on *a priori* grounds, which take no account of the real facts of the case. It is unfortunately true that, in spite of all the labour that has been expended on them, our knowledge of Imperial mints is still far from satisfactory.   Even where we can identify groups of coins not struck in Rome, we are often at a loss for an exact attribution to their locality.   But sufficient ground has already been won to justify the highest hopes ; and here, as often, it will be found that the path of greatest difficulty is also the path of highest promise.

CHAPTER II

THE CONTENT OF THE EARLY IMPERIAL COINAGE.
TYPES AND LEGENDS

1. **Transition from the Republic**—By the end of the Republic we found that the coinage was fast outgrowing the stereotyped and conventional forms in which it had begun. The official religion of the State still played an important part ; but more often than not religious forms conveyed definite topical allusions and the minor deities, or " Virtues," were beginning to appear beside the greater gods. A great part of the space was allotted to mythological and antiquarian allusions, in which the families of the moneyers played an important rôle, while, beside the family allusions, reference to contemporary history was becoming increasingly common. Above all, interest in the individual was steadily on the increase ; the portraits of great men of old are soon succeeded by the portraits of living statesmen and generals, and, even before the Empire, the coinage was assuming an Imperial tinge. The coming of the Empire marks no violent breach in the development, though, in the natural course of events, some features received new emphasis, while others fell into abeyance. With the disappearance of the moneyers from the coins, the glorification of the great families ceases ; Augustus, indeed, allowed the moneyers of gold and silver to follow to some extent the old practice, but he had no intention of making it permanent. The interest in the individual was to be focussed on the Emperor and the members of his family.

2. **General Principles**—The movement of the later Republic had been all away from the stereotyped form to the free illustration of the life of the State, and the Empire, in the long run, only accelerated this movement. There was a moment in the early Empire, however, when a new set of conventions appeared likely to settle down on the coinage. The " Aes " of

Augustus hardly varied from one or two fixed patterns. On the gold and silver the type of the two princes, C. and L. Caesar, remained in use for a long term of years, and Tiberius used the one reverse type of Livia as Pax Augusta during the greater part of his reign. With Caligula the tradition begins to give way. More and more freedom is introduced into the choice of types and by the reign of Vespasian we find ourselves in the full development of the Imperial coinage. Only on the half piece of aureus and denarius, the quinarius or victoriate, was the standard type of Victory normally retained. The Imperial coinage, in fact, served not only the end of currency, but most of the uses of the modern medal. The accession of a new Emperor, the adoption of a successor, important concessions to Senate or people, buildings of temples, roads or harbours, journeys in the provinces or victories over the foreign foe—one and all are brought to the public notice on the coins. In this use of the coin as a means of publicity is implied its use as an agency of propaganda. The Emperor ruled by tradition and consent, as much as by force ; it was most important for him to have public opinion on his side. He therefore seized the opportunity that the issue of coins presented of representing events in the light in which he wished them to appear and of definitely announcing not only his actual achievements, but also his hopes and policy. A certain reserve is clearly needed in accepting such official bulletins, but their value for history is obvious.

Remembering that one branch of the coinage, the " Aes," was reserved to the Senate, we naturally look to find some evidence of the division of authority in the coins. At no time, till the collapse of the old " Aes " coinage under Gallienus, do we fail to notice some difference in the choice of types ; certain events and policies were specially chosen for commemoration here, particularly such as illustrate the statesmanlike and constitutional side of an Emperor's activities. But it is only in the very first days of the Empire that we can really talk of two distinct policies in the coinage : from the time of Caligula onwards we can trace more and more clearly an underlying unity of direction. Under Augustus and Tiberius the influence of the Senate was something more than a form. The head of the Emperor only appears on one denomination, the As. Great prominence is given to the Senatorial stamp *S.C.*, which ranks rather as a main type than as a subsidiary part of one ; the title of the Emperor takes a subordinate place, and reference to him lays stress on his constitutional policy ; we see the oak-wreath voted to him by the Senate as " Saviour of his Country," the laurels planted on either side of his door, the emblems of his chief pontificate, the statue and the quadriga of elephants assigned to the honour of the deified Augustus. But, as we have just stated, this is only a passing phase ; the theory of the " dyarchy " did not long enjoy the respect to which it had a claim.

No clear picture of the varied wealth of allusion in the Imperial coinage can be given, except by a detailed study under various heads ; but, before we proceed to this, we must clear the ground by stating some general guiding principles.

The obverse is normally given up to the " image and super-scription " of the reigning Emperor ; only on the smaller denominations of " Aes " are other obverses commonly found. The right of portraiture could, however, be extended either to a colleague in the Imperial power (e.g. Agrippa, Plate XXXV, 3), to the Empress or to a prince or princess of the house, or to some deified Emperor or other Imperial personage after death. Portraiture on the reverse, as a less important honour, was more freely delegated. Of the importance of this privilege there can be no question. The Emperor replaces the goddess Roma of the Republic as the visible head of the Roman State ; he is chary in the first place of sharing his right with others ; when he begins to allow it freely to other members of his house, it clearly marks the fact that the Empire was gradually being transformed from an elective office into an hereditary monarchy. The illustrious dead of the Imperial house receive the honour at first more freely than the living ; they were not to be feared as rivals. Obverses other than portraits hardly occur except on the " Republican " issues of the Civil Wars of A.D. 68-69.

The legend of the obverse is normally in the nominative, marking the Emperor as the issuer of the coin. A dative, of dedication, is much less commonly found. The genitive of Republican tradition hardly occurs except on the issues of L. Clodius Macer in Africa. In the form of the Imperial name and in the choice of Imperial titles the greatest variety prevails. The praenomen is frequently omitted, the gentile name commonly, the family name seldom, if ever. The title " Augustus," the most common designation of the reigning Emperor, is normally present ; the family name of the first Emperors, " Caesar," came to be associated with the successors of the Julio-Claudian line, and was frequently combined at the beginning of the title with the praenomen of imperator. That praenomen, which marked the Emperor as the one holder of supreme military power, was only occasionally used at first ; later, it became more and more the common form. The use of the same title " imperator " as cognomen, often with a numeral to denote the number of times that the Emperor had been acclaimed for victories won by himself or his legates, is particularly common in some reigns.[1] The consulship, the tribunician power, the chief priesthood, often figure in the title, and with them such titles of honour as " Germanicus," " Dacicus," " Britannicus," conferred in honour of particular victories. The title of " Pater patriae," the most distinguished that an Emperor could bear, was often added as a particular compliment. The kinship of the Emperor to his predecessors in office is often indicated by such titles as " Divi F.," " Divi Augusti F.," " Divi Nervae Nepos," or by the use of the dead Emperor's name as part of the new Imperial title.[2] Other titles, such as censor (Vespasian, Titus, Domitian) or proconsul (Nero (?), Diocletian), are far less common. In the third century the epithets " Pius Felix " (P.F.) were freely embodied in the official style. The Empress or princess is regularly " Augusta," the prince, who is not actually a colleague, " Caesar ; " the use of this family title to mark the prince of the blood can be traced as early as Titus and Domitian. The epithets, " Divus," " Diva," mark the consecrated Emperor or Empress.

The legend of the reverse is sometimes a mere continuation of the obverse ; it completes the Imperial title, without reference to the type. Normally, the legend is direct and descriptive, defining the deity or " Virtue " or event portrayed in the type. Frequently we have a deictic nominative—simply

---

[1] E.g. under Septimius Severus.

[2] Cp. Nerva Traianus, Traianus Hadrianus, Hadr. Antoninus, etc.

pointing to the type. Less commonly we have a dative of dedication or a genitive of possession ; the ablative of attendant circumstances is excessively rare.[1] An occasional accusative without government must be understood as governed by a verb implied. The Emperor of the obverse, for instance, erects a statue of Mars and expresses the fact by the accusative " Martem " on the reverse.[2] Often legends are formed by complete phrases, or even sentences, describing an elaborate type ; we need only instance Nero's " Pace P.R. terra marique parta Ianum clusit " or Trajan's " Regna Adsignata " or " Armenia et Mesopotamia in potestatem P.R. redactae." The types demand a fuller and more classified treatment, to which we can now proceed.

3. Types Classified—(a) *Types of the Emperor and his Family*—A very large part of the whole Imperial coinage might be brought under this heading ; for convenience, however, we will confine ourselves here to types having a more special reference to the Imperial family, leaving to the separate sections on religion, the State, the provinces, the army, those types in which the interest is divided between the Emperor and such other themes.

The mere fact of striking a coin with one's portrait constituted as definite a claim to Empire as can well be imagined.[3] Special honours would often be commemorated (cp. Plate XXXV, 1, 2), but there was no one special reverse type that represented a claim to Empire. Such an one has been seen in the oak-wreath, presented by the Senate to the Emperor as " Saviour of his country " (Plate XXXV, 4) ; but this type was only struck for some Emperors, and not always at the beginning of the reign. Each Emperor celebrated his accession by such choice of types as seemed to answer the immediate

---

[1] Cp. coins of the Civil Wars of A.D. 68, " florente fortuna P.R."

[2] So Caracalla.

[3] The pretender in the provinces—e.g. Pescennius Niger, Albinus, Pacatian—regularly issues coin. It was unusual, however, for an Emperor to take the trouble to suppress such issues. History records usurpation of right of portraiture in a number of cases where the coins are silent—e.g. for Perennis under Commodus (*Herodian*, I, 9, 7), Valerius Paetus under Elagabalus (*Dio Cassius*, LXXIX, 4). Many of the " Thirty Tyrants " of Gallienus's day have left no record on coins : perhaps in some cases the usurper only knew of his usurpation when the order for his execution arrived : we remember that Gallienus was responsible for excluding senators from provincial governorships.

needs of the time. The most distinctive Imperial title, " Augustus," is regularly assumed by the claimant to Empire ; reference to the component parts of the Imperial power, the " imperium " and the " tribunicia potestas," though common, is by no means universal.

A certain number of types present the Emperor in a variety of formal aspects, as " rector orbis " with rudder on globe (Plate XXXV, 9), as priest sacrificing, as general armed or haranguing the troops, as guardian of the Empire, with spear and globe, or globe and sceptre (Plate XXXV, 15), or as maintainer of peace with branch and sceptre. We see him as a warrior riding, sometimes hunting wild beasts, sometimes riding down a foeman. Similarly the Empress appears as priestess, as " mother of the camp," as " mother of the Senate " (Plate XXXV, 12), as goddess (Vesta, Venus, Ceres, Cybele) or as " Virtue " (Constantia, Pax Augusta). The harmony in the Imperial family, particularly the wedded bliss of Emperor and Empress, is represented by types of Concordia or by figures clasping hands, sometimes presided over by Concordia (cp. Plate XXXV, 13). Other types are more definitely dynastic. The " Aeternitas Imperi," of Septimius Severus, with the heads of the Emperor and his family (Plate XXXV, 11, cp. also 17), the later " Felicitas Saeculi," " Felicitas Temporum," all point to the members of the Imperial house as the surety for the continuance and the prosperity of the Empire. The " Pietas Augusti " of Titus (Plate XXXV, 6), that shows him clasping hands with Domitian, represents a pious hope of fraternal concord that was only imperfectly realized. The vital question of the succession was always to the fore. Apart from adoption type of a formal nature, as, for instance, that of Hadrian adopted by Trajan (Plate XXXV, 5) [1] or Trajan adopted by Nerva, we find the type of Providentia used with special reference to the wisdom that leads the Emperor to arrange for the succession (cp. Plate XXXV, 7). The " Providence " is usually that of the Emperor himself : occasionally the thought of the Divine Providence, which is behind him, receives emphasis. The same idea, regarded rather from the point of view of the successor, is conveyed by the types of Spes, either

[1] Cp. Pl. XXXV, 10, Hadrian adopting Antoninus Pius.

alone or presiding over a group of Emperor and heir. The "Concordia" of L. Aelius, who rests her arm on a statue of Spes, represents the harmony existing between the Emperor and his chosen successor. The idea of Providence implies some thought of conscious selection and is specially appropriate to the period in which the Emperor was succeeded by an adopted, rather than by a natural son. It is less to the fore when the dynastic principle gains strength and the Empire passes from father to son ; the "dynastic" types of which we spoke above then tend to take its place.

The princes of the Imperial house, and particularly the heir apparent, regularly bear the title "Caesar" and are honoured as "Principes Iuventutis," or "Chiefs of the Knights" (cp. Plate XXXV, 14, 16). The Knights, the second order of the State, were organized in "turmae" under leaders called "severi ;" they bestowed the title of "Princeps Iuventutis" by acclamation on princes, who were certainly, as a rule, "severi" of the first troop. Gaius and Lucius, the young grandsons of Augustus, were the first to be so acclaimed ; then followed Nero and Domitian and most of the princes of the Imperial house. It is noteworthy, however, that the title was felt to be suitable only for a young man : Tiberius as Caesar never held it, nor did L. Aelius Caesar—even the young Marcus Aurelius, though he has a type of "Iuventus," is never directly honoured as "Princeps Iuventutis." The insignia of the office, as shown on coins, are naturally of a military character, —shields, spears, standards, trophies,—most characteristic of all, a small wand or baton. Often, naturally enough, the prince is represented on horseback. In the third century, the original use of the term was to some extent forgotten, its types are confused with those of the Emperor himself (Philip II, for example, carries the globe of Empire) and finally the title is occasionally borne by the Emperor himself.[1]

The Emperor who had deserved well of the State regularly received divine worship after death. He was consecrated, bore the title of "Divus" and was worshipped as a god, with a *flamen* and *sodales* of his own. Temples were erected in his honour and sacrifices were offered at his altars. The bad

---

[1] E.g. by Probus.

Emperor suffered condemnation of his memory and had his acts annulled, except in so far as considerations of equity and expedience restricted so extreme a measure. A few Emperors —such as Tiberius and Galba—were left in a limbo between the imperial heaven and hell ; though not consecrated, they were not condemned and might in some cases receive honours of coinage after death. Consecration was at first strictly reserved for the Emperor himself. The idea was certainly borrowed from the Eastern kingdoms of Syria and Egypt, where the king, even in his lifetime, ranked as a god. The consecration of Julius Caesar [1] was a powerful weapon in the hands of his avengers. The precedent once set was naturally repeated for Augustus and became a fixed part of the imperial tradition. The first woman to receive consecration was Livia,— not, however, immediately after her death from Tiberius, but some years later under her grandson Claudius. Nero consecrated his baby daughter, and Domitian, not content with consecrating his father and brother, extended the honour to his own infant son (Plate XXXVI, 3) and to Julia, daughter of Titus. He built a special temple to the " Flavian house " and seems to have claimed divinity as an hereditary right of the family. Trajan himself consecrated his sister Marciana and his father, Trajan senior, as well as his predecessor Nerva. In the long run, however, the honour was usually confined to Emperor and Empress, and, when we reach the third century, mainly to the Emperor alone. Towards the close of that century, consecrations became few, whether because the violent successions precluded such honour of predecessors or because the popular interest in the cult was on the decline. The series of coins of the " Divi " struck by Trajan Decius (Plate XXXVI, 11, 12) is probably the sign of a general endeavour to revive interest in the old forms of religion and has a definite relation to the persecution of the Christians in that reign. The symbolism of consecration is varied and picturesque (Pl. XXXVI, 1-10).[2] There are such obvious types as the pyre, the altar, the temple, the statue of the new

[1] Cp. Pl. XXXVI, 1, for the star which was taken to be the soul of the divine Julius. Pl. XXXVI, 2, shows a sort of unofficial consecration of Agrippa.

[2] Pl. XXXVI, 4, consecration of Vespasian ; the " divus " is placed under the special protection of Jupiter and Mercury.

god. The soul of the dead Emperor was conceived of as borne skywards by an eagle (cp. the eagle of Divus Augustus, the eagle carrying Emperor, e.g. Hadrian) to the heaven of stars, which was to be his future home. Prominent therefore are the symbols of the sky and the sky-gods—the star, the rays of the sun, the thunderbolt of Jupiter. Particularly, in the case of the Empress, the new deity was assimilated to the divine powers, and we find as consecration types, Diana Lucifera with her torches, Ceres with her corn-ears and torch, Juno with her peacock, or the peacock as her emblem. The consecration of Faustina I was celebrated by a gallery of types of "Aeternitas" (cp. Plate XXXVI, 9), represented with the attributes of goddesses, with the immortal bird, the phoenix, or with the mantle of the starry sky. A charming fancy of a moneyer of Domitian shows us the baby Caesar, the infant Zeus of Crete,[1] seated on the globe of the earth and stretching up his hands to the stars. Finally, to return from heaven to earth, a favourite theme of consecration types was the appearance of an effigy of the dead Emperor borne by a quadriga of elephants, the imperial beasts, in the "circensis pompa" or solemn procession before the games in the circus.

The travels of the Emperor were matter of direct public concern. Apart from the importance of the duties, military or civil, that demanded his presence in the provinces, his coming or going had an interest for the people of Rome; did not their material wants and their pleasures depend largely on him? The arrival or departure of the Emperor is usually represented by a type on horseback,—the prancing horse usually suggesting the riding abroad, the pacing horse the slow and solemn entry in procession (Plate XXXVI, 14, 17). In "profectio" types the Emperor often holds a spear in rest, in "adventus" types he often raises his right hand in acknowledgment of the plaudits of the crowd. More elaborate groups sometimes show the Emperor accompanied on his way by soldiers. Journeys by sea are represented by types of galleys (Plate XXXVI, 15, 16). Septimius Severus and Gordian actually use the legend "traiectus," "crossing."

Of great importance in the social and economic life of

---

[1] Cp. A. B. Cook, *Zeus*, I, p. 51 f.

Rome were the imperial largesses or " liberalitates." The custom of supplying the poor of Rome with necessaries such as corn or wine at reduced prices had been common under the Republic—partly as a form of private display, partly as a measure of state relief. The corn-doles of the Republic were carried on under a systematized form by the Emperors and are constantly referred to under the symbolism of Ceres, goddess of corn, and Annona and Abundantia, the presiding spirits of the corn-supply. Above and beyond this the Emperors proceeded to distributions of money to the Roman poor, on the analogy of the donatives given to the troops. These " congiaria " or " liberalitates " (Plate XXXVII, 1, 2), as they came later to be called, were in the first century only sparingly given. Trajan increased the sums distributed and Hadrian and his successors made the distribution a prominent feature of their policy. These " liberalitates," given at accession, at the return from travel, at the adoption of a successor, constituted a serious burden on the exchequer and contributed their share towards state bankruptcy. Necessary they may have been, popular they necessarily were and figure to a corresponding extent on the coinage. The most direct form of celebration is a distribution scene in which the Emperor, seated on a platform, presides over the distribution to citizens. Liberalitas, the spirit of the bounty, a normal subsidiary feature of these scenes, is often used as an independent type and to the attached legend, " Liberalitas Augusti," a number denoting the particular bounty is often added. The type of Spes has sometimes a similar reference : here it is not " Spes Augusta " but " Spes P.R." that is represented, the hopes of the people for the rising generation, who are to profit by the imperial generosity. The exact relation of the types of " Aequitas " and " Moneta "[1] to these distributions is not quite so certain ; but there can be no doubt that these types are not simply of general interest, but refer to the qualities of the Emperor that lead him to use his resources with regard to the needs of his poorer subjects. In the third century a " Moneta " or " Aequitas " type, with three figures holding scales and cornucopiae and having beside them small piles of metal, becomes normal for

[1] The allusions here are probably to distributions of corn and donatives.

the medallions of base silver. In that age of debasement, there was little to boast of in the quality of the coinage ; the reference is probably rather to the Emperor's due heed to the claims of the poor on his purse.[1]

At the beginning of every year vows were undertaken and paid for the health and well-being of the Emperor,—with special ceremony and solemnity at intervals of five or ten years ; the Empire had at first been conferred not for life, but for terms of years, and some memory of this may survive in the Imperial vows. As occasions of public rejoicings and merry-making these vows figure largely on the coinage,—sometimes with general types such as " Pietas," sometimes with more specialized "vota" types, explained by the legend, "Vota P.R.," " Vota Soluta V," " Vota Suscepta X," etc. (Plates XXXV, 9, XXXVII, 8, 9). The usual type is a sacrifice scene, with the Emperor sacrificing over an altar or in front of a temple, sometimes accompanied by other figures, a prince, attendants at the sacrifice, flute-players. Beside the regularly recurring " vota," special vows were undertaken for particular occasions,—for the recovery of the Emperor from illness, for his safe return from travelling abroad. The Roman State, which undertakes these vows, is sometimes represented by the Genius of the Senate and the Genius of the Roman people sacrificing together.

The triumphs of the Emperor, though springing from his connexion with the army, belong rather to his activities in Rome. They were celebrated with great pomp not only for victories won by the Emperor, but also at times for victories won by his lieutenants in the field. The normal type to celebrate them is the triumphal quadriga, in which stands the Emperor, holding the laurel-branch of victory and the eagle-tipped sceptre ; sometimes more elaborate scenes, such as the " Triump. Aug." of Vespasian (Plate XXXVI, 13), offer some picture of the accompanying procession. An empty quadriga seems sometimes to stand for a triumph offered to the Emperor by the Senate, but not accepted by him. A more permanent record of imperial victories is seen in the triumphal arches which were usually erected after successful campaigns, and appear

---

[1] Unless these medallions were standard pieces, to show the exact alloy recognized in use.

on coins, inscribed with the name of the defeated enemy
(" De Brit." " De Germ.").

(b) *Types relating to the Senate and People of Rome*—The
direct control of the " Aes " coinage by the Senate is regularly
attested by the *S.C.* of the reverse. On the gold and silver
the Senate appears only indirectly, as the voter of honours,
which the Emperor thinks fit to commemorate on his coinage ;
among such honours are the oak-wreath given to the " Saviour
of the State " or the posthumous honours of a quadriga in the
" circensis pompa," voted to the deified Emperor. The more
constitutional Emperors took pains to emphasize the harmony
existing between them and the Senate. Galba celebrates the
restoration of constitutional government (Plate XXXVII, 3).
Vespasian won the goodwill of the body by restoring to honour
the Senate's favourite, Galba ; the occasion is commemorated
by sestertii of Vespasian,—one with posthumous portrait of
Galba—with the legends " Concordia Senatui " and " Senatus
Pietati Augusti " [1] and the type, a Senator crowning the Emperor. Trajan for years placed on his reverses the legend
" S.P.Q.R. Optimo Principi," in joyful recognition of the
grateful acceptance that his wise government found. The
personified Senate, represented by its Genius, a venerable elder,
appears both on coins of Trajan and Antoninus Pius (Plate
XXXVII, 7). In the third century the Senate naturally falls
into the background,—finally losing its very privilege of issuing
" Aes."

Consideration for the people of Rome was never far from
the minds of the Emperor's advisers. The bad Emperor
might neglect or flout the Senate ; some respect for the people
was essential unless he was to be exposed to constant unpleasant-
ness and danger. Apart from the many types, such as the
" liberalitates," which directly concern the citizens of Rome,
the Roman people finds direct mention on coins either under
the guise of the " Genius P.R." (Plate XXXVII, 5) or in
those personifications which are directly related to it, " Spes
P.R.," " Felicitas P.R.," " Hilaritas P.R." ; to these we may
add " Salus Publica," " Fides Publica," " Libertas Publica,"
and others. In all these cases the government is at pains to

---

[1] The thought apparently is, " Concordia suggests to the Senate the offer of a
wreath to the Emperor for his piety towards his predecessor " (cp. Pl. XXXVII, 6).

show that the interests and needs of its people are not forgotten by it : the tradition of the Empire, which began as the defender and inheritor of the rights of the people, is steadily maintained.

(c) *Types relating to Rome, Italy, and the Provinces*— If in many points the cautious policy of Augustus commands more respect than the bold innovations of Julius Caesar, this can hardly be claimed for his treatment of the provinces. Julius Caesar, carrying out the policy of the democrats, seemed ready to hasten on the equalization of privilege and the broadening of the base of Empire. Augustus drew back on to the old conservative basis and initiated a policy of cautious reserve, which remained in force long after his death and fatally cramped and confined the possibilities of the Empire. The inevitable equalization of the provinces with Rome and Italy was delayed, until it was too late to bear much fruit.

The coinage faithfully mirrors this development. In the first century, the provinces hardly appear on coins, except as defeated subjects of Rome,—represented by captive figures seated under trophies with bound hands and dejected mien (cp. Plate XXXVIII, 2, 3). The making of Emperors in Gaul and Spain brought these provinces to the fore ; Gallia and Hispania appear as warrior goddesses, armed in defence of their claimant (cp. Plate XXXVIII, 1). Trajan devotes a peaceful type to his new province of Arabia, with her aromatic canes and her camel, and, after the multitude of Victory types showing the crushing of Dacia, presents Dacia as a new member of the Roman Commonwealth of nations (cp. the Danuvius type. Plate XXXVIII, 4). Only under Hadrian, however, do the provinces really come into their own,—and Hadrian was an isolated genius, whose ideas for the Empire found no successor to carry them out. Hadrian was the first of the Emperors to regard his Empire from any but a purely Roman point of view. His provincial birth, his natural curiosity, his far-sighted ability, combined to give him a wide outlook. He spent a large part of his reign in personally visiting the provinces, learning their problems at first hand, winning their confidence and satisfying their material needs. His magnificent series of types, struck in A.D. 134 to 135 as the crown of his life's work, shows the arrival of the Emperor in the various provinces (Plate XXXVIII, 16),—a scene of sacrifice,—the restoration of the provinces,—the Emperor raising a kneeling figure to her feet—the provinces themselves, represented as women in peaceful or warlike guise, with native dress and attributes (Plate XXXVIII, 6-11, 15, 17-19). Emphasis is deliberately laid on the local characteristic,—the ibis of Egypt, the games of Achaea, the cities of Asia, the curved sword of Dacia. The Empire according to Hadrian was to be keenly alive not only at its centre but in all its parts. But Hadrian, as we have said, found no true successor. Antoninus Pius has, indeed, a series of provincial types, struck in connexion with the offering of crowns at his succession ; but he was at heart a Roman and, with all his nobility of character, lacked something of understanding of what the Empire required. The series of later provincial types mainly refers, as before, to victories over rebels. The one great exception is the sudden rise of the Balkan provinces to imperial importance with the accession of Trajan Decius ; he introduces the types of Dacia, the two Pannoniae, and the Genius of the army of Illyricum (Plate XXXVIII, 12, 13)—a break with custom and no doubt no small shock to the civilians of Rome.

Direct reference to Italy, in spite of her privileged position, is not very common—we naturally think first of the " alimentary " institutions of Trajan and his successors. Roma, the Amazon goddess, who typifies in some aspects the Roman state, was probably felt to stand for Italy as well.[1] She is commonly represented as a goddess armed, with short tunic, spear or parazonium and shield,—occasionally with a Victory or inscribing a shield. An extension of the *pomoerium* finds its records in Trajan's type of colonist ploughing [2] (Plate XXXVII 4).

The province is normally represented as a woman, sometimes in a long dress, with attributes of peace, sometimes as an Amazon armed : her character is defined by the attributes which she holds, by her head-dress and costume and by such adjuncts as camel, rabbit, or corn-ears in the field. To the same order of types belong Oriens, the rising sun, radiate, as representative of the East, and the river and Ocean gods of the coinage of Hadrian.

(*d*) *Types relating to the Army*—The Empire was not from

[1] For Rome of the seven hills, cp. Pl. XXXVIII, 14.
[2] For Trajan's new road, cp. Pl. XXXVIII, 5.

the first a military despotism. It began by performing the very necessary duty of reducing the army to its right position in the State, that is to say, of recognizing its just needs and demands, but of shutting it off from any serious influence on politics. The presence of the praetorian guard in Rome and the revolts of rival Emperors in the provinces led at last to the complete breakdown of the sound old tradition and to a reign of military lawlessness. Some trace of this development may be seen on the coinage, where the reference to the army becomes more and more insistent as the Empire advances and culminates in the period of Aurelian, where the army may be said to dwarf the State in importance. Even in that period, however, some facts were allowed to pass in silence. The Emperor at all times had to purchase the loyalty of the troops with donatives,—moderate under most good rulers, excessive under the weak and feckless. Every one has heard of the auction of the Empire held by the praetorians, when Didius Julianus was highest bidder. It is remarkable that these donatives do not figure on coins unless they are included under the general head of " Liberalitates ; " they were a matter between the commander-in-chief and his men and were not considered to interest the general public at all.[1]

Despite the firm pacific policy, which characterized the Empire as a whole, the military tradition was strong. Even when all was quiet within the Empire, the guard on the frontiers could never be relaxed ; and, although after a time separatist movements in the provinces are rare, wars of succession were disastrously common. The military element in the coinage is always, then, an important one. One important class of types celebrates victories in the field ; we find Victory inscribing a shield with the record of triumph, Victory crowning the Emperor, Trajan presenting a Dacian captive to the Senate, the troops acclaiming their victorious commander (cp. Plate XXXIX, 17). Another series of types, characterized often by the legend " Virtus Aug.," lays stress on the valiant achievement that has led to victory ; the Emperor is represented on horseback in the field or surrounded by a group of soldiers. A favourite theme for representation is the harangue given to

---

[1] But the type of *Moneta Aug.* may have something to do with them.

the soldiers by the Emperor,—whether to the guard in Rome, or to the armies in the provinces.   Hadrian has a fine series of types, which show him haranguing his troops, not only from a platform in the camp, but also on horseback in the field after the completion of their manœuvres (Plate XXXIX, 15, 16). Claudius strikes the type of " Imperator receptus," the Prae- torian camp, and " Praetor Receptus," a praetorian clasping hands with the Emperor, in honour of the guard who gave him the throne (Plate XXXIX, 1).   Nero on his " Decursio " type is seen sharing in the military exercises of the praetorians (Plate XXXIX, 13).   Domitian, who relied so largely on the loyalty of his army, represents the taking of the military oath or " sacra- mentum" (Plate XXXIX, 14).   Hadrian's " Disciplina," which shows him leading a file of soldiers, attests the fact of the ex- cellent spirit and discipline which he induced in his troops (Plate XXXIX, 5, cp. 6).   The class of types represented by such legends as " Concordia," " Fides Exercituum,"—whether simple figures of Fides and Concordia with standards or more elaborate groups,—hides a wealth of meaning under a simple form.   Coin types have often to be interpreted on the theory of opposites, —the type expresses a desired result which is quite different from the actual reality.   These types first become common in the Civil Wars of A.D. 68 to 69 (Plate XXXIX, 3), where everything hung on the adhesion of the guard and main legions to the Emperor's cause.   The " Concordia " types of Nerva are the one comment in coinage on the fierce discontent of the guard, which forced Nerva against his will to surrender Domitian's murderers to execution (Plate XXXIX, 4).   A " Concordia Exercituum " of Hadrian in A.D. 119 suggests fears of trouble in the army after the execution of the rebel marshals. A " Concordia Militum " type of Commodus marks the end of a bitter and dangerous quarrel between the armies of Gaul and Spain (Plate XXXIX, 7).   The almost uninterrupted sequence of similar types in the third century tells a clear story of anxiety and insecurity ; military loyalty, the basic virtue of a soldier, was chiefly conspicuous by its absence in a period when more Emperors perished by the hands of their friends than by those of their enemies.   Of the triumph types we have spoken above.   One remarkable type of Gallienus, showing Victory in a biga of mules, with the astounding legend, " Ubique pax," is perhaps the one example of satire on an Imperial coin. It belongs to a date after the loss of the East and the secession of Gaul, when the most flattering of optimists could scarcely have spoken without mockery of " Universal Peace." [1] The coin is hardly intelligible, unless it was issued after Gallienus's death by Claudius II, as a justification of the murder of his predecessor.

The most distinctive class of military coins remains to be discussed. Mark Antony had been the first to strike coins with types of eagle and standards and galley and the names of his individual legions. The practice was revived by Clodius Macer in A.D. 68, by Septimius Severus in his fight for the throne in A.D. 193, and repeated by Gallienus in A.D. 257-258, by Victorinus in A.D. 268 or 269, and by Carausius in A.D. 188-189 (Plate XXXIX, 2, 8-12). On all these occasions the Emperor was particularly dependent on the support of the army and was led to give it an importance above what was usually considered fit. Septimius strikes with one unaltering reverse, eagle and standards, varying only the name of the legion ; he strikes for the legions which espoused his cause against Pescennius Niger. Gallienus varies his type from legion to legion, employing one form or another of regimental badge. His coinage was evidently designed mainly to confirm the loyalty of the Western legions just before the revolt of Postumus. Victorinus follows the practice of Gallienus in using legionary badges as types. Among the legions named are several which could never by any possibility have been under his command. It seems certain that the coins record an event, unknown in the scraps of history that have come down to us—an abortive attempt by the Gallic Emperor, in alliance with Palmyra in the East, to overcome the Roman centre of the Empire. [2] Carausius seems to have copied the policy of Victorinus, striking coins for a number of legions, on whose allegiance he could only base the most shadowy of hopes. It is highly probable that these legionary coins were largely used in the pay of the particular legions whose names they bear. Gold coins of these

---

[1] My friend, Dr. Alföldy, reminds me that the coins often express the desire for the reverse of the actual state of things ; but what are we to make of the *Gallienae Augustae*, which is sometimes on the obverse of these coins ?

[2] Cp. Oman in *Num. Chron.*, 1924, pp. 53 and especially 56 ff.

series are always excessively rare if they are struck at all
—they were perhaps meant only for presentation to senior
officers. Victorinus's legionary coins are all of gold and are
very rare—a fact that would suggest that he may have been
intriguing rather with the commanders of armies than tampering
with the loyalty of the rank and file.

We have now made some attempt to survey the Imperial
coinage in its relation to the different parts of the State—the
Emperor, the Senate, the people, the army, the provinces.
To complete our study we must adopt a more formal classification and consider types in their classes as religious, historical,
animate and inanimate, and buildings. Some of these formal
types will be found to bear on the subjects we have already
discussed.

(e) *Religious Types* (Plates XL, XLI, XLII)—Types of this
character continue to occupy a large space in the coinage.
The Empire opened with a definite revival of old Roman
religion : we are in fact impressed with the persistence of
the old mythology in days when it was losing its grip on men
of all classes alike. The religious symbolism of the coins is
still that of the Roman-Greek Olympians—Jupiter [1] with his
thunderbolt and eagle, Juno with her sceptre and peacock,
Neptune with his trident, Apollo with his lyre and bow, Mars
with his spear and trophy, Mercury with his caduceus and
purse, Hercules with club and lion-skin, Janus, Minerva,
Venus, Vesta and the rest. It is not often, however, that the
deity is present in a mere formal capacity, without reference
to particular functions related to current events. Jupiter
appears as Victor (Plate XL, 14), giver of Victory in war
(Domitian, Hadrian), as " Custos " (Nero), or " Conservator "
(Domitian, Valerian I), the deliverer of the Emperor from
imminent danger, as " Fulgerator " (M. Aurelius, Septimius
Severus), destroying the rebel enemy, as once the giants. A
favourite type shows him sheltering the Emperor under his
outstretched arm (Trajan—Plate XL, 11, Marcus Aurelius).
Mars [2] may be either " Pater," the ancestor of the Roman
State, or " Ultor," the god of war in action against the enemy,
" Propugnator," the defender from danger, " Victor," the giver

---

[1] Cp. Pl. XL, 1, 11, 14.   [2] Cp. Pl. XL, 2.

of victory, or " Pacator," the giver of peace. Hercules [1] was
a natural type of the Emperor, who laboured in the arts of war
and peace for the good of mankind, and plays a considerable
part in the coinage (cp. Plate XL, 12). His honour culminates
under Commodus, who accounted himself a Roman Hercules
and dared to identify himself with the god (Plate XL, 17).
Apollo is honoured by Augustus as " Actius," the giver of the
victory that founded the Empire, by Nero as " Citharoedus "
in honour of Nero's own artistic accomplishments (Plate XL,
4), later by Commodus as patron of the Roman mint. On
coins of Trebonianus Gallus and Volusian (Plate XLI, 5), he
appears as the god of healing. Neptune is sometimes honoured
as " Redux," when he is implored to protect the Emperor
travelling by sea (Plate XL, 5). Minerva, the goddess of wisdom,
culture, and war, held a place of honour throughout, particularly
under Domitian, who placed the whole of his activities under
her protection (Plate XL, 9, 10). Juno usually appears as
the divine counterpart of the Empress (" Regina "), occasionally
as " Lucina," the giver of easy child-birth (Plate XL, 16).
Diana figures either as the goddess of the night-sky (" Lucifera "), often in connexion with " consecration," or as huntress,
—patroness of a sport which was taken very seriously by the
Romans and which fascinated more than one Emperor. Roma
constantly appears as an Amazon goddess, often as giver of
victory. From the time of Hadrian on she is worshipped with
the epithet " Aeterna " as the symbol of the eternity of the
Empire (Plate XL, 13). Ceres is either a type of the Empress
(Plate XL, 15) or the presiding spirit of the corn-supply.
Castor is a suitable type for the young prince, as " princeps
iuventutis " (Commodus, Geta). Cybele, as " Magna Mater,"
is a type for the Empress (Plate XLI, 2), who comes to be known
as " Mother of the Senate " and " Mother of the Camp." Vesta
at all times represents the religious side of State life, often in
close association with the Empress, while Venus, the ancestress
of the first Imperial line, remains a natural type for the woman
who has won the love of the master of the world. She is represented under various aspects as " Felix," " Victrix " (Plate
XL, 6), " Genetrix." Bacchus appears rarely—but one must

[1] For types of labours of Hercules, cp. Pl. XLI, 7, 8.

not forget his appearance on a coin of Gallienus, with the truly wonderful legend, " Conservator Exercitus."

The celebration of sacred banquets in honour of the chief gods (*lectisternium*), after the great eruption of Vesuvius, is represented by types showing the " pulvinaria," or couches on which the attributes of the gods were displayed (Plate XL, 7, 8).

The study of the attributes, which, even where legends are wanting to identify it, indicate the character of the type, is far too intricate to approach here. Its general principles are simple enough—the small Victory held in the hand on a globe marks the " Victor," the branch the " Pacator " or " Pacifer," [1] the spear and trophy the " Ultor." Venus is marked out as " Victrix " by the helmet held in her hand, Ceres as " Frugifera " by her ears of corn, Diana as " Lucifera " by her torch. Only a long experience can determine the interpretation in cases where real doubt is possible.

Hitherto we have spoken only of the old Olympian mythology ; what of the newer developments, the Eastern religions, including Christianity, and the worship of the man-god, the Emperor ? The emotional cults of Syria and Egypt, which were so popular among certain grades of society in Rome, were but slowly admitted to the official world. Serapis and Isis appear once under Hadrian, then again under Commodus and more freely later (Plate XLI, 3). The Dea Caelestis of Syria comes in with the dynasty of Severus who married into a Syrian priestly family. The special worship of the sun-god of Emesa, Elagabalus, was confined to the reign of the Emperor who bore his name (Plate XLI, 4). The worship of the sun-god in a more general aspect was familiar from the cult of Apollo ; the Eastern cults of the god first take root in Rome under Septimius Severus and gradually grow in power, until under Aurelian Sol ranks as the chief divinity, the " lord of the Roman world." There is no single definite reference to Mithraism, but the worship of " Sol Invictus Comes " under the later Emperors (cp. Plate XLI, 8) undoubtedly suggested Mithraic associations to the troops who brought the worship of Mithras westward.

---

[1] Cp. Minerva Pacifera, Pl. XLI, 1.

The worship of Cybele, the great mother, became prominent under the Antonines and the Severi, but seems to have fallen into disrepute after the reign of Elagabalus. The type of " Hilaritas P.R." has often, if not always, a definite reference to the great spring festival, the " Hilaria," which celebrated the resurrection of Attis. Its reappearance on the coins of the Gallic and British Emperors is probably a sign of the importance of the worship of Cybele in those provinces. Curiously enough there are no clear signs on coins of that syncretism, or deliberate blending of several deities in one, which was so marked a feature of the religious thought of the third century.[1] Judaism naturally figures only as a vanquished enemy of the Roman State, not as a religion. Christianity before Diocletian had hardly spread widely enough among the upper classes to win a place on the coinage ; officially, it was at best tolerated. The one possible Christian reference is in the reverse of Salonina, with the distinctly Christian legend, " Augusta in Pace " (Plate XLI, 6) ; Salonina ranks in tradition as a Christian, but how much is implied in the legend we cannot say.

The worship of the Emperor is more important. We have already spoken of the highly organized State-cult of the deified Emperors. But the living Emperor too was freely worshipped in the provinces and even in Rome worship might be offered to his spirit or " Genius." In the coinage we can trace a growing tendency to bestow divine attributes on the Emperor and to assimilate him to, if not actually to identify him with, particular divinities. The laureate crown, the usual head-dress of the Emperor, is borrowed from Apollo, the radiate crown from the sun-god, the aegis from Jupiter or Minerva ; however little the real meaning of this symbolism may be remembered, there is no question as to its origin. So too the Emperor might be assimilated to Jupiter, the lord of the world, or to Hercules, the great benefactor of mankind, whose merits were crowned with immortality. The divine types, in these cases, suggest the Emperor, who is the earthly counterpart of the god. The idea was most at home in the Greek East, where Mark Antony had been acclaimed as a " Νεὸς Διόνυσος," —an avatar of the

---

[1] But cp. the medallion of Julia Mammæa, described in Gnecchi, *I Medaglioni Romani*, II, p. 83, Pl. 100, 8.

wine-god, and Nero as " Νεός 'Αγαθὸς Δαίμων " ; in Rome the same idea is implied rather than expressed. Augustus was especially assimilated to Apollo and Mercury, Nero to Apollo, Commodus to Hercules, the late Emperors of the third century to the sun-god. The Empress, even in her lifetime, was freely associated with the divine world,—particularly with Ceres, with Vesta, and with Venus ; the crown of corn-ears, which she so often wears, is borrowed directly from Ceres. When the adjective "Augustus (a)" is applied to a deity, we seem to have something very like identification, but this use is mainly late and at no time really common.

In estimating the importance of the religious ideas involved in these uses, it is most important not to exaggerate. A large part of the Roman Empire was far more prepared to worship an immanent than a transcendent god and found it easy to find divinity in men who were distinguished for exceptional power or virtue ; the influence of Euhemerism, which saw in the gods of the State only great men of olden times, reinforced this tendency. But in other parts of the Empire, and particularly in Rome, there was a far clearer sense of distinction between the human and the divine. Many Romans regarded even the established practice of "consecratio" with a certain humorous reserve. General common-sense hung back from the extremes of Eastern religion or court flattery. The megalomania of Caligula has left no trace on his Roman coins. The sculpture of the Arch at Beneventum might represent Jupiter as handing over to Trajan his thunderbolt, in token of abdication : the coins, which must surely come nearer to average popular belief, still show a colossal Jupiter, extending his arm with its thunderbolt in protection over the Emperor. Domitian might be "dominus et deus" in the language of flattery, starting from his freedmen ; but the two titles never appear on coins till the reign of Aurelian and then only on a very rare issue of the small mint of Serdica. The worship of the Emperor, then, marks an important stage in the development of religious thought ; Rome herself contributes little to its development and exercises a salutary check on it, by maintaining beside it the older religious beliefs.

There was, however, one side of Roman religious belief which lent itself to the new tendencies,—the worship of minor deities, personified conceptions or virtues, by the side of the major deities. Primitive Roman religion drew an exact parallel between the concrete world of experience and its somewhat shadowy spiritual world. Every occurrence and act of life was related to a spiritual power or " numen." In time certain ranges of activity were attributed to a major deity, who includes in himself a number of potential minor powers. Mars, for example, in his various aspects of " Propugnator," " Victor," " Ultor," may be considered to be a combination of powers associated with the acts of repulsing the enemy, gaining victory and wrecking vengeance on the defeated. Definite traces of this can be seen in the Maia Mercurii, the Heries Junonis, the Moles Martis of primitive Roman religion ; the name in the nominative represents one particular aspect of the god, whose name is given in the genitive. Apart from the major deities the Romans worshipped a number of other powers —such as Victoria, Virtus, Salus, Pax, Fortuna—which, though less vividly realized and less potent than the great gods, had something more than a momentary character and presided over well-defined branches of life. The Empire took over the cult of these minor divinities and developed it to an enormous extent in the coinage ; in them it had ready to hand a convenient form of symbolical reference to almost every possible activity of the State, which had the extra advantage of possessing a real hold on popular belief. Fortuna, to the Roman, was no mere linguistic abstraction ; she was an actual power, influencing human life, to whom sacrifices might be offered and vows made. Each of these powers might be worshipped under some particular aspect, with reference to some particular branch of its activity ; and here the relation to the worship of the Emperor comes in. With the person of the Emperor is associated a wide range of powers, which can be divided over a number of personifications ; the " Victoria Augusti " is his capacity for gaining victory, the " Virtus Augusti " his spirit of courage in the field, the " Libertas Augusti " his spirit of constitutionalism at home. Where the genitive " Augusti " is used we are probably strictly correct in regarding the personification as a definite quality of the Emperor himself ; when the adjective " Augustus (a) " takes its place, the association is a looser one and only relates the personification in a general way to the imperial system.   " Pax Augusti," as distinguished from " Pax Augusta," should denote rather the pacific temper of the Emperor than the vaguer idea of " imperial peace."

We have now to define more closely the particular ideas associated with these virtues in the coinage and the attributes by which they are defined ; a few attributes such as the cornucopiae, representing abundance, and the sceptre, representing dignity, are common to many—but most attributes are proper to particular powers and are only transferred to others by a conscious or unconscious blending of ideas.   Let us start with the more general conceptions and then go on to those that are associated with more limited sides of national life.   Concordia (Plate XLI, 14), with her attribute, the patera of sacrifice, represents harmony,—in the imperial family, in the State, in the army (" Concordia Augusta, P.R., Exercituum ").   Felicitas (Plate XLI, 17, 19), with her caduceus, suggests prosperity, with particular reference to material welfare ; she is closely associated with Mercury, the god of trade.   Fides (Plate XLII, 1), usually described as " Publica," with her dish of fruit and corn-ears, seems to denote " Public credit " and to be associated particularly with the censorial functions of the Emperor. " Fides Militum," with distinct attributes, the military standards, has our modern meaning of " loyalty."   Fortuna (Plate XLII, 2), with her rudder and globe, may be related either to Emperor or State.   She is the power that raises or abases men, seen at her height when she raises a man to the pinnacle of Empire.   As " Redux " she is invoked to give the Emperor a safe home-coming from his travellings.   Pax (Plate XLII, 12, 13, 14), with her attribute, the olive-branch, is the power who presides over the Augustan peace ; the constant reference to her on the coins attests the general pacific policy of the Empire. Pietas (Plate XLII, 15, 16) represents a favourite Roman virtue, in a variety of applications.   As piety in a religious sense, she appears sacrificing over an altar ; as piety in a family sense, she is specially represented by a woman with children (Plate XLII, 15) ; with her types are occasionally associated the stork, her bird, or the traditional group of Aeneas, Anchises and Ascanius.   Salus (Plate XLII, 19), feeding her snake, is usually related either to the Emperor or to the State ; she suggests particularly the deliverance of the Emperor from serious illness

or danger or of the State from disaster.   A similar conception
is conveyed by Securitas (Plate XLII, 20) resting her head on
her hand or leaning on her column ; she follows after Salus
and suggests the peace of mind which comes when danger is
past.   Victory (Plate XLII, 23, 24), with her wreath and palm,
is the commonest of all these imperial virtues.   She represents
the victorious quality of the Roman Emperor and State ; often
she stands on the globe of the world or on a prow, to denote
sea-victory,—she is associated, by epithet, with particular
triumphs (Britannica, Parthica) and often inscribes a shield
with the title of the triumph.   Specially characteristic of her
are her wings, which bear her abroad in triumph over the
world.   Associated with Nemesis, she represents the vengeful
and warning aspect of imperial victory.

Many of the virtues are closely associated with particular
events or classes of events.   The all-important corn supply is
represented by Annona (Plate XLI, 11), with corn-ears, modius
and the prow of a sea-going ship, or Abundantia, with similar
attributes, or with a cornucopiae, which she empties on the
ground.   Ubertas (Plate XLII, 22), with her purse, is a third-
century personification denoting wealth,—probably with reference to imperial largesses.   Liberalitas (Plate XLII, 8), with
her tessera or, perhaps better, her account-board (*abacus*),[1] represents the bounty of the Emperor in providing the customary
largesses.   Aequitas (Plate XLI, 10), with her scales and measuring rod, and Moneta, with her scales and cornucopiae, are
kindred conceptions, associated with the giving of due measure
in the corn-doles and the coinage.   Their exact relation to
Liberalitas has yet to be determined.   The public games and
shows, which were frequently given by the Emperors on occasion
of public rejoicing and were as much expected of him as the
corn-doles, may be represented by Laetitia (Plate XLII, 7),
with her wreath and anchor ; the anchor expresses the idea
often expressed directly in the epithet " Fundata."   This personification refers directly rather to the joyful occasion than to
its celebration ; for the latter the term is " Munificentia Aug.,"
usually expressed by some type chosen from the show, as for example the elephant of Antoninus Pius.   Hilaritas (Plate XLII, 3)

---

[1] Cp. Dodd in *Num. Chron.*, 1911, p. 246.

was especially associated with the " Hilaria," the great spring festival of rejoicing in the cult of the Great Mother. Aeternitas (Plate XLI, 12) with her heads of sun and moon, her mantle inwrought with stars, or her phoenix, has reference either to the immortality of the blessed dead, the " divi " and other members of the imperial house, or to the eternity of Rome. The military virtues are well represented. The commonest after Victory is Virtus (Plate XLII, 26), usually a female, occasionally a male figure, with spear and parazonium,— the symbol of the active courage of the soldier,—and Honos (Plate XLII, 4), with his sceptre, who stands for the dignity of the military profession. Concordia and Fides, when definitely related to the army, express the idea of comradeship and loyalty and bear standards as attributes. The Constantia of Claudius (Plate XLI, 15) represents rather the idea of steadfast endurance. The important question of the succession is represented by Providentia, the wise foresight of the Emperor, with her wand and globe (Plate XLII, 17), and by Spes (Plate XLII, 2) with her flower, the hope centred on the heir. Nobilitas (Plate XLII, 10) suggests the high rank of the prince, who came to be known distinctively as "nobilissimus Caesar." With the epithets " P.R." or " Publica," Spes has a different shade of meaning and looks rather to the rising generation as the hope of Rome.

A group of virtues, usually associated closely with the Emperor, represent various sides of the activity of a good ruler. Libertas (Plate XLII, 9), with her pileus and wand (*vindicta*) stands for the constitution or the constitutional temper of the ruler. Then follow Clementia, Indulgentia, Justitia, and Tranquillitas (Plates XLI, 13 ; XLII, 5, 6, 21), expressing the idea of mercy, readiness to grant favours, just dealing and calm judgment. These powers are not very clearly defined ; Clementia and Justitia hold patera and sceptre, Indulgentia extends her right hand in a gesture of friendliness, Tranquillitas holds in her arms a capricorn.[1] Patientia (Plate XLII, 11) represents the heroism of Hadrian in enduring his last illness. Closely associated with the Empress are Fecunditas (Plate XLI, 16), with a reference to the blessing of children, and Pudicitia

---

[1] Is there a reference to Augustus, whose natal sign it was ?

(Plate XLII, 18), with her veil,—a reference to the personal sanctity of the Empress, who, as consort of the Pontifex Maximus, shares in the honours of the Vestal Virgins. The uncommon type of " Iuventus " has special reference to the youthful promise of the heir. A few remain to be noted—Bonus Eventus (Plate XLI, 18), with his patera and corn-ears, the giver of success in all undertakings, the various " Genii," of the Emperor, the Roman people, the Senate, the army, most commonly represented with the patera, but sometimes with the sceptre or the standard, the " Fata Victricia " of Diocletian, the " Bona Mens " of Pertinax, the " Ops Divina " of Antoninus Pius and Pertinax, the " Tellus Stabilita " of Hadrian. The " Saeculum Frugiferum " of Septimius Severus and Albinus seems to be a Roman expression for a native African god of Hadrumetum, presiding over agriculture.

A few general rules governing the use of these personifications on coins need to be remembered. They are usually represented by female figures, standing or seated, seldom by busts on the reverse ; when busts occur, the attribute usually carried in the hand is sometimes placed by the neck. They have often several forms of activity, which are defined by descriptive epithets—" Augusti " or " Augustus (a) "—adjective, " P.R." or " Publica," " Militum " or " Exercitus." They have for the most part definite distinguishing attributes, which can however be transferred for special reasons to other powers. Thus we find under Hadrian Pax with a miniature Victory as " Pax Victrix " and Nemesis—Victory with the olive-branch, as " Victoria Pacifera." Providentia under Severus Alexander has the corn-ears and modius of Abundantia, and evidently looks to the provision for the corn supply. Pax often borrows the caduceus of a closely related power, Felicitas. Examples of such transferred attributes always deserve careful study, for it may be safely assumed that there is some particular meaning to be expressed by it. The patera, the commonest of all symbols of sacrifice, is naturally borne by Pietas, in the sense of piety towards the gods—it is less obvious why it should be attributed to such powers as Securitas, Clementia, Justitia, and, occasionally, Victory. In some cases the idea of sacrifice is probably present ; in others, it is the virtue herself that is worshipped—the patera, the implement of worship, is, by a curious transference, assigned to her instead of to her priest.

Mythology, as distinct from religion, no longer plays the part that it played on the later Republican coins. On the bronze medallions of the second century, which were not destined for currency, it holds a large place—a sign that they were something apart from the ordinary coins. Antoninus Pius has an interesting series relating to the early history of Rome—the landing of Aeneas, the story of Hercules and Cacus.[1] On the coins themselves, we have the she-wolf and twins on aurei of Hadrian, Aeneas and Anchises on the sestertius of Antoninus Pius, Romulus and Mars and Rhea on aurei of the same reign. A few references on the coins of the moneyers of Augustus—to Tarpeia (Plate XL, 3), to the treaty with Gabii—must be considered to belong rather to the Republican tradition.

(f) *Historical Types*—Historical types are common at all periods of the empire and, as we have seen, give the coinage something of the character of a medallic series. The history of the Republic is not unnaturally neglected ; interests ran in new channels and there was always the danger of reviving old bitternesses. Trajan, the most Republican in sentiment of all Roman Emperors, on the occasion of the calling in of the old Republican silver, reissued a chosen series of types with his own legend of restoration : he deliberately represented the Empire as the natural outcome of the Republic and included among his restorations types of Sulla, Pompey, and Brutus,— the foremost enemies of the founders of the Empire. The issue represents a notable attempt to see Roman history as a whole, emphasizing its continuity and harmonizing its discords, but it exercised no permanent influence on the choice of imperial coin-types. History for the mint-masters of the Empire meant primarily the history of the present,—the performances of imperial government, which must be presented—and presented in the proper light—to its subjects. Some reference to earlier Emperors is occasionally found, whether in commemorative issues, in echoing of types or in definite restorations of earlier coins ; interest in the past even here is dwarfed

---

[1] These were issued in preparation for the games celebrating the 900th year of Rome.

by the present. A brief chronological survey, under the general headings of Rome and Italy—the provinces—foreign powers—will give a good idea of this aspect of the coinage.

(1) *Rome and Italy.*

Augustus celebrates his surrender of his exceptional powers and the honours voted to him by the Senate in return, his restoration of the roads of Italy, his election as " pontifex maximus." Tiberius, with his type of wreath and curule chair, refers to the transference of the election of magistrates from the " comitia " to the Senate. The " R.C.C." of the quadrans of Caligula (Plate XLV, 3) stands for the " remission of the two-hundredth," the tax of ½ per cent. on sales. The " P.N.R." [1] of the quadrans of Claudius attests the restoration of the true weight of the " Aes " coinage, with which Caligula seems to have tampered. We have already spoken of the types that refer to the share of the praetorian guard in making Claudius Emperor. Nero's " Roma " and " Vesta " types allude to the great fire of Rome, his " Port of Ostia " to the great harbour begun under his predecessor, his closed temple of Janus to the peace following the successful termination of the Parthian War. Nerva chronicles a series of popular measures, the abolition of the vexatious exaction of the tax on the Jews, the remission of the charges of the imperial post on Italy (Plate XLV, 8), and the distribution of corn to the people of Rome. Trajan records the building of his new harbour at Centumcellae, the laying out of the " Via Trajana " from Teanum to Brundisium, and, above all, the alimentary institutions (Plate XLV, 9), which served at once to provide for the education of Italian orphans and to encourage Italian agriculture. These institutions grew and prospered under his successors ; a rare and beautiful aureus of the deified Faustina I records the granting of a charter by her husband to the " Puellae Faustinianae," orphan girls for whom he provided in her honour (Plate XLV, 14). Hadrian records the burning of the bonds of arrears of debt in the forum of Trajan (Plate XLV, 13). His " Libertas Restituta," with the type of a woman presenting two children to the Emperor (Plate XLV, 10), may refer to his approval of the principle, that the children of mixed marriages

---

[1] " Pondus Nummorum Restitutum " (?).

should be free, even when it was the mother who was a slave ; an alternative explanation would see in the type a reference to the restoration, of the freedom of testation, by the refusal of the Emperor to accept legacies from fathers, who left children behind them. In A.D. 121 Hadrian celebrated the *Parilia* under the new name of *Natalia Urbis* and opened thus a new age of gold (Plate XLV, 11, 12). The various games established from time to time at Rome find occasional mention on the coinage, notably the " Neronia " of Nero, represented by the type, table of the games, urn and palm. The Secular Games, celebrated by Augustus in 17 B.C., by Domitian in A.D. 88 and by Septimius Severus in A.D. 202, were marked by a succession of moving scenes of sacrifice and prayer, calculated to make a deep impression on the minds of the onlookers. Augustus, whose Secular Games served as a kind of ritual of inauguration of the Empire, strikes several commemorative types (Plate XLV, 1, 2), including one of the preliminary distribution of purifying substances (" suffimenta "). Domitian celebrates his performance with types on gold and silver, showing the herald who announced the games, and a magnificent series of types on sestertius and " As," showing the distribution of " suffimenta " by the Emperor and his colleagues, the reception by them of " fruges " from the people, the sacrifices to Jupiter, Juno, the Moerae, Terra Mater, and the Eilithyiae, and the choral procession of boys and girls in honour of Apollo and Diana (Plate XLV, 4-7). Septimius Severus strikes a coin with type of Hercules and Bacchus and legend announcing his celebration of the games (Plate XLV, 15) ; he must, it would seem, have introduced into the ritual some special honours to his two protecting deities. The " Secular Games " of Claudius in A.D. 48 were distinct in character from these— they celebrated the eight-hundredth anniversary of Rome : it is curious that they have left no numismatic record. The nine-hundredth anniversary in A.D. 148 was celebrated by Antoninus Pius with various mythical types—struck some years before in anticipation.[1] The great event of A.D. 248, the end of the thousand years of Rome, was celebrated by Philip with magnificent games,—represented on the coins by types of the

---

[1] Cp. Miss Toynbee in *Cl. R.*, 1925, pp. 170 ff.

beasts exhibited,—lions, hippopotami, and various kinds of
deer ; the she-wolf and twins of the foundation legend are rather
curiously inserted among them.

It may perhaps seem that the record of events of the capital
on coins is a meagre one.   The explanation lies partly in the fact
that the life of Rome, under the Empire, moved as a rule on
quiet lines, the violent interruptions in the shape of new Emperors being represented by the new coinage,—often with no
special reference to the violent transition—partly by the other
fact, that many events were of the kind that is liable to occur
at regular intervals and were therefore represented by more or
less stereotyped reverses.

The foreign policy of the Empire, its diplomacy and its
wars, finds a full and usually explicit record.   Augustus com-
memorates his recovery of the East by the types of Asia
Recepta and the crocodile of Egypt (Plate XLIII, 3).   His
great diplomatic triumph over Parthia and Armenia is represented by the kneeling Parthian offering a standard and by
the suppliant Armenia (Plate XLIII, 4., cp. 2).   His wars in
Rhaetia and Noricum and on the German frontier are depicted
in the type of the soldiers acclaiming him as " imperator "
(Plate XLIII, 1), in the type of the barbarian offering a hostage
and the German kneeling to surrender a standard (Plate XLIII,
5).   The quelling of the Pannonian revolt is only celebrated
by the triumph type of Tiberius.   Caligula records the great
exploit of his father Germanicus in the East—the crowning
of Artaxias king of Armenia (Plate XLIII, 6).   Claudius places
on his coins a triumphal arch erected for the victory " De
Britannis " (Plate XLIII, 7).   The subjection of Britain after
the revolt of Boadicea under Nero finds no mention beyond
that implied in the general type of Victory ; the government was
perhaps unwilling to call public attention to a success so hardly
won.   The successful war against Parthia, on the other hand,[1]
finds its record in the triumphal arch, the closing of the temple
of Janus, and the adoption of the praenomen of " imperator "
by the Emperor.   The civil wars of A.D. 68-69 are fully represented by the local coinage of Spain and Gaul (Plate XLIII, 10),
with their glorification of the Senate and people of Rome and

[1] For Armenian Victories, cp. Pl. XLIII, 8.

of the militant provinces; by the coins of L. Clodius Macer, with reference to Africa, Carthage and Sicily and to the legions that supported Macer; by the coinage of the rebellious legions of Germany, with their insistence on the devotion of the armies and their appeal to the praetorian guard to assist them in making a new Emperor; by the issues of Vespasian in Illyricum, the East, Gaul and Spain, and by the coinage of the rebels of the Gallic Empire, who celebrate the capture of the legion at Vetera, the new loyalty to Gaul, and the restoration of national liberty. An Eastern aureus, showing Vespasian as restorer, is shown on Plate XLIII, 9. The conquest of Judaea, the great exploit of Vespasian and Titus, is recorded by types of the captured province mourning; the " Victoria Navalis " on which Vespasian lays such emphasis probably refers to the pressure of sea-power brought to bear on Rome to end the civil war. The victories of Agricola in Britain find their record in types of a formal character under Vespasian and Titus. Domitian chose rather to direct attention to the more personal triumph won over the Chatti on the middle Rhine. We find Germania mourning with her broken spear beneath her (Plate XLIII, 11), a barbarian kneeling to ask for mercy, the Rhine prostrate at Domitian's feet. The wars against the Dacians, the Suevi, and the Sarmatae, with their doubtful issues, are hardly touched upon. Trajan, the greatest of all the aggressive Emperors, celebrates his Dacian triumph with types showing a Dacian mourning defeat, presented by Trajan to the Senate (Plate XLIII, 12), or crushed beneath the heel of Peace. His Eastern wars are presented in all their main phases—the appearance of Parthamaspates before Trajan at Elegeia (" Rex Parthus "), the assignment of kingdoms to the princes of Osrhoene, Characene, etc. (" Regna Adsignata ") (Plate XLIII, 13), the bestowal of the crown of Parthia on Parthamasiris (" Rex Parthis Datus "), the addition of new provinces (" Armenia et Mesopotamia in potestatem P.R. reductae "). The type of Arabia with her camel records the addition of that province to the Empire in A.D. 106. Hadrian, as a lover of peace, prefers to lay emphasis on his work in building up and developing the Empire; the Jewish revolt, the one serious blot on the pacific record of the reign, is recorded only by a type of the Emperor with standards and by a Victory-Nemesis, with the branch of Peace. The

building of the wall in Britain is perhaps suggested by the stone,
—showing distinct traces of courses—on which Britain rests.
Antoninus Pius records the suppression of a revolt in Britain
and the peaceful diplomacy, which enabled him to assign rulers
to Armenia and the Quadi (" Rex Armeniis Datus "—Plate
XLIII, 14, " Rex Quadis Datus "). The Parthian war of
M. Aurelius and L. Verus finds record in a " Profectio " type
for L. Verus, in types of Mars and Victory (Plate XLIV, 1),
and finally in the giving of a king to conquered Armenia
(" Rex Armeniis Datus.") The bitter wars on the Danube
frontier, which caused Marcus Aurelius, the philosopher Emperor, to exchange his study for the camp, gave rise to types of
arms and trophy, recording the victories " De Sarmatis "
(Plate XLIV, 2) and " De Germanis." A " Victoria Britannica "
records the suppression of a revolt in Britain under Commodus.
The civil war of Pescennius Niger and Septimius Severus is
reflected in the Eastern coinages of the two rivals, while the
victorious Septimius has further victories to record over Arabia,
Adiabene, and, later, over Parthia herself (Plate XLIV, 3).
A Lugdunum coinage of Albinus bears witness to his short
independent rule in Gaul. Finally the British campaign, in
which Septimius ended his days, produces types of " Victoria
Britannica " (Plate XLIV, 4), of the crossing of a river, of the
acclamation of the victorious Emperors by their troops.

The troublous history of the third century, with its succession
of short-lived Emperors, of usurpations in the provinces, of wars
with the new Persian Empire that rose on the ruins of the
Parthian, with the wars on the Rhine and wars on the Danube,
that culminated in the great Gothic invasions, is written full
in the military types of the Emperors and in the coinage of
the usurpers abroad (cp. Plate XLIV, 5, 8, 9, 12, 13). The
more picturesque style of reference in the form of special scenes
of the campaign or special acts, such as the bestowal of the
crown on a subject king, is hardly to be found ; we find mainly
formal types of Mars, of Fides Militum, of Pax and Victory,—
occasionally made more explicit by explanatory legends, such
as the " Pax Fundata cum Persis " of Philip I (Plate
XLIV, 7), the " Victoria Carpica " of the same Emperor
(Plate XLIV, 6), or the " Victoria Gothica " of Claudius II
(Plate XLIV, 11). Among the more remarkable coinages of

usurpers we may signalize the issues of Uranius Antoninus at Emesa,[1] the uncouth over-struck coins of Regalian in Dacia, the ample coinage of the Gallic Emperors, and the coinage of Carausius and Allectus.   Carausius celebrates his welcome in Britain (" Expectate Veni "—Plate XLIV, 14), his establishment of peace (" Pax Aug."), the peace and recognition that he extorted from his " brothers " Diocletian and Maximian. Allectus emphasizes the store set by him on his navy, with types of a galley and legends expressing the " Delight " and the " Valour " of the Emperor.

Rome in these anxious years had come very near the brink of disaster ; the " Ubique pax " type of Gallienus (Plate XLIV, 10) can hardly be anything but an indignant gibe at a government which had rather attained a state of universal war. The " Restitutor " types of Aurelian mark the beginning of a happier era and, by the time of Diocletian and Maximian, we are in the full revival of Roman military prowess, which was to start the new form of the Empire under auspices that must have seemed entirely favourable.

(g) *Animate and Inanimate Objects*—Animate types, other than those of living persons, gods and personifications, play a large part in the imperial coinage but can only be briefly reviewed here.   The priest ploughing, a type of the founder of the city, is used by Augustus, Trajan and Commodus : the first two seem to refer by it to their extension of the " pomoerium," Commodus to his foundation of Rome as the " Colonia Herculea Commodiana."   The herald of the secular games appears on coins of Augustus and Domitian.   Soldiers clasping hands stand for military harmony under Vespasian.   As a subordinate part of the type, we find citizens attending to receive the imperial largesses, soldiers listening to the Emperor's harangues, acclaiming him as " Imperator " or aiding in the celebration of his triumphs.   The clasped hands are a natural symbol of concord (Plate XLVI, 18), whether in a civil or military sense,—and the further meaning of prosperity can readily be added by a winged caduceus and corn-ears held in them. The sphinx on the coins of Augustus is his signet-ring, the capricorn his natal sign (Plate XLVI, 1).   The Pegasus and Siren

---

[1] These gold pieces are held by some to be false.

of Augustus's moneyer, Turpilianus, referring directly to an
ancestor, Turpilius, may convey an indirect reference to the
great poet Virgil, who had just died in 19 B.C.   The phoenix
on consecration coins of Trajan is a symbol of immortality
(Plate XLVI, 6).   The she-wolf and twins stand for the foundation legend of eternal Rome (Plate XLVI, 7).   The eagle, the
bird that is conceived of as carrying the soul of the dead
Emperor heavenwards, will represent consecration.   The crocodile of Augustus represents the province of Egypt. The butting
bull of Augustus has a double reference—a local one to South
Gaul and a personal reference to Augustus, who was nick-
named " Thurinus "—we remember that a bull was the typical
reverse of Thurii (Plate XLVI, 3).   Often a bird or animal
represents the deity with whom it is associated—the eagle
Jupiter, the gryphon Apollo (Plate XLVI, 8), the peacock
Juno (Plate XLVI, 5), the owl Minerva, the dove Venus
(Plate XLVI, 9).   The games of the arena are also fully symbolized by the animals there displayed to public view—the lion,
(Plate XLVI, 11),[1] the rhinoceros (Plate XLVI, 4), the hippopotamus (Plate XLVI, 10), the elephant, the elk, and the stag.
A remarkable type of Septimius Severus, with legend " Laetitia
temporum," shows us a vessel disgorging its freight of animals
for the public show.

Inanimate objects are used both as literal expressions of
current events and as symbols.   We may begin with the little
columns, set up and inscribed to commemorate acts of the
Emperor or decrees of the Senate (cp. Plate XLVI, 25), the
triumphal chariots and arches which celebrate the imperial
triumphs, the chariots drawn in the " pompa circensis," or the
" carpentum," voted in honour of the dead or living Empress.
In the same class we may put the laurel-branches planted on
either side of Augustus's doorposts, the oak-wreath, " Ob Civis
Servatos," so often decreed by the Senate to the " Father of
the Country."   An altar may be a general symbol of religious
worship or may commemorate a particular dedication, such as
that of the altar of " Fortuna Redux " to Augustus in 19 B.C.
The chief priestly offices of the State may be represented by
emblems of the priests—the simpulum, jug and sprinkler for

---

[1] The lion of Postumus is probably a symbol of strength (Pl. XLVI, 12).

the pontifex, the lituus for the augur, the tripod and raven for the " quindecimviri sacris faciundis," the patera for the " sep-timviri epulones " (Plate XLVI, 19, 23, 24). Standards natur-ally symbolize the army (cp. Plate XLVI, 16), piles of arms or a trophy the victory over a foreign foe (Plate XLVI, 15). A galley may stand for the travels of the Emperor by sea, for sea-power or for the service of corn ships from over seas to Rome. The eruption of Vesuvius in A.D. 79 was expiated by solemn supplications and banquets at the table of the chief gods (" supplicatio," " lectisternium "). The couches or " pulvin-aria " of the gods appear on the coins of Titus and Domitian. We know from our literary sources that the gods were usually re-presented on these occasions, not by statues,[1] but by " exuviae " —i.e. the various trappings, which we usually describe as attri-butes. The great gods figured in pairs at these " lectisternia " and we may take the procedure after Trasymene as a possible model for this occasion. There is one couch for Jupiter and Juno—represented by thunderbolt on throne ; one for Neptune and Minerva, represented by dolphin and anchor and by helmet on throne ; one for Ceres and Mercury, represented by corn-ears on throne ; one for Apollo and Diana, represented by dolphin, raven and tripod, and by crescents and stars on throne. Vesta and Vulcan will be represented by the altar type, Mars and Venus by the wreath on throne, composed of two curule chairs ; wreaths (" struppi ") were sometimes used to symbolize the heads of the gods. On other occasions, too, the divine attributes may stand for the god—the thunderbolt for Jupiter, the helmet, aegis and olive-branch for Minerva. The caduceus of Mercury is a regular symbol for prosperity and the cornucopiae, the common attribute of so many " Virtues," for abundance (Plate XLVI, 20).[2]

(h) *Buildings*—The Romans, both individually and as a State, always displayed a passion for building, which finds its full expression in the imperial coinage. The delineation is often, of course, very imperfect and conventional, but, in the

---

[1] But cp. A. B. Cook, *Zeus*, II, pp. 1170 ff.

[2] Further illustration of this subject will be seen on Pl. XLVI: No. 13 : tiara, bow-case, and quiver as a symbol of Armenia ; No. 14 : rudder on globe, repre-senting the government of the world ; No. 17 : the table of the games for Nero's festival ; No. 21 : a statue on a rostral column ; No. 22 : the twin sons of Marcus Aurelius in horns of plenty.

12

absence of other memorials, the coin record of imperial buildings is of the highest value. Temples are naturally well represented —the temples of Mars Ultor (Plate XLVII, 1), of Jupiter Tonans, of Diana Sicilia, of Divus Julius under Augustus, the temple of Concordia under Tiberius, the temple of the deified Augustus under Caligula, the closed temple of Janus under Nero (Plate XLVII, 10), the restored Capitol under Vespasian and Domitian (Plate XLVII, 11, 12),[1] the round temple of Vesta under Nero and Vespasian (Plate XLVI, 3), the temple of Jupiter under Trajan (Plate XLVII, 15), the temple of Roma and Venus under Hadrian, the temple of Faustina the elder and the restored temple of Divus Augustus under Antoninus Pius. After the second century, this class of reverse falls off in frequency ; the most interesting types are the temples of Apollo and Roma under Philip I and the round temple of Juno Martialis under Trebonianus Gallus. The Altar of Roma and Lugdunum under Augustus and Tiberius is worthy to be ranked among the buildings, for the coins show not so much the altar itself as its surroundings—an elaborately ornamented plinth, flanked right and left by Victories on pillars. An " Ara Pacis " of Nero is shown on Plate XLVII, 9. The triumphal arches, which have already claimed a place among military types, are sometimes very slightly rendered : or again they are given on the large scale, with a full rendering of the details of statuary. Chief among these are the Arches of Nero Drusus, Nero, Trajan and Severus. Columns are found under Augustus and Nero— the great column of Trajan does not fail to appear. A memorial column to Antoninus Pius appears on his " consecration " coins. We have further the " Macellum " or meat-market of Nero, the praetorian camp of Claudius (Plate XLVII, 2), the harbours of Ostia under Nero (Plate XLVII, 8) and of Centumcellae under Trajan, the Coliseum of Titus (Plate XLVII, 13), the Danube bridge of Trajan, the Basilica Ulpia and Forum Traianum (Plate XLVII, 7), the Circus Maximus of Trajan (Plate XLVII, 14), Caracalla and Gordian III, the baths of Alexander Severus. Augustus's legate, P. Carisius, gives a bird's-eye view of the Spanish colony of Emerita.

4. **Relation of Early Imperial Coinage to Art**—The relation

---

[1] For other temples, built or restored by Domitian, cp. Pl. XLVII, 4, 6.

of the imperial coinage to art on the grander scale is a question of high interest and importance. The debt of the coins to sculpture is obviously very great : the portraits of the Emperors must have been modelled at times on well-known busts, and the same will hold good of many divine types of the reverses. Republican Rome had already ransacked the provinces to enrich herself with statuary and the Emperors showed something of the same taste for art, if less of the rapacious brutality allied to it. Augustus placed a wealth of statuary in the temples of Mars Ultor and Concord and Vespasian's temple of Pax was something not unlike an Art Museum. Pliny the Elder gives us a very vivid idea of the treasures assembled in Rome to delight the heart of the art-collector : in his own appreciation there is present what we may perhaps without offence term a Transatlantic element—he is impressed by costs and curiosities, as well as by sheer artistic merit. The most famous statue that has been identified on imperial coins is perhaps the Cow of Myron (Augustus—Plate XLVI, 2—and Vespasian), brought by Augustus to Rome and placed in the portico of Apollo and, it seems, transferred by Vespasian to the temple of Peace. The province types of the coins must owe much in the way of general conception, if not of exact execution, to the statues of the nations placed by Augustus in the " porticus ad nationes," and afterwards by Hadrian in the " Basilica Neptuni." The elaborate reverse of Geta, Bacchus with his crew finding Ariadne, is clearly derived from a group of statuary.

The historical bas-relief,—developed from Pergamene and Alexandrian models but, as far as choice of subject goes, a creation of the Empire—has certainly had a profound influence on some of the more elaborate compositions on coins—on such types as the distribution scenes, the " adlocutiones," the burning of bonds by the lictor under Hadrian, the procession of soldiers in his " Disciplina " type. The acclamation type of Trajan may be closely paralleled in the sculptures of his column.

Materials for comparison with paintings and mosaics are not very plentiful and do not, so far as we know, suggest any close relation. Very different is the case with metal work in silver and gold and above all with the art of gem-cutting. There are striking parallels to coin-types in such rare survivals of ancient plate as the Bosco Reale cups and the patera of

Rennes.   The art of the engraver of gems is hardly to be distinguished in kind from that of the die-sinker—the principles
are the same, only the material differs.   Extant gems show the
closest of parallels both to the portraits of the Emperors and
to the reverse figures on coins : it stands to reason, of course,
that the standard of gem engraving is technically on a higher
level than that of the ordinary coin.

Here we may leave our discussion of this fertile and fascinating subject.   We have hardly done more than touch its fringes
—to master its wealth of detail requires a lifetime of study.
It is not too much to say that there is hardly a branch of study
connected with the Empire which cannot be deepened and
enriched by a study of the coins.

COINAGE IN THE GENERAL LIFE OF THE EARLY EMPIRE

1. The Outside World and the Provinces—For this third chapter we have reserved the full discussion of the influence of the imperial coinage on the general history of the Empire. The range of our inquiry will be wider than in the corresponding chapter on the Republic. The imperial currency travels far beyond the bounds of the Empire and influences foreign powers. The provinces now form an integral part of the system and must be included in our survey. And on the life of the State itself,—on trade, on the army, on the people of Rome—the reactions of the coinage are, if not more important, at any rate easier to follow than in the preceding period.

The foreign politics of the Empire were usually very simple in character. The only civilized power with which Rome had regular diplomatic relations was Parthia. For the rest, her territory marched with barbarian nations, which, if not in a state of war against Rome, were usually subject to her tutelage. Roman gold soon became a world currency and found acceptance beyond Roman territories in the Parthian Empire and as far as India. The Parthian kings struck silver and copper independently, but never gold : to this extent, they recognized the claim of the Roman Emperor to be " King of Kings." The only gold coinage, other than that of Rome, was struck in the vassal kingdom of the Bosphorus, which was accustomed to a coinage in gold and copper and did not use silver. It was felt as a sign of the new independence of the Sassanian monarchs, that they struck in their own name in gold. The Roman silver circulated beyond the Empire. Britain, which first learned the art of coinage from Gaul, betrays Roman influence from the invasion of Julius Caesar to the conquest under Claudius. The German tribes never developed an indigenous coinage ;

in the time of Tacitus they were still addicted to the use of Republican silver, particularly of the older issues, the " bigati," and of the later " serrati." The evidence of finds shows that imperial denarii in time succeeded the Republican in this field. In Africa the vassal kingdom of Mauretania had its own silver currency : when this ceased, the Roman coinage reigned supreme. On the Danube, as on the Rhine, we find no native coinage ; even the Dacia of Decebalus stopped short before this point. In the East, we find Roman silver, as well as Roman gold, penetrating as far as South India. Rome, then, supplied the needs of coinage, so far as they were at all felt, over a very wide area. She became a great importing nation, drawing raw materials such as hides from the North and, far more important, the costly spices and perfumes from the East. To pay for them she had no great mass of manufactured goods to offer— payment had to be made, for the most part, in bullion. The result was a steady drain on the Roman treasury, a steady depletion of the stocks of precious metal, which played its part in the production of the crisis of the third century. The decrease in the purchasing power of gold and silver, which was a main feature of the Republic, reached and passed its height. The government endeavours by reduction of the weight of gold and silver and by debasement of the silver to protect its stocks of metal. It does nothing to correct the adverse balance of trade and finds itself involved, through the expedients it devises, in worse ills than those originally feared.

How far considerations of foreign trade influenced the imperial government in its issues of coin is very hard to determine. We must not assume a negative result, because our evidence is scanty. It has been suggested that plated denarii of the early Empire, particularly of the famous " C.L. Caesares " type of Augustus, were expressly issued for the trade with the far East. The evidence quoted for this view is subject to serious question and it seems improbable that Rome can have seriously considered a policy so certain in the long run to defeat its own aims. The practice of subsidizing native princes, in return for their acceptance of Roman suzerainty, was adopted as early as the reign of Domitian for Dacia and is a familiar device of state-craft later. As the debasement of the silver progressed, such subsidies would more and more need to be paid in gold, and we may conjecture that this fact partly accounts for the marked scarcity of gold in the third century.   The extreme rarity of aurei of Maximin I is perhaps to be accounted for on this assumption.

Turning to the provinces of the Empire, we find ourselves on surer ground.   The details of the arrangements for provincial coinage must be reserved for a separate chapter ; all that we are concerned with for the moment is the general principles at stake.   Roman gold circulated over the whole Empire without a rival, except in the Bosphorus.   Roman silver dominated the market in the West, but in the East had to compete with the old coinage still in circulation, provincial issues in Asia Minor, Syria and Egypt and occasional issues of towns.   Roman " Aes " was at first issued for Rome and Italy ; its use soon extended to Sicily, Africa, Spain and Gaul, but not till the reign of Nero was the transition from local coinage here complete.   In the East it played a very subordinate part.   Small change was issued regularly from a limited number of provincial mints and a vast number of city mints,—usually bearing the head of the Emperor or Senate, as token of allegiance, but, in form, the independent coinage of the people or city.   At many towns there exists, often beside an " imperial " coinage, one purely autonomous in form, only betraying its imperial date by its general style and fabric.   Rome was evidently only too thankful to decentralize this difficult question of supply and to profit by the long experience in coinage of her Eastern subjects.   The vassal states of the Empire struck gold (in Bosphorus only), silver (in Macedonia, Thrace, Pontus Polemoniacus), and copper (Thrace, Pontus, etc.).   These vassal coinages are mainly a feature of the first century of the Empire ; only in Bosphorus does gold and copper continue to be struck down into the third century.

The decay of the Roman silver currency brought down this system in ruins.   Bankers became reluctant to give small change for the wretched billon of Gallienus.   Local and provincial coinage declined and came to an end under Tacitus. The tendency that already existed to establish provincial mints received an immense impetus—the only solution was to carry the debased imperial silver over the whole Empire.   Mommsen has assumed on inconclusive evidence that the silver coinages of the East were given general currency in the third century to eke out the failing imperial stocks. It is perhaps enough to suppose that the government was unwilling to reserve special funds for provincial use. Egypt, which was the last province to maintain its independent issues, coined its base billon till the reign of Diocletian; its tetradrachm, already a base coinage in the reign of Tiberius, ends as a small dump of metal indistinguishable from copper. This was obviously the only alternative to a change to imperial issues; and the Roman government seems to have shown wisdom in making one form of debased silver standard for the whole Empire, instead of attempting to maintain it in various provincial forms in relation with the imperial.

The Roman Emperors, then, made some serious attempt to consider the coinage problems of the Empire as a whole. They based all reckonings, even in the East, on the Roman standards. They supplied an imperial coinage in gold and silver, eked out by Eastern issues of silver. They solved the problem of small change by calling in the aid of the city state. So far as this policy gave a chance for local cults and interests to survive, we may be thankful that they were not more thorough; and, however attractive the idea of a uniform system of coinage for East and West may appear, we must remember that its introduction in the East would have involved a difficult breach with a multitude of old traditions and connexions. A more serious complaint may be urged against them for neglecting at times to provide an adequate supply of coinage. The existence of local imitations of imperial coinage, particularly in the West under the early Empire, seems to point directly to a failure in supply. And the provincial silver of the East, supposing it to have served a really useful end, should have been coined with far greater regularity than we find to be the case.

2. Occasions of Coinage. Legal Tender—With the settled peace, established by Augustus and preserved with little break for many years after him, trade began to develop on a scale unknown before. Not only were raw commodities freely transported from place to place, but a trade grew up in such manufactured articles as tiles and pots. It was only suitable, then, that the Emperors should regularize the supply of coinage and keep the mints permanently at work. In the early years, it is true, we still find occasional intermissions of coinage ; by the end of the first century, regular issues in all metals had become the rule, fuller at some times than at others, but at no time entirely in abeyance. The money was put on the market either in the form of payments to the army, civil service, and state creditors or through the banks (*mensae*) ; the existence of " nummularii " among the mint officials suggests that some of these banks were official. Tiberius, at the great financial crisis of A.D. 33, placed 100,000,000 HS in the banks, to be lent free of interest to those in need of money, on the giving of sufficient security.[1] The supply of bullion was maintained partly from the mines, partly from the existing stocks of coined metals, as the coins became obliterated and were called in : it is probable that individuals could bring bullion to the mint to be coined for them for a small royalty.

In this connexion we have to face the problem of legal tender. Over what areas and for how long a period were coins under the Empire current ? Our evidence must be drawn mainly from finds, countermarks, " restored " issues, and some general considerations ; without dogmatizing as to theory we shall be able to form an approximate idea of the practice.

Finds show us that Republican denarii circulated beside the imperial down to the time of Nero and, less commonly, beyond it ; the last to continue in use are the base pieces of Mark Antony, which still occur in hoards of the middle of the third century. After the reduction of the weight of the denarius by Nero pre-Neronian coins are usually absent—they must have gone in masses to the melting-pot. Even in the third-century hoards stray coins from Nero onwards occur—they evidently ranked as equal to the later denarii. " Antoniniani " and denarii are quite commonly found in the same hoards. The

---

[1] The action taken by Tiberius in A.D. 33 demands a closer investigation. A financial crisis had been brought about by an enforcement of the laws governing usury, which were being widely infringed. To put their affairs in order, creditors called in their debts. The money lent had been largely invested in Italian land ; the forced sales that followed led to a collapse in prices and a great scarcity of ready money. Tiberius came to the rescue by lending 100 million sesterces, free of interest, on security. This is an isolated case, in our present state of knowledge ; in reality, it is probably only one of many similar cases. The Emperors seem to have been ready to make a wise use of their control of coinage to meet the financial needs of their times.

increasing debasement of the silver has no influence at first :
only at the complete breakdown under Gallienus do we find
a clear line drawn—the utterly debased billon of Gallienus,
Claudius II and the Gallic Emperors is found in vast quantities
in hoards, but seldom in conjunction either with earlier or
later pieces. The Gallic money found admission to a limited
extent to the Roman market and the Roman to the Gallic :
the standard of the coins was approximately the same in both.
The reformed coinage of Aurelian and his successors is normally
kept distinct in hoards from the base money preceding it.
Hoards then indicate three critical dates for the silver, A.D. 65,
A.D. 258, and A.D. 272-273.[1] Gold is not very commonly found
in hoards. Mommsen has concluded from the evidence of a
few hoards that gold was very soon withdrawn from circulation.
The evidence of other finds such as that of Corbridge (Nero-
Antoninus Pius) suggests that the period of circulation was
fairly long. The reform of Nero of A.D. 65 marks a critical
division for gold as for silver : the pre-Neronian gold was
largely melted down. The brass coinage was not often hoarded
until the third century, when, with the debasement of the silver,
it began to have a real value. Eastern coinages, so far as their
denominations fitted in with the imperial, are occasionally
included in imperial hoards ; the Lycian drachm of Trajan
not infrequently appears with denarii.

Countermarks on Roman coins are practically confined to
the early brass from Augustus to Nero ; they are common on
the As, less common on dupondius and sestertius and unknown
on the quadrans. A series of countermarks of the reign of
Augustus and early Tiberius seems to serve the purpose of making
Roman pieces current in Gaul and Gallic in Italy : other
countermarks of the same period mark Roman pieces for
circulation in Sicily and Africa. A second series of the reign
of Claudius, occurring only on coins of Caligula and Claudius
himself, probably stamped coins for circulation in Britain.
A third series under Nero represent a revision of the existing

---

[1] Nero, in A.D. 65, may have called in the old coinage, and Aurelian in A.D. 272-
273 certainly did so. Whether Gallienus did the same in A.D. 258 is very doubtful ;
it seems more probable that he did not intend to make a break with the past, but only
to profit by the issue of base metal ; it was the refusal of the commercial world to
accept his coinage at the old rates that led to the cleavage.

coinage and a stamping of part of it for continued circulation. This revision may have begun under Claudius, but belongs mainly to the early years of his successor. The countermark *NCAPR* (" Nero Caesar Augustus Probavit ") is never found on coins of Augustus—they were already obsolete : it is found freely on coins of Tiberius to Claudius. The old coin was sometimes continued in circulation at a reduced rate,—a sestertius as a dupondius, a dupondius as an As. A fourth class belongs to the period of the Civil Wars of A.D. 68-69 ; coins of Nero are countermarked by the rebels in Gaul and Spain (*S.P.Q.R.*, *P.R.*), by Vitellius and by Vespasian. Here the countermarks practically cease ; a rare countermark of Trajan may have marked coins to circulate in Dacia.

Roman countermarks, however imperfectly we know them as yet, teach some most valuable lessons. They prove to us that the senatorial coinage had at first only a limited circulation, probably in Rome and Italy, and had to be countermarked for circulation outside. After the reign of Tiberius, no more countermarks of this class occur and we may conjecture that the *S.C.* money had currency at least over the West. They further teach us that the brass wore out rapidly and was withdrawn from circulation : by the reign of Nero, the coinage of Augustus had, practically speaking, disappeared. It is probable, however, that there was no rigid rule—i.e. that it was the worn coins that were withdrawn, not coins earlier than a certain date. We cannot prove that the Romans knew the meaning of legal tender in this stricter sense. The countermarks of the fourth class, which mark a change of issuing authority, rather than a change of circulation, are interesting from a different point of view.

The " restored " coins require a word of explanation. Vespasian and his sons deliberately revived a number of types of Augustus in all metals. Titus and Domitian struck a series of brass, with a formula announcing that they had restored them, from Augustus to Galba ; the coins, apart from this formula, are closely copied from the originals. Nerva restored the " capricorn " type of the denarius of Augustus and various types of his in brass, but with a freedom not met with under Titus and Domitian. Trajan, in A.D. 107, in connexion with the melting down of the old " worn-out " silver,

issued a " restored " series of Republican denarii and imperial
aurei—the former close to their originals, the latter in most
cases essentially new coins, except for the portrait. This great
issue certainly marks an extensive calling-in of the old coinage ;
but it has another purpose, in the presentation of Roman history
as a whole—the Empire succeeding in natural order to the
Republic : obviously the coins of Nerva, if not those of Vespasian and Titus, cannot have been yet out of date. Hadrian
restruck great numbers of " cistophori " of Mark Antony,
Augustus and Claudius with his own types. Finally, Marcus
Aurelius and L. Verus restored the type of one legion of Mark
Antony.

Finally, there are a few general considerations that seem
to bear on the case. The withdrawal of worn-out coin is a
natural and almost inevitable measure at any time. Again,
after a change in the money-system, old and new coins can
hardly circulate together, unless they are definitely tariffed to
one another in terms acceptable to the general public. And
the existence or non-existence of provincial coinages in silver
and brass enables us to form conclusions as to the range of
circulation of the imperial money.

Let us try to extract from the above evidence the rules
of circulation under the Empire. First, as regards range of
circulation in place. Imperial gold is current everywhere ;
so too is imperial silver, but only in competition with provincial coinages in the East. The *S.C.* coinage of Rome is at
first restricted to Rome and Italy, then extended over the
whole West ; it may have been current in the East, but certainly
had no large circulation there. In Syria its place seems to have
been taken by an analogous coinage of Antioch, bearing the
same mark of senatorial control (*S.C.*). Secondly, as regards
period of circulation. Money was withdrawn as it became
obliterated by wear or as it was ousted by new denominations.
Trajan certainly withdrew the mass of Republican denarii
from circulation ; it is possible that he definitely demonetized
them. In the third century, the coinages of A.D. 258 and 272
were definitely separated off both from the earlier and later
coinage. Aurelian certainly demonetized the coins of Gallienus in the sense that he did not give them parity with his
new money : if he allowed them any legal status, it must have

been on a scale unsatisfactory to the owners,—only so can we account for the immense quantities of them that were buried away.

3. Financial Policy.   Largesses and Donatives—The general policy of the early Empire was, it seems, a sound one.   The gold and silver were struck true to weight and of an exceptional fineness.   They could command acceptance on their merits, without any pressure on the part of government. The brass and copper only represented part value, but, as they were not ordinarily used in large payments, this did not seriously matter.   Serious doubts, however, are raised by the existing masses of plated denarii of the period.   If these were official issues, the government largely stultified its own endeavours, by secretly going back on its own avowed policy.   A definite decision is hard to reach.   We shall probably not be far wrong, if we credit Augustus and Tiberius with a faithful maintenance of their policy, while admitting that official debasement, by means of the expedient of plating, may have to be debited to the account of Caligula and Claudius. For the most part the plated coins are the work of false moneyers whether or not in official connexion with the mint.   After the debasement of the silver under Nero had begun, the plated coin as an official issue lacks a *raison d'être*.

How was it that the imperial government left the sound lines which it had at first followed and took the devious path that led to the financial collapse ?   We have already seen one cause of this in the loss of precious metal in foreign trade and in articles of luxury : the stocks of metal were no longer adequate for the needs of coinage, and the government under Nero began to protect itself by reduction of weight and debasement of the silver.   But some further cause must be sought and this we shall find in two directions—in the ever-increasing demands of the poorer citizens of Rome and of the armies.   The practice of giving gifts in kind to the poor of Rome goes well back into the Republic.   Caesar introduced the practice of distributing money and his successors followed in his footsteps.   It was not, however, till the reign of Trajan that these " liberalitates " assumed such proportions as to constitute a serious drain on the exchequer.   Trajan distributed no fewer than 650 denarii per head, Hadrian 1000, Antoninus Pius 800.   From

this time on the " liberalitates " were a heavy item in the debit
account of the imperial budget. The motives that underlay
them were mixed and, to some extent, pardonable or even
laudable. The Emperors, who did most to increase the burden
of the " liberalitates," were among the best and wisest that
Rome ever had. They still respected the position of Rome
as head and centre of the imperial system and they found in her
masses of citizens hardly able to bring up their families to a
decent standard of livelihood. What more fitting than that the
imperial funds should contribute to the material well-being of
the Roman people, on which the supply of a healthy and
vigorous population depended ? The mischief, of course, lay
in the fact that these doles only palliated, without relieving
the cause of the trouble. The people of Rome were not taught
to be self-supporting, but only to depend more and more on
the imperial bounty. The consequence most to be desired—
the rearing of a large and vigorous population of native Romans
—was only imperfectly realized, though the " Spes P.R." types,
representing all the hopes reposed on the rising generation, bear
eloquent witness to the good intention. We in our day, who
have seen the necessity of doles as an alternative to worse
evils, are not likely to condemn the Romans too hastily. All
we can say is that the empire of the Antonine and succeeding
period found itself burdened with a permanent expenditure on
the poor of Rome, which brought in no adequate return.

To this must be added the needs of the army. Augustus
had put the soldier in his right place ; he had shut him out
of interference in politics and, whilst providing for him gener-
ously on his discharge, had compelled him to serve for a long
term at a very modest rate of pay (225 denarii—9 aurei per
year—for the legionary). Domitian, who depended so much on
the support of the army, raised the pay by a quarter—to twelve
aurei. Then, after an interval of a century, Commodus and
Septimius Severus again raised the pay and Caracalla followed
him with a further increase. And to all these regular payments
fell to be added the donatives which corresponded to the doles for
the civil population, which, like them, were always increasing
and came more and more to be looked on by the soldiers as their
right. The story of the putting up of the Empire to auction by
the praetorians after the death of Pertinax is certainly in its

essence true. The accession of Severus brought no real improvement. His dying advice to his sons " to enrich the army and care nothing for anybody else " sufficiently well indicates the trend of his policy. In one way and another, direct and indirect, the army was becoming an ever heavier burden on the budget, and the third century, with its lack of long settled dynasties and its quick transferences of power, only made matters worse. With the increased pay of the troops, with the donatives and doles, the expenses of the government were brought to a dangerous height. What could be done to balance the budget ? Our knowledge of provincial taxation is too imperfect to allow of a very positive answer, but we can feel fairly safe in saying that no great increase in taxation was possible. The provinces were already paying as much as could reasonably be required of them and, at times, a remission of old bad debts was considered necessary. The government, then, perhaps hardly realizing the full scope of its action, plunged deeper and deeper down the dangerous path of debasement and reduction of weight. It had the command of the coinage and could apparently increase its resources by these expedients ; it did not sufficiently realize that it was only attempting to raise by an inequitable form of indirect taxation what it could not trust itself to raise by direct.

    4. **The Crisis of the Third Century. Attempts at Recovery**— The debasement of the denarius, we have seen, proceeded by a series of regular drops from Nero to Caracalla. The weight of the aureus, reduced by Nero, was restored by Domitian— probably out of regard for people and army,—but was again reduced by Trajan. Caracalla reduced the weight again to $\frac{1}{50}$th of a pound and, to increase the profits of the silver coinage, introduced his new " Antoninianus," or double denarius, at less than the weight of two denarii. The victory of this new coin over the denarius after Balbinus and Pupienus marks a critical stage : it was a victory for immediate necessities over a further-sighted policy. Even so, however, a stand was not called ; debasement of the silver proceeded and, at last, Gallienus, at the crisis of his reign, broke clean away from sound tradition and attempted to impose the basest of bad billon in place of a silver currency. Up to now, the imperial silver seems to have been accepted at its normal face value ; the evil

day was postponed and the owner of debased silver could still flatter himself with the hope that his coin was exchangeable for its equivalent in good metal. Now at last the harvest had to be reaped. The imperial silver was no longer accepted as what it pretended to be—its course must have fluctuated up and down, till it reached bed-rock. Moneychangers in the East refused to give small change for it and had to be commanded to do so—with how much permanent success we can readily imagine—by imperial edict. The gold coinage lost all stability and regularity : it could not bear the impossible burden thrown on it by the collapse of the silver. The Empire had, in all but words, declared itself bankrupt and thrown the burden of its insolvency on its citizens. It had begun, in the third century, to attempt to collect provincial taxes in bullion, so as to escape itself the consequences of its own debasement. Obviously there were limits to the unjust gains that could be procured thus : in the long run the government must have been compelled to accept payment for the most part in its own coin and so find itself no better off than before. The results of the crash must have been disastrous. Trade must have been shaken to its foundation, prices must have risen to fabulous heights and individual fortunes must have been swallowed up in the cataclysm. No doubt, then as in our own time, the violent disturbance of credit gave occasion to the daring speculator to build up gigantic fortunes. The net result for the hard-working citizen must have been, almost without mitigation, evil.

By the time that Aurelian was ready to reform the coinage, the worst of the mischief must already have taken place. Any hopes that the holders of the old billon may have had of recouping their losses were certainly buried, when he refused to admit the old coin on a parity with his new. Many owners, sooner than part with their money at unfavourable rates, hoarded it in the ground—to make up those huge finds, which are constantly coming to light. Demonetization of this kind, however, was a necessary step towards any reform. All that Aurelian could hope to do was to leave the past with its losses and build for a happier future. The local and provincial silver and copper of the East had begun to collapse with the break-down of the imperial silver under Gallienus. Aurelian made no

attempt to restore them—they cease entirely under Tacitus—
but prepared to supply the whole Empire with imperial coin.
For the senatorial copper of Rome he substituted new imperial
issues, while leaving the East as a whole without any fresh
supplies of small change. Only in Egypt did the old provincial
coinage continue, reduced in weight and debased to match the
imperial. Aurelian's reform cannot be accounted an entire
failure—it provided a makeshift coinage and paved the way for
the more far-reaching reform of Diocletian. But he gave the
world no regular and dependable coinage either in gold or in
silver ; the main supply was still to consist of a billon coin,
with a delusive coating of silver, not much more valuable
intrinsically than the worst productions of the mint of Gallienus.
Prices must have remained at an abnormally high level and,
worse than this, there must have been all the uncertainty
and instability that attends a coinage which does not rest on
an adequate reserve. The one genuine remedy—the restoration
of a regular coinage of gold and silver—was not yet resorted
to. The supplies must have been inadequate and, in the case
of the silver, the good metal had been frittered away over the
supply of vast masses of inferior billon. How Diocletian found
sufficient gold and silver to inaugurate his reform must remain
to some extent a mystery : probably his Eastern conquests
actually placed fresh supplies of bullion at his disposal. With
his new attempt to reform the coinage and with the doubtful
success that attended it we shall have to deal in the first chapter
of our third book.

Looking back then we see that the financial miseries of
the third century amounted to a formal state-bankruptcy,
brought about by a long failure to adjust expenses to income.
The best of all remedies would have lain in a cutting down
of expenditure, but the political conditions of the time forbade
any saving on the least justifiable of the charges—those for the
poor of Rome and for the army. A second alternative would
have been the recognition of the deficit and the funding of a
national debt. This was something as much beyond the ken
of the imperial as of the Republican statesman. The real insolvency of the State was dissimulated up to the last possible
moment and then the whole burden was thrown on the private
citizen. The State emerged, as modern Germany has emerged
from a similar crisis, but only at a cost of individual happiness
and well-being that is well-nigh incalculable.

13

CHAPTER IV

THE PROVINCIAL AND LOCAL COINAGE OF THE EARLY EMPIRE

1. **General Principles**—The place of the local and provincial issues in the coinage of the Empire has already been defined in general terms in the preceding chapter. Our present task is to pursue this inquiry into further detail and to give some idea of the conditions under which these coins were struck, the denominations which they represented and the subjects which were chosen for their types. In no part of this handbook is the author more aware of the imperfection of his equipment for his task and of the inadequacy of the space at his disposal. Some indulgence may perhaps reasonably be claimed for an attempt, however imperfect, to draw a faithful sketch of a subject which really requires a book to itself.

The task of providing coinage in all metals for the whole Empire was not even attempted by the early imperial government. Coinage in gold was almost entirely imperial. Coinage in silver was imperial over almost the whole of the West ; but in the East local and provincial issues helped out the demand. Coinage in base metal was issued by the Senate, first for Rome and Italy, after Nero for the whole of the West ; in the East, local and provincial issues took its place and continued in use till late in the third century. We will try to give some idea of the arrangements made, province by province, first for the Western, then for the Eastern provinces.

Spain had a large number of city mints striking bronze under Augustus (cp. Plate XLVIII, 1, Emerita), many of which were still active in the reign of his successor ; under Caligula (cp. Plate XLVIII, 2, Caesaraugusta) only a handful are still at work and after him the mints are closed. It is probable, however, that here and in Gaul the supply of senatorial " Aes " was inadequate and was eked out by local imitations till the reign of Nero, who provided a more satisfactory supply for local needs. Gaul, in the latest period of the Republic, had had a silver coinage at Lugdunum, Nemausus and Cabellio and a coinage in bronze at Lugdunum and Vienna. Under Augustus the coins of Nemausus formed something like a provincial currency for Gallia Narbonensis (Plate XLVIII, 3). In Gaul, however, the city played a much smaller part than in Spain ; and in 11 B.C. Augustus instituted the provincial issues of the " Commune Galliarum " at Lugdunum, with the famous reverse type of the " Altar of Rome and Augustus." This coinage was suspended by Tiberius out of fear of nationalist movements and only resumed for a moment by Claudius ; but the branch of the Roman mint, opened by Nero at Lugdunum for the supply of the West, may be regarded as in some sense the successor of the provincial mint. Britain had no provincial coinage of its own ; in the days preceding the Roman conquest, however, the influence of Roman types is clearly to be seen on the silver and bronze issues of the native princes. Africa had a local city coinage in bronze under Augustus and Tiberius, Mauretania had a silver coinage under its kings, Juba II (Plate XLVIII, 7) and Ptolemaeus, and very rare coins in gold ; after Claudius its only coinage is that of the little town of Babba (Plate XLVIII, 6) which struck down to the reign of Galba. Sicily has a few issues of bronze down to Tiberius (cp. Plate XLVIII, 5, Panormus), and to these we may add a group of coins of the moneyers of Augustus, counter-marked for local use. The Sardinian coins of C. Atius have sometimes been attributed to the reign of Augustus ; the small coinage of the Balearic Isles extends down to the reign of Claudius. Italy itself depended on the mint of Rome ; only in the South did the mint of Paestum issue small bronze coins down to the reign of Tiberius (Plate XLVIII, 4).

The general lines of the development are clear enough. Coinage in the West was not highly developed and there was never any question of establishing regular mints for the supply of gold and silver. For the base metal Augustus made an experiment in local issues. But the nationalist movements in Gaul and Africa led Tiberius to revise this policy and in the end we find it completely abandoned. The imperial coinage itself was largely issued by Augustus from Spanish and Gallic mints. Here too a change of policy set in ; after the reign of Caligula provincial issues of imperial coin are a symptom only of the Civil Wars, not a permanent part of the system. Authority to coin was given either by the Emperor himself for a town or even for a whole province or by the provincial governor.

The East presents us with a mass of coinage of diverse kinds, which by its detail baffles any attempt at a full description here. The vassal kings, held in a relation of dependence on the Emperor, issued semi-independent coinage, on which the heads of the local ruler and Emperor often appear on opposite sides of the coin. The kingdom of the Bosphorus is remarkable in having a coinage of gold (Plate XLIX, 1) and bronze, but no silver. Silver coinage is found in Thrace, Galatia, Cappadocia, Nabathaea—bronze in the same kingdoms and also in the small principalities round Palestine and in Commagene. These coinages, for the most part, came to an early end and represent a passing and unimportant phase.

2. **Provincial Issues**—Of far greater interest are the provincial issues. Under the Republic the East had never fallen under the sway of the denarius ; it still maintained local standards and possessed masses of struck coin. The Roman Empire accepted the *status quo* and issued coins, imperial as far as the authority was concerned, but provincial in their standard and in their general style and appearance For the province of Asia Augustus, Claudius (Plate XLVIII, 8, 9), Vespasian, Domitian, Nerva and Trajan struck tetradrachms of the cistophoric standard, equated in value to three denarii. Hadrian struck similar coins for Asia and also for Bithynia and recoined masses of earlier pieces (Plate XLVIII, 10) ; after him, except perhaps for a moment under Septimius Severus, the series ends. Crete has a silver coinage from Caligula to Trajan (cp. Plate XLIX, 3), Cyprus under Vespasian (Plate XLIX, 7) and his sons. Caesarea in Cappadocia strikes silver, mainly drachms, from Tiberius to Gordian III (cp. Plate XLIX, 9-11) ; [1] these drachms seem to belong to the same system as the tetradrachms of Syria. These Syrian tetradrachms were struck mainly at Antioch, later at a number of other mints (cp. Plates XLIX, 12, 13 ; L, 1, 2). Mesopotamia had a

[1] The coin shown on Pl. XLIX, 8, was possibly struck at Caesarea, but for circulation in Cyrene.

small silver coinage under Marcus Aurelius and L. Verus. Finally, the great mint of Alexandria in Egypt from the reign of Tiberius issued its base billon tetradrachms (Plate L, 3), to which no higher value than that of one denarius was assigned.[1] The Lycian League had an autonomous silver coinage down to Claudius and a provincial coinage after him under Domitian, Nerva and Trajan (Plate XLIX, 5). As an appendix to these provincial issues we may place a few sporadic issues of cities— Byzantium under Claudius (? Plate XLIX, 2), Chios under Augustus, Stratonicea under the same Emperor, Amisus in Pontus under Hadrian (Plate XLVIII, 12), Aegeae in Cilicia under Hadrian, Mopsus under Hadrian and Antoninus Pius, Nicopolis under Antoninus Pius (Plate XLVIII, 11), Thessalonica under Commodus, Cydonia, Hierapytna (Plate XLIX, 4), and other Cretan cities under Tiberius, Tarsus under Domitian and succeeding Emperors down to Caracalla (cp. Plate XLIX, 6). In the Syrian district we find autonomous silver of Seleucia, Laodicea and Tyre during the first century A.D. and coins with the heads of Emperors later at Tyre, Berytus, Damascus, Emesa, Heliopolis, Tripolis, etc. Some of these town issues are really to be regarded as provincial issues, struck at a number of centres. In general we may say that silver was restricted to a few great provincial issues and formed no part of the general local coinage.

With bronze the case is entirely different. We find associated with the provincial " concilia " a number of issues for such provinces as Bithynia (Plate L, 7), Asia, Crete, Cyprus, Galatia, Macedon (Plate L, 6) and Pontus. Alexandria (Plate L, 5) has a great coinage of bronze, running parallel to its billon coinage, and Antioch strikes bronze with the Latin legend S.C. on the reverse (Plate L, 4). This S.C. can only refer to the Senate of Rome, and, strange as the fact may appear, we must recognize in this coinage a sort of Eastern counterpart of the senatorial " Aes " of the West. Dacia (Plate L, 9) from Philip I to Valerian has its own provincial coinage and the coinage of Viminacium (Gordian III to Valerian—Plate L, 8) should perhaps be regarded as a provincial coinage for Moesia Superior. There are other instances (e.g. Corinth and

---

[1] Perhaps the passage in the *Gnomon of the Idios Logos*, s. 106 : νόμισμα πλέον οὗ ἰσχύει οὐκ ἐξὸν κερματίζειν, implies an attempt to keep the denarius down to par.

Patrae) in which the coinage of some important city seems to take the place of a provincial.

3. **Local Issues**—These provincial issues of bronze, however, fade into insignificance before the vast masses of coin struck by a number of city mints over the whole of the East. Of special grants of the right to coin we hear little [1]—we may quote the " indulgentia Augusti moneta impetrata " of Patrae and the " perm. Imp." of Corinth under Domitian. As a rule we must suppose that the right to coin in bronze was conceded almost as a matter of course to every organized civic body, capable of meeting its own needs of small change. Such coinage, while bearing the " ethnic " or city name as a mark of authority, indicates its dependence on the Empire by complimentary reference to the Emperor, the Senate, or, less commonly, to the people of Rome. Many cities, however, strike a coinage, either alone or parallel with that just described, which is purely autonomous in character. Such a display of independence has nothing to surprise us at a city like Athens that still enjoyed nominal independence. But the autonomous coinage is far too widespread to be fully explained on this one hypothesis. The explanation perhaps is that local coinage was always in theory autonomous and that the omission of any reference to Rome had no constitutional significance. A special place is taken by the coinage of the Roman colonies and by the " municipia," which, though not actually colonies, were organized on the Roman model. The theory of the Republic had made the colony dependent on the capital for its coins. Under the Empire all this was changed. The colony strikes like any other city, but is distinguished by its use of Latin instead of Greek and by the selection of types of a more Roman character, particularly such types as the priest ploughing which bears directly on colonization.[2]

To study the distribution of mints over the Eastern provinces is more than we can attempt here. The foundations of the coinage were almost everywhere laid by Augustus, but scarcely a reign passed without some addition to the number

---

[1] The governor certainly enjoyed general powers of supervision; cp. Digest, XLVI, 31-2, bad silver demonetized by governor.

[2] The type of Marsyas, taken from the statue in the Roman forum, was used as a symbol of the " ius Latii."

of mints.   At certain periods in particular provinces the increase is peculiarly marked—e.g. under the Flavians in Bithynia, under Trajan in Lydia, under Septimius Severus in Achaea, under Gordian III in Lycia.   If ever the great task of presenting the local coinage of the Empire chronologically is successfully achieved, it is certain to add considerably to our knowledge of the imperial government in its relation to the provinces.   In some provinces, such as Asia, the mints are extremely numerous, in others the burden falls mainly on a few cities, which must have ministered to the needs of large country-sides.

This is perhaps the best place in which to refer to the important and difficult question of countermarks.   In coinage, as elsewhere, things are not always what they seem and the countermarked coin is an excellent example of this truth. In every case the countermark effects some alteration in the piece on which it appears ; it may bring an obsolete coin up to date, it may alter the nominal value of a coin, it may claim the coin of one city for the use of another.[1]   The last mentioned is probably the most common function of the countermark. For example EPYX and LILYB on moneyers' coins of Augustus appropriate the pieces to the local uses of Eryx and Lilybaeum. Spanish countermarks of a number of towns (C.A.—Acci, CAS—Cascantum, CLV or boar—Clunia, ꓘR—Turiaso, etc.) were probably affixed after the cessation of the Spanish city coinage ; there was a dearth of money and cities, forbidden to strike new money, had to content themselves with seizing as many as possible of the worn pieces already in circulation. In Bithynia coins of Nicaea of the early third century A.D. seem to have been countermarked for use in other towns during the distressful years of the reign of Gallienus.   Other countermarks, such as those of a governor (e.g. VAR at Laodicea in Syria, KOP—Corbulo (?)—on Commagene coins of Tiberius) or of a legion seem to be used to extend the circulation of local issues for particular purposes.

4. **Mint Authorities**—We pass on to the question of the authorities controlling these coinages.   The provincial issues of silver, which bear no " ethnic," may safely be assigned to

---

[1] Cp. *Num. Chron.*, 1913, pp. 389 ff. ;   1914, pp. 5 ff. ; *N.Z.*, 1915, p. 86 ; 1921, p. 144 ; *R.N.*, 1911, p. 423 f. ; *M.N.*, 1875, pp. 101 ff. ; *Bull. Soc. Num. Rom.*, 1924, pp. 53 ff.

the provincial government ; they are essentially imperial in nature, only the standard being provincial. The coinages of the provincial councils were presumably issued by those bodies under the supervision of the governor. The issue of local coinage was a part of the local administration and fell to the local senates and to local magistrates. Reference to the governor is common enough, but it is normally in the form of ἐπί with the genitive case—a date, not a mark of authority. Portraits of governors only appear for a very short period in the reign of Augustus and are restricted to Asia and Africa ; they seem to mark a temporary grant of privilege by the Emperor. The local arrangements were very various. Most often one of the permanent boards of magistrates was entrusted with the issue. Thus we find στρατηγοί, ἄρχοντες, γραμματεῖς in Asia, ephors at Sparta, suffetes at Carthage, duumviri in Spain, and elsewhere. The name of the authority is either in the nominative case, or in the genitive with the preposition ἐπί or διά, less commonly παρά. The issuer of coin sometimes adds other titles of honour, not relevant to his function as moneyer, either the name of some other office held by him, or simply some general title of honour, such as πρῶτος πόλεως, Ὀλυμπιονίκης, or φιλόκαισαρ. The expense of an issue was sometimes borne by a private citizen and is then distinguished by the description ἀνάθημα or by the verb ἀνέθηκε. A dative may denote the person to whom an issue is dedicated or an accusative the person who is complimented thereby. Such formulae as αἰτησαμένου or εἰσαγγείλαντος seem to mean that a coinage was decided upon on the request or proposal of some individual. For many provinces the evidence on these points is almost nil ; for the province of Asia there is a mass of evidence, which gives us a considerable insight into the way in which the cities of the Empire managed their finances.

5. **Systems of Reckoning**—Our knowledge of the systems of reckoning in use is very slight indeed. It is, however, tolerably certain that Roman reckoning was in use over the whole Empire, at any rate for all larger transactions, either alone or beside local systems. All the coinages of gold and silver were undoubtedly tariffed in terms of aureus and denarius. The gold piece of the kingdom of the Bosphorus was equated with the aureus. In the late second and the third centuries

it came to be very heavily alloyed with bronze and ends as little more than a piece of base metal ; it may perhaps have retained its nominal value in terms of sestertii, while the Roman aurei of good metal were at a very great premium. The " cistophoric " tetradrachm was equated to three denarii, its fourth part, the " Rhodian " drachm, to twelve Asses, three-quarters of a denarius ; a lower value of ten Asses is also attested, but is certainly exceptional.[1] The drachm and didrachm of Caesarea in Cappadocia were probably equated to one and two denarii, whilst the Syrian tetradrachm, heavier than the " cistophoric " but less pure, was, like it, valued at three denarii. The Alexandrian tetradrachm, struck in very poor billon, was valued at one denarius only and was often at a discount. The fact, however, that there was an official prohibition against giving more small change for a coin than it was worth seems to indicate that it tended itself to stand at a premium. The drachm of Crete was, by weight, only equal to about two-thirds of the denarius ; Mommsen inclines to the belief that it was valued at three-fourths of that coin, but the facts of the coinage seem to be against him. Turning to the bronze, we find the Italian As in common use as a unit of reckoning ; whether there were other Asses in use beside it, e.g. an As that is one-sixteenth of the Rhodian drachm, is extremely doubtful. In the case of great provincial issues like that of Antioch it is possible that denominations were actually known by the Latin names of Dupondius, As, etc. In the case of the small change of the cities we do not know to what extent Latin names replaced local ones—all we can say with certainty is that all such coins were tariffed in terms of the denarius. Chios has a system in which Roman As and Greek chalcus appear side by side ; the As seems to be the sixteenth part of the denarius, the chalcus the forty-eighth part of the " Rhodian " drachm or one sixty-fourth of the denarius. Marks of value are never common on the local coins.[2] We find δίδραχμον on copper of Rhodes, ὄβολος on a coin of dupondius size of Seleucia in Pieria. In the early third century Sparta has pieces of 2, 4, 6 and 8 Asses, Argos of 6, 7 and 10 Asses, Syros of 1½ Asses, Thessaly of 3 and

---

[1] Cp. here and below, Mommsen in *Z.f.N.*, 1887, pp. 40 ff.

[2] Cp. Imhoof Blumer, *Griechische Münzen*, pp. 680 ff. ; L. Cesano in *Analecta Numismatica*, pp. 3 ff. ; *Num. Chron.*, 1876, pp. 307 ff., 1923, p. 225.

4 Asses, Thessalonica of 2 and 4 Asses. On the Western coast of the Euxine from Septimius Severus to Philip I we find pieces of 1, 2, 3, 4, 4½ and 5 Asses. In the South of Asia Minor from the reign of Valerian and Gallienus we find a reckoning, apparently in Asses, with pieces of 2, 3, 4, 6, 8 and 12, later with pieces of 5 and 10 Asses. Here there seems to be a transition from a duodecimal to a decimal reckoning. A private letter, in an unpublished papyrus, probably of the reign of Diocletian, shows that Italian money was reduced to one-half of a νοῦμμος;[1] the reduction was probably absolute, not merely relative to Egyptian coins. At the end of this period local coinage decays and Roman coin, as well as Roman reckoning, holds the field unchallenged.

6. Occasions of Issue—The occasions of issue were no doubt determined mainly by the needs of everyday life and trade. Religious ceremonies seem, however, to have played no inconsiderable part,—in particular, the great festivals and games which formed so remarkable a feature of the life of the Empire. Such occasions as an imperial visit would call forth special issues ; and the so-called alliances of cities in the same or in different provinces, which represent acts of courtesy rather than real diplomatic engagements, are frequently commemorated by large bronze coins, or " medallions." In general, we can distinguish with some certainty the smaller unpretentious pieces of everyday use from the larger show-pieces, struck to celebrate special occasions. In the case of the provincial silver military considerations seem to have played a very large part in determining the extent of the output.[2]

When we come to the types of the local and provincial coinage we feel like a man who should take a bucket to draw up the sea. The utmost that we can hope to achieve is to draw the main lines of the picture and to supply a little illustrative detail from widely separate sources.

7. Obverse Types and Legends—The general rule of the obverse is that it is given up to the portrait of the Roman Emperor, with his appropriate style, expressed in Greek, but modelled on the Latin. It is certainly not as mint-authority

---

[1] *N.Z.*, 1920, p. 158.

[2] Cp., for example, the extensive issues of Caesarea in Cappadocia for Nero's Parthian war.

that the Emperor appears ; the right of coinage was vested in the local senate.   The imperial portrait is rather a sign of loyalty to the Empire as expressed in the person of its ruler ; and, as the worship of the living Emperor was accepted over a large part of the Empire as a perfectly natural form, we may see in it something very much like religious veneration. In the names and styles of the Emperors irregularities and curiosities occur—the local authorities were not always very well informed about such matters.   Thus we find names like Βηρίσσιμος for Marcus Aurelius, Βασσιάνος for Caracalla, Χρυσογόνη for Salonina.   Occasionally a picturesque phrase, like the Κομμόδου βασιλεύοντος ὁ κόσμος εὐτυχεῖ of Nicaea relieves the monotony of formal etiquette.[1]   Beside the Emperor a place is found for Empresses and princes and princesses of the imperial house.   In the early Empire we find Agrippa, C. and L. Caesares, Livia, Drusus and Germanicus, Nero and Drusus Caesares in Spain and elsewhere.   Later all persons enjoying rights of coinage in Rome, and some who do not, regularly find a place in the local issues.   Apart from these cases portraits of Romans are very rare ; there are a few portraits of governors of Asia and Africa during a short period in the reign of Augustus, a portrait of Cicero (Plate LI, 4) struck when his son was governor of Asia, a portrait of Corbulo at Dioshieron.   Quite by itself stands the series of coins commemorating Antinous, the favourite of Hadrian.

In senatorial provinces the bust of the senate (cp. Plate LI, 1) or of Rome may replace that of the Emperor, and, in these cases, the titles Θεὰ Σύγκλητος, Θεὰ Ῥώμη are often found.   The personification of the Roman people is rather less common. The formulae S.C., S.P.Q.R. seem to refer to the senate or to the Senate and people of Rome ; whether they imply in every case that the issue was something more than an ordinary city one is not quite certain.

The " autonomous " coinage, which is found in many cities, either alone or parallel to the issues with head of Emperor, has generally on the obverse the head of some divinity.   An interesting variation consists in the substitution of the portrait of some local celebrity—real or mythological.   Thus we meet

---

[1] Cp. Muensterberg in N.Z., 1925, pp. 37 ff.

with representations of Homer at Chios (Plate LI, 2), of Anacreon at Teos, of Herodotus at Halicarnassus, of Sappho at Mytilene (Plate LI, 3), of Theophanes at the same mint, of Chrysippus and Aratus at Soli. Sometimes later personages are introduced, as for example Pancratidas and Dada at Mytilene (Plate LI, 5). Very common in some parts of the East is the bust of the city "Tyche" or "Fortune,"—the symbol of the city life, characteristically represented with her crown of towers.

8. Reverse Types and Legends—If the rules governing the choice of obverse type are relatively simple, the same cannot be said of the reverse. These reverse types are a treasure-house of information about the religious and social life of the Empire ; and the scholar who really commanded this subject would be in a very favourable position to understand what local life in the first three centuries of our era was really like.

(a) *Religious*—The predominating interest is undoubtedly religious. Most of the great Olympian deities—Zeus, Hera, Apollo, Artemis and the rest—are frequently represented. Asclepius enjoys a very wide worship, and so too, in particular districts, do Demeter, Kore and Dionysus. Ares, the war-god, is rather neglected under the peace that was the prevailing atmosphere of the Empire. As a rule the gods are Greek ; specifically Roman forms are occasionally found—we may quote the Capitoline Triad, Jupiter, Juno and Minerva at Cadi in Phrygia. Very often it is neither the Greek nor the Roman deity that is honoured, but some local divinity, loosely identified with one of the Olympians, but really enshrining the memory of some older power. Asia Minor, in particular, is the home of a vast system of cults, in which qualifying epithets, attached to the name of the Olympian deity, still preserve something of the original character of the local god. Zeus Labrandeus, the god of the double axe, has a special worship in Caria, for example at Euromus and Mylasa (Plate LI, 6). Zeus Osogoa, a blend of Zeus and Poseidon, has a special cult at Mylasa. Laodicea and Heliopolis worship each a special Zeus of its own. And further we find special by-names of the god at many towns —Panameros at Stratonicea in Caria, Larasios at Tralles, Ammon at Beroea, Lydios at Sardis, Hyetios at Ephesus, Hagios at Tripolis in Phoenicia, Syrgastes at Tium. Apollo too has many secondary names—Smintheus at Alexandria Troas, Clarios at Colophon, Didymeus at Miletus, Amyclaeus at Sparta, Tyrimnaeus at Thyateira, Propylaeus at Cremna. Leto and the Python appear on coins of Mastaura in Lydia. Artemis, the many-breasted, is the great " Diana of the Ephesians " and of other Asiatic cities. Artemis of Perga is only another form of the same great nature-goddess. We find Artemis Leucophrene at Magnesia in Ionia, Artemis Anaitis at Hypaepa in Lydia. Cybele enjoys high honour in many towns of Asia, as do also Demeter and Kore. The worship of the moon-god, Men, is particularly widespread in Phrygia (Plate LI, 8). The worship of the triple Hecate (Plate LI, 7) and of Hades has a similarly wide extension. The cult of the Dioscuri has special local importance at Tripolis in Phoenicia. Others of the Olympians figure less prominently in the local cults. We find Hera at Samos, Athena at Athens, Athena and Hephaestos at Thyateira, Aphrodite at Aphrodisias in Caria and at Paphos in Cyprus ; Bacchus and Hercules are worshipped together at Leptis Magna in Africa. The rude cultus-statues, which are often used to represent these local deities, force us to realize what very primitive idols were worshipped under the dignity of great Olympian names. In many cases the local deity seems to have little beyond the name in common with the Olympian and we find it hard now to understand how the identification was originally arrived at.

(b) *Mythological*—Close to religion in importance and in breadth of diffusion comes mythology. The local coins provide a remarkable set of illustrations of a great number of legends— some purely local, others drawn from the great Greek stock. The Trojan war is represented by a group of Hector, Priam and Patroclus at Ilium (Plate LII, 1), by Ajax at Prusa in Bithynia, by Aeneas and Anchises at Apamea, at Dardanus and at Otrus in Phrygia. Diomedes with the palladium appears at Argos. We find reference to the myths of Io at Gaza, of Marsyas at Apamea, of Cadmus at Tyre, of Amphion, Zethus and Dirce at Acrasus in Caria, of Ganymede and the eagle at Ilium, of the rape of Proserpine at Elaea. Corinth honours her mythical hero, Bellerophon, and Athens her Theseus. Atalanta and the Calydonian boar figure appropriately on the coins of Tegea. Other examples of local mythology are to be seen in Dido at Tyre (Plate LI, 12), Hero and Leander at Sestos (Plate LI, 11), and the dutiful brothers, who saved their aged parents from an eruption of Etna, at Catana in Sicily. Halfway between the religious and the mythological may be placed the types referring to the labours of Heracles at Aspendus in Pamphylia and at Heraclea Pontica, to Apollo and Daphne at Apollonia ad Rhyndacum, to Apollo and Marsyas at Germe, to Dionysos and Ariadne at Perinthus, to Theseus at Troezen, to Athena and the giants at Seleucia ad Calycadnum. Somewhere between myth and history falls the vision of Alexander represented on coins of Smyrna (Plate LII, 2). This is but a small selection from an immense repertory, but it will give some idea of the extent to which Greek mythology had permeated the East and had associated itself with the life of the cities. A most remarkable type is that of the Ark with a Noe, actually identified by name, at Apamea in Phrygia. Why this one selection from an alien mythology should have been made is not exactly known ; presumably there was a local legend of a flood, which could be aptly fitted on to the Bible story, and we naturally suspect that Apamea had a strong Jewish colony. Various local myths are represented by the bull at Nysa, the radiate horseman at Mostene, the winged horse at Lampsacus, the sacred serpent at Aboniteichus (Plate LII, 3), Cabirus at Thessalonica and Tylos and Masnes at Sardes.

(c) *Emperor-Worship*—Before passing on from the sphere of religion we must ask ourselves what part in the religious life of the Empire was played by the cult of the deified Emperors. Curiously enough " consecration " issues do not enjoy the importance that we might have expected. Θεὸς Σεβαστός is widely honoured, Divus Claudius appears on a series of silver coins struck at Caesarea in Cappadocia, and other Emperors are, here and there, honoured after death. But, whereas in Rome the imperial worship only began at death, in the provinces it would naturally begin at accession. The posthumous issues have therefore relatively a much smaller importance, as worship is naturally offered first to the living occupant of the imperial throne. One remarkable case of consecration, unknown to the Roman series, is that of Θεὸς Μάρεινος, the father of Philip I, at Philippopolis in Arabia (Plate LI, 10). A striking series of types of deified Emperors, with Latin legends, has been assigned to Patrae,[1] but should perhaps be given to Philip-popolis in Thrace (Plate LI, 9).   It seems to belong to the reign of Trajan Decius and, if so, finds its parallel in his Roman series of the " Divi." It seems not improbable that the ardent belief in immortality, which we know to have been a character-istic of the Dacians, lived on in the Balkans and ensured a special respect for the cult of the deified Emperors.

(d) *Personifications*—The personifications, which are so prominent on the imperial coins, play a very subordinate rôle on the local.   At one or two mints—e.g. Alexandria in Egypt and Caesarea in Cappadocia—something like the Roman custom prevails ; but these two mints strike provincial coinage in the imperial tradition and cannot be held characteristic of the East at large.   The commonest of personifications found else-where are Salus ('Υγίεια), the attendant spirit of Asclepius, who was extensively worshipped, and Fortuna (Τύχη), whose cult was world-wide.   Victory (Νίκη) and Virtus ('Αρετή) occur not infrequently, as for example at Antioch in Pisidia. Aequitas (Δικαιοσύνη) appears at Prymnessus, and her dis-tinctive attribute, the pair of scales, is often used as an indepen-dent coin-type.   Quite unusual for the East is the Ὁμόνοια Αὐτο κρατόρων of Marcus Aurelius and L. Verus at Pautalia in Thrace. A rare instance of allusion to the genius of the Emperor is seen under Commodus at Apamea.   The worship of Nemesis or of the two Nemeses is common in Asia, particularly at Smyrna ; but here we should speak rather of goddesses than of personi-fications.   So far as this evidence goes, it seems to bear out the conclusions at which we arrived in Chapter II of this book, that there was something peculiarly Roman in the worship of these secondary powers, associated with particular areas of human life—that we have, in fact, the later development of beliefs in the spiritual counterpart of the material world which were never very familiar in the Greek East.   If so, this is perhaps the most important contribution that Rome made to the religious and philosophical thought of the world.

(e) *General History*—Direct references to the general his-tory of the Empire are not very numerous, though indirect references are probably common enough, if only we were able

---

[1] Muensterberg in *Bl. f. Mzfr.*, 1923, pp. 361 ff.

to detect them. Philippi has a type of Augustus and Divus Julius (Plate LII, 4), Mytilene a figure of Augustus in a car drawn by elephants, Philippi a type of the children of Claudius. A " Parthia Capta " type of Ephesus celebrates the chief Eastern success of Trajan (Plate LII, 5), while Tripolis in Phoenicia shows the same Emperor as conqueror of Dacia, with a Dacian captive. The Emperor crowned by Victory appears at Maeonia, a triumph type of Macrinus at Nicopolis ad Istrum. Commodus in a triumphal procession and later, the imperial brothers, Caracalla and Geta, appear on coins of Mytilene, and Septimius Severus is represented striking down a foeman on a coin of Bageis in Lydia. Phocaea has a type of Maximin I and his son Maximus seated on curule chairs. A series of large bronze at Edessa shows Gordian III granting the crown of Osrhoene to Abgar X (Plate LII, 6). Imperial journeys and arrivals are not infrequently celebrated by types of ships, etc., sometimes with explanatory legend. The provincial issues, not unnaturally, reflect contemporary history far more closely. The " Cistophori " of Augustus refer to his Parthian successes, those of Domitian to his restoration of the Capitol. Alexandria, in particular, offers a commentary on Roman affairs, which is sometimes comparable to that of the imperial series.[1] But the general rule of the local coinage is absorption in local interests, with very scant heed paid to the larger movements in the Empire.

(f) *Local Interests*—What then are the local interests which to such an extent monopolize attention ? They are in the main religious—celebrations of sacrifices in honour of special deities, the adoption of the official worship of " Roma and Augustus " or of the deified Emperors, offices which earn for the city the title of Νεωκόρος, Δὶς Νεωκόρος and the like, alliances which have barely any political significance, but which indicate relations of special goodwill between states. Asia, the home of the most intense development of city life, is the best source from which to illustrate this phase of the coinage. Finally, there were the athletic games and contests of various kinds, which spread from Greece Proper over the East and made up perhaps the chief interest of the inhabitants of the Empire.

---

[1] Cp. here Vogt, *Die Alexandrinischen Münzen*, Stuttgart, 1924.

They were calculated to occupy men's minds and to inspire healthy rivalries and, as such, they were definitely encouraged by the Emperors, who often contributed to the prize-money and, in the case of the important games, the Εἰσελαστικοί, victory in which earned the winner an entry in triumph through a breach in the city walls, actually settled pensions on the victors. The connexion of these games with religion was, as in the case of the Greek prototypes, a very close one. The most common types that celebrate these were the vases, wreaths or urns, which we find, for example, at Anazarbus and Perinthus ; the purses that were given as prizes may be seen on coins of Magnesia in Caria, of Perge and of Corycus. The parsley-wreath, the prize of victory at the Isthmian games, appears on coins of Corinth. A table set for the games, with urn, vase and palm (?), is seen on coins of Nicaea. Not infrequently more graphic views of the games are given,—a group of three athletes at Aphrodisias, an athlete with urn at Cyme, a group of athletes at Nicaea (Plate LII, 8). Cyzicus shows both a show at a festival and a race, Nicomedia a body of spectators looking on. Games in the arena are shown at Synnada (Plate LIII, 1).

To the Roman, games of the Greek type seemed foreign and unmanly ; and, although the Emperors found it politic to encourage them in the East, they never introduced them to any great extent in Rome itself. To modern tastes these bloodless shows, which at worst encouraged interest in insignificant themes and a certain vanity and at best developed healthy qualities of body and ministered to general culture, appear vastly preferable to the bloody gladiatorial shows which most Romans justified as ministering to the military spirit. The games of the circus, the other madness of the capital, were of course familiar in all great cities of the East, notably at Antioch and Alexandria where they formed the centre of men's interests.

It would not appear from the coins that interest in local politics was very lively ; but perhaps we must not press this negative evidence too far. Reference to the local senate is found at Tiberiopolis and Sagalassus, at Miletus and Alexandria Troas, to the Demos at Sagalassus. Indirectly, the connexion with local politics is no doubt close ; particular issues would

14

be determined by the accession of particular men to office. The legends here teach us more than the types.

(g) *Military Types*—Direct military references are rare except in a few series like that of Alexandria. The worship of the legionary eagle is shown on a coin of Tomi (Plate LII, 7), an eagle in a temple on a coin of Perga, an eagle between standards at Amorium. But the Empire was after all predominantly an age of peace and it was precisely the most settled provinces that developed the art of coinage to the fullest extent. On the Balkan frontiers there is more suggestion of military activity in the favourite type of city-gates, to which we shall come back in a moment.

(h) *Buildings, Statues, etc.*—The representations of buildings are extraordinarily numerous and interesting and might well form the subject of an independent study. The temples claim the first place of importance,—we may instance the temple of Aphrodite Paphia in Cyprus, the temple of Astarte at Berytus, the temple of Artemis Ephesia at Ephesus, the temple of " Roma et Augustus " of the Κοινὸν Βιθυνιῶν at Pergamum, the temple of the " gens Iulia " at Corinth. Nicomedia with its three temples claims the proud title of Τρὶς Νεωκόρος. Neapolis in Samaria has an interesting type showing the sacred buildings connected with Mount Gerizim (Plate LIII, 3). The common council-hall (Κοινοβούλιον) appears on a coin of Tarsus. Buildings of local interest are common enough — the city gates at Nysa, bridges at Mallus, Zeugma, Antiochia ad Maeandrum, the harbour at Caesarea Germanicia, the circuit of walls at Nicaea, a view of the city at Amasia, the acropolis at Corinth (cp. Plate LIII, 6), Argos and Troezen. Corinth also shows its harbour and the celebrated tomb of the courtesan, Lais. The Theatre of Dionysus is shown on a coin of Athens (Plate LIII, 5). The city gate, as a symbol of the defence of the city against barbarian attack, is particularly popular in Thrace and Moesia (at Anchialus, Nicopolis ad Istrum—Plate LIII, 4— and elsewhere)—the problem had there an immediate practical bearing. Of special antiquarian interest is the Labyrinth at Cnossus in Crete (Plate LIII, 2).

For examples of illustrations of ancient statues on coins we may refer to the " Numismatic Commentary on Pausanias " of Imhoof-Blumer and Gardner. Athens is perhaps the richest mine of such information, but instances occur sporadically at many places and often yield valuable information about works of art, not otherwise known in picture.

(*i*) *Various Types*—Miscellaneous types of local reference are far too numerous to summarize here. The lion of Miletus is the badge of the city, the camel of Bostra suggests the caravan trade. Mons Argaeus, the sacred mountain of Caesarea in Cappadocia, is the most characteristic type of that town. Crescent and star or stars, as symbols of sun and moon or of the sky, are common at many cities, such as Smyrna. Signs of the Zodiac are seen on coins of Amastris, Perinthus, Rhesaena, Singara and Sidon.

9. Types of Colonies and " Municipia "—The coinage of the colonies and " municipia " demands a word to itself. Here the language was normally Latin ; the communities considered themselves definitely Roman. This fact was expressly commemorated by particular types, such as the she-wolf and twins, Aeneas and Anchises, the priest ploughing to mark out the boundaries of the new colony. Reference to matters of Roman interest is in general more common here than in the rest of the local coinage. The coinage of the Western provinces, short-lived as it was, was mainly of the colonial or municipal pattern (cp. typical coin of Bilbilis, Plate LIII, 8). The worship of Roma and the Emperor was the main theme of the coinage of Lugdunum, the temple of Divus Augustus is shown at Tarraco (Plate LIII, 10). In Spain there is lively interest in the Emperor and his family—Livia (cp. Plate LIII, 9), Agrippa, C. and L. Caesares, Drusus and Germanicus, Nero and Drusus Caesares. Types drawn from the ordinary Roman symbolism are common : globe, globe and cornucopiae, capricorn, shield in laurel-wreath, she-wolf and twins, Roma, the Genius of the Roman people (Plate LIII, 7). The early extinction of this coinage deprives us of a most valuable side-commentary on Roman affairs.

Of the use of the two imperial languages, Latin and Greek, something has already been said. Latin was in universal use in the West, except in Africa where Phoenician legends still occur. In the East, Latin was the language of the colonies and " municipia," but only occurs quite exceptionally elsewhere. In the third century there are definite traces of a decline of Latin ; Greek begins to intrude on the coinages of colonies,—as for example at Thessalonica, Philippopolis in Arabia and the colonies of Mesopotamia. The Byzantine coinage, as is well known, developed a strange mixed alphabet, in which Latin and Greek forms are blended together in strange confusion.

10. **Local Art**—The art of the provincial and local issues is of interest for the study of local styles, but falls a long way behind the best imperial standards. Evidently the best skill of the Empire, whatever the nationality of the artists, was steadily drawn in to the capital. The West supplies little of artistic value ; in Spain we can trace what may be termed a distinct provincial style, but it has small artistic merit. It is more surprising to find a low standard prevailing in the local coinage of the East. Fine work is occasionally found on the " Cistophori " and on the silver and billon of Alexandria ; the large bronze " medallions " of Asia sometimes present portraits that may rank with the better work of the imperial mint. As a rule the claims of art are not much considered ; the coinage of the Roman period in the East falls as far behind that of earlier ages in beauty as it rises above it in the wealth of its subject-matter.

11. **Local Coinage in the Third Century, A.D.**—The local coinage of the West, we have seen, did not survive the first century of the Empire. In the East it struck firm root in the early Empire and actually extended its range steadily throughout the second and early third centuries. In spite of the official policy of developing imperial coinage at local mints, there seems to have been no discouragement of local coinage. As late as the reign of Gordian III we find a number of new mints bursting into activity in Lycia. It was the financial crash under Gallienus that ruined the local currency of the East. The debased Antoninianus was still supposed to circulate at its former value, and, naturally enough, bankers began to refuse to give change for it. We have an Egyptian papyrus, giving us the terms of an imperial edict, requiring bankers to accept this money, unless it was " altogether bad and rotten." Had the government taken timely steps to withdraw the bad money or to assign to it a suitable market-value, all might still have been well. As a matter of fact, it did neither, with the

result that vast masses of bronze coin were hoarded and issues stopped abruptly over a large part of the East under Gallienus. Eastern bronze is said to appear occasionally in hoards along the Western frontiers, and it is thought that it was at this time that it came West. Now, too, may have originated the practice of collecting great sums of bronze coin in purses or " folles," to effect large payments. In Egypt the provincial money continued to be issued ; but the trouble was to some extent met by debasement and reduction of size in the tetradrachm ; the later tetradrachm of Alexandria was a fair match for the basest of Roman billon. After Gallienus local coinage lingered on only at a limited range of mints in the South of Asia Minor— particularly in Pamphylia, Pisidia, and Cilicia, provinces which were not near the supplies of any one of the new imperial mints, such as Cyzicus. This coinage extends as late as the reign of Tacitus and bears a number of marks of value,—Greek letters denoting 2, 3, 4, 5, 6, 8, 10 and 12. The mark IA, which seems to be interchangeable with I, cannot therefore denote eleven, and must mean ten Assaria. The reckoning, then, is in Asses, and a decimal reckoning supplants the duodecimal of the earlier period. The letter ε (five) occurs commonly as a countermark on coins on which we should expect the mark I (ten). This seems to involve a reduction of face values by a half, and can be paralleled both by the Egyptian papyrus, which records a reduction in value of Italian money (cp. above, p. 202), and by the marks I, X, which occur occasionally on coins of Tacitus and Carus, in place of the normal K, XX. The debasement of the denarius and of its multiple, the Antoninianus, seems to have led to the abandonment of reference to these coins in the local currency. The attempt was made to base a new system on the As ; and after the reform of Aurelian this As was, it appears, identified with his new unit of account, the " libella " of the sestertius. It may well be that the system of Aurelian was really one that had gradually been growing up in the East, during the financial miseries under Gallienus.

It has been maintained by Mommsen that the Emperors, during the financial crisis, drew on the silver issues of the East to help out the imperial coinage as it became more and more debased. The question centres round the billon tetradrachms of Antioch. Now, it is true that in the reign of Philip I we

find some tetradrachms signed in the exergue " Mon. Urb.,"
while others are marked " Antiochia ; " the style of the former
series is vastly superior to that of the second and recalls that
of the Roman mint. It certainly appears probable that
" Mon. Urb.," " Moneta Urbica " denotes mint or coinage of
the capital, and marks a part of the coinage as coinage of the
Empire. So far Mommsen's theory seems to be correct, though
we may question the reason that he has assigned to it. Perhaps
all that was intended was to introduce a larger denomination
than the denarius,—a step that might well appear desirable,
when prices were rising so high.

The decay of local coinage was, we have seen, rather the
unforeseen result of a vicious financial policy, than the outcome of a direct official endeavour. The process once accomplished, however, the Emperors made no attempt to restore
the old conditions. Bronze was not suited to be an independent
coinage, and the good silver, in terms of which it had been
tariffed, was steadily being lost. It seemed a simpler matter
to substitute everywhere for silver and bronze the intermediate coinage of base billon, which Aurelian tariffed on what
we might call a " nickel " basis. In point of policy, too, there
was no difficulty. The government was tending in the direction
of a dead uniformity, and, finding so much effected, as it were
by accident, in the coinage of the East, it readily fitted this in
with its general aims. The fact that Diocletian closed the
one remaining mint of the old style, Alexandria, shows in what
direction his wishes lay. While recognizing the naturalness
and the expediency of such a policy in the long run, we need
feel no regret that the Emperors were so slow in coming to it.
Had uniformity been established earlier, we should be without
one of our most important sources of information for the local
life of the cities of the East.

BOOK III

THE EMPIRE—DIOCLETIAN TO ROMULUS AUGUSTULUS

CHAPTER I

THE EXTERNAL HISTORY OF THE LATER IMPERIAL COINAGE : MINTS, MONEY-SYSTEMS, ETC.

1. Reform of Diocletian and its Developments : Mints—
In A.D. 296 Diocletian carried through a reform of the coinage, which may have been in preparation for two or three years before. He closed the one remaining provincial mint of the old style, Alexandria, and arranged for the supply of the whole Empire from a number of imperial mints in the provinces, all issuing coins of the same general types and the same denominations, but distinguishing their issues by letters or signs denoting mint, officina, and series. At the same time he made sweeping changes in the money-system, striking in place of the old aureus a new one of one-sixtieth of a pound and a pure silver coin, corresponding to the denarius of Nero. The details both of this reform and of its subsequent developments are very obscure and will be discussed fully a little later on ; for the moment we can only note the salient features of each change as it occurs. The mint-system of Diocletian was the logical completion of the developments of the third century and faithfully represented the changes that had come over imperial institutions. The centre of the Empire now lay, not so much in any one site, as in the " sacra domus," the entourage of the two Augusti and the two Caesars of Diocletian's tetrarchy. The exact local *habitat* of the " domus " mattered little—in the nature of the case there were bound to be several capitals. Rome (Plate LVIII, 3) was still one of these, the headquarters of the Augustus of the West ; but beside it stood Treveri, as the capital of the Western Caesar, while Diocletian made Nicomedia his capital in the East, leaving Antioch to his Caesar, Galerius. The imperial coinage was now uniform and without a rival ; the local and provincial issues disappeared. So far as institutions could affect the case this meant the loss

of local traditions and peculiarities and the spreading of a monotonous culture over the whole of the Empire. The practical advantages gained by the unification of administration and control were obviously great ; supplies of coin were now everywhere available without any great expense or difficulty of transport. As we study the allocation of local mints, we shall find that it does not correspond exactly to the system of provinces and dioceses. Britain had its one mint of Londinium (Plate LVII, 9)—the " C " mint of Carausius and Allectus was closed. Gaul had two mints—Treveri (Plate LVII, 10) and Lugdunum, Spain none ; in Africa the mint of Carthage (Plate LVIII, 11) was closed after the revolt of Alexander (A.D. 308-311). Italy had Rome, Ticinum and the new mint of Aquileia (Plate LVIII, 5)—important for the service of the armies on the North-eastern frontier. In the Balkans we find Siscia and Serdica (Plate LVIII, 7), in Macedonia Thessalonica (Plate LVIII, 8), in Asia Minor Heraclea Thracica, that is to say, the old Perinthus, Nicomedia (Plate LVIII, 10) and Cyzicus, in Syria Antioch (Plate LVIII, 13), in Egypt Alexandria (Plate LVIII, 12). Evidently the general plan of supplying the needs for coinage locally was modified by considerations of movements of troops and trade. The most striking feature is the absence of a regular mint for Spain and after A.D. 308 for Africa. Both these provinces stood outside the main movements of the age and were dependent for their supplies on Gaul and Italy respectively.

The coinage system of Diocletian was the model for all that succeeded it, but in itself it only achieved a partial success. The introduction of reliable denominations of gold and silver was a permanent gain. But the silver-washed bronze, which was certainly tariffed too high for its intrinsic value and was apparently used as legal tender for large amounts, was less satisfactory. Prices again rose to absurd heights, and Diocletian felt himself called upon to interfere with direct legislation in the shape of his famous edict, " De maximis pretiis," fixing prices above which articles must not be sold and proposing savage penalties for infringements of his law. We need hardly say that force was impotent to effect permanent improvement here. And matters became worse when Diocletian's successors, A.D. 305-312, began to diminish the weight of the follis or twenty denarius piece. The " denarius communis," the new unit of reckoning, fixed by Diocletian at one fifty-thousandth of the gold pound, rapidly fell to much lower values. When Constantine I and Licinius divided the Empire in A.D. 312, there was a partial break between East and West ; while Licinius in the East still struck the gold and silver of Diocletian, with a follis of reduced size and value, Constantine instituted a new system, based on solidus and siliqua. The victory of Constantine in 324 led to the spread of his system over the whole Empire. His sons, on his death, introduced a new follis of about eighty grains weight (5·18 gm.). This piece disappeared for the time in 352-353 but was revived by Julian and appeared at intervals down to 395. After this the only base-metal coin is a small piece of about twenty grains (1·3 gm.) which gradually dies out in the Western mints and in Illyricum, and is only found in Rome and Italy, at Thessalonica and the other Eastern mints. Beside the siliqua appears a new denomination, the miliarense, originally perhaps the thousandth part of the gold pound and nominally the eighty-fourth of the silver, but afterwards raised in value to represent the twelfth of the solidus and twice the siliqua. The later miliarense and siliqua represented nominally the sixtieth and the hundred-and-twentieth part of the silver pound but were struck consistently light ; that is to say, they were to some extent token-money. For some reason not yet clearly understood, the silver of the late fourth century is rare except at the Western mints and hardly appears in any but British finds. The decay of the coinage of silvered bronze in the West and in Illyricum faithfully represents the weakening of Roman grip on these parts of the Empire. In the general plan of mints laid down by Diocletian no radical change was made. Ostia (Plate LVIII, 1) was opened as a mint by Maxentius ; after his defeat in 312 the mint was transferred bodily to Arelate (Constantina) in Southern Gaul (Plate LVII, 12). Ticinum ceased striking a little after 326—its functions were now fully covered by the mint of Aquileia. The mint of Londinium was closed at about the same date—not to reopen except for a brief space under its new name of Augusta under Magnus Maximus. The staffs of these two mints were possibly drawn upon for the new mint of Constantinople—opened by Constantine in 330 (Plate LVIII, 9). In the Balkans Siscia remained the chief mint ; Serdica closed in about 306, while Sirmium was opened as a mint by Constantine and struck at intervals down to the reign of Theodosius I (Plate LVIII, 6). Ambianum (Amiens) struck for a short time for Magnentius (Plate LVII, 11). After about 386 the Balkan mints one and all began to suspend operations ; the Romans never fully recovered from the Gothic disaster of Valens at Adrianople in 378. Thessalonica, Heracleia, Nicomedia and Cyzicus continue to strike busily into Byzantine times. To these must be added the mint of the Eastern capital, Constantinople. Antioch continued to supply the needs of Syria, as did Alexandria those of Egypt ; but the latter scarcely issued any but base-metal coins after 324—an arrangement which led to curious local developments of currency. The mint of Mediolanum (Plate LVIII, 4) in North Italy was opened by Theodosius I about 390—that of Ravenna (Plate LVIII, 2) by his son, Honorius, in about 400. Both of these two mints play a prominent part in the coinage of the last century of the Western Empire.

A marked feature of the coinage after Diocletian is the rigid control now exercised. Every coin now bears not only a mint-mark, usually the first letter or letters of the city (e.g. L for Londinium, TR for Treveri, L or LD for Lugdunum, AR or CONST for Arelate, R for Rome, T for Ticinum, AQ for Aquileia, K for Carthage, SISC for Siscia, SD or SERD for Serdica, SIRM for Sirmium, TS for Thessalonica, CONS for Constantinople, HT for Heracleia Thracica, K for Cyzicus, N for Nicomedia, A or ANT for Antioch, ALE for Alexandra), but also a mark (Latin or Greek letters or Latin numerals) for the officina and further marks to distinguish the particular issue. The letters S.M. ("sacra moneta") often accompany the mint signature. The marks that define the issue are as yet only imperfectly understood. They consist sometimes of symbols, sometimes of combinations of letters, often apparently arbitrary. References to Jupiter and Hercules, as patrons of Diocletian and Maximian, have been traced, and other similar references probably await discovery.[1] Despite these doubts as to the exact meaning of these formulæ, their general meaning is clear ; they serve to facilitate control, by marking

[1] Note ΕΡΩΣ (= AMOR, anagram of ROMA) on Roman issue of about A.D. 324. Such letters as S F, T F, may stand for " Saeculi," " Temporum Felicitas."

the exact period of a mint's activity to which the individual coin belongs. Jules Maurice has claimed to have found traces of the employment of groups of workmen, outside the regular personnel of the mint. His arguments—based on the recurrence of characteristic mis-spellings in particular issues (e.g. at Londinium)—are perhaps not quite conclusive.[1] His general theory is, however, attractive ; but we must also remember that forgery was rife—as is proved by the moulds that are so frequently found and by a string of edicts in the Codex of Theodosius. Curiously enough, the system of mint-marks is far more fully developed on the silvered bronze than on the gold or silver. It would appear as if in each mint the striking of the precious metals was reserved for particular groups of workmen, to whom any fraud could at once be brought home ; the possibility of the use of secret marks too must not be forgotten. Towards the close of the fourth century the marks OB and PS begin to appear on gold and silver respectively. They certainly denote pure gold (*obryziacum*) [2] and pure silver (*pusulatum*) respectively, and were affixed by special officers responsible for the quality of the metal. In the West the letters OB are attached to the mint name ; in the West the formula COMOB becomes universal after about 395—a single official of high rank, the " comes auri " or " comes obryziacus " vouched for the quality of the gold, wherever struck. Bars of gold and silver, stamped with the names of the control-officers, are occasionally found.

2. Administration—Administration, we have said, was highly centralized. Under the tetrarchy of Diocletian the division of the Empire into four great districts was decisive. The mints in each received their orders to strike from the Chancellory of their own Augustus or Caesar. When no reliable portrait of a distant colleague was available the portrait of the lord of the mint was often made to serve for him. From 312-324 there was the division into East under Licinius and West under Constantine. After the death of Constantine the one great division of East and West becomes normal and, with only short exceptions, permanent. On the death of Theodosius I the schism proceeds to become final. The West drifts

---

[1] *Numismatique Constantinienne*, Vol. II., pp. c ff.
[2] Probably also denotes 72—the number of solidi in a pound.

slowly along to its inevitable decay, occasionally brought into line with the East by political considerations, but for the most part running an independent course. The East begins to develop the new tradition, which ends in the fully developed Byzantine coinage of Anastasius and his successors. The close dependence of the provincial mints on instructions from head-quarters rules out the possibility of real autonomy. Individual styles are still well-marked and enable the trained eye to dis-tinguish mintage, even without the aid of mint-marks. Fabric, however, tends to become more and more uniform, and special local references and allusions on the reverse, though still oc-casionally prominent, as for example in the mint of Carthage from 296 to 308, are in general on the decline. The main feature of the age is a stale uniformity, which proves at least that the central control, however destructive of local vigour, was functioning well.

3. **Money-systems**—We can no longer postpone the diffi-cult adventure of seeking to find our way through the tangled money-systems of the fourth and fifth centuries. As the system of Diocletian, modified by Constantine, remained the basis of all subsequent developments, it seems advisable to begin with a careful description of the coins actually struck by Diocletian and of the changes in them introduced by his successors. The way will then be clear for a discussion of the relations of the coins to another and of the systems of reckoning then in vogue. The evidence is imperfect and often obscure and certainty is not always to be reached ; but, with a know-ledge of the coins themselves behind us, we shall not be so likely to wander far astray. From time to time we will sum up in tabular form the result of our inquiries, showing the systems probably in use at different times in our period.

[1] We must here mention certain monetiform objects of the period, which are not actually coins :—

(*a*) Medallions of bronze, still struck occasionally for presentation, but not representing regular coin-denominations. The medallions of gold and silver, though also struck for presentation, were regularly multiples of the ordinary gold and silver pieces. The large gold pieces were often given as presents to native princes.

(*b*) Contorniates—pieces of base metal, of about the size of a sestertius, with turned-up edge (hence the name) and an incised circle round the rim. They are cast and chased and occasionally inlaid with small pieces of gold. The obverses show heads of Emperors—Nero, Vespasian, Trajan, Caracalla, or later Emperors

In gold Diocletian struck an aureus of one-sixtieth of a pound of gold, sometimes marked with its value in Greek (Ξ) (Plate LIV, 1).[1] In the East this coin continued to be struck till 324 ; but in the West Constantine introduced in 312 a lighter coin, the solidus, a seventy-second of a pound, which after 324 became the standard coin for the whole Empire and lasted on into late Byzantine times (Plate LIV, 5, 7, 12).[2]

In silver Diocletian struck a piece of one-ninety-sixth of a pound, which, in all but name, was the denarius of Nero restored (Plate LV, 1).[3] We do not know what it was now called ; it may have been known as the " argenteus " simply. This coin was struck both in East and West till early in the reign of the sons of Constantine I.[4] In 312 Constantine introduced a new denomination, the siliqua (Plate LV, 7) or the one-thousand seven hundred and twenty-eighth part of the pound of gold. A larger piece, the miliarense, was struck from about 330 (Plate LV, 4, 5). These two coins dominate the silver coinage from that time on, though larger pieces, " medallions," and a smaller, a half-siliqua, are also occasionally found.

In bronze, or rather in a very poor alloy of silver and bronze, thinly coated with silver, Diocletian struck three denominations, (1) the well-known " Genio populi Romani " coin, weighing about 150 grains (9·72 gm) (Plate LV, 8, 9), with laureate head of Emperor, (2) a coin, weighing about 60 grains (3·89 gm.), with radiate head on obverse, which looks like a continuation of the famous " twenty-one " coin of Aurelian (Plate LV, 12), (3) a small coin, weighing about 20 grains (1·3 gm.) with laureate head on obverse (Plate LVI, 2).

down to about 450, of famous men of letters—Homer, Horace, Sallust—or of charioteers ; the reverses have reference to the games of the circus, to historical types, to mythology, or to more general subjects. In front of the head is often found the symbol ₽, with one or more bars. There can be little doubt that the contorniates were used for some kind of game, played on a board, and the predominance of allusions to the circus suggests that the game itself had some connexion with racing.

[1] Multiples occur not infrequently. A piece of a fiftieth of a pound is found rarely under Diocletian. The piece of a seventieth of a pound goes out of use. For a third of an aureus, cp. Pl. LIV, 3.

[2] For double-solidus, cp. Pl. LIV, 4, 9 ; for half-solidus, Pl. LIV, 6, 10 ; for third of solidus, Pl. LIV, 11. A medallion of five (?) solidi, Pl. LIV, 8.

[3] It often bears the number XCVI in token of this ; its actual weight is usually well below the normal. For a four-argenteus piece, cp. Pl. LV, 6. A half-piece also occurs early in the fourth century (Pl. LV, 2).

[4] Between c. A.D. 307 and 330 scarcely any silver was struck.

The first of these denominations began to lose weight in about 308 and fell by degrees, often hardly perceptible, to 120 grains (7·77 gm.), 100 (6·48 gm.), 70 (4·53 gm.), and then to 50 (3·24 gm.) (Plate LV, 8-11 ; LVI, 1, 7, 8,). Since the loss in weight is gradual and since the types and general appearance of the coins do not change with the change in weight, it is probable that it was supposed to be the same denomination throughout. When it had fallen to about 50 grains (3·24 gm.) the radiate crown, which was the distinguishing mark of Diocletian's second denomination, occasionally reappears on this coin and it seems probable that at that stage its value was reduced towards that of second denomination (Plate LVI, 9 ; cp. LVI, 3). A smaller denomination was struck at intervals down to about 324 (Plate LVI, 4-6).[1] The piece of 50 grains (3·24 gm.) remained at the same standard till about 330 when it again dropped, this time to about 40 grains (2·59 gm.) ; in 335 it fell further to 30 grains (1·94 gm.) (Plate LVI, 9-12). In 340 Constantius and Constans made a decided change. The piece of 30 grains (1·94 gm.) was little, if at all, struck, and a new and larger coin of 80 grains (5·18 gm.) took its place (Plate LVI, 13). In the years after 350 this denomination, like the first of Diocletian, began to lose weight and fell to 70 grains (4·53 gm.) and later to 40 grains (2·57 gm.). From 361 we can trace four denominations of bronze, (1) weighing c. 120 grains (7·77 gm.)—apparently the follis of Diocletian in a slightly reduced form—struck by Julian,[2] Jovian (Plate LVII, 3, 4), Valentinian I, and Valens, (2) weighing c. 80 grains (5·18 gm.)—apparently the piece of Constantius II and Constans restored—struck by Gratian (Plate LVII, 5), Valentinian II, and Theodosius I, (3) weighing c. 40 grains (2·59 gm.)—struck by most Emperors after Julian (Plate LVII, 6, 7), (4) weighing c. 20 grains (1·3 gm.)—struck particularly in the closing years of the century by Theodosius I and his sons (Plate LVII, 8).

We must now endeavour to assign some meaning to the facts of the coinage which we have been surveying. The first point

---

[1] The value of these small pieces is uncertain. They are heavier than the piece of Diocletian, which we have tariffed at two denarii, at a time when the larger pieces were much reduced in weight. They may therefore represent five-denarii pieces.

[2] Perhaps first introduced by Magnentius.

to be determined is the unit of reckoning. Down to 296, as we have seen, the sestertius was still in use. In the edict of Diocletian of 301 reckoning is in denarii, and 50,000 of these denarii go to the pound of gold. Values in multiples of 2, 5, 20 and 50 denarii are common. Later we find in general use a division of the solidus into 6000 (sometimes into 7200 or more) minute parts, called nummi. There is some reason for regarding the nummus as the two-fifth part of the denarius. The siliqua, one twenty-fourth of the solidus, equalled 250 nummi, and in the Vandal coinage a piece that seems to correspond to the siliqua is tariffed at 100 denarii. Egyptian documents show a marked drop in the value of the denarius in terms of the gold pound ; [1] after 324 the drop is abrupt and immense and the solidus is finally tariffed at millions of denarii.

We have already suggested that Aurelian had based his money-system on a sestertius,[2] reckoned as the five-thousandth part of the gold pound and containing ten smaller units or " libellae." Diocletian continued to build on the foundation of the sestertius. But he identified its tenth part, the " libella," with the " denarius communis," and introduced a new silver coin worth forty denarii, and a new double sestertius worth twenty : Aurelian's " twenty-piece " was reduced to a fourth of its value. This seems to be the most reasonable explanation of the fact that Diocletian continued to strike a coin very closely resembling the " twenty " piece of Aurelian as a subdivision of his largest piece of silvered bronze. The unit of the later systems is much smaller than that of Diocletian. This is to be explained by two facts, (1) the depreciation of the " denarius communis," due in the first place to the reduction of weight in the main bronze denomination of Diocletian, and (2) the introduction of a smaller unit, a subdivision—the nummus—perhaps two-fifths of the denarius.[3] This coin may

---

[1] 8328 denarii to the pound of silver (i.e. over 100,000 to the pound of gold) in 307 ; 313,508⅓ denarii to the pound of gold in 323 (cp. *N.Z.*, 1918, pp. 211 ff.). For later figures see Wessely, quoted p. 232, n. 2. Conditions in Egypt, however, were probably peculiar. The Alexandrian tetradrachm, formerly equal to the silver denarius, was perhaps treated simply as a bronze coin and equated with the " denarius communis."

[2] For denarius reckoning, cp. *C.I.L.*, V, 1880, " denariorum folex sescentos ; " cp. also *C.I.L.*, VIII, 5333.

[3] See above.

15

have been originally the smallest denomination of the kingdom of the Bosphorus, the uncia of bronze, one forty-eighth of the sestertius. The piece of twenty denarii seems to have been identified with the sestertius of the Bosphorus (equals 48 nummi), and from this a relation of denarius to nummus as five to two is easily derived.

Let us now consider what can be known about the tariffing of the various coins in terms of the unit of reckoning and their relations to one another.[1] In the system of Diocletian the gold pound was worth 50,000 denarii and sixty aurei. The silver coin of one ninety-sixth of the silver pound was probably one-twentieth of the aureus. The largest denomination of silvered bronze, which is commonly and perhaps rightly called the follis, contained twenty denarii ; we find the mark of value, XX, at Alexandria and Siscia (Plate LV, 8). The second denomination of bronze is in weight about two-fifths of the first ; but weight in this token coinage is not the only criterion and it is probable that the relation was rather that of one to four. The smallest denomination, over one-third of the second in weight, may have been two-fifths of it in value. We thus reach some such system as this :—

one gold pound = 60 aurei = 1200 argentei

= 2400 folles = 9600 " radiate " coins

= 24,000 smallest bronze = 48,000 denarii.

Various methods of adjusting this system to the value of the gold pound (50,000 denarii) of the Edict might be suggested ; but it is perhaps safer to be content with the approximation given above.[2]

[1] Various statements of the price of pork will supply a rough and ready method of testing values at different times.

In the " Edict " of Diocletian the pound of pork is valued at 12 denarii. In a law of 363 it is rated at 6 folles. In 389, 80 pounds of pork are equated with a solidus, and in 419 20 pounds of pork are worth 1000 denarii. We have then four values for the pound of pork—12 denarii (301), 6 folles (363), 30 denarii ($\frac{24000}{800}$) (389), 50 denarii (419). The chief difficulty lies in the value of 6 folles—we expect a value of about 30 denarii and no follis of suitable value has yet been identified. Perhaps the price was exceptionally high in 363.

There can be little doubt that all systems from Aurelian onwards depend on units that are sub-divisions of the sestertius. Anastasius's solidus seems to have contained 150 M (40 nummia) pieces, 6000 nummia ; the M piece ranks as the sestertius, the nummus as its " teruncius " or fortieth part. The name " terentiani," applied to these coins of Anastasius, is very probably intended for " terunciani."

[2] One might suppose, for example, that Diocletian contemplated the introduction of an aureus of one-fiftieth of the gold pound, containing 1000 denarii.

For the period from 305-324 we are reduced to something little better than guess-work. All we have to go on are the certain depreciation of the denarius, a few documents of doubtful interpretation, and a few marks on the coins, which appear to denote value—notably $C\text{M}\text{H}$ on coins of the first bronze denomination at Nicomedia (Plate LVI, 10) and Cyzicus, of a reduced weight of 100 grains (6·48 gm.) or less, and the $\frac{x}{\text{II}\Gamma}$, which is found from about 317 on the same coin in the Eastern mints of Licinius (Plate LVII, 9), when it had fallen to the weight of about 50 grains (3·24 gm.).[1] The $C\text{M}\text{H}$ is perhaps to be read as C MH, C = centenionalis denoting the coin as the hundredth part of the solidus, and MH (48) giving its value in nummi ; it will still be equal to twenty denarii.

The gold pound then would equal 60 aurei = 6000 centenionales = 120,000 denarii = 288,000 nummi. We are assuming that the drop in the value of the denarius was reflected in a decline in the value of the twenty denarius piece in relation to the aureus.[2]

The $\frac{x}{\text{II}\Gamma}$ on coins of Licinius is perhaps best read as " ten—a sestertius," i.e. the coin is a sestertius, containing ten smaller units, denarii.[3] The decline in weight of the piece has led to its being finally degraded from its original value of two sestertii to that of one. Since the denarius was still depreciating there is some probability that the following system is not far wide of the mark :—

one gold pound = 60 aurei = 1200 argentei = 16,800 $\frac{x}{\text{II}\Gamma}$ pieces
= 168,000 denarii = 420,000 nummi.

In the West, where the solidus and siliqua were replacing the aureus and argenteus, the reckoning will run a little differently :—

[1] The meaning of the signs NK ΥXC on aurei of Nicomedia (Pl. LIV, 2) is quite doubtful ; NK should stand for Nicomedia, LX for the number of aurei in the pound, C for the number of centenionales in the aureus. The meaning of the V in ΥX is uncertain.
[2] Other marks on the coins probably denoting value are : VI on the largest bronze at Siscia (c. 306 ; weight c. 150 gr.—9·72 gm.) ; KV, XK, O on the same denomination at Alexandria (c. 308 ; weight c. 100 gr.—6·48 gm.) ; CI | $\frac{H}{S}$ on the same denomination at Lugdunum (c. 308 ; weight c. 100 gr.—6·48 gm.). (Pl. LVI, 1.)
[3] Or, possibly, the IIΓ represents the value of the denarius in nummi ($2\frac{1}{2}$).

one gold pound = 72 solidi = 1728 siliquae = 17,280 $\overset{x}{\text{iir}}$ pieces [1] = 172,800 denarii = 432,000 nummi.

A welcome piece of confirmatory evidence is provided by the " Stiftung aus Feltre," a document which shows us a sum of 60,000 denarii supplying payments probably amounting to 25 solidi 3 siliquae ; [2] a value of 172,800 denarii for the gold pound gives a value of 25 solidi to 60,000 denarii ($72 \times \frac{60000}{172800}$ = 25).

If we have been correct in these latest guesses, the reckoning of 6000 nummi or 2400 denarii to the solidus had already been established before 324. When Constantine reunited East and West under his rule in that year, the old aureus of one-sixtieth of the pound disappeared and the argenteus of one ninety-sixth of the pound was but sparingly struck. In place of the latter appear the siliqua, equal to the 1728th part of the pound of gold, or one twenty-fourth of the solidus, weighing about 40 grains (2·59 gm.), and the miliarense, equal to one-thousandth of the gold pound, a fourteenth of the solidus in value and weighing about 60 grains (3·89 gm.). Later we find a heavier miliarense, nominally a sixtieth of the silver pound, actually weighing about 70 grains (4·53 gm.), equal in value to two siliquae or one-twelfth of the solidus ; the siliqua is supposed to be one hundred-and-twentieth of the pound, but is actually struck very light.

The one coin of silvered bronze struck between 324 and 340 weighed at first about 50 grains (3·24 gm.), later 30 grains (1·94 gm.). It was probably the same denomination as before, the reduced follis, identified with the sestertius, containing ten denarii communes or 25 nummi. The larger coin of about 80 grains (5·18 gm.) introduced c. 340, must be the " centenionalis " [3] of the Edict of Theodosius—the hundredth part

---

[1] The mark does not actually occur in the West ; but the contemporary coin of Constantine is hardly to be distinguished in weight and appearance from that of Licinius and occurs with it in finds.

[2] The bequest (cp. *N.Z.*, 1909, pp. 47 ff.) provides for an annual expense of " aurei den. et sil. sing." plus an additional amount of " n. CCCLXII ; " the only suitable value that can be assigned to the second amount is " 362 siliquae," and we thus get a total of 10 × 24 + 1 + 362 siliquae = 603 in all, or 25 solidi 3 siliquae.

[3] A passage in the *Cod. Theod.* (IX, 23) of 356 speaks of the " nummus qui in usu publico perseverat," and apparently defines this as the " pecuniae quas more solito maiorinas vel centenionales appellant." The " centenionalis " then was a

of the solidus, containing 60 nummi or 24 denarii (Plate LVI, 13). The largest denomination of all, introduced perhaps by Magnentius (Plate LVI, 14) and struck after him by Julian and his successors, was called the " nummus decargyrus " or " pecunia maior ; " another term for it was, perhaps, " pecunia maiorina," but this word may have applied rather to the " centenionalis " before the introduction of the larger coin. Its value was perhaps 100 nummi or 40 denarii,[1] one-sixtieth of the solidus. The term " follis " was not always applied to the same coin ; it seems occasionally to have denoted the " centenionalis," [2] sometimes, as under Constantine I, the piece of ten denarii or twenty-five nummi ; but towards the end of the fourth century it is specially used for the smallest denomination of bronze, the piece of 20 grains (1·3 gm.), containing perhaps four denarii or ten nummi.[3]

The system of the late fourth century was, therefore, something like this :—

One pound gold = 72 solidi = 864 miliarensia = 1728 siliquae ; one solidus = 12 miliarensia = 24 siliquae = 60 decargyri nummi = 100 centenionales = 240 " third bronze " (of 10 denarii, 25 nummi each) = 600 " fourth bronze " (of 4 denarii, 10 nummi each) = 2400 denarii = 6000 nummi.

current coin in 356, and may be the same as the " pecunia maiorina." Another edict in the same codex of the year 395 (IX, 23, 2) calls in the " pecunia maior " or " decargyrus nummus," leaving the " centenionalis " in circulation. It is obviously a mistake to identify the " centenionalis " with either of the two smaller denominations of the late fourth century.

Whether the reduced form of this coin, struck *c.* 353, was considered as representing the same value or not, must remain doubtful. The figures LXII, which occur on it at the mint of Aquileia, probably mark it as the seventy-second part of the pound, i.e. with a normal weight of 70 odd grains (4.56 gm.). (Pl. LVII, 1, 2.)

[1] Or 80 nummi and 32 denarii (?).

[2] A passage in the *Cod. Theod.* (VI, 4, 5), 340, shows allowances of 25,000 folles and 50 silver pounds, 20,000 folles and 40 silver pounds, 15,000 folles and 30 silver pounds for the expenses of the various prætorships. It will be seen that the sum of 500 folles balances the silver pound and may well be equal to it. Later we find the pound of silver equal to five solidi or 500 centenionales—hence the deduction that centenionalis here equals follis.

[3] Augustine (*Sermons*, 389, 3) tells of a man who, whenever he sold a solidus, gave 100 folles—a trifling proportion of the total—to the poor ; this follis must obviously represent a very small value. Brambach (*Mitth. f. Münzsammler*), 1925, suggests that it is a *libella*, $\frac{1}{10}$th sestertius—so presumably $\frac{1}{10}$th centenionalis = 6 nummi.

The solidus was normally rated at 6000 nummi, but the tariff varied and in the fifth century definitely rose to 7200 nummi.

A number of metrological texts seem to show us a λεπτόν (the nummus) = $\frac{1}{6000}$th solidus, a κοδράντης = two λεπτά, a follis = four κόδραντι or eight λεπτά. We have no coins that we can identify with either λεπτόν or κοδράντης ; but our " third bronze," to which we have assigned a value of ten nummi, may be identical with this follis, and its value may have been reduced from ten to eight nummi or λεπτά.

Of the relative values of the metals we have some certain knowledge. Late in the fourth century gold was to silver as 1 to 14·4 and silver to bronze as 1 to 125—gold therefore to bronze as 1 to 1800.[1] The later miliarense of one-sixtieth of the silver pound was exactly equal to the one eight hundred and sixty-fourth part of the pound of gold. The nummus, a six thousandth part of the solidus, represented a bronze value of one two hundred and fortieth part of the pound of bronze ($\frac{1}{72} \times \frac{1800}{6000}$). The silvered bronze certainly bore a value much in excess of that of bronze ; but this surplus value was probably to some extent arbitrary and varied with the denomination.[2]

We come to other systems of reckoning—notably to the follis reckonings of the metrological writers. The pound of gold was sometimes itself described as a follis ; it contained 72 solidi, 1000, later 864 miliarensia, 1728 siliquae. The silver pound seems also to have served as a basis for reckoning, possibly known as ἀργυρισμός. Like its fifth part, the solidus, it was divided into 6000 smallest parts, or λεπτά.[3] It contained 100 denarii, as the solidus contained 100 centenionales. The silver follis contained 125 miliarensia and was therefore equal to the eighth part of the pound of gold.[4] The term

---

[1] Five solidi for a pound of silver (*Cod. Theod.*, XIII, 2, 1, 397), four for the pound, 422. An edict of 396 made the solidus the equivalent of 25 pounds of bronze.

[2] For a value of one-hundredth of that of gold, cp. *Cod. Theod.*, X, 21·3.

[3] The talent of the metrological writers, which weighs 125 pounds, is nothing but this silver pound. It contains 100 denarii of one and a quarter pounds each, 6000 λεπτά of one-quarter ounce each. This denarius of reckoning must, of course, be distinguished from the " denarius communis."

[4] Brambach in *Mitth. fur Münzsammler*, 1925, June, makes some very interesting suggestions. Eight purses of 125 miliarensia each make up 1000 miliarensia or a pound of gold. But the solidus is worth 14 miliarensia, the pound of gold, therefore, 1008. The eight odd miliarensia represent the costs of making up the purses. Further, 1728 siliquae of fine silver are actually struck into 2016 siliquae

δηναρισμός, which is contrasted with ἀργυρισμός,[1] may possibly denote the reckoning by the solidus with its 6000 nummi. We meet it in the Codex Theodosianus (" denarismo vel unciis "), apparently as the description of a tax ; if the nummus was originally, as we have suggested above, the uncia of the Kingdom of the Bosphorus, the term " denarismus vel unciae " may have denoted the reckoning by denarii and nummi. A metrological writer tells us that the φολλίς equals two λεπτὰ κατὰ τὸν δηναρισμόν—a mysterious phrase, which suggests that the " third bronze " of the late fourth century may have been tariffed much lower than we have assumed—at two, instead of ten (or eight) nummi ; such a low value, however, seems to be inconsistent with what we should deduce from other considerations. The true explanation is clearly connected with the method of raising taxes at the time—and of this the details are lost. There was another follis weighing $312\frac{1}{2}$ pounds and containing 250 denarii of $1\frac{1}{4}$ pounds each. This is generally taken to be the follis or purse of bronze coin, made up to represent quite large sums.[2] This use of base-metal coin for large payments probably began after the great debasement of the coinage under Gallienus and is attested on various occasions in the fourth century. It is natural then to see in the follis just mentioned the equivalent of the " sestertium " or 1000 sestertii of the old reckoning. For the period of Diocletian, then, the follis would contain 1000 sestertii of ten denarii each, 10,000 denarii or $\frac{1}{48}$th of the gold pound, and the gold pound would be equal to 1500 pounds of bronze : the actual weight of the large follis, expressed as it was in terms of silvered bronze, would naturally be much less. The denarius is equal to $1\frac{1}{4}$ pounds of bronze ; this gives a relation of silver to bronze as 1 to 120 ($\frac{1}{96}$th pound, Æ = $1\frac{1}{4}$ pounds bronze). The ratio of gold to silver would then be 1 to 12·5. It is perhaps too much to

as coin ; the miliarense therefore equals two siliquae. Brambach supports his assumption that one-sixth of alloy is added to the pure metal by a passage in the Cod. Theod. (XII, 7, 1), which requires seven-sixths of an ounce of gold to be paid in for every ounce of pure gold.

[1] Excerpta ex Epiphanii libro, 49 (Hultsch, Metrol. Script. Reliquiæ, I, p. 267 ; see also Hultsch, Griechische und römische Metrologie, pp. 340 ff.). φόλλις δύο λεπτὰ κατὰ τὸν δηναρισμόν, ἀλλ᾽ οὐ κατὰ τὸν ἀργυρισμόν.

[2] Cp. the Gesta apud Zenophilum consularem (Dec. 13, 320). The investigation deals with the alleged sale of a presbytery for 20 folles : the money, we are told, had been seen by witnesses brought in bags or in a " sacellum." Cp. other examples in Z.f.N., 1890, p. 53, n. 1.

expect that this statement of a very obscure question will carry conviction to all ; but it is fair to hope that the setting out of the evidence of the coins beside that of the literary authorities and the papyri may contribute to that final solution of which, as numismatists, we must refuse to despair.

4. Success and Failure—The great gain of the fourth century was the improved supply of the precious metals—due in part to the Eastern conquests of Diocletian, in part to the ruthless calling in of private stocks for the imperial account, in part again to the release of temple treasures at the decline of paganism. The rise in value of gold as compared to silver in the late fourth century is very remarkable,[1] for it occurs at a time when the silver coinage was beginning to decline and when the silver coins, miliarense and siliqua, were both being struck below standard weight. And then, too, there is the curious fact that silver of the period is very rarely found except in Britain. The calling in of the " pecunia maior," too, in 395 suggests that the government wished to recover the silver content of that coin. Everything, in fact, except the ratio of gold to silver, points rather to a scarcity than to a superabundance of silver. A possible explanation might be that silver was replacing gold on a large scale for articles of luxury in trade, and that, for this reason, silver, though not actually scarce, was not readily available for the coinage. The Byzantine Empire, we must remember, was run mainly on a coinage of gold and bronze.

One evil inheritance from the third century was the use of bronze, with a coating and slight admixture of silver, to represent amounts above those of the ordinary bronze. All the systems of the fourth century suffered to some extent from this evil, and to it we may attribute the instability of values and the tendency of the unit of account to keep on falling. Constantine I in 324 seems to have arrested the fall of the denarius at the figure of 172,800 to the gold pound. But, in one province, Egypt, he did not back the silvered bronze with money of gold and silver. The result was that, in Egypt, and, so far as we can tell, nowhere else, the unit of account fell further and further away, till many millions were reckoned to the gold pound.[2] Evidently the bronze coinage was quite

---

[1] Cp. above, p. 230.

[2] Cp. Wessely, *Ein Altersindizium in Philogelos*, Abh. d. Kais. Ak. d. Wiss., Vienna, Phil.-hist. Klasse, CXLIX, pp. 1 ff.

unfitted to bear the whole burden of the currency. It was treated more and more as a pure token or " paper " currency, which hardly represented real value at all and to which ever-increasing nominal values were attached, without increasing its actual purchasing power. We shall see below in Chapter III, how the general policy of the Empire made it possible for one province to run a course so far distinct from the general course of the Empire. The decay of the bronze coinage in Illyricum and the West in the closing years of the fourth century is simply a symptom of the decline of Roman authority in those parts. The government had not yet abandoned its claim to possession, but showed itself more and more incapable of minis-tering to the requirements of local trade, of which the bronze coinage was an essential part.

The financial administration was simplified by the elimina-tion of the senate from all imperial affairs ; it was now no more than the city council of Rome and Constantinople. The only divisions of authority were those that resulted from the division of the imperial power—at first between the two Augusti and the two Caesars of the tetrarchy of Diocletian, afterwards between the Augustus of the East and the Augustus of the West. Even so, a large measure of uniformity was secured by conference between the heads of departments. It is only after the final division of the Empire under Arcadius and Honorius that the coinages of East and West really parted company. The chief financial officer was the " comes sacrarum largitionum," as-sisted by some subsidiary " comites," such as the " comes auri." The individual mints were controlled by the " rationales," who took the place of the procurators of the early Empire. For the personnel of the mint we find the term " monetales " employed. Service in the mint came to be an hereditary profession, from which no one could escape except by providing a substitute. The system of control was now most elaborate and aimed at nothing less than the fixing of responsibility for every issue. But the question here was that of Juvenal, " quis custodiet ipsos custodes ? " In spite of all the machinery of control fraud of various kinds was rampant.[1]

Looking on the system as a whole, we must grant it a certain

[1] See below, Chapter III.

limited success.   No financial crisis on the scale of that of the
third century recurred.   The financial resources of the Empire
were carefully husbanded and the gold coinage in particular
enjoyed a well-deserved respect even beyond the bounds of
the Empire.   The main weakness was the prevailing corrup-
tion in and about the mint and the unsatisfactory character
of the coinage of silvered bronze, which could not be maintained in stable relations with the gold and silver.

5. **Organization of the Mints**—Of the details of mint organization we know little.   There was a careful sub-division
of the work of the mints over a number of officinae and perhaps
a distribution of the work inside the officinae to smaller groups
of workmen.   Fabric becomes more and more uniform everywhere.   The style is on the decline.   Portraiture, the " chef
d'oeuvre " of the early Empire, is still on a high technical level.
But the growth of the " hieratic " principle—the principle, that
is to say, of representing the Emperor rather in his formal aspect
than as a living individual—is in the long run fatal to real life.
Stress is laid more and more on the attributes of power, the
diadem, the mantle, the sceptre, the orb ;   these attributes,
which assume ever more stereotyped forms, crowd out the
living interest, and Emperor after Emperor is represented with
little to distinguish him from his fellows.   In the reverse types
we have to report a growing barbarism both of theme and of
rendering.   In the East a new life gradually pushed through
and blossomed in the development of Byzantine art, which has
a conscious theory of its own, unlike the Greek, but not un-
worthy of respect.   In the West the life impulse slowly died
and left at the last little beyond an elaborate formalism.
When the early mediaeval art appears in the West it is found
to be aiming at a beauty of ornament and pattern rather than
of life.

6. **Mints and Chronology**—Questions of mint hardly trouble
us in this period, when the mint-mark is a regular part of the
coin.   Each mint, however, has an individual style of its own,
marked enough to allow of the attribution of unsigned issues.
Dating, of course, still depends mainly on the imperial portrait,
though the omission of imperial titles with numbers makes it
often difficult to attribute coins with certainty to their exact
place in a reign.   A few cases of attribution where knowledge

is required, may be noted. The coins of " Divus Claudius," " Divus Maximianus " and " Divus Galerius " were issued partly by Constantine I, partly by Maxentius, at war with their rivals. The coins of Theodora were struck after her death by Constantine I (c. 336-7). The coins of Helena and Fausta with obverse title " N(obilissima) F(emina) " and reverse type, star, have been the theme of a long controversy.[1] There can be little doubt, however, that they were struck for Helena, the mother, and Fausta, the wife of Constantine I ; but they may possibly have been issued some time after their deaths, possibly by Julian, c. 361 ; the star suggests some lingering thoughts of consecration, and the title, " Nobilissima Femina," which is found nowhere else on coins, might well be used to distinguish the dead Empresses from the living. A remarkable series of anonymous types, with reference to Egyptian religion,—Serapis, Isis Pharia and Anubis,—is attributed with strong probability to the reign of Julian. A similar, but smaller, series of Antioch, has also been attributed to an earlier date.

Our knowledge of the finds of this period is far from satisfactory as yet. The chief facts that emerge are (1) the separation of the coins of Diocletian from the coins of Aurelian and his successors down to the reform of 296 ; examples of sestertii, however, in finds of the age of Diocletian have been recorded ; (2) the co-ordination of the small bronze issues of Constantine I and Licinius I in the period from 312 to 324. A curious problem, as yet unsolved, is presented by the imitations of the bronze coinage. When the module of the imitation is approximately the same as that of the original we may attribute the imitation to contemporary forgery. More puzzling are the " minimi," pieces of very small module and, often, of great barbarism of style, copying not only the diademed heads of the fourth century, but also the radiate heads of the third. Certain Egyptian " minimi," known chiefly from Egyptian hoards, copy closely the small bronze coins of Eastern mints of the late fourth century, and were possibly issued irregularly in Egypt—perhaps by the great landowners, who asserted a half-independence of the Imperial Government.[2]

[1] Cp. Maurice, *Numismatique Constantinienne*, Vol. II, pp. 451 ff.
[2] Cp. J. G. Milne in *Num. Chron.*, 1926, pp. 43 ff., especially p. 61.

More familiar to us are the " minimi," diademed or radiate,
of the West, which are peculiarly plentiful in some British
finds. Failing any definite evidence of date, we are inclined
to see in them an emergency local coinage in Gaul and Britain
during the latter years of the fourth century and perhaps even
more in the early years of the fifth, in the decay of the Roman
power.   If anyone objects to this view that the types imitated
are often of much earlier date, we may remind him that the
earliest Anglo-Saxon sceattas, which occasionally show some
points of resemblance to the " minimi," often hark back to
much earlier types—to the radiate heads of the Gallic Emperors
or to the type of the she-wolf and twins of the years 330 to 337.

CHAPTER II

THE CONTENT OF THE LATER IMPERIAL COINAGE.
TYPES AND LEGENDS

1. **General Tendencies**—Gradual as was the actual transition from the Empire of the third century to the new Empire of Diocletian, the change once made was soon found to be a decisive one. It was not so much that new features were introduced, as that the whole emphasis was shifted to a new class of subjects. The forms of the Empire down to Diocletian had been, with few exceptions, those of the free state under its " Princeps ; " those of the new Empire were those of an Eastern monarchy under its king. The types of the new age faithfully mirror its new tendencies. Apart from changes in detail, we find a new conception of the imperial office, a new relation towards religion, a new attitude towards the celebration of contemporary history ; and, perhaps as striking as any other change, a new spirit, tainted with savagery and boastfulness, informs the whole coinage. Before we come to the more de-tailed discussion of different classes of types, a few words on these main changes will help to clear the way.

The principate of Augustus was dead. The Emperor of the fourth and fifth centuries is the traditional " Great King," the master of his subjects, worshipped almost as a god. The triumph of Christianity, it is true, forced into the background the divinity of the Emperor or rather shaded it off into some-thing like the doctrine of the " divine right of kings." But the word " sacer " is now used as an almost exact equivalent of " imperial," and the personality of the Emperor dominates the entire coinage. The exact form of division of the imperial power designed by Diocletian was not permanent. But the fundamental distinction between East and West, which had never been entirely overcome, was definitely recognized by the

237

foundation of the Eastern capital of Constantinople in A.D. 330. The restorations of the imperial unity under Constantine I, Constantius II and Theodosius I were only provisional, and the East, in the end, disengaged itself from the sinking Empire of the West and carried over its own age-long history, touched with something of the Roman tradition, into the Middle Ages. The West gradually relapsed into the barbarism from which Rome had raised it, while Rome herself and Italy stood in an equivocal middle position, partly saved from barbarism by the influence of the East. The Senate, of course, had now lost its last remnants of political power. It has no influence on the coinage and is entirely confined to its local dignity in the two capitals.

The age was one in which religion occupied a great place in men's thoughts and emotions. It began with the decisive battle between paganism and Christianity ; it continues with the intestine struggles of the Christian Church and the abortive pagan revival of Julian : it ends with the stamping of a definite Christian mark on the coinage. Diocletian attempted to associate his dynasty in the closest possible way with the old paganism in the persons of Jupiter and Hercules. Then follows a short period in which the " invincible Sun-God," now, it may be, closely associated with the worship of Mithras, comes to the front. Then follows an interval of neutrality, in which, as if by common consent, direct religious references were banned and the field was left to vague allegorical conceptions of neutral character. Finally Christianity, which had already begun to find expression in the form of symbols on the coins, gained the day and definite Christian types appear. The labarum, or standard, emblazoned with the monogram of Christ (☧) became the sign of the Christian Emperor. Julian's apostasy is represented by his " Apis bull " type and by local Alexandrian coins illustrating Egyptian myths. After his death the invasion of the coinage by Christian forms proceeds to its completion. The cross and labarum constantly appear and the Emperor is celebrated as the Defender of the Faith. The full exploitation of the symbolism of the new faith was, however, reserved for the Byzantine Empire.

One or two points deserve special notice. Mithraism would appear to have been more or less in alliance with Christianity against the older forms of pagan faith.   Only after the attempt to crush Christianity had failed does there seem to have been a brief but sharp fight between it and Mithraism.   Bitter rivals as the two religions were, they had undoubtedly much in common—in particular in their general moral outlook.   The bitter factions of the Christian Church, distracted between Arians and Athanasians, have hardly left a mark on the coinage —unless there still remain allusions to be discovered that have as yet escaped us.   In fact, Christianity, in the early day of its triumph, seems to have been singularly moderate in its self-assertion ; we may safely conclude that there were powerful pagan elements still surviving in the official classes.

The worship of the personifications or " Virtues " is, on the whole, on the decline.   It had always been closely associated with the person of the Emperor and it may be that Christian belief interposed difficulties here.   One personification, that of the Genius of Emperor or State, plays a very large part and we know from literature that it held a central position in the thought of the time.   We shall see later how Christianity took over under its own forms the great conception of the " Victory," who accompanies the march of Rome from age to age.

The coinage of the fourth century did not cease to offer some kind of medallic history of the Empire, but something definite was lost for ever.   The propagandist element is still strong—the government is concerned to present its policies in an attractive light to its subjects.   But there is on the whole a decline in active political interest and in the commemoration of particular events : vague general conceptions associated with formal types tend to supplant the definite portrayal of current happenings.   The army, now strongly felt to be the only protection of civilization against insurgent barbarism, is constantly in the picture and, in the incessant references to the " Safety," the " Security," the " Glory " of the State we see the genuine concern of the government to steer the ship safely through to its haven.   As we advance, we find the forms of the coinage gradually stiffening into a lifeless conventionality.   Each denomination tends to gain a type of its own which remains unchanged for years at a time.   It is perhaps a feature of the exhaustion of the time that interest could not be shifted from year to year over the moving course of events, but had to be

concentrated on the contemplation of a few quasi-permanent
features of the life of the State.

The general change in the moral tone of the coinage is
easier felt than described. Rome of the great days had indeed celebrated her victories, but usually with a strict sense of
proportion and reality and without any vainglorious mouthings.
Now we are constantly hearing of the " Glory of the Romans,"
the " Glory of the State "—the word " Gloria " itself is new
to the language of the coins. This is, however, at worst a
minor fault of taste. More serious is the element of savagery,
which the conflict with a barbarian world introduced. The
Emperor is portrayed, with a special complacency, as the
" Conqueror of the whole world," the " Conqueror of the
barbarian nations," and is shown setting his foot in triumph
on a crouching captive. The famous " Fel. Temp. Reparatio "
of Constantius II shows a Roman legionary in act to transfix
with his spear a fallen Persian : in the " Gloria Romanorum "
of Valentinian I the Emperor drags a captive by the hair.
We are familiar with the thought that the Empire fell, not by
the barbarians without, but by the barbarians within : such
types as these are an eloquent comment on the justness of that
reflexion.

The obverse of the coin is, of course, reserved for the
Emperor, though, in the new order of things, several Emperors
often strike concurrently at the same mint. The right of
portraiture is still extended to the Caesars, the Emperors to
be, and occasionally, but not so commonly, to the ladies of the
imperial house. Remarkable is the small coinage of Hannibalianus, the nephew whom Constantine I appointed King of the
Bosphorus but who was murdered after Constantine's death by
the troops. The foundation of Constantinople was commemorated by special issues with the heads of Roma, Constantinopolis,
and the people of Rome on the obverses. Such substitutions
of other obverses for the imperial are decidedly rare. Almost
the only other exceptions are in the little series of coins, with
religious types, of the mints of Alexandria and Antioch, struck,
in part at any rate, under Julian.

The imperial title is much less open to variety than before.
The title " Imperator " gives place to that of " D(ominus)
N(oster) " under the sons of Constantine I and the description

" P(ius) F(elix) " becomes an invariable part of the style. The praenomen is seldon given, the gentile name (cp. " Iulius," " Valerius ") more commonly. The consulship is occasionally mentioned on the reverse and so too the proconsular power, which in the early Empire had hardly ever found expression. The tribunician power, the chief pontificate, the title of " pater patriae " are almost obsolete. There is one exceptional use of the cognomen " imperator " with a number to represent the regnal years of Theodosius II. The Caesar is regularly designated by that name with the distinguishing epithet " Nobilissimus." With Gratian the custom was introduced of giving the full imperial title " Augustus " to the junior colleague : the title " Augg. Aug." which Gratian bears on his earliest coins seem to describe him as the " Augustus dependent on the two (senior) Augusti." The Empress is still the " Augusta." The title " N(obilissima) F(emina)," which is given on rare issues to a Helena and Fausta, has been discussed above.[1]

The laureate wreath is still at first the normal wear for the Emperor. Later the diadem of Eastern monarchy, interwoven with flowers or pearls, takes its place. The radiate crown of the sun-god is still found under Constantine I, while military portraits, with helmet, spear and shield, become increasingly common. Common too is the portrait with imperial mantle and eagle-tipped sceptre, later with the sceptre and orb, which became the choice symbols of imperial power. With Constantius II comes in the facing military portrait, which was to play so large a part in the Byzantine coinage. In general, we notice a great elaboration of ornament and ritual—the Emperor is represented less as an individual than as the holder of a great symbolic office.

2. Types Classified—The reverses can only be studied satisfactorily under different subject groups. We may adopt the following provisional classification :—

(a) Types in which the person of the Emperor is the main interest.

(b) Types showing the care of the Emperor for the State.

(c) Types relating to provincial and foreign affairs.

---

[1] See above, p. 235.

(*d*) Military types.

(*e*) Religious types, with personifications and the " consecration " issues, so far as they continued to exist.

(*f*) Various animate and inanimate types.

(*g*) Buildings.

The reverse legends naturally, as a rule, describe the types ; but the practice becomes more and more common of associating with a composite type a legend vaguely characterizing, rather than describing it : to take one or two examples,—Constantine and his sons are described as the "Safety and Hope of the State," a warrior spearing a fallen foe symbolizes the " Restoration of Happy Times," a Victory stands for the " Security of the State," the Emperor setting his foot on the " ancient serpent " is an emblem of the " Imperial Victory." The tendency deserves close attention, for it is markedly characteristic of the age.

(*a*) *Types of the Emperor*—The Emperor, in his formal aspect of head of the State, is mainly represented by the portraits of the obverse. On the reverse he is occasionally represented in his robes as consul or in his chariot, scattering largess to the people. In an age where there were usually several colleagues in the imperial power, there was a strong preference for types emphasizing the good relations of the colleagues : such are the " Perpetua Concordia Augg." of the aureus that shows Diocletian crowned by Jupiter and Maximian crowned by Hercules, the "Gloria Romanorum" of the aureus that shows Valentinian I and Valens throned together, holding their orbs, or the " Victoria Augg." of the later solidi, showing the two Emperors seated side by side, while over them broods the imperial Victory. Maxentius took pains to commend himself to his subjects, by picturing on his coins the divine powers that help him to preserve his cities (Plate LIX, 2) or his ceremonial appearance at his consulship (Plate LIX, 3). A series of " Pietas " types shows the Empress Fausta with her children, and Constantine and his sons often appear together in military dress, with such legends as " Felicitas Romanorum " or " Salus et Spes Reipublicae." Anthemius and Leo I are represented together, holding spears and crosses, with the legend " Salus Reipublicae." The Empress Aelia Flaccilla, wife of Theodosius I, appears standing, with her hands clasped on her breast in prayer, as " Salus Reipublicae," and the marriage of Marcian and

Pulcheria is represented by figures of the two rulers, united in holy wedlock by Christ, with the remarkable legend " Feliciter Nubtiis." The princes still bear the title " Princeps Iuventutis " (Plate LIX, 1, 10) and appear with such military attributes as spear, shield and standards ; sometimes the legend reads " Principia Iuventutis," the first stage of military training for the career of Emperor. The " Spes " type still bears witness to the hopes centred in the heir (Plate LX, 2),[1] and Arcadius is acclaimed on a solidus as the " Nova Spes Reipublicae." Gratian, with labarum and spear, is hailed as the " Gloria Novi Saeculi " on his accession to the throne ; another type shows him as the " Spes P.R." standing between his seated senior colleagues (Plate LX, 9). A new turn is given to the same thought by the legend " Bono Reipublicae " or " Bono Reipublicae Natus " (cp. Plate LIX, 4), which was used by Constantine I and Magnus Maximus and continues in use in the fifth century.

The imperial largesses are no longer represented by scenes of distribution with the Emperor on a platform : the new equivalent is the scattering of coins by the Emperor from his chariot (Plate LIX, 14). The occasion of the arrival of the Emperor in one of the chief towns of the Empire is still represented by the Emperor riding on horseback and such legends as " Felix Adventus Aug."

The imperial vows were celebrated as ever with especial emphasis at the expiry of each five years of the reign, with such formulae as " Vot. V. Mult(iplicatis) X " or " Sic X Sic XX." The most common type is the plain legend in a wreath (cp. Plate LXI, 1, 2), but the allusion to the vows is often introduced as a detail of a larger type,—on the base of a statue, on the shield held by two Victories—or associated with a type of Victory (Plates LX, 18 ; LXI, 4). The " Vota " legend is sometimes illustrated by more elaborate types,—by the two Emperors enthroned together (Valens), by the figures of Roma and Constantinopolis (Honorius—Plate LXI, 3), by the Emperor and a kneeling figure of Rome (Valentinian III —Plate LXI, 5). An unusually full expression of the vows appears on the solidus of Constantine I, with the legend

---

[1] Cp. Pl. LIX, 9, Fausta and children.

" Vota orbis et urbis sen(atus) et p(opuli) R(omani)." A remarkable series of " Vota publica " types of the period of Julian at the mint of Alexandria celebrates various Egyptian deities,—Osiris, Isis, Serapis, Anubis : the exact occasion is unknown but there is no mistaking the relation of the types to the pagan restoration of Julian. These " Vota " types are of great importance as a help to chronology ; we have to remember, however, that the vows were sometimes celebrated in advance of the right time and that vows, appropriate to a senior Emperor, may sometimes appear on the coins of a junior colleague.

Of the consecration issues we shall have to speak under religious types. The special occasion of the abdication of Diocletian and Maximian is appropriately marked by coins, celebrating the " Quiet Retirement of the Emperors," and the " Providence " that had arranged for the succession. The anticlimax of the return of Maximian to active political life is represented by coins, giving him the title of " senior " Augustus.

(b) *Types of Emperor and State*—The care for the State, which seems to have been ever present in the mind of the rulers, is reflected in the number of legends acclaiming the " Peace " (Plate LX, 1), the " Happiness " (Plate LIX, 8, 15), the " Glory " (Plate LX, 7, 11, 12, 14, 15, 16), the " Safety " (Plate LX, 8), the " Security " (Plate LX, 4), of the State. Constantine I (Plate LIX, 6, 8) and Magnentius claim the credit of having restored the liberty of Rome, Vetranio appears as " Saviour " (" Salvator "—Plate LX, 3), Valentinian I and Valens as " Restorers " (" Restitutores ") of the State (Plate LX, 5, 6). Under Theodosius I the conception of the " Reparatio Reipublicae " is conveyed by a type, showing the Emperor stretching out a hand to raise a kneeling woman. The well-known series of types of Constantius II and Constans with the legend " Fel(icium) Temp(orum) Reparatio " presents the general idea of " reconstruction " under a variety of aspects—by the Roman legionary spearing a fallen Persian, by the Emperor dragging a barbarian from his forest hut—presumably to settle within the Empire—by Victory steering the Emperor's bark, by the phoenix as the type of eternal Rome (Plate LIX, 11-13). Magnentius repeats the same conception, with fresh emphasis, when he represents himself, a victorious general, as "Gloria et reparatio temporum." Very commonly the idea of the "Glory of the State" is conveyed by the old and new capitals, Rome and Constantinople, seated enthroned side by side. Later the idea of the "Victory of the Augusti" is expressed by a figure of the Emperor, trampling down a foeman or a human-headed serpent (Plate LX, 10, 13). Many similar types have a definite military setting and will be considered below under the military heading. We may almost say that the thought of the State was an obsession with the government, which devoted so much effort to preserve it intact, at whatever cost to individuals. The remarkable types of Constantine I. representing the "Senate" by a man in robes of state and the Roman knights by a figure on horseback (Plate LIX, 5) show the interest of Constantine I in the Roman aristocracy. For the most part the orders are confounded in the one general conception of "respublica."

(c) *Types of Provinces and Foreign Powers*—We have already mentioned that definite and particular reference to current events tends to yield place to more general forms of allusion. Exceptions, however, still occur. The great hoard recently discovered at Arras has enriched us with some splendid medallions of gold, commemorating the recovery of Britain by Constantius I : one of the largest and finest of them shows Constantius riding up to the gates of a town at which kneels a suppliant woman, expressly identified as "Lon(dinium,") while on the river below a boat with armed men is in attendance. The mint of Carthage celebrates the city herself and the province of Africa (Plate LXI, 6, 7). Constantine I celebrates by name his Sarmatian victory and represents "Francia" and "Alamannia" (Plate LXI, 8), seated with hands bound behind the back, in the old tradition of the "capta provincia." A type of a sea-god for Hannibalianus represents his kingdom of the Bosphorus (Plate LXI, 9). Julian honours the valour of the Gallic army, which fought for him so gallantly to recover the province from its German invaders, and later the valour of the Roman army with which he sought to conquer Persia. Honorius has a type of the solidus, in which the lion under his foot symbolizes his African victory of A.D. 413. The remarkable type of Constans, "Bononia Oceanensis," that shows his departure for the campaign in Britain, is only found on a contorniate and has, strictly speaking, no place in our present discussion. The great victory of Aetius over the Huns at Chalons comes too late to receive the numismatic commentary that its signal importance deserves.

Events of a more peaceful character find even scantier commemoration. One or two interesting types record the transference of the mint of Ostia to Arelate by Constantine the Great. The foundation of Constantinople was, as we have already seen, commemorated by special issues in honour of the two capitals, the old and the new, and Roma and Constantinopolis constantly appear as types of the " Glory " or the " Safety " of the State. The " Invicta Roma Aeterna " on the coins of Priscus Attalus, the puppet-Emperor of the Visigoths, has a curiously ironical sound. A small silver coin of Julius Nepos shows Ravenna, the last capital of the West, as a towered woman, with her foot set on a prow, holding spear and cornucopiae.

(d) *Types of the Army*—The all-important rôle of the army, the bulwark of Rome against the insurgent barbarians, is faithfully represented by the general character of the coinage. The Emperor is depicted, commonly in military garb, often setting his foot on a captive, under the proud title of "Debellator," " Triumphator gentium barbararum." A multitude of " Victoria " and " Virtus " types (Plate LXI, 12, 15) [1] celebrates the victorious course of Roman arms and the Roman valour by which it is secured. Favourite types are the Victories supporting a shield, Victory with trophy and captive, the Emperor setting his foot on a captive, a Roman legionary dragging a prostrate foeman, the Emperor standing armed or riding on horseback, the legionary standards (Plate LXI, 16) : these types are associated with such legends as " Pax Aeterna Aug," " Pacatores Gentium," " Ob Victoriam triumfalem," " Ubique Victores," " Victor omnium gentium," " Victor totius orbis," " Victoriae Laetae Princ(ipum) Perp(etuorum)," " Virtus Exercitus Romanorum," " Salus Reipublicae," or " Securitas Perpetua." The military attendance of the Emperor is shown by mounted figures on the aureus of Maximian (Plate LXI, 10).

---

[1] Pl. LXI, 13, seems to show the plan of a camp.

A remarkable solidus of Constantine I represents the " Safety of the State " by a group of the Emperor crowned by Victory and attended by nine soldiers.   The famous fort on the Danube, "Constantiniana Dafne," is celebrated on a coin (Plate LXI, 11). Very prominent is the conception of the " Glory of the Army," which is represented by two soldiers with spears and shields on the common copper coins of Constantine and his family (A.D. 330-337).   There is no mistaking the importance attached to military prowess in this age of the decline of the Roman arms.   But one evil of the previous century had to some extent been overcome.   The legions had been taught their place and were no longer so ready to seize the first opportunity of putting a pretender on the throne ;   the establishment of the dynastic principle no doubt contributed its share here.   Pretenders indeed there still were : but, considering the opportunities for rebellion provided by the general unsettlement of the times, we are disposed rather to wonder at the loyalty of the troops to the established régime.   The period of the ascendancy of the barbarian " magistri militum " in the fifth century has left little mark on a coinage that was gradually falling mute.

(e) *Religious Types*—We have first to consider the records of the last rallies of paganism on the imperial coinage.   Diocletian associated himself in a special way with the great father of the Roman gods, Jupiter, and was commonly known as " Jovius ; " his colleague, Maximian, added to the wisdom and foresight of the imperial Jupiter the strength and valour of his patron Hercules, after whom he was named " Herculius." The worship of these two great deities is the keynote of the religious types of the tetrarchy.   Jupiter is usually represented simply with his thunderbolt, sceptre and eagle : the myths relating to Hercules gave scope to more varied treatment and a number of his labours figure on the gold of Maximian (Plate LXII, 3, 4).   The only other deities to claim a large part are Mars, the god of war, and " Invictus Sol," the Eastern divinity so closely associated with Mithraism and so deeply enshrined in the affections of the troops.   In the period after the defeat of Maxentius, " Invictus Sol " became for a moment the dominant power in the Roman religious world, but his ascendancy ended with the growing devotion of Constantine to the Christian Church.   The Dioscuri appear on coins of Constantine I and Maxentius (Plate LXII, 1, 2). The cult of the Roman goddesses is hardly represented except by the " Venus Victrix " of Galeria Valeria, wife of Galerius (Plate LXII, 15). Roma, as the patron-goddess of the old capital, enjoyed a special worship under Maxentius and held her place,—perhaps as a personification rather than as a true divinity—even later (Plates LXII, 9-12 ; LXIII, 13). Jupiter is honoured by preference with the title " Conservator " (Plate LXII, 5), as also is Mars (cp. Plate LXII, 6, 7, 8) : Sol is " Invictus," " Invictus Comes " (Plate LXII, 13, 14), or " Aeternus," or may appear as " Claritas reipublicae." Jupiter as " Fulgerator " is the triumphant conqueror of the giants, Hercules takes various titles from his various labours. The decline in the cults of goddesses, no doubt, is partly accidental—due to the comparative unimportance of the ladies of the dynasty of Diocletian. It may, however, be symptomatic of the strongly virile and military character of the later paganism. Mithraism, which was peculiarly a religion of the troops, hardly allowed women any place at all and, to that extent, it has been conjectured, suffered in its final struggle for mastery with Christianity.

Christianity first insinuates itself on the coins in the form of minor symbols,—cross or Christian monogram. A type of Constantinople shows the cross set on a serpent as the emblem of the " Safety of the State " (Plate LXIII, 7). The upward turned heads of Constantine and his sons on late solidi of his reign were meant very probably to suggest an attitude of prayer and aspiration. The Christian Emperors assumed the " labarum," the standard emblazoned with the monogram of Christ, as their distinctive emblem, and with Magnentius and Vetranio we reach such definitely religious types as " Salus Dd. Nn. Aug. et Caes." the ☧ between A and Ω, or the " Hoc signo victor eris." Later the hand of God, which is sometimes shown extending a crown over the Emperor's head, has a definitely religious flavour, and the fifth century type, with the Emperor setting his foot on a human-headed serpent, probably represents him as the Defender of the Faith, the guardian of Christian civilization, against the ancient serpent of spiritual evil (Plate LX, 13). The cross (Plate LXIII, 3) or the ☧ (Plate LXIII, 9, 10) become common types. The " Salus Mundi " solidus of Olybrius, with the cross as main type, has an almost mediaeval character (Plate LXIII, 12). What strikes one most is the guarded nature of religious reference on the coinage.   The pagan revival of Julian is hardly signalized by anything beyond the " Apis bull " reverse of his copper and the types of Egyptian deities at Alexandria (Plate LXII, 16, 17).   The world under the early Christian Emperors remained fundamentally pagan in its conceptions.   Christianity first adopted pagan forms and interspersed them with its own symbols : only very slowly and tentatively did it proceed to substitute types that had no foundation in Paganism.   The general policy followed was one of compromise and assimilation, rather than of direct change.

The worship of the Emperor, forbidden at Rome under the Early Empire, was almost undisguised under Diocletian, and he and his colleagues enjoyed all the honours of the earthly representatives of the great gods.   Had paganism held its own, the divinity of the Emperor would unquestionably have become a main tenet of the orthodox.   The triumph of Christianity interrupted the development.   The Emperor is closely associated with the emblems of the new faith, cross and labarum, —he is crowned by the hand of the Lord or by the Angel of Victory—but he remains a man.   The conception of the divine in human nature was for ever dissociated from mere place and power.   The consecration of the dead Emperor naturally continued so long as paganism held the field, though the merits of the great Diocletian missed this particular form of recognition in the party strife after his death.   Constantine paid divine honours to his father (cp. Plate LXIII, 1), and to his ancestor, Claudius Gothicus,—Maxentius to his father Maximian (cp. Plate LXIII, 3, 4) and his son Romulus (Plate LXIII, 2), Maximin II to Galerius.   Even Constantine himself, though he died a Christian, was celebrated as " Divus " after his death— a new shade of meaning must have been attached to the term (Plate LXIII, 5, 6).   The reverse types show him as a standing figure, with the legend " Veneranda Memoria" (*VN. MR.*), or in a chariot beckoned on by the hand of God ; some reminiscence of the ascent of Elijah may be mingled in the latter type.   These are the last formal issues of consecration, but there are still certain issues, with star on reverse as main type or symbol (cp. Plate LXIII, 8), which were probably

struck in honour of the dead (so for Helena, Fausta, Theodosius I).[1] The conception of immortality in the world of the
stars was deeply rooted in the imagination and could easily be
provided with Christian parallels.

The worship of the minor deities or Virtues has still a place,
though only a restricted one, on the coinage. Fortuna still
appears with her rudder and globe (Plate LXIII, 18), Spes
with her flower, Securitas leaning on her column (Plate LXIV, 6).
Moneta with her scales still stands under Diocletian for the
activities of the imperial mint (Plate LXIV, 4).[2] These virtues,
however, had usually been associated with the person of the
Emperor as a semi-divine being. With the triumph of Christianity this conception declines and the Virtues, so far as they
are worshipped, tend rather to be associated with the State or
the people of Rome. The use of abstractions to convey general
conceptions of the State was actually a main feature of the time ;
but the abstraction is frequently not personified, but expressed
instead by a symbolical type. We have already spoken of the
types associated with such ideas as " Pietas," " Salus,"
" Felicitas," " Felicium Temporum Reparatio," " Victoria "
and " Virtus." Specially characteristic of the times is the
thought of the " Glory of Rome " or " the Army," which is
exceptionally personified as a woman holding branch and
leaning on a column (Plate LXIII, 17) ; more often the idea is
conveyed by a type of Rome and Constantinople or of the Emperor as a victorious general. The worship of the Genius of
the Emperor, or of the people of Rome, was especially popular ;
the Genius is usually represented as a youth holding cornucopiae and patera for sacrifice. The history of one personification, Victoria (cp. Plate LXIV, 7-14), is peculiarly interesting
in the development of religious belief. The Roman people
clung closely to this great power that symbolized the triumphant
progress of Rome in the world, and over the great statue of
Victory in the senate-house at Rome one of the main struggles
between Christianity and paganism developed. The Christian

---

[1] References to the immortality of the good Emperors are common in Claudian.
Cp. *On the Third Consulship of Honorius*, IV, 105 ff., 158 ff.

[2] For other examples, cp. Pl. LXIII, 14, Concordia ; 15, Fata Victricia ; 16,
Fides Militum ; LXIV, 3, Pietas ; 5, Providentia deorum Quies Augg.—the
abdication type of Diocletian and Maximian.

party succeeded in A.D. 382 in inducing the Emperor Gratian to order the removal of the statue ; but, to our surprise, we find the Victory type still appearing on the coinage and even being associated in the closest possible way, not only with the person of the Emperors but also with the symbol of the cross.   We can easily guess what it was that happened.   Christianity was unable to eradicate the worship of Victory entirely ;   there remained a second course—to retain it with a definitely Christian stamp.[1]   The pagan goddess becomes the Christian Angel of Victory, retaining her wings and her emblems, wreath and palm, and now bearing as a new emblem, the Christian cross.   It is a striking example of the same subtle policy that merged the worship of pagan gods in the veneration for Christian saints.

(f) *Animate and Inanimate Objects*—The use of various animate and inanimate types as symbols of general ideas is decidedly on the decline ;   fond as the age was of abstractions, it was forgetting the art of clothing them in symbols.   The she-wolf and twins still suggests the legend of Rome (Plate LXIV, 15).   The lion, as a type of strength, appears on the reverse of Divus Maximian, and again, with an added punning reference, on the coins of Leo the Great.   The eagle, associated from of old with consecration, appears on posthumous coins of Constantius I.   The phoenix is associated with the two kindred conceptions of renewal (" Fel. Temp. Reparatio "—Plate LXIV, 16) and durability (" Perpetuitas ").   The wreath is freely used as a frame for the " Vota " reverses and occasionally to enclose a star ;   but the old use of the " corona civica " can no longer be traced.   The military standards still convey the idea of the reliability of the army, and the altar, associated with the legend " Beata Tranquillitas," suggests offerings of thanksgiving for the blessing of peace.   The Christian monogram, ☧, is first associated on the coins of Magnentius with the idea of the " Salvation of the State : " the A and Ω that flank it refer to the description of Christ in the Book of Revelations. In the fifth century both ☧ and cross were used freely as main types,—the cross becoming the set type of the gold tremissis. The idea associated with it is usually that of the " Victory of

---

[1] Cp. St. Augustine, *De Civitate Dei*, Bk. IV, Ch. 14.

the Augusti,"—we have already noticed the remarkable legend " Salus Mundi " of Olybrius.

(g) *Buildings*—Apart from these Christian types, the most remarkable creation of the new age was the type of camp or city-gate, which occurs at intervals throughout the fourth century (Plate LXIV, 17-19). The frontier-defence was no longer a solid bulwark as it had been in the great days : it was at best a serviceable sea-wall, which could bank back the normal tides but was liable to be overflooded when the tide was at the spring. The defensibility of the great cities of the Empire became a prime necessity and the care of the Emperors for their defence is symbolized by the type of a city-gate with such legends as " Providentiae Augg." or " Virtus Augg."; it is the wisdom and valour of the Emperor that ensures defence. The types of the silver of the tetrarchy that show a scene of sacrifice outside a gate are probably to be taken rather as types of thanksgiving for victories in the field ; they are associated with the legends " Victoria Sarmatica " and " Virtus Militum." Magnus Maximus in Gaul defines the city gate as the " Hope of the Romans " (Plate LXIV, 17), and contemporary coins of Theodosius and his sons at Thessalonica mark it as " the Glory of the State " (Plate LXIV, 18). Representations of actual individual buildings are now very rare. The two most famous occur on the double solidus of Constantine I, showing with some attempt at fidelity to detail the bridge and gate of Treveri, and the newly discovered medallion of Constantius I, showing Londinium kneeling before her gates to welcome the deliverer.[1] The remarkable legend " Redditor lucis aeternae " has probably no special Mithraic symbolism, but draws on the natural thought of light as an equivalent of good, which was familiar enough to the Romans and was afterwards to supply the inspiration of some of the noblest Christian hymns. The representation of the gate and walls of London is no doubt conventional, but it may at least convince us that the city was not unwalled in A.D. 296.

We have seen that the coinage of the age was rich in its comment on the persons of its rulers, on the valour and renown of the army, on the happiness and safety of the State. We

---

[1] Cp. A. Alföldy, *Die Donaubrücke Konstantins des Grossen und verwandte historische Darstellungen auf spätrömischen Münzen*, Z.f.N. 1926, pp. 161 ff.

miss the full record of contemporary events and the full series of Virtues of the earlier period.   We miss too the interest in mythology, archaeology and in the past history of Rome, which at various times played an important rôle in the coinage. Some allowance must be made for the influence of the new faith ; but we may still conclude with safety that interest was more closely concentrated on the immediate present than in early times.   If we read the coinage superficially, we may gather the impression of a certain preoccupation with immediate necessities, coupled with a poverty of new ideas, that leads to bombastic phrases that convey little meaning and to the re-peated use of a few well-worn types.   We need to look a little deeper into the history as revealed by such historians as Ammianus Marcellinus and such an historical document as the great *Codex Theodosianus* to learn something of the des-perate struggle of civilization to maintain itself against an increasing weight of difficulty, the ever-repeated effort to hold the frontiers against the barbarians, the fettering of individual life in the system of hereditary castes, the terrible burden of the machinery of civil and military government, which gave the Empire the chance to live on but almost crushed it in the process.   These were the dominant facts of life as they pre-sented themselves to the subjects of the Empire and we, who are living in a time of not dissimilar stress, should find no diffi-culty in entering into sympathy with their struggles and in judging with leniency a world so hard put to it in the fight for sheer existence.   The language of the coins has little to say of the reverse side of the picture ; it gives us rather the great watchwords of encouragement that were used to buoy up sinking courage.   " The Happiness of the State," " The Safety of the State," " The Restoration of Prosperity," the " Glory of the Army," the " Joy of the Romans "—all these no doubt con-veyed some positive meaning to the men who handled the coins ; but we shall understand them better if we see their bright encouragement in black contrast with the dark abyss of national danger and humiliation, of misfortune and misery, into which the Western Empire finally sank and from which the East was only saved by what sometimes appears to us almost as a miracle.

CHAPTER III

COINAGE IN THE GENERAL LIFE OF THE LATER EMPIRE

ONCE again we must try to discover the importance of the facts of coinage which we have been investigating in the general life of the State. The uncertainties with which we have had to contend will still occasion difficulties, but we shall be helped by a number of precise indications in the *Codex Theodosianus* and other documents.

1. **Foreign Powers**—Let us look first at the relations of the imperial coinage to the world outside the Empire. The failing reputation of the Roman arms was for a time triumphantly restored by Diocletian ; and it is perhaps to this, as well as to the intrinsic merits of the coin, that we may attribute the world-wide reputation of the Roman solidus. Even the Sassanian kingdom of Persia, with its strong nationalist bias, struck gold but seldom ; apart from this one exception the whole world gladly accepted the Roman standard. Never, even in the days of Augustus, had the right of the Roman Emperor as King of Kings over gold coinage been so completely recognized. So strongly was this unwritten law established that, even after the fall of the Western Empire, its barbarian successors continued to strike with the head of the Emperor of the East, adding at most their own monogram ; and it was felt to be a grave violation of tradition when a Merovingian king took the bold step of stamping his own portrait on the solidus. Many of the large gold pieces, "medallions," or multiples of the solidus, seem actually to have been struck for presentation to native princes—a fact which is attested both by definite testimonies and by the appearance of such pieces in hoards found outside the imperial frontiers. A passage in the *Codex of Justinian* (IV, 63, 2), which may well have some

meaning for earlier times too, forbids the supply of gold to barbarians and recommends the use of craft to recover it for imperial use ; evidently the export tended to reach dangerous dimensions.

Of Roman silver outside the Empire we have nothing to say. The Roman silvered bronze was freely imitated both in East and West. In the West we are familiar with the so-called " minimi "—pieces of very small module, bearing types more or less loosely copied from Roman coins of the fourth and even of the third century. These pieces are particularly common in finds in Britain and Gaul and it seems highly probable that these imitations filled the place of a regular currency after the departure of the Romans. The fact that radiate heads of the third century are among the imitations need not seriously alarm us ; the series of Anglo-Saxon sceattas, beginning about A.D. 600, is partly dependent for its types on coins quite as early. In the East somewhat similar imitations of imperial bronze are found in great quantities in Egypt. They have been assigned, somewhat hastily, to the Vandal occupation of Africa. We prefer to follow J. G. Milne in giving them a local Egyptian origin and regarding them as the token-money of the great landed proprietors, striking in practical independence of the government.[1] The types imitated in Egypt are on the whole decidedly later than those imitated in the West —a fact which may be fully accounted for, when we contrast the continuance of the official coinage in the provinces of Egypt and Syria with the closing of all the Roman mints outside Italy in the West soon after the beginning of the fifth century.

The curious imitations of late fourth-century Roman coins which are found occasionally in Ceylon rouse our curiosity about this little chapter of forgotten history. They are all of bronze, and, as the one Roman province (Egypt) in close touch with Taprobane was precisely the one in which gold and silver coinage came to an early end, we need not wonder at this. It seems that Roman merchants still carried on a lively trade with the distant island and that they actually found it convenient to export small change with them which was then multiplied by imitations on native soil.

[1] Cp. *Num. Chron.*, 1926, pp. 43 ff.

2. The Provinces—We turn to the provinces. In the early Empire we found a definite centre—Rome and Italy—and round it the provinces, moving but slowly to full political and economic equality. With Diocletian this movement is complete. The Empire has no longer one centre, but a number of foci—residences of the Augusti and Caesars and of their praetorian prefects. Beside Rome we can now set Nicomedia, Antioch, Treveri, Constantinople and other cities which at one time or another were raised by imperial favour to special importance. All the subjects of the Empire, as far as geographical position is concerned, have now equal rights—or, perhaps we should rather say, equal responsibilities. This new unity and equality, however, has nothing to do with true local independence. The provinces are made equal to Rome and Italy in servitude and not in freedom ; the same omnipotent central government grips all alike and demands a general obedience to its stereotyped instructions.

The advantages of the new system in its relation to coinage are obvious and indisputable. There is no longer a confusion of imperial, provincial and local issues, involving constant difficulties in tariffing and exchange : the same imperial coinage is current everywhere. The supply too is well adapted to local needs. Almost every province has its own mint or mints and the need for the transport of coin from a distance is removed. The government, however, seems to have impaired the value of this well-planned system by occasional displays of capricious tyranny and by a general lack of sense in its legislation regarding coinage. Let us look at one or two cases of capricious tyranny. While the Roman world at large was carefully supplied with coinage, a few provinces were excluded from the general boon. Spain had no mint of its own and depended on Southern Gaul for its supplies. Africa had no mint after the brief activity of Carthage from A.D. 296-311 and was dependent on Italy. The military insignificance of these provinces no doubt explains the lack of mints, but the effect on local trade must have been depressing. Britain had its mint of Londinium from A.D. 296-324, but no coinage thereafter except for a moment under Magnus Maximus. The military argument hardly applies here, and we are forced to accuse the government of a lack of consideration for a province from which no important income was derivable. A curious fact of late fourth-century hoards—the finding of miliarensia and siliquae in Britain and very seldom elsewhere—may find its explanation in the arrangements made for coinage. We may conjecture that Britain was but scantily supplied with gold and therefore thrown back on the use of silver for all larger business transactions. This alone would account for the prevalence of silver in British hoards ; and, if we may credit the government with the intention of withdrawing the silver as well as the gold from the island, the hoards may be regarded as evidence of an attempt to preserve treasure not so much from the barbarian invader, as from the even more terrible government official. That the government was capable of ruthlessness in its policy is proved beyond question in the case of Egypt. After about A.D. 324 Egypt has, practically speaking, no gold or silver of her own. Forced to trade with no better medium than the small silvered bronze the Egyptians found it impossible to maintain the standard of reckoning. Prices rose to fabulous heights and there was no remedy but to assign ever higher values to the almost worthless coins. Such a process of collapse has theoretically no limit, and in Egypt, in fact, depreciation reached an amazing pitch. Now two things are obvious here at once. Such conditions must cause a vast amount of unnecessary misery ; and for such conditions the government is primarily responsible. Perhaps it was fear of the unruliness of Egypt that made the Romans inflict this policy on the province ; the Egyptian taxes were collected mainly in kind and the poverty of the province in metal would not react immediately on its oppressor. The mere omission to strike gold and silver in a province is not in itself enough to bring it to this sorry pass ; we should naturally expect supplies to flow in from outside as required, in the ordinary course of trade. We conclude that the government must have made it a part of its policy to hinder the free movement of money ; and this conclusion is in fact confirmed by ancient evidence.[1] Merchants are definitely forbidden to carry with them more than a very modest allowance of money for their personal requirements ; the selling of coin is strictly forbidden ; coin is to be an instrument of public use, not an article

---

[1] *Cod. Theod.*, IX, 23 (speaking primarily of bronze).

17

of commerce. Let us reflect for a moment on what is involved in this policy. Each province is condemned to subsist on such supplies of coin as the government thinks fit to provide. If the supply is anywhere inadequate either in quantity or in quality there is no help to be had; any definite attempts to remedy it are punishable in law. We catch an alarming glimpse of that tyrannical control, so characteristic of the age, which entirely subordinated the interests of the individual to those of the State. We suspect that the government in its issues of money for the provinces was mainly concerned with its own interests, not with those of trade or of private life. Where the requirements of the army particularly demanded it or where the government itself needed masses of coined money, there the supply was ample; where these conditions did not exist, it refused to go to the trouble and expense of supplying trade with its most vital necessity.

3. **Occasions of Coinage**—What then were the main occasions for which coin was issued? In the first place we must set the supply of pay to the troops and, perhaps even more, to the Civil Service,[1] which after Diocletian was almost a heavier burden on the State than the army. The mint of Aquileia is a good example of a mint serving military needs, supplying, as it did, the pay for troops moving eastwards from Italy into the Balkans. The mint of Sirmium, which is often found striking gold and silver with very little bronze, is another example, the mint of Treviri after Valentinian I is a third. In the second place will come the supply of coinage for the doles to the people, whether made by the Emperor himself or by leading officials in the big cities. Legislation has come down to us, regulating the size of the coins to be used in these largesses; the miliarense was particularly used for such purposes and, according to one etymology, certainly a false one, got its name from being distributed to the "milites." The formal bounties of the early Empire cannot be traced beyond Diocletian and Maximian, but the practice of winning popular goodwill by a display of generosity was too valuable to be lightly discarded. We have coins of Valentinian I and II showing the Emperors

---

[1] But we must remember that the government made a determined stand for paying salaries in kind and against payment in cash, " adaeratio ; " in the age of Valentinian I it was beginning to give way on the general principle.

in their chariots flinging largess to the mob.   Such gifts seem now to be restricted to a series of special occasions, such as the visit of the Emperor to a town ;   the regular provision for the poor of the capitals by this means was apparently abandoned.   Whether more was gained or lost by the change is hard to determine.   Probably only in the third place came the requirements of trade and private life.   Taxes were now so commonly collected in bullion or in kind that the lack of coined money caused little embarrassment to the treasury ;   and, as we have seen above, of a far-sighted and disinterested care for private needs there is very little trace.   We shall see later how this policy gave rise to false coinage on the largest scale and to the irregular extension of mint privileges to private individuals—practices which the government first stimulated by its unwise regulations and then endeavoured to repress with the utmost rigour.

4. **Supplies of Precious Metal**—One notable feature of the period was the restoration of an ample coinage in the precious metals—in itself an excellent thing for trade.   Whence these new supplies came is not at first quite obvious, as the State mines were in many cases approaching exhaustion and new metallic resources within the Empire were not easily to be found.   It is highly probable that Diocletian's Eastern victories placed large new stocks of gold and silver at his disposal.   Even more importance must be attached to the severity of government methods of inquisition and taxation.   Little by little the metallic reserves of the Empire must have been drawn into imperial use ;   the vast quantities of precious metal, hitherto immobilized in articles of luxury, must to a large extent have found their way to the melting-pot.   Another most important source of supply was the temple treasures, which, as paganism died, came again into the market.   Towards the close of the fourth century the supplies of silver began to fail and later we find the Byzantine Empire with a coinage of gold and bronze. The reasons for this relative scarcity of silver are not hard to guess.   The gold coinage was the main concern of the government and the inquisition for gold was correspondingly keen. Further, silver was being continually squandered on the silvering of the bronze.   And finally, as articles of luxury cannot have gone entirely out of vogue, the less costly silver probably

tended to replace gold in this field. That the decline of silver coinage was not due to an absolute scarcity of the metal is proved by the fact that the relation of gold to silver, far from declining, was actually on the rise.

The supply of small change, ample in the early stages, became meagre towards the end of our period. Here there was no question of larger imperial needs—it was private convenience that was mainly at stake, and private convenience, as we have already seen, did not lie very near the heart of the government. It is in its treatment of this branch of the coinage that the administration is most open to criticism ; such criticism will lead us naturally on to our next subject—that of the general financial theories prevailing in this age.

5. **Financial Theory**—The Emperors of the third century, unable to balance their budget, had resorted to the fatal expedient of assigning fictitious values to their coinage. They exploited the false theory that the State can, by an act of will, enforce the circulation of its own money at its own rates. This theory needs no refuting to-day ; such inflation is no more than a dishonest form of taxation, when the government pays in bad money and exacts payment in good. What was the attitude of Diocletian and his successors to this problem ? The bad old practice lasted after them down into mediaeval times ; were they responsible for endorsing it themselves ? The answer to this question cannot be quite simple. To a certain extent—particularly in the supply of a pure gold and silver coinage—they seem to have adopted the sound policy of giving the world a currency that could command confidence on its merits. That the silver was constantly struck below its normal weight was, perhaps, no very serious disadvantage, since it was tariffed in terms of a reliable gold coinage. It was the smaller change—the coinage of silvered bronze—that was now as before the weak point of the system. It had originated in the third century as a fraudulent substitute for silver. Diocletian, indeed, distinguished it sharply from the coinage of pure silver and assigned to it values more in accordance with its actual worth. The fact, however, remained that a coinage, essentially of bronze, was offered to the world at rates well above its bronze values. The bitter memories of the third century still survived and expressed themselves in a steady distrust of the new coins.

The result was a continuous decline in the value of the new unit of reckoning, the denarius, from 50,000 to the pound under Diocletian to 172,800 under Constantine. With Constantine relative stability was attained, but even now the value of the denarius tended to fall and, in the fifth century, we find as many as 2880 denarii (7200 nummi) to the solidus. If we ask why the government was not content to treat this silvered bronze as a token coinage, dependent on the gold, we may hesitate for an answer ; gold, we should have thought, was plentiful enough to carry the weight of the whole coinage. The government must have insisted on making the bronze a source of profit. As a matter of fact, the silvered bronze seems to have been used, not merely as small change, but as real money to effect large payments ; and, when put to this use, its inherent defects became obvious.

The difficulties of maintaining two metals in the same system are sufficiently well known. How much more serious was the problem, when, beside gold and silver, a place had to be found for silvered bronze ! In the long run, the government seems to have abandoned the attempt as hopeless. In the system of Constantine after A.D. 324 there was no convenient relation between solidus and miliarense or between miliarense and siliqua.[1] Even later when satisfactory relations between these coins had been established,[2] the silvered bronze remained a difficulty. The solidus, nominally worth 6000 nummi, reached a value of 7200.[3] It became more and more the custom to make the pound of metal—gold, silver or bronze—the unit and to treat the individual coins simply as fractions of those pounds.[4] The pound of metal would rise or fall in market value and the coins would vary with it. The coin is, in fact, relapsing from a measure of value to an article of commerce like any other. The tendency was accentuated by the practice of collecting a large proportion of the taxes in kind. The

---

[1] The solidus equals 14 miliarensia nearly ; the miliarense equals about $1\frac{5}{7}$ siliquæ.

[2] The solidus equals 12 miliarensia, equals 24 siliquæ.

[3] The *Cod. Justin.*, XI, 11, 2, shows an attempt to make the solidus a standard for all prices ; " pro imminutione, quae in aestimatione solidi forte tractatur, omnium quoque specierum pretia decrescere oportet."

[4] The proof of this is to be found in the constant reckoning in pounds in the *Codex Theodosianus*. The *Historia Augusta*, which reckons similarly, probably often reflects the practice, rather of the fourth than of the third century.

taxpayer found himself called upon to pay over either certain amounts of necessaries in the form of foodstuffs, clothing or the like or certain values of metal ; the payments might be made either in bullion or in coin indifferently. The system, in this respect, represented a decided relapse from that of the earlier Empire ; the needs of the government may have been satisfied by it, but the ordinary requirements of trade must have suffered serious loss.

6. **False Coinage**—On a number of points relating to the coinage, the *Codex Theodosianus* preserves for us valuable information. False coinage was remarkably prevalent and was met with correspondingly severe penalties. It took various forms and was perpetrated, partly by the mint officials themselves, partly by irresponsible persons outside.[1] One form of abuse consisted in the clipping of the edge of the solidus and called forth a special edict of repression. The clipping of the silver, which, as our coins show us, was extensively practised, was less serious, as the silver was in any case partly token money. Another form of abuse consisted in the melting down of the bronze, to extract the silver and, no doubt, reissue a baser bronze in its place. In general, it was the bronze that was most open to attack ; the general public can have had no ready method of distinguishing between coins containing the full official allowance of silver and forgeries with an inferior proportion. The penalties for the forger were severe. Offenders were held to be guilty of high treason and were liable to the death penalty or to long terms of penal servitude. They were expressly excluded from the amnesty granted to ordinary malefactors on Easter Day. Not only the forger himself, but the owner of the property on which forgery took place, was liable to give account, though here some merciful allowance was made in the case of minors. The *Codex* leaves us with the impression of a very widespread evil, which defied the efforts of the law to repress it.

---

[1] Cp. *Cod. Theod.*, IX, 21 ff., penalties for forgers, 21, 6 ; penalties for " flaturarii," who separate the silver from the bronze in the " pecunia majorina," 21, 9 ; forgery is " maiestas," high treason, 22 ; penalties for clippers of the solidus, XII, 7, 2 ; " zygostatai " appointed in each city to test solidi that have been cut or rubbed down.

The most exact description of the commonest form of forgery is " nummum falsa fusione formare "—the casting of silvered bronze, no doubt of inferior quality.

We have seen above that the state supply of money for trade purposes was probably often inadequate. It is not surprising to find, then, that private persons contrived to secure licences to have money coined for them at the mint.[1] An edict of Valentinian I revokes all such licences in existence at the time and another edict confiscates all private bullion brought to be struck at the mint ; as this second edict defeated its purpose by its severity, a further edict decreed that two ounces only in the pound should be appropriated by the State.[2]

The government certainly seems to have claimed the right to determine exactly how and where money should circulate. The transport of coin from province to province for purposes of sale was expressly forbidden by an edict of A.D. 354. In A.D. 395 one of the two larger bronze coins then in circulation, the so-called " pecunia maiorina," was withdrawn from currency, only the " centenionalis " being retained. The prohibition of the transport of coin was a serious matter ; it meant that the government insisted on the validity of its arrangements even when experience clearly demonstrated their inadequacy.

7. Control of Prices—The standard example of the attempt to control prices by legislation is the famous edict " de maximis pretiis " of Diocletian (A.D. 301). It was probably by no means the only attempt of the kind ; but it is the only one any details of which have come down to us, and it may stand here for its class. Diocletian had in A.D. 296 provided what he regarded, with some justification, as a satisfactory coinage. The business world could not reject it, but it refused to accept the values assigned to the coins by Diocletian ; prices in fact rose to enormous heights. To Diocletian this seemed nothing more or less than downright villainy, calling for drastic remedies. He accordingly issued an edict, dealing with all commodities in the greatest detail and fixing a maximum price for each. We hear—and we are not surprised to hear—that the edict was a failure ; prices remained as they were or rose even higher. It is easy to blame Diocletian for his short-sighted folly in thinking that he could enforce by legislation the acceptance of a coinage that could not win respect on its merits. But there is something to be said for his point of view, if not for his method of enforcing

---

[1] *Cod. Theod.*, IX, 21, 10.
[2] *Ibid.*, 21, 7 (A.D. 369), amended IX, 21, 8 (A.D. 374).

it.   We know from experience how much room for conscienceless profiteering is provided by a sudden change of money-values. During the whole of the third century the world had seen falling values and soaring prices.   The reform of Aurelian had brought only partial relief ; prices had again risen, reducing the real, if not the nominal, values of the coins.   We may well believe that it was partly a matter of bad habit and deliberate fraud, if the well-judged reform of 296 was at once followed by a new rise in prices.   Lactantius, indeed, accuses Diocletian of causing dear prices himself by " various unfair measures ; " but, in the absence of more exact information, we cannot determine what weight to attach to this charge.[1]   All we can say is that the reform of 296 appears to have provided a possibility of financial stability.

The collection of taxes was another matter calling for continual legislation.   It was a particular hardship of the time that the demands were not regular and constant, but that, in addition to fixed charges, there were requisitions to be made, varying from time to time both in quality and in amount.[2] Here too edict after edict was issued, prescribing how payments were to be effected and at what rates payments in one metal might be expressed in terms of another.

8. The Caste of Moneyers—It is a well-established fact that Roman society from the time of Diocletian came to be organized more and more on a basis of caste.   A man was born into a caste or profession and could only with the very greatest difficulty escape from it.   It seemed as if nearly every one was engaged in the sad attempt to escape out of the frying-pan into the fire.   The State was so distrustful of its reserves that it feared to leave any gaps to be filled by natural processes.   The caste of mint officials, " monetales," was no exception to this rule.   It became an hereditary profession, recruited from the families of the moneyers ; various edicts expressly forbid any moneyer to resign his functions, unless he can provide a substitute.   We gather that attempts at evasion were common and

[1] If we were right in attributing to Diocletian a reduction of the " twenty " piece of Aurelian from two sestertii to half a sestertius, that measure may have led to a rush to spend the old money before its devaluation, and so to a rise in prices; cp. above, p 225.

[2] Cp. *Cod. Theod.*, XI, 21, 3.

infer that the normal emoluments were poor, however tempting might be the prospects of illicit gain to such bold spirits as chose to brave the penalties for forgery.

9. **Success and Failure**—To sum up the results of our inquiry, we find that the government of the period after Diocletian were at least partially successful in overcoming the evils inherited from the third century and in preventing the recurrence of any desperate financial crisis.   It established a uniform system of coinage for the Empire and secured a steady supply of good gold and silver.   So far we must give it credit for excellent intentions, not so poorly expressed in action.   But there is a reverse side to the medal.   The needs of the individual were subordinated to those of the State and, in the long run, the State suffered with him.   Where abuses occurred the State proceeded by edict, instead of by a careful examination and removal of the causes.   The government aspired to regulate everything and leave nothing to chance.   It hindered the free movement of coin and, in so doing, cramped trade.   It failed to secure a satisfactory supply of small change and, by its continual experiments, contributed to instability and unsettlement.   We are not in a position to estimate exactly the weight of the difficulties with which it had to contend.   But, in general, we must admit that a judicious comment which has been made on the general policy of Diocletian and Constantine applies to the coinage as well.   The Emperors felt themselves unable to preserve the interests of both individual and State ; and, as the lesser of the two evils, they allowed those of the individual to go to the wall.   That this meant nothing better than a postponement of the evil day for the State as well, was a misfortune which it lay beyond their power to prevent.

EPILOGUE

THERE is no one fixed date which can be taken to mark the end of the Roman Empire. We have here taken the fall of the Western Empire in 476. But the West still acknowledged the supremacy of the Eastern Emperor; it was not until the Western kings began to strike independently that the fall of Rome can be regarded as an accomplished fact. It is obviously impossible for us to follow Byzantium, as the successor of Rome, into the Middle Ages. Byzantium is, of course, a bridge between the ancient and the modern worlds; but it is convenient to treat the later history from the fall of the Western Empire as a separate episode, while never forgetting that there is historical continuity with Rome.

We saw the coinage of Rome beginning as that of a city-state, which gradually rises to supremacy in Italy and then crosses the seas to extend its sway little by little over the whole of the Mediterranean world. The first coinage is indigenous— a coinage of bronze; soon the Greek use of silver is borrowed, later gold is struck in the tradition of Philip and Alexander of Macedon. Rome begins her career as a part of Western barbarism; she develops a civilization under Etruscan and Greek influences and hands it on to the more backward peoples of the West. She wins political, but never cultural, supremacy over the Greek East. Finally she first shares her sway with an Eastern capital, then resigns her sceptre to the " New Rome " of the East. The West relapses towards barbarism but the memory of imperial Rome and the example and power of Byzantium save Rome and Italy and even the more Western peoples from a complete submersion in the barbarian night. Let us see how these changes expressed themselves in coinage. Byzantine coinage carries on in direct line the traditions of the late Roman Empire. But there was fresh life awaiting expression that was not Roman and the later developments of

Byzantium, interesting as they are, are certainly not Roman in inspiration. It is noteworthy that the full development of the Christian element in coins was reserved for Byzantium. The position of the Emperor changed little, but that was only because Oriental despotism had already won the day over Roman liberty before Rome fell. All that is really characteristic of Rome in coinage steadily declines. The alphabet is more and more infected with Greek forms ; and the reform of the money-system by Anastasius made the breach palpable.

We have to look more closely at the course of development in the West.[1] The first stage is that of coinage of the barbarians in imitation of Roman and Byzantine models. The Vandals strike gold only with Roman types, silver and bronze with their own types and legends. The Visigoths in Gaul imitate the coins of Valentinian III ; in Spain they develop a coinage of their own on the Roman model, giving name of mint as well as of king. A somewhat similar coinage is attributed to the Suevi in Spain. The Burgundians and Merovingians begin with Byzantine imitations ; the Merovingian kings pass on to royal coinage in their own names and thence to the typical coinage of tremisses, with name of town and moneyer. Odoacer and the Ostrogoths copy Byzantine types, then develop silver and bronze of their own. Quasi-independent coinage is issued by Rome itself. The Lombards copy Byzantine coins and only advance slowly to coinage in their own name, both in the North and in their South Italian duchy of Beneventum. Coins of the Gepidae on Byzantine models have only recently been identified. Britain at the Roman retirement was left without a coinage ; all that we can place in the dark years between c. 410 and 600 are one or two imitations of Roman solidi with runic legends and, conceivably, some of the " minimi," tiny bronze coins imitating the radiate heads of the Gallic Emperors and the diademed heads of Constantine I and his successors. Out of this confusion of coinage the feudal coins of the Middle Ages and after them the national issues of the West gradually emerged.

The fact that strikes us most forcibly is the vast prestige of Rome—a prestige so great as to impose itself on the

---

[1] Cp. C. F. Keary, *The Coinages of Western Europe*, London, 1879.

barbarian successors of the Empire. But, by the side of this, another fact becomes prominent; the Roman tradition, potent in the appeal of its great past, is weak and unprogressive in the present. The influence of that great past is slowly forgotten. The Roman tradition is involuntarily and insensibly lost and new independent forms arise. There is no longer sufficient vigour in the remains of Roman life in the West to give a Roman stamp to these new developments. There is very little of Rome, except the language, in the coinage of the later Merovingians and of the Carolingians. However high we assess the debt of the West to Rome, there is nothing gained by obscuring the fact that the world of the sixth and following centuries found itself unable to develop on Roman lines and was forced to branch off on many new paths of its own. If we look at the last few years of the Western Empire we find this view confirmed. The impulse of Roman civilization had spent itself internally—the Empire was penetrated through and through by barbarian elements, long before its political structure broke. There was an unhappy discord between the brain and the body of the world. The educated and cultured classes lacked strength, the barbarian intruders lacked depth of culture. Italy herself, with her concentrated traditions of political life, was deeply influenced racially by barbarian settlement. Out of the blend of strong unexhausted races and old political and social conditions has risen our modern Europe, redeemed from barbarism by the heritage of the ancient world, but reinvigorated by the new blood of the barbarians who had knocked for so long at the doors of the Empire.

INDEX

A

Actium, battle of, 85.
Aediles, curule, 33.
— plebeian, 33.
Aerarium Saturni, 29, 61, 132.
Aes, 18 n., 111.
— Grave, 3 ff., 9 ff., 16, 21, 50 ff., 99.
— Signatum, 8 f., 50 and n.
Africa, 102, 112, 114, 183, 195, 218, 256.
Alexandria, 130 and n., 197, 218, 220.
Alimenta Italiae, 170 f.
Animate types, 85 f., 175 ff., 251 f.
Anniversaries, of Rome, 171 f.
Antioch, 115, 117 ff., 214.
Antoninianus, 125 ff., 191 f.
Architecture, 86 f., 177 ff., 210 f., 252.
Army, pay of, 24, 93 f., 122, 190 f.
— types relating to, 155 ff., 166 f., 172 ff.,
    177, 210, 239, 246 ff.
Art, 38 f., 45, 86 ff., 135 f., 178 ff., 212,
    234.
As, 3 f., 10 ff., 13 f., 16 f., 19 ff., 23 ff., 49,
    53, 92 ff., 97, 122 ff., 130, 201 f.
Asia, 103 f., 196.
Attributes, 161, 168 f.
Augustus, 110 ff.
Aurelian, reform of, 128 ff., 192 f., 225,
    264.
Aureus, 18, 25, 121 ff., 200 ff., 223, 226 f.
Autonomous coinage, 198.

B

Bankruptcy, State, 91 ff., 96 ff., 191 ff.,
    212 ff.
Banks, 185.
Bes, 25, 52.
Biga types, 55 ff.
Billon coinage, 126 ff., 193, 218 f., 223 ff.,
    230, 232, 260 ff.
Brass coinage, 27, 111 ff., 121 ff., 131 ff.,
    189.
Britain, 103, 118, 120, 172 ff., 176, 180,
    195, 256, 267
Bronze coinage, 3 ff., 9 ff., 16 and n., 17 ff.,
    27.
Buildings, 86 f., 177 ff., 210 f., 252.
Bullion, supply of, 36 f., 182, 193, 259 f.

Burgundians, 267.
Byzantium, 234, 237 f., 240, 246, 266 f.

C

Canting badges, 61, 74.
Capua, 6 ff., 16, 99.
Caracalla, reform of, 125 f., 191 f.
Carthage, 7 f., 50 ff., 54, 94, 102, 218, 256.
Censors, 28 f.
Centenionalis, 227 ff., 263.
Centralization at Rome, 116 ff., 217.
Ceylon, 255.
Christianity, 149, 161, 238 f., 248 ff., 267.
Chronology, 39 ff., 137 ff., 234 ff.
Cimbrian War, 60, 78, 90.
Circus races, 57.
Civil wars, 79 ff., 82 ff., 114 ff.
Clipping, 262.
Colonies, 32 f., 65, 77 ff., 90, 95, 98 f.,
    198, 211 f.
Comes auri, 233.
— sacrarum largitionum, 233.
Commemorative coins, 137.
Concilia, provincial, 197 f.
Congiaria, 52, 65, 78 f., 83, 151.
Consecration, 137 f., 145, 148 ff., 162 f.,
    167, 176, 205 ff., 235, 244, 249 f.
Conservatism in types, etc., 52 ff., 58,
    142 f., 239 f.
Consular coins, 31.
Consuls, 33 f.
Contemporary history, 41, 57 f., 63 f., 72,
    77 ff., 169 ff., 206 f., 239, 252 f.
Contorniates, 222 f., n.
Control of Mint, 28 ff., 134 f., 199 f., 262.
Copper coinage, 111 ff., 121 ff., 130 ff.,
    189, 195 ff.
Corn distributions, 34 f., 52, 65, 78 f., 83,
    87, 90, 95, 151, 160, 166.
Countermarks, 186 f., 199 f.
Curator denariis flandis, 35.

D

Dacia, 172 ff., 182.
Debasement of coinage, 24, 26 ff., 92 ff.
    124 ff., 134 f., 189 ff.

KEY TO THE PLATES

PLATE I (pp. 5 ff., 19 ff., 50 ff.).

1.	" Romano-Campanian " coinage.	Didrachm, *c.* 278 B.C.
2.	,,	,,	,,	Didrachm, *c.* 275 B.C.
3.	,,	,,	,,	Bronze (half-litra ?), *c.* 275 B.C.
4.	,,	,,	,,	Bronze (quarter-litra ?), *c.* 275 B.C.
5.	,,	,,	,,	Bronze (double-litra ?), *c.* 275 B.C.
6.	,,	,,	,,	Didrachm, after 268 B.C.
7.	,,	,,	,,	Drachm, *c.* 220 B.C. (?).
8.	,,	,,	,,	Gold piece (6 scruples), 209 B.C.
9.	,,	,,	,,	Gold piece (3 scruples), 209 B.C.
10.	,,	,,	,,	Triens, after 268 B.C.
11.	,,	,,	,,	Quadrans, after 268 B.C.
12.	,,	,,	,,	Sextans, after 268 B.C.

PLATE II (pp. 5 ff., 19 ff., 49 ff.).

1. " Romano-Campanian " coinage.   Uncia, after 268 B.C.
2.   ,,   ,,   ,,   Semuncia, after 268 B.C.
3. Denarius (heavy standard), before *c.* 217 B.C.
4. Quinarius (heavy standard), before *c.* 217 B.C.
5. Sestertius (heavy standard), before *c.* 217 B.C.
6. Victoriate (heavy standard), *c.* 235-217 B.C.
7. Denarius (reduced standard), *c.* 215 B.C.
8. Gold piece of 60 sestertii (3 scruples), 217 B.C.
9. Gold pieces of 40 sestertii (2 scruples), 217 B.C.
10. Gold piece of 20 sestertii (1 scruple), 217 B.C.
11. Semuncia (" semi-libral " standard), *c.* 268-245 B.C.
12. Quartuncia (" semi-libral " standard), *c.* 268-245 B.C.
13. Sextans (" semi-libral " standard), *c.* 268-245 B.C.
14. As (uncial standard), *c.* 190 B.C.
15. Uncia (" semi-libral " standard), *c.* 268-245 B.C.

PLATE III (pp. 3 ff., 19, 49).

1. As (libral standard), before 268 B.C.

PLATE IV (pp. 3 ff., 19, 49).

1. Semis (libral standard), before 268 B.C.
2. Triens (libral standard), before 268 B.C.
3. Quadrans (libral standard), before 268 B.C.

PLATE V (pp. 10 ff., 20 ff., 49).

1. Dupondius ("semi-libral" standard), *c.* 268-245 B.C.
2. Semis ("semi-libral" standard), *c.* 268-245 B.C.

PLATE VI (pp. 14 ff., 23 ff., 49 ff.).

1. Dextans, *c.* 215 B.C.
2. Quincunx, *c.* 215 B.C.
3. Sextans (local issue), *c.* 217 B.C.
4. Triens (M. FABRINI.), *c.* 140 B.C.
5. Quadrans (P. MAE. ANT.), *c.* 140 B.C.
6. Dodrans (C. CASSI.), *c.* 123 B.C.
7. Bes (C. CASSI.), *c.* 123 B.C.
8. As (M. FONTEI. C. F.—semuncial standard), *c.* 87 B.C.
9. Quinarius (Anonymous), *c.* 105 B.C.
10. Quinarius (L. PISO), *c.* 90 B.C.
11. Sestertius (A. LICINIVS MACER.), *c.* 47 B.C.
12. Aureus (Sulla), *c.* 83 B.C.
13. Aureus (Julius Caesar), *c.* 45 B.C.
14. As (Julius Caesar—Q. OPPIVS), *c.* 45 B.C.
15. Cistophoric Tetradrachm (= 3 denarii, Mark Antony), *c.* 37 B.C.

PLATE VII (pp. 14 ff., 23 ff., 31 ff., 54 ff.).

1. Denarius (VAR.), *c.* 217 B.C.
2. Denarius (L. PORCI. LICI., L. LIC. CN. DOM.), *c.* 118 B.C.
3. Denarius (M. CALID. Q. METE. CN. FL.), *c.* 125 B.C.
4. Quadrans (M. SILA. Q. CVRT.), *c.* 120 B.C.
5. Denarivs (M. SERGIVS SILVS Q. EX S.C.), *c.* 125 B.C.
6. Denarius (A. ALB. S. F. L. METEL. C. MALL.), *c.* 99 B.C.
7. Denarius (C. VAL. FLA. IMPERAT. EX S.C.), *c.* 84 B.C.
8. Denarius (M. FAN. L. CRIT. AED. PL.), *c.* 87 B.C.
9. Denarius (Q. ANTO. BALB. S.C.), *c.* 82 B.C.
10. Denarius (P. GALB. AED. CVR. S.C.), *c.* 70 B.C.
11. Denarius (M. PLAETORIVS CESTIANVS AED. CVR. EX S.C.), *c.* 68 B.C.
12. Denarius (L. FVRI. CN. F. BROCCHI IIIVIR), *c.* 55 B.C.
13. Denarius (T. CARISIVS—MONETA), *c.* 45 B.C.
14. Aureus (L. PLANC. PRAEF. VRB.—C. CAES. DIC. TER.), *c.* 45 B.C.
15. Denarius (L. FLAMINI. CHILO IIIIVIR PRI(mus) FL(avit)), 44 B.C.
16. Denarius (Q. SICINIVS IIIVIR—C. COPONIVS PR. S.C.), *c.* 49 B.C.
17. Denarius (METEL. PIVS SCIP. IMP.—CRASSVS IVN. LEG. PRO PR.), *c.* 46 B.C.
18. Denarius (M. ANTON. COS. IMP.—M. LEPID. COS. IMP.), *c.* 43 B.C.
19. Aureus (L. MUSSIDIUS T. F. LONGVS IIIIVIR A.P.F.—C. CAESAR IIIVIR R.P.C.), *c.* 42 B.C.
20. Denarius (C. CAESAR IMP. S.C.), *c.* 43 B.C.

PLATE VIII (pp. 31 ff., 35 ff., 59 ff.).

1. Denarius (LENT. MAR. F. P.E.S.C.), *c.* 99 B.C.
2. Triens (L.P.D.P.P.), *c.* 89 B.C.
3. Denarius (Ex A.P.—anonymous—types of L. IVLI. BVRSIO), *c.* 87 B.C.
4. Denarius (M. LVCILI. RVF. Pv.), *c.* 117 B.C.
5. Denarius (M. VOLTEI. M.F. S.C.D.T.), *c.* 80 B.C.
6. Denarius (L. SATVRN.—·C.), *c.* 110 B.C.
7. Denarius (L. PISO FRVG.—XIIII-XXV), *c.* 90 B.C.
8. Denarius (M. SERVEILI. C.F.—ω—A.), *c.* 111 B.C.
9. Denarius (C. FVNDAN. Q.—A.), *c.* 112 B.C.
10. Denarius (L. IVLI. BVRSIO—Anchor), *c.* 87 B.C.
11. Denarius (C. MALLE. C. F., L. LIC. CN. DOM.—serrate), *c.* 118 B.C.
12. Denarius (L. COT.—o—serrate), *c.* 102 B.C.
13. Denarius (L. PAPI.—pulley with hook, rope—serrate), *c.* 82 B.C.
14. Denarius (L. VOLT. L. F. STRABO.—serrate), *c.* 81 B.C.
15. Denarius (C. HOSIDI. C. F. GETA IIIVir—serrate), *c.* 55 B.C.
16. Denarius (M. PLAETORIVS CEST. S.C.), *c.* 70 B.C.
17. Denarius (M. PLAETORI. CEST. S.C.), *c.* 70 B.C.
18. Denarius (M. PISO M. F. FRVGI), *c.* 70 B.C.
19. Denarius (CN. PLANCIVS AED. CVR. S.C.), *c.* 57 B.C.
20. Denarius (L. PLAVTIVS PLANCVS), *c.* 47 B.C.

PLATE IX (pp. 30 ff., 40, 44 f., 54 ff.).

1. Denarius (no mint-mark), *c.* 250 B.C.
2. Denarius (caduceus), *c.* 260 B.C.
3. Denarius (palm), *c.* 245 B.C.
4. Denarius (MA.), *c.* 230 B.C. (?)
5. Denarius (C.), *c.* 220 B.C. (?).
6. Denarius (caduceus), *c.* 240 B.C.
7. Denarius (knife), *c.* 220 B.C.
8. Denarius (D.), *c.* 215 B.C.
9. Denarius (GR.), *c.* 215 B.C.
10. Denarius (Q.L.C.), *c.* 215 B.C.
11. Victoriate (CROT.), *c.* 225 B.C.
12. Quinarius (H.), *c.* 225 B.C.
13. Victoriate (MP. ?), *c.* 225 B.C.
14. Victoriate (MT. ?), *c.* 225 B.C.
15. Victoriate (Q.), *c.* 225 B.C.
16. Victoriate (VIB.), *c.* 225 B.C.
17. Denarius (SX. Q.), *c.* 215 B.C.
18. Denarius (fly), *c.* 210 B.C.
19. Denarius (PVR.), *c.* 205 B.C.
20. Denarius (C. MAIANI.), *c.* 180 B.C.

PLATE X (pp. 31 ff., 40 ff., 56 ff.).

1. Denarius (P. CALP.), *c.* 145 B.C.
2. Denarius (CARB.), *c.* 145 B.C.

3. Denarius (C.F.L.R.Q.M.), *c.* 135 B.C.
4. Denarius (CN. DOMIT.), *c.* 130 B.C.
5. Denarius (M. CIPI. M.F.), *c.* 120 B.C.
6. Denarius (L. CAESI.), *c.* 110 B.C.
7. Denarius (L. IVLI L.F.), *c.* 105 B.C.
8. Denarius (C. MALL.), *c.* 99 B.C.
9. Aureus (L. MANLI. PROQ.—L. SVLLA IMP.), *c.* 81 B.C.
10. Aureus (L. SVLLA IMPER. ITERV.), *c.* 83 B.C.
11. Denarius (Q.), *c.* 81 B.C.
12. Denarius (C. ANNI. T.F.T.N. PRO COS. EX S.C.—L. FABI. L. F. HISP. Q.), *c.* 81 B.C.
13. Denarius (L. TORQUAT. IIIVIR), *c.* 70 B.C.
14. Denarius (Q. SICINIVS IIIVIR), *c.* 49 B.C.
15. Denarius (Q. METELL. PIVS SCIPIO IMP.), *c.* 46 B.C.
16. Denarius (MAG. PIVS IMP. ITER.—PRAEF. CLAS. ET ORAE MARIT. EX S.C.), *c.* 38 B.C.
17. Denarius (C. ANTONIVS M. F. PROCOS.), *c.* 43 B.C.
18. Aureus (C. CASSI. IMP.—LENTVLVS SPINT.), *c.* 43 B.C.
19. Denarius (C. CAESAR IIIVIR R.P.C.—Q. SALVIVS IMP. COS. DESG.), *c.* 40 B.C.
20. Denarius (M. ANTONIVS AVG. IMP. IIII. COS. TERT. IIIVIR R.P.C. —D. TVR.), *c.* 31 B.C.

PLATE XI (pp. 54 ff.).

1. Denarius (Victory crowning Dioscuri), *c.* 242 B.C.
2. Denarius (Dioscuri—griffin), *c.* 217 B.C.
3. Denarius (Diana in biga—Av.), *c.* 212 B.C.
4. Denarius (Dioscuri—Victory crowning Roma), *c.* 189 B.C. (?).
5. Denarius (Victory in biga—S. AFRA.), *c.* 170 B.C.
6. Denarius (Victory in biga—C. TAL.), *c.* 180 B.C.
7. Denarius (Juno in biga of goats—C. RENI.), *c.* 150 B.C.
8. Denarius (Juno (?) in quadriga—C. CVR. TRIGE.), *c.* 150 B.C.
9. Denarius (Hercules in biga of centaurs—M. AVRELI. COTA), *c.* 149 B.C.
10. Denarius (Dioscuri—L. IVLI.—XVI), *c.* 149 B.C.
11. Denarius (Victory in biga—C. VAL. C. F. FLAC.—XVI), *c.* 149 B.C.
12. Denarius (Corn-monument and statues—C. AVG.), *c.* 146 B.C.
13. Denarius (Apollo in quadriga—CN. BAEBI. Q.F. TAMPIL.), *c.* 146 B.C.
14. Denarius (Juno (?) in quadriga—C. CVR. F. TRIGE.), *c.* 140 B.C.
15. Denarius (Jupiter in quadriga—L. ANTES. GRAG.), *c.* 140 B.C.
16. Denarius (Sol in quadriga—M. ABVRI. M. F. GEM.), *c.* 134 B.C.
17. Denarius (Venus, crowned by Cupid, in biga—SEX. IVLI. L. F. CAESAR), *c.* 138 B.C.
18. Denarius (Victory in biga—corn-ear—T. CLOVLI.), *c.* 130 B.C.
19. Denarius (Pax in biga—elephant's head), *c.* 123 B.C.
20. Denarius (Corn-monument and statues—TI. MINVCI. C. F. AVGV-RINI.), *c.* 123 B.C.

PLATE XII (pp. 52 ff.).

1. Sextans (Uncial standard—Victory above prow), *c.* 217 B.C.
2. As (Uncial standard—Victory crowning trophy—CN. BLASIO CN. F.), *c.* 110 B.C.
3. Quadrans (Uncial standard—Club in wreath—L. OPEIMI.), *c.* 136 B.C.
4. As (Semuncial standard — Victory on prow—L. PISO FRVGI.), *c.* 90 B.C.
5. As (Semuncial standard—Numa Pompilius and Ancus Marcius— prows and column—C. CENSO.), *c.* 88 B.C.
6. As (Semuncial standard—triple prow—C. PANSA), *c.* 87 B.C.
7. Quadrans (Semuncial standard—rudder and anchor—L. PISO), *c.* 90 B.C.
8. Dupondius (?), (Crocodile—rostrum—CRAS.), *c.* 31 B.C.
9. As (?), (Apollo—fasces—CRA.), *c.* 31 B.C.

PLATE XIII (pp. 59 ff.).

1. Denarius (Apollo—C. PISO L. F. FRVGI), *c.* 66 B.C.
2. Denarius (Apollo—M. METELLVS Q.F.), *c.* 81 B.C.
3. Denarius (Bacchus (Liber)—Libera—L. CASSI. Q.F.), *c.* 80 B.C.
4. Denarius (Ceres—L. CASSI. CAEICIAN.), *c.* 98 B.C.
5. Denarius (Cybele—C. FABI. C.F.), *c.* 108 B.C.
6. Aureus (Cybele—C. NORBANVS L. CESTIVS), *c.* 44 B.C.
7. Denarius (Diana—TI. CLAVD. TI. F. AP. N.), *c.* 78 B.C.
8. Denarius (Diana—C. POSTVMI. TA.), *c.* 75 B.C.
9. Denarius (Diana—C. HOSIDI. C. F. GETA IIIVIR.), *c.* 55 B.C.
10. Denarius (Dioscuri—M. FONTEI.), *c.* 110 B.C.
11. Denarius (Dioscuri—M. CORDIVS RVFVS), *c.* 46 B.C.
12. Denarius (Juno—L. RVBRI. DOS.), *c.* 88 B.C.
13. Denarius (Juno Sospita—L. THORIVS BALBVS), *c.* 110 B.C.
14. Denarius (Juno Sospita—L. ROSCI. FABATI), *c.* 57 B.C.
15. Denarius (Juno Moneta—L. PLAETORI. L.F.Q.S.C.), *c.* 84 B.C.
16. Victoriate (Jupiter—MAT.), *c.* 212 B.C.
17. Denarius (Jupiter—L. PROCILI. F.), *c.* 81 B.C.
18. Denarius (Jupiter—Q. POMPONI. RVFVS), *c.* 74 B.C.
19. Denarius (Jupiter—L. VALERIVS ACISCVLVS), *c.* 45 B.C.
20. Denarius (Jupiter (Veiovis)—GAR. VER. OGVL.), *c.* 87 B.C.

PLATE XIV (pp. 59 ff.).

1. Didrachm (Mars—club), *c.* 275 B.C.
2. Denarius (Mars—CN. LENTVL.), *c.* 87 B.C.
3. Denarius (Mars—P. SATRIENVS), *c.* 75 B.C.
4. Denarius (Mars—L. AXSIVS L. F. NASO S.C.), *c.* 75 B.C.
5. Denarius (Mars—ALBINVS BRVTI F.), *c.* 49 B.C.
6. Denarius (Medusa—L. COSSVTI. C. F. SABVLA), *c.* 70 B.C.
7. Denarius (Minerva (on rev.)—C. VIBIVS C. F.), *c.* 88 B.C.
8. Denarius (Neptune—L. LVCRETI. TRIO), *c.* 75 B.C.

9. Denarius (Silenus—D. SILANVS L. F.), *c.* 90 B.C.
10. Denarius (Pan-Silenus—C. VIBIVS C. F. PANSA), *c.* 89 B.C.
11. Denarius (Pan—C. VIBIVS C. F. PANSA), *c.* 49 B.C.
12. Denarius (Priapus—Q. TITI.), *c.* 87 B.C.
13. Denarius (Roma—C. SCR.), *c.* 195 B.C.
14. Denarius (Roma—C. CVR. F. TRIGE.), *c.* 140 B.C.
15. Denarius (Roma—L. POST. ALB.), *c.* 138 B.C.
16. Denarius (Roma—C. POBLICI. Q.F.), *c.* 80 B.C.
17. Aureus (Roma—C. VIBIVS VARVS), *c.* 43 B.C.
18. Denarius (Sol—M'. AQVIL.), *c.* 108 B.C.
19. Denarius (Venus—L. CENSORIN. P. CREPVS. C. LIMETAN.), *c.* 86 B.C.
20. Denarius (Vesta—Q. CASSIVS), *c.* 58 B.C.

PLATE XV (pp. 67 ff.).

1. Denarius (Bonus Eventus—LIBO), *c.* 55 B.C.
2. Denarius (Concordia—L. MUSSIDIVS LONGVS), *c.* 42 B.C.
3. Quinarius (Felicitas—PALIKANVS), *c.* 46 B.C.
4. Denarius (Genius P.R.—CN. LENT. Q. EX S.C.), *c.* 75 B.C.
5. Denarius (Libertas—Q. CASSIVS), *c.* 59 B.C.
6. Denarius (Fides—A. LICINIVS MACER), *c.* 48 B.C.
7. Aureus (Fortuna (rev.)—TI. SEMPRON. GRACCVS IIIIVIR Q.D.), *c.* 41 B.C.
8. Denarius (Honos et Virtus—KALENI—CORDI.), *c.* 55 B.C.
9. Denarius (Honos—PALIKANVS), *c.* 46 B.C.
10. Quinarius (Pax(s)—L. AEMILIVS BVCA IIIIVIR), *c.* 44 B.C.
11. Denarius (Pietas—M. HERENNI.), *c.* 108 B.C.
12. Denarius (Salus—D. SILANVS L.F.), *c.* 90 B.C.
13. Denarius (Triumpus—L. PAPIVS CELSVS IIIVIR), *c.* 46 B.C.
14. Denarius (Victory (rev.)—M. CATO), *c.* 100 B.C.
15. Denarius (Victory—L. VALERI. FLACCI), *c.* 108 B.C.
16. Aureus (Victory—L. PLANC. PR. VRB.), *c.* 45 B.C.
17. Aureus (Victory—C. NVMONIVS VAALA), *c.* 43 B.C.

PLATE XVI (pp. 71 ff.).

1. Denarius (Scipio Africanus—CN. BLASIO CN. F.), *c.* 108 B.C.
2. Denarius (Philip V. of Macedon—L. PHILIPPVS), *c.* 115 B.C.
3. Denarius (Jugurtha—FAVSTVS), *c.* 61 B.C.
4. Denarius (C. Coelius Caldus, consul—CALDVS), *c.* 60 B.C.
5. Denarius (Brutus—Ahala—BRVTVS (?)), *c.* 59 B.C.
6. Denarius (Marcellus—MARCELLINVS), *c.* 45 B.C. (?).
7. Denarius (Numonius Vaala (?)—C. NVMONIVS VAALA), *c.* 43 B.C.
8. Aureus (Sex. Pompey, Cn. Pompeius Magnus and Cn. Pompeius iun. MAG. PIVS IMP. ITER, etc.), *c.* 38 B.C.
9. Denarius (Cn. Pompeius Magnus—M. MINAT. SABIN. PR. Q.), *c.* 46 B.C.
10. Denarius (L. Regulus the praetor—L. REGVLVS), *c.* 42 B.C.
11. Denarius (Dog—C. ANTESTI.), *c.* 155 B.C.

12. Denarius (Faustulus, she-wolf and twins—Sex. Pomp. Fostlvs.),
    c. 145 B.C.
13. Denarius (Macedonian shield—T.Q.), c. 123 B.C.
14. Denarius (Mars and Nerio—Cn. Gel.), c. 146 B.C.
15. Denarius (Macedonian shield—M. Metellvs Q.F.), c. 133 B.C.
16. Denarius (Perseus of Macedon (?)—Q. Pilipvs), c. 135 B.C.
17. Denarius (Quirinus—N. Fabi. Pictor), c. 123 B.C.
18. Denarius (Ulysses and dog Argos—C. Mamil. Limetan.), c. 86 B.C.
19. Denarius (Acca Larentia (?)—P. Accoleivs Lariscolvs), c. 43 B.C.
20. Aureus (Venus Victrix—C. Vibivs Varvs), c. 42 B.C.

PLATE XVII (pp. 75 ff.).

1. Denarius (Roma, she-wolf and twins, birds—Anonymous), c. 115 B.C.
2. Denarius (Quirinus—Games of Ceres—C. Memmi. C.F.), c. 56 B.C.
3. Denarius (Numa Pompilius and Ancus Marcius—C. Censo.), c.
   87 B.C.
4. Denarius (Titius Tatius—Rape of Sabines—L. Titvri. Sabini), c.
   88 B.C.
5. Denarius (Purification after Sabine War—L. Mvssidivs Longvs),
   42 B.C.
6. Aureus (Brutus the first consul—M. Brvtvs—Costa Leg.), c. 42 B.C.
7. Denarius (Brutus the first consul—Brvtvs), c. 42 B.C.
8. Aureus (Tusculum—L. Servivs Rvfvs), c. 43 B.C.
9. Denarius (Lepidus, guardian of Ptolemy V.—M. Lepidvs), c. 67 B.C.
10. Denarius (Perseus and his sons—Pavllvs Lepidvs), c. 55 B.C.
11. Denarius (M. Lepidus, the warrior of fifteen—M. Lepidvs), c. 67 B.C.
12. Denarius (Games of Flora — Gladiators—C. Serveil. C.F.), c.
    60 B.C.
13. Denarius (M'. Aquillius, restorer of Sicily—M. Aqvil. M'.F.M'.N.
    IIIVir), c. 53 B.C.
14. Denarius (Bocchus surrendering Jugurtha to Sulla—Favstvs.),
    c. 61 B.C.
15. Denarius (Trophies of Cn. Pompeius Magnus—Favstvs), c. 61 B.C.
16. Denarius (Games of Victory founded—Sex. Noni. Svfenas.), c.
    60 B.C.
17. Denarius (Oath-Scene—C. Svlpici. C.F.), c. 101 B.C.
18. Denarius (" Provocatio "—P. Laeca), c. 110 B.C.
19. Denarius (Voting-scene—P. Nerva), c. 112 B.C.
20. Aureus (Vestal Virgin—C. Clodivs Vestalis), c. 43 B.C.

PLATE XVIII (pp. 77 ff.).

1. Denarius (Ahala and Sp. Maelius—Ti. Gracchus—C. Serveil.), c.
   133 B.C.
2. Denarius (Ahala and Sp. Maelius—Ti. Gracchus—C. Serveil.), c.
   81 B.C.
3. Denarius (War against Bituitus—Cn. Dom.), c. 123 B.C.

4. Denarius (Cn. Domitius in Gaul—C. METELLVS.), *c.* 122 B.C.
5. Denarius (Cimbrian War—C. SERVEILI. M.F.), *c.* 114 B.C.
6. Denarius (Victories in Illyricum (?)—M. FOVRI. L. F. PHILI), *c.* 115 B.C.
7. Denarius (War in Gaul (?)—L. TORQVA. EX S.C.), *c.* 125 B.C.
8. Denarius (Cimbrian War—Q. THERM. M.F.), *c.* 110 B.C.
9. Denarius (Triumph of Marius—LENT. MAR. F.), *c.* 100 B.C.
10. Denarius (Social War—Rebels—ITALIA.), *c.* 89 B.C.
11. Denarius (Social War—Rebels—VITELLIV), *c.* 89 B.C.
12. Denarius (Social War—Rebels—C. PAAPIVS C. F. MVTILVS.), *c.* 89 B.C.
13. Denarius (Social War—Despatch-rider—L. PISO L. F. FRVGI), *c.* 90 B.C.
14. Denarius (Largesse of curule aedile—P. FOVRIVS CRASSIPES AED. CVR.), *c.* 87 B.C.
15. Denarius (Marians and Italians—C. EGNATIVS CN. F. CN. N.), *c.* 83 B.C.
16. Denarius (Marians and Italians and Pirates (?)—C. EGNATIVS CN. F. CN. N.), *c.* 83 B.C.
17. Denarius (Marians and Italians—L. FARSVLEI. MENSOR.), *c.* 85 B.C.
18. Denarius (Sertorius in Spain—A. POST. A.F.S.N. ALBIN.), *c.* 79 B.C.
19. Denarius (Sertorius in Spain—A. POST. A.F.S.N. ALBIN.), *c.* 79 B.C.
20. Denarius (Sertorius and Pirates—Q. CREPER. M. F. ROCVS), *c.* 75 B.C.

PLATE XIX (pp. 81 ff.).

1. Denarius (Sale of slaves—Pirates—SER. SVLP.), *c.* 66 B.C.
2. Denarius (Surrender of Aretas—Capture of Privernum)—M. SCAVR. AED. CVR. EX S.C.—P. HYPSAEVS AED. CVR.), *c.* 58 B.C.
3. Denarius (Bacchius Iudaeus—A. PLAVTIVS AED. CVR. S.C.), *c.* 56 B.C.
4. Denarius (Consulship of Messalla—MESSAL. F.), *c.* 53 B.C.
5. Denarius (Pompeians at Ephesus—L. LENTVLVS MAR. COS.), *c.* 48 B.C.
6. Denarius (Caesar's 52nd birthday—CAESAR.), *c.* 49 B.C.
7. Aureus (Caesar's 4th year as dictator—CAES. DIC. QVAR. COS. QVINC.), 44 B.C.
8. Denarius (Cato at Utica—M. CATO PRO PR.), *c.* 46 B.C.
9. Denarius (Julius Caesar—P. SEPVLLIVS MACER.), 44 B.C.
10. Denarius (Julius Caesar dictator for life—L. BVCA.), 44 B.C.
11. Denarius (Cn. Pompeius jun. welcomed in Spain—M. MINAT. SABIN. PR. Q.), *c.* 45 B.C.
12. Denarius (Sex. Pompeius in Spain—SEX. MAGNVS IMP. (SAL.)), *c.* 45 B.C.
13. Denarius (Dream of Sulla—L. BVCA.), 44 B.C.
14. Aureus (M. Lepidus—L. MVSSIDIVS LONGVS), 42 B.C.
15. Denarius (Julius Caesar—L. MVSSIDIVS LONGVS), 42 B.C.
16. Denarius (Battle of Philippi—L. MVSSIDIVS LONGVS), 42 B.C.
17. Aureus (Brutus in the East—Q. CAEPIO BRVTVS IMP.—M. SERVEILIVS LEG.), *c.* 42 B.C.

18. Aureus (Cassius in the East—C. Cassei. Imp.—M. Serveilivs Leg.), *c.* 42 B.C.
19. Denarius (Murcus in Asia—-Mvrcvs Imp.), *c.* 42 B.C.
20. Denarius (Q. Labienus and the Parthians—Q. Labienvs Parthicvs), *c.* 40 B.C.

Plate XX (pp. 83 ff.).

1. Denarius (Antony in Gaul—M. Anto. Imp.), *c.* 43 B.C.
2. Denarius (Octavian in Italy—C. Caesar IIIVir R.P C.), *c.* 43 B.C.
3. Denarius (Antony in the East—M. Antonivs IIIVir R.P.C.), *c.* 41 B.C.
4. Denarius (Q. Cornuficius in Africa—Q. Cornvfici. Avgvr Imp.), *c.* 43 B.C.
5. Denarius (P. Ventidius Bassus in Italy—P. Ventidi. Pont. Imp.—M. Ant. IIIV. R.P.C.), 41 B.C.
6. Denarius (Antony and Octavian—M. Ant. Imp., etc.—M. Barbat. Q.P.), 41 B.C.
7. Denarius (Antony and L. Antonius—M. Ant. Imp., etc.—P. Nerva Proq.P.), 41 B.C.
8. Denarius (L. Antonius; " Pietas,"—Ant. Avg. Imp., etc.—Pietas Cos.), 41 B.C.
9. Denarius (Octavian in Gaul—M. Agrippa Cos. Desig.), *c.* 38 B.C.
10. Denarius (Victory of Sex. Pompeius—Q. Nasidivs), *c.* 36 B.C.
11. Denarius (Triumph of Metellus in Spain—P. Lent. P.F.L.N.), *c.* 77 B.C.
12. Aureus (Antony and Octavia—M. Antonivs M.F.M.N. Avgvr, etc.), *c.* 37 B.C.
13. Denarius (Antony's Armenian triumph—Antonivs Avgvr Cos. Des. Iter. Et. Tert), *c.* 35 B.C.
14. Denarius (Antony's Armenian triumph (?)—Ant. Avgvr IIIVir R.P.C.), *c.* 35 B.C.
15. Aureus (Antony and Antyllus—M. Antoni. M.F.M.N. Avg., etc.), *c.* 34 B.C.
16. Denarius (Antony and Cleopatra—Antoni. Armenia Devicta, etc.), *c.* 32 B.C.
17. Denarius (Actium (fleet and army)—praetorian cohorts—Ant. Avg. IIIVir R.P.C.), *c.* 32 B.C.
18. Denarius (Actium (fleet and army)—Leg. XVIII Libyca—Ant. Avg. IIIVir R.P.C.), *c.* 32 B.C.
19. Denarius (Actium (fleet and army)—Cohors speculatorum—Ant. Avg. IIIVir. R.P.C.), *c.* 32 B.C.
20. Denarius (Scarpus in Cyrene (?)—Leg. VIII.—-Scarpvs Imp.), *c.* 31 B.C.

Plate XXI (pp. 85 ff.).

1. Denarius (Thunderbolt and cornucopiae—Q. Max.), *c.* 133 B.C.
2. Denarius (Marsyas—L. Censor.), *c.* 88 B.C.

3. Denarius (Corn-ears, fasces, caduceus—C NORBANVS), *c.* 86 B.C.
4. Denarius (Knife, simpulum, axe—P. GALB. AED. CVR. S.C.), *c.* 70 B.C.
5. Denarius (Curule chair, etc.—Q. POMPEI. RVF.), *c.* 57 B.C.
6. Denarius (Curule chair—C. CONSIDIVS PAETVS), *c.* 45 B.C.
7. Aureus (Crescent and five stars—P. CLODIVS M.F.), 42 B.C.
8. Denarius (Wreath, sceptre and *sella castrensis*—M. ARRIVS SECVNDVS), *c.* 43 B.C.
9. Aureus (Clasped hands—C. VIBIVS VAARVS), 42 B.C.
10. Denarius (Curule chair and fasces—L. LIVINEIVS REGVLVS), 42 B.C.
11. Denarius (Caduceus and cornucopiae on globe—M. ANT. IMP. IIIVIR R.P.C.), *c.* 38 B.C.
12. Aureus (Star and prow—ANT. IMP.—CN. DOMIT. AHENOBARBVS IMP.), *c.* 40 B.C.
13. Quinarius (Clasped hands holding caduceus—M. ANTON. C. CAESAR IIIVIR R.P.C.), *c.* 40 B.C.
14. Denarius (Lituus, jug—thunderbolt, jug, caduceus—M. ANTON. IMP. . . . L. PLANCVS PROCOS.), *c.* 40 B.C.
15. Denarius (Temple of Jupiter Capitolinus—M. VOLTEI. M.F.), *c.* 80 B.C.
16. Denarius (Basilica Aemilia—M. LEPIDVS AIMILIA REF. S.C.), *c.* 67 B.C.
17. Denarius (Temple of Venus Erycina—C. CONSIDI NONIANI), *c.* 60 B.C.
18. Denarius (Villa Publica—P. FONTEIVS IIIVIR—T. DIDI. IMP. VIL. PVB.), *c.* 58 B.C.
19. Denarius (Rostra—PALIKANVS), *c.* 46 B.C.
20. Denarius (Temple of Jupiter Capitolinus—PETILLIVS CAPITOLINVS), *c.* 43 B.C. (?).

PLATE XXII (Introduction, p. 12, and n., pp. 100 f.).

1. Tetradrachm (Syracuse-Agathocles), *c.* 310-306 B.C.
2. Tetradrachm (Syracuse), *c.* 287-278 B.C.
3. Didrachm (Syracuse—Hiero (Gelo.)), *c.* 260 B.C.
4. Tetradrachm (Carthage), *c.* 330 B.C. (?).
5. Electrum stater (Carthage), 330-264 B.C.
6. Drachm (Massalia), *c.* 250 B.C.
7. Drachm (Rhoda), *c.* 200 B.C.
8. Drachm (Emporiae), *c.* 200 B.C.
9. Silver piece of five units (Etruria), *c.* 400 B.C.
10. Silver piece of five units (Etrurua), *c.* 300 B.C.
11. Silver piece of twenty units (Etruria), *c.* 260 B.C.
12. Silver piece of ten units (Etruria), *c.* 260 B.C.
13. Silver piece of five units (Etruria), *c.* 260 B.C.
14. Silver piece of two and a half units (Etruria), *c.* 260 B.C.

PLATE XXIII (pp. 99 ff.).

1. Didrachm (Metapontum), *c.* 310 B.C.
2. Drachm (?) (Bruttium), *c.* 275 B.C.

3. Hemidrachm (Bruttium), *c.* 275 B.C.
4. " Corinthian " stater (Syracuse), *c.* 275 B.C. (?).
5. Didrachm (Arpi), *c.* 275 B.C.
6. Didrachm (Cales), *c.* 275 B.C.
7. Didrachm (Naples), *c.* 280 B.C.
8. Didrachm (Nuceria), *c.* 275 B.C.
9. Didrachm (Suessa), *c.* 275 B.C.
10. Didrachm (Tarentum), *c.* 275 B.C.
11. Didrachm (Tarentum—" Campanian " coinage), *c.* 275 B.C.
12. Copper (Beneventum), *c.* 268 B.C.
13. Didrachm (Tarentum—reduced weight), *c.* 272 B.C.
14. Didrachm (Syracuse), *c.* 212 B.C.

PLATE XXIV (pp. 99 ff.).

1. Sextans (Capua), *c.* 215 B.C.
2. Copper (Canusium), *c.* 215 B.C.
3. Gold drachm (Capua), *c.* 215 B.C.
4. Semis (Syracuse), 2nd century B.C.
5. Semis (Panormus), 2nd-1st century B.C.
6. Denarius (Oscan money), 2nd century B.C.
7. As (?) (Valentia), *c.* 135 B.C.
8. As (?) (Saguntum), *c.* 135 B.C.
9. As (?) (Sardinia), *c.* 58 B.C. (or later).
10. Victoriate (Massalia), 2nd century B.C.
11. Quinarius (Cabellio), *c.* 40 B.C.
12. Quinarius (Lugdunum), 43 B.C.
13. Quinarius (Nemausus), *c.* 40 B.C.
14. Victoriate (Apollonia Illyrici), 2nd century B.C.
15. Denarius (Corcyra), 2nd-1st century B.C.

PLATE XXV (pp. 103 ff.).

1. Tetradrachm (Perseus of Macedon), *c.* 175 B.C.
2. Tetradrachm (Macedonia—first division), *c.* 160 B.C.
3. Tetradrachm (Macedonia—AESILLAS Q.), *c.* 93-92 B.C.
4. Gold stater (Philip III. of Macedon), *c.* 340 B.C.
5. Copper (Macedonia—Brutus ?), *c.* 42 B.C.
6. Tetradrachm, Cistophoric (Q. METELLVS PIVS.), *c.* 49-48 B.C.
7. Tetradrachm (Philip Epiphanes of Syria), 92-85 B.C.
8. Tetradrachm (Tyre), 63 B.C.
9. Tetradrachm (Athens), 2nd century B.C.
10. Drachm (Rhodes), 3rd-2nd century B.C.

PLATE XXVI (pp. 121 ff.).

1. Aureus (Augustus), *c.* A.D. 8.
2. Gold Quinarius (Augustus), *c.* 6 B.C.
3. Silver Quinarius (Augustus), *c.* 27 B.C.

4. Denarius (Tiberius), *c.* A.D. 24.
5. Aureus (Nero), *c.* A.D. 66.
6. Denarius (Nero), *c.* A.D. 66.
7. Silver Quinarius (Galba, struck by Vespasian), *c.* A.D. 71.
8. Double Aureus (Caracalla), A.D. 216.
9. Aureus (Caracalla), A.D. 217.
10. Antoninianus (Double denarius) (Caracalla), A.D. 217.
11. Antoninianus (Double denarius) (Balbinus), A.D. 238.
12. Denarius (Gordian III.), *c.* A.D. 242.
13. Aureus (Trajan Decius), *c.* A.D. 250.
14. Gold triens (Saloninus), *c.* A.D. 257.
15. Silver Quinarius (Trajan Decius), *c.* A.D. 250.

PLATE XXVII (pp. 126 ff.).

1. Antoninianus (Double denarius) (Gallienus), *c.* A.D. 258.
2. Antoninianus (Double denarius) (Gallienus), *c.* A.D. 267.
3. Aureus (Postumus), *c.* A.D. 260.
4. Aureus (Aurelian), A.D. 270-275.
5. Double sestertius (Aurelian), A.D. 270-275.
6. Sestertius (Aurelian), A.D. 270-275.
7. Half-sestertius (Probus), A.D. 276-282.
8. Aureus ($\frac{1}{70}$th lb.) (Diocletian), *c.* A.D. 286.
9. Eight denarius piece (Domitian), A.D. 85.
10. Seven-denarius piece (?) (Hadrian), *c.* A.D. 119.
11. Five-aureus piece (Gallienus), *c.* A.D. 265.

PLATE XXVIII (pp. 121 ff.).

1. Sestertius (Augustus), *c.* 22 B.C.
2. " Triumphal " Coin (Augustus), *c.* 7 B.C.
3. As (Tiberius), A.D. 22-23.
4. Quadrans (Augustus), *c.* 11 B.C.
5. As (orichalcum) (Nero), *c.* A.D. 65.
6. Semis (copper) (Nero), *c.* A.D. 65.
7. Semis (orichalcum) (Nero), *c.* A.D. 65.
8. Quadrans (orichalcum) (Nero), *c.* A.D. 65.
9. Semis (Trajan Decius), *c.* A.D. 250.
10. As (Probus), A.D. 276-282.
11. Quadrans (Probus), A.D. 276-282.

PLATE XXIX (pp. 127 ff.).

1. Double sestertius (Trajan Decius), *c.* A.D. 250.
2. Dupondius (Aurelian), A.D. 270-275.
3. Dupondius (Trajan Decius), *c.* A.D. 250.
4. Sestertius (Interregnum ?), A.D. 275.
5. Sestertius (Postumus), *c.* A.D. 260.
6. Billon " medallion " (Probus), A.D. 276-282.

KEY TO THE PLATES

PLATE XXX (pp. 109 ff., 139 ff.).

1. Aureus (Augustus—Rome), 8 B.C.
2. Denarius (Augustus—Emerita Lusitaniae), c. 23 B.C.
3. Denarius (Augustus—Emerita Lusitaniae), ? c. 22 B.C.
4. Denarius (Augustus—Caesaraugusta Tarraconensis ?), c. 18 B.C.
5. Aureus (Augustus—Colonia Patricia Baeticae ?), c. 18 B.C.
6. Denarius (Augustus—Asia), c. 30 B.C.
7. Aureus (Augustus—Pergamum), c. 28 B.C.
8. Denarius (Augustus—Samos ?), c. 21 B.C.
9. Aureus (Caligula—Lugdunum), A.D. 37-38.
10. Aureus (Caligula—Rome), A.D. 37-38.
11. Aureus (Nero—Rome), A.D. 56.
12. Denarius (Clodius Macer—Africa), A.D. 68.
13. Denarius (Civil Wars—Spain), A.D. 68.
14. Denarius (Civil Wars—Gaul), A.D. 68.
15. Denarius (Civil Wars—Upper Germany), A.D. 68 (end).
16. Aureus (Galba—Tarraco), A.D. 68.
17. Denarius (Galba—Narbo ?), A.D. 68.
18. Aureus (Vitellius—Tarraco), A.D. 69.

PLATE XXXI (pp. 115 ff., 139 ff.).

1. Aureus (Vespasian—Tarraco), A.D. 69.
2. Aureus (Vespasian—Lugdunum), A.D. 72.
3. Denarius (Vespasian—Aquileia ?), A.D. 69.
4. Denarius (Vespasian—Ephesus), A.D. 71.
5. Aureus (Titus—Tyre ?), A.D. 69.
6. Aureus (Vespasian and Titus—Antioch), A.D. 69.
7. Aureus (Vespasian—Antioch ?), A.D. 72.
8. Denarius (Domitian—O mint—Lycia ?), A.D. 76.
9. Aureus (Trajan—East ?), A.D. 117.
10. Denarius (Hadrian—Antioch ?), c A.D. 124.
11. Denarius (Hadrian—Asia), A.D. 138.
12. Aureus (L. Verus—Rome), A.D. 164.
13. Denarius (Pescennius Niger—Antioch), A.D. 193.
14. Aureus (Septimius Severus—Syria), A.D. 194.
15. Aureus (Septimius Severus—Antioch), A.D. 202.
16. Denarius (Albinus—Lugdunum), A.D. 195-196.
17. Aureus (Elagabalus—Syria), A.D. 218.
18. Antoninianus (Double denarius) (Gordian III—Viminacium), c. A.D. 244.
19. Antoninianus (Double denarius) (Philip I—Viminacium), A.D. 244-249.

PLATE XXXII (pp. 118 ff., 139 ff.).

1. Antoninianus (Double denarius) (Philip I—Antioch), A.D. 247.
2. Antoninianus (Double denarius) (Pacatian—Viminacium), A.D. 248-249.

3. Antoninianus (Double denarius) (Jotapian—Syria), *c.* A.D. 248.
4. Antoninianus (Double denarius) (Trebonianus Gallus—East), A.D. 251-253.
5. Antoninianus (Double denarius) (Valerian I—Lugdunum), *c.* A.D. 256.
6. Antoninianus (Double denarius) (Valerian I—Antioch), *c.* A.D. 256.
7. Antoninianus (Double denarius) (Gallienus—Mediolanum), *c.* A.D. 260.
8. Antoninianus (Double denarius) (Gallienus—Rome), *c.* A.D. 259.
9. Antoninianus (Double denarius) (Gallienus—Cyzicus ?), A.D. 266.
10. Antoninianus (Double denarius) (Quietus—East), A.D. 259-260.
11. Antoninianus (Double denarius) (Regalian—Carnuntum), *c.* A.D. 260.
12. Aureus (Postumus—Lugdunum), *c.* A.D. 259.
13. Antoninianus (Double denarius) (Postumus—Colonia Agrippina), *c.* A.D. 266.
14. Aureus (Victorinus—Mogontiacum ?), A.D. 268.
15. Aureus (Tetricus I—Lugdunum ?), A.D. 270-273.
16. Antoninianus (Double denarius) (Claudius II—Cyzicus), A.D. 268-270.

PLATE XXXIII (pp. 110 ff., 119 ff.).

1. Double sestertius (Aurelian—Ticinum), *c.* A.D. 274.
2. Double sestertius (Aurelian—Serdica), *c.* A.D. 270.
3. Double sestertius (Florian—Ticinum), A.D. 276.
4. Double sestertius (Probus—Rome), A.D. 276-282.
5. Aureus (Probus—Siscia), A.D. 276-282.
6. Aureus (Probus—Antioch), A.D. 276-282.
7. Double sestertius (Julian—Siscia), *c.* A.D. 283.
8. Double sestertius (Probus—Cyzicus), A.D. 276-282.
9. Double sestertius (Carus—Lugdunum), A.D. 282-283.
10. Double sestertius (Carausius—Rotomagus), *c.* A.D. 287.
11. Double sestertius (Carausius—London), *c.* A.D. 289.
12. Double sestertius (Carausius—Camulodunum ?), *c.* A.D. 289.
13. Quadrans (Augustus—Rome), *c.* 11 B.C.
14. Sestertius (Nero—Lugdunum), *c.* A.D. 66.

PLATE XXXIV (pp. 111 ff.).

1. Dupondius (Augustus—Lugdunum), *c.* A.D. 11.
2. Dupondius (Claudius I—Western imitation), A.D. 41-42.
3. Dupondius (Tiberius—Commagene), A.D. 20-21.
4. As (Vitellius—Tarraco), A.D. 69.
5. Sestertius (Vespasian—Tarraco), A.D. 71.
6. Dupondius (Vespasian—Commagene), A.D. 74.
7. Dupondius (Vespasian—Lugdunum), A.D. 77-78.
8. Sestertius (Domitian—Lugdunum), A.D. 81.

PLATE XXXV (pp. 146 ff.).

1. Denarius (Augustus—quadriga-insignia), c. 17 B.C.
2. Aureus (Augustus—doorway, laurels and oak-wreath), c. 12 B.C.
3. Aureus (Augustus—M. Agrippa), c. 13 B.C.
4. Aureus (Galba—oak-wreath), A.D. 68-69.
5. Denarius (Hadrian—adoption), A.D. 118.
6. Sestertius (Titus—" Pietas " group), A.D. 80.
7. Sestertius (Titus—" Providentia " group), A.D. 80.
8. Aureus (Hadrian—" rector orbis "), A.D. 121.
9. Aureus (Hadrian—" vota publica "), c. A.D. 135.
10. Aureus (Hadrian—adoption of Antoninus Pius), A.D. 138.
11. Aureus (Septimius Severus—Julia Domna and sons), c. A.D. 202.
12. Aureus (Julia Domna—" Mater Augg, etc."), c. A.D. 211.
13. Denarius (Plantilla—" Concordia "), c. A.D. 202.
14. Denarius (Diadumenian—" Princeps Iuventutis "), A D 217-218.
15. Antoninianus (Double denarius) (Philip I—Emperor with orb and sceptre), A.D. 245.
16. Aureus (Philip II—" Princeps Iuventutis "), c. A.D. 245.
17. Aureus (Postumus—" Aeternitas Aug."), c. A.D. 260.

PLATE XXXVI (pp. 148 ff.).

1. Denarius (Augustus—" sidus Iulium "), c. 17 B.C.
2. Denarius (Augustus—" consecration " of Agrippa), 12 B.C.
3. Aureus (Domitia—" divus Caesar "), c. A.D. 83.
4. Aureus (Vespasian, restored by Trajan—Jupiter, Mercury and star), c. A.D. 107.
5. Aureus (Nerva, restored by Trajan—biga of elephants), c. A.D. 107.
6. As (Augustus, restored by Titus—altar), A.D. 80.
7. Aureus (Hadrian—" divis parentibus "), c. A.D. 138.
8. Aureus (Sabina—Empress borne aloft by eagle), A.D. 138 (?).
9. Aureus (Faustina I—AETERNITAS, Fortuna), c. A.D. 141.
10. Aureus (Antoninus Pius—pyre), A.D. 161.
11. Antoninianus (Double sestertius) (Divus Augustus, struck by Trajan Decius), c. A.D. 251.
12. Antoninianus (Double sestertius) (Divus Marcus—struck by Trajan Decius), c. A.D. 251.
13. Aureus (Vespasian—Triumph), A.D. 71.
14. Aureus (Septimius Severus—" adventus "), A.D. 195-196.
15. Denarius (Caracalla—" adventus "), c. A.D. 202.
16. As (Hadrian—galley, FELICITATI AVG.), c. A.D. 132.
17. Aureus (Trajan—" profectio "), c. AD. 114.

PLATE XXXVII (pp. 151 ff.).

1. Sestertius (Nero—" congiarium "), c. A.D. 66.
2. Denarius (Hadrian—" liberalitas "), A.D. 121.

3. Sestertius (Galba, struck by Vespasian—" libertas restituta "), c. A.D. 71.
4. Sestertius (Trajan—Emperor as colonizer), c. A.D. 111.
5. Aureus (Civil Wars—" Genius P.R."), A.D. 68.
6. Sestertius (Galba, struck by Vespasian—"Senatus Pietati Augusti"), c. A.D. 71.
7. Dupondius (Antoninus Pius—" Genio Senatus "), A.D. 140-144.
8. As (Antoninus Pius—" vota suscepta dec. III "), A.D. 157-158.
9. As (Antoninus Pius—" primi decennalas "), A.D. 147-148.

PLATE XXXVIII (pp. 154 ff.).

1. Denarius (Galba—" Tres Galliae "), A.D. 68.
2. Aureus (Vespasian—" Iudaea "), A.D. 70.
3. Aureus (Domitian—" Germania Capta "), A.D. 86.
4. Denarius (Trajan—" Danuvius "), c. A.D. 107.
5. Denarius (Trajan—" Via Traiana "), c. A.D. 111.
6. Aureus (Hadrian—" Africa "), c. A.D. 134.
7. Denarius (Hadrian—" Asia "), c. A.D. 134.
8. Denarius (Hadrian—" Germania "), c. A.D. 134.
9. Aureus (Hadrian—" Hispania "), c. A.D. 134.
10. Aureus (Hadrian—" Nilus "), c. A.D. 134.
11. Aureus (Hadrian—" Tiberis "), c. A.D. 121.
12. Antoninianus (Double sestertius) (Trajan Decius—" Pannoniae "), c. A.D. 250.
13. Antoninianus (Double sestertius) (Trajan Decius—" Gen(ius) Illyrici "), c. A.D. 250.
14. Sestertius (Vespasian—Roma of the Seven Hills), A.D. 71.
15. As (Hadrian—Antioch ?), c. A.D. 126.
16. Sestertius (Hadrian—" Adventus Aug. Iudaeae "), c. A.D. 134.
17. Sestertius (Hadrian—" Britannia "), c. A.D. 134.
18. Sestertius (Hadrian—" Cappadocia "), c. A.D. 134.
19. Sestertius (L. Aelius Caesar—" Pannonia "), c. A.D. 137.

PLATE XXXIX (pp. 155 ff.).

1. Aureus (Claudius I—" praetor. recept."), A.D. 41-42.
2. Denarius (Clodius Macer—" leg. III. Aug."), A.D. 68.
3. Denarius (Civil Wars—" fides exercituum "), A.D. 68 (end).
4. Aureus (Nerva—" concordia exercituum "), A.D. 97.
5. Aureus (Hadrian—" disciplina Aug."), c. A.D. 135.
6. Aureus (Hadrian—Emperor in the field), c. A.D. 135.
7. Aureus (Commodus—" concordia militum "), A.D. 186.
8. Aureus (Septimius Severus—" leg. VIII Aug."), A.D. 193.
9. Antoninianus (Double sestertius) (Gallienus — " leg. III Ital."), c. A.D. 257.
10. Antoninianus (Double sestertius) (Gallienus—" leg. XI Cl."), c. A.D. 257.
11. Aureus (Victorinus—" leg. IIII Flavia p.f."), c. A.D. 268.

12. Double sestertius (Carausius—" leg. I. Min."), *c.* A.D. 287.
13. Sestertius (Nero—" decursio "), *c.* A.D. 66.
14. Sestertius (Domitian—the " sacramentum "), A.D. 85.
15. Sestertius (Hadrian—address to British Army), *c.* A.D. 134.
16. Sestertius (Hadrian—address to Spanish Army), *c.* A.D. 134.
17. Sestertius (Geta—Princes in the field), A.D. 210.

PLATE XL (pp. 159 ff.).

1. Denarius (Augustus—youthful Jupiter), *c.* 29 B.C.
2. Denarius (Augustus—Mars), *c.* 16 B.C.
3. Denarius (Augustus—Tarpeia), 18 B.C.
4. As (Nero—Apollo Citharoedus), *c.* A.D. 66.
5. Aureus (Vespasian—Neptune), A.D. 72.
6. Aureus (Titus—Venus Victrix), A.D. 80.
7. Aureus (Domitian—*pulvinar* of Jupiter), A.D. 81.
8. Aureus (Titus—*pulvinar* of Venus and the Divi ?), A.D. 86.
9. Aureus (Domitian—Minerva), A.D. 83.
10. Aureus (Domitian—Minerva), A.D. 92.
11. Aureus (Trajan—Jupiter protecting Emperor), A.D. 113.
12. Aureus (Hadrian—Hercules Gaditanus), A.D. 119.
13. Aureus (Hadrian—Roma Aeterna), *c.* A.D. 135.
14. Aureus (Hadrian—Jupiter Victor), *c.* A.D. 136.
15. Aureus (Sabina—Ceres), *c.* A.D. 138.
16. Aureus (Faustina II—Juno Lucina), *c.* A.D. 164.
17. Aureus (Commodus—Hercules Commodianus), A.D. 191.

PLATE XLI (pp. 159 ff., 163 ff.).

1. Denarius (Albinus—Minerva Pacifera), A.D. 194.
2. Aureus (Julia Domna—Cybele), *c.* A.D. 204.
3. Antoninianus (Double denarius) (Caracalla—Serapis), A.D. 216.
4. Aureus (Elagabalus—sacred stone of Emesa), *c.* A.D. 220.
5. Antoninianus (Double denarius) (Volusian—Apollo), A.D. 251-253.
6. Antoninianus (Double denarius) (Salonina—" Aug. in Pace "), *c.* A.D. 265.
7. Denarius (Postumus—Hercules), *c.* A.D. 266.
8. Denarius (Postumus—Hercules), *c.* A.D. 266.
9. Aureus (Probus—Sol.), A.D. 276-282.
10. As (Vespasian—Aequitas), A.D. 72.
11. Sestertius (Titus—Annona), A.D. 80.
12. Aureus (Faustina I—Aeternitis ?), *c.* A.D. 141.
13. Aureus (Vitellius—Clementia), A.D. 69.
14. Aureus (Vitellius—Concordia), A.D. 69.
15. Aureus (Claudius I—Constantia), A.D. 41.
16. Denarius (Julia Maesa—Fecunditas), A.D. 218-222.
17. Aureus (Laelian—Felicitas Temporum), *c.* A.D. 268.
18. Denarius (Titus—Bonus Eventus), *c.* A.D. 80.
19. Aureus (Marius—Sae(culi) Felicitas), *c.* A.D. 268.

19

PLATE XLII (pp. 163 ff.).

1. Denarius (Hadrian—Fides), *c.* A.D. 135.
2. Aureus (Hadrian—Fortuna—Spes), A.D. 137.
3. Aureus (Didia Clara—Hilaritas Temporum), A.D. 173.
4. Aureus (Augustus—M. Durmius—Honos), 18 B.C.
5. Denarius (Hadrian—Indulgentia), A.D. 132-134.
6. Denarius (Hadrian—Iustitia), A.D. 132-134.
7. Double sestertius (Tacitus—Laetitia), A.D. 275-276.
8. Denarius (Commodus—Liberalitas), A.D. 186.
9. Denarius (Galba—Libertas), A.D. 68.
10. Antoninianus (Double denarius) (Philip I.—Nobilitas), A.D. 248-249.
11. Denarius (Hadrian—Patientia), A.D. 138.
12. Denarius (Albinus—Pax), A.D. 195-196.
13. Denarius (Vespasian—Pax ?), A.D. 72.
14. Denarius (Hadrian—Pax Victrix), *c.* A.D. 119.
15. Denarius (Domitia—Pietas), *c.* A.D. 81.
16. Aureus (Antoninus Pius—Pietas), A.D. 138.
17. Antoninianus (Double denarius) (Claudius II—Providentia), A.D. 268-270.
18. Antoninianus (Double denarius) (Herennia Etruscilla—Pudicitia), *c.* A.D. 250.
19. Denarius (Severus Alexander—Salus), A.D. 222-235.
20. Antoninianus (Double denarius) (Gordian III—Securitas), A.D. 238-244.
21. Denarius (Hadrian—Tranquillitas), *c.* A.D. 132-134.
22. Antoninianus (Double denarius) (Trajan Decius—Ubertas), *c.* A.D. 250.
23. Denarius (Augustus—Victoria), *c.* 29 B.C.
24. Aureus (Otho—Victoria), A.D. 69.
25. Denarius (Hadrian—Victoria—Nemesis), *c.* A.D. 135.
26. As (Domitian—Virtus), A.D. 95-96.

PLATE XLIII (pp. 169 ff., pp. 172-174).

1. Aureus (Augustus—Conquest of Rhaetia), *c.* 14 B.C.
2. Aureus (Augustus—Conquest of Armenia), *c.* 19 B.C.
3. Aureus (Augustus—Conquest of Egypt), *c.* 28 B.C.
4. Aureus (Augustus—Recovery of captives and standards from Parthia), *c.* 16 B.C.
5. Denarius (Augustus—German returning standards), *c.* 12 B.C.
6. Didrachm (Caligula—Germanicus crowning Artaxias), *c.* A.D. 38.
7. Aureus (Claudius—Conquest of Britain), A.D. 46.
8. Didrachm (Nero—Armenian victories), *c.* A.D. 60.
9. Aureus (Vespasian—Vespasian as restorer), A.D. 72.
10. Denarius (Civil Wars—Gaul and Spain allied), A.D. 68.
11. Aureus (Domitian—Victory over Chatti), A.D. 85.
12. Aureus (Trajan—Trajan presenting Dacian to Senate), *c.* A.D. 110.
13. Aureus (Trajan—Assignment of kingdoms in East), A.D. 116.
14. Sestertius (Antoninus Pius—King given to Armenia), *c.* A.D. 143.

PLATE XLIV (pp. 169 ff., 174 ff.).

1. Aureus (L. Verus—Armenian victory), A.D. 163.
2. Aureus (Marcus Aurelius—Sarmatian victory), A.D. 175.
3. Aureus (Septimius Severus—Victories in Parthia, Arabia and Adiabene), c. A.D. 195.
4. Aureus (Septimius Severus—British victory), c. A.D. 211.
5. Denarius (Maximin I—German victory), c. A.D. 137.
6. Antoninianus (Double denarius) (Philip I—Carpic victory), c. A.D. 247.
7. Antoninianus (Double denarius) (Philip I—Peace established with Persia), c. A.D. 244.
8. Antoninianus (Double denarius) (Trajan Decius—German victory), c. A.D. 251.
9. Antoninianus (Double denarius) (Gallienus—" Gallienus and his army to Jupiter Victor "), c. A.D. 257.
10. Aureus (Gallienus—" Universal Peace "), c. A.D. 268.
11. Antoninianus (Double denarius) (Claudius II—Gothic victory), c. A.D. 269.
12. Aureus (Probus—" Pacator orbis "), A.D. 276-282.
13. Double sestertius (Probus—German victory), A.D. 276-282.
14. Silver coin (Carausius—Carausius welcomed in Britain), c. A.D. 287.

PLATE XLV (pp. 170 ff.).

1. Aureus (Augustus—Saecular Games), 16 B.C.
2. Aureus (Augustus—Saecular Games), c. 17 B.C.
3. Quadrans (Caligula—" remissa ducentesima "), A.D. 39-40.
4. As (Domitian—Saecular Games), A.D. 88.
5. Denarius (Domitian—Saecular Games), A.D. 88.
6. As (Domitian—Saecular Games), A.D. 88.
7. Sestertius (Domitian—Saecular Games), A.D. 88.
8. Sestertius (Nerva—" vehiculatione Italiae remissa "), A.D. 96-98.
9. Aureus (Trajan—" alimenta Italiae "), c. A.D. 107.
10. Sestertius (Hadrian—" libertas restituta,"), A.D. 119.
11. Aureus (Hadrian—" Golden Age "), c. A.D. 121.
12. Aureus (Hadrian—" Natalia Urbis "), A.D. 121.
13. Sestertius (Hadrian—Burning of old bonds), A.D. 119-120.
14. Aureus (Faustina I.—" Puellae Faustinianae "), c. A.D. 144.
15. Denarius (Septimius Severus—Saecular Games), A.D. 204.

PLATE XLVI (pp. 175 ff.).

1. Aureus (Augustus—capricorn), c 20 B.C.
2. Aureus (Augustus—cow), c. 20 B.C.
3. Aureus (Augustus—bull), c. 8 B.C.
4. Quadrans (Domitian—rhinoceros), c. A.D. 85.
5. Aureus (Julia Titi—peacock), c. A.D. 89.
6. Aureus (Divus Traianus—phoenix), A.D. 118.

7. Aureus (Hadrian—she-wolf and twins), *c.* A.D. 126.
8. As (Hadrian—griffin), *c.* A.D. 126.
9. Aureus (Faustina II.—dove), *c.* A.D. 164.
10. Antoninianus (Double denarius) (Otacilia Severa—hippopotamus), A.D. 248.
11. Antoninianus (Double denarius) (Philip I.—lion), A.D. 248.
12. Aureus (Postumus—lion), *c.* A.D. 258.
13. Denarius (Augustus—tiara, bow-case and quiver), *c.* 20 B.C.
14. As (Tiberius—rudder on globe), A.D. 36-37.
15. Aureus (Nero Drusus—vexillum, shields, spears), *c.* A.D. 42.
16. As (Galba, struck by Vespasian—aquila and standards on prows), *c.* A.D. 70.
17. Semis (Nero—table of games), *c.* A.D. 65.
18. Denarius (Civil Wars—clasped hands), A.D. 68.
19. Aureus (Vitellius—tripod, dolphin and raven), A.D. 69.
20. Aureus (Domitian—cornucopiae), A.D. 76.
21. Aureus (Vespasian—statue on rostral column), A.D. 79.
22. Aureus (Antoninus Pius—twins in cornuacopiae), *c.* A.D. 150.
23. Aureus (Caracalla—sacrificial implements), *c.* A.D. 197.
24. Antoninianus (Double denarius) (Herennius Etruscus—sacrificial implements), *c.* A.D. 250.
25. Antoninianus (Double denarius) (Philip I—column), A.D. 248.

PLATE XLVII (pp. 177 ff.).

1. Aureus (Augustus—temple of Mars Ultor), *c.* 18 B.C.
2. Aureus (Claudius I—praetorian camp), A.D. 41-42.
3. Aureus (Vespasian—temple of Vesta), *c.* A.D. 73.
4. Denarius (Domitian—temple of Cybele), *c.* A.D. 95.
5. Denarius (Domitian—temple of Serapis), *c.* A.D. 95.
6. Denarius (Domitian—temple of Jupiter), *c.* A.D. 95.
7. Aureus (Trajan—forum of Trajan), *c.* A.D. 112.
8. Sestertius (Nero—harbour of Ostia), *c.* A.D. 66.
9. As (Nero—altar of Peace), *c.* A.D. 66.
10. Sestertius (Nero—closed temple of Janus), *c.* A.D. 66.
11. Sestertius (Vespasian—temple of Jupiter Capitolinus restored), A.D. 78.
12. Tetradrachms, cistophoric (Domitian—temple of Jupiter Capitolinus restored), *c.* A.D. 85.
13. Sestertius (Titus—the Colosseum), A.D. 80.
14. Sestertius (Trajan—the Circus Maximus), *c.* A.D. 111.
15. Sestertius (Trajan—temple of Jupiter), *c.* A.D. 111.
16. Sestertius (Trajan—bridge), *c.* A.D. 111.

PLATE XLVIII (pp. 181 ff., 194 ff.).

1. *Aes* (Augustus—Emerita), *c.* 20 B.C.
2. *Aes* (Caligula—Caesaraugusta), *c.* A.D. 37.

3. *Aes* (Augustus and Agrippa—Nemausus), *c.* 20 B.C.
4. *Aes* (Tiberius—Paestum), *c.* A.D. 20.
5. *Aes* (Divus Augustus—Panormus), *c.* A.D. 20.
6. *Aes* (Nero—Babba), *c.* A.D. 65.
7. Drachm (Juba II—Mauretania), 25 B.C.-A.D. 23.
8. Tetradrachm, cistophoric (Augustus—Asia), *c.* 25 B.C.
9. Tetradrachm, cistophoric (Claudius I—Asia), *c.* A.D. 50.
10. Tetradrachm, cistophoric (Hadrian—Asia), *c.* A.D. 136.
11. Drachm (Antoninus Pius—Nicopolis), A.D. 138-161.
12. Drachm (Hadrian—Amisus), *c.* A.D. 131.

PLATE XLIX (pp. 181 ff., 194 ff.).

1. Drachm (Rhescuporis I and Tiberius—Pontus), A.D. 28.
2. Didrachm (Divus Augustus—Byzantium), *c.* A.D. 45.
3. Tetradrachm (Claudius I—Crete), *c.* A.D. 45.
4. Drachm (Tiberius—Hierapytna), A.D. 14-37.
5. Drachm (Trajan—Lycia), A.D. 98-117.
6. Tetradrachm (Hadrian—Tarsus), A.D. 117-138.
7. Tetradrachm (Vespasian—Cyprus), A.D. 69-79.
8. Drachm (Trajan—Cyrene ?), A.D. 98-117.
9. Didrachm (Nero—Caesarea Cappadociae), A.D. 54-68.
10. Tetradrachm (Trajan—Caesarea Cappadociae), A.D. 98-117.
11. Drachm (Septimius Severus—Caesarea Cappadociae), A.D. 193-211.
12. Tetradrachm (Nero—Antioch), A.D. 54-68.
13. Tetradrachm (Trajan—Tyre), A.D. 98-117.

PLATE L (pp. 181 ff., 194 ff.).

1. Tetradrachm (Caracalla—Heliopolis), A.D. 211-217.
2. Tetradrachm (Philip I—Antioch), A.D. 244-249.
3. Tetradrachm (Nero—Alexandria), A.D. 54-68.
4. *Aes* (Augustus—Antioch), 27 B.C.-A.D. 14.
5. *Aes* (Antoninus Pius—Alexandria), A.D. 144-145.
6. *Aes* (Hadrian—Macedonia), A.D. 117-138.
7. *Aes* (Vespasian—Bithynia), A.D. 69-79.
8. *Aes* (Hostilian—Viminacium), *c.* A.D. 251.
9. *Aes* (Philip I—Dacia), A.D. 248-249.

PLATE LI. (pp. 202 ff.).

1. *Aes* (Erythrae—ΙΕΡΑ ΣΥΓΚΛΗΤΟΣ), 1st century A.D.
2. *Aes* (Chios—Homer), 1st century A.D.
3. *Aes* (Mytilene—Sappho), 1st century A.D.
4. *Aes* (Magnesia Lydiae—Cicero), 27 B.C.
5. *Aes* (Mytilene—Pancratidas and Dada), 1st century A.D.
6. *Aes* (Septimius Severus—Mylasa—Zeus Labrandeus), A.D. 193-211.
7. *Aes* (Otacilia Severa—Mastaura—the triple Hekate), A.D. 244-249.
8. *Aes* (Gordian III—Alia Phrygiae—Mên), A.D. 238-244.

9. *Aes* (Uncertain mint—C.P.—Divus Marcus Aurelius), *c.* A.D. 250 (?).
10. *Aes* (Philip I—Philippopolis Arabiae—Divus Marinus), A.D. 244-249.
11. *Aes* (Caracalla—Sestos—Hero and Leander), A.D. 211-217.
12. *Aes* (Trebonianus Gallus—Tyre—Dido building Carthage), A.D. 251-253.

PLATE LII (pp. 205 ff.).

1. *Aes* (Septimius Severus—Ilium—Hector and Patroclus), A.D. 193-211.
2. *Aes* (Philip I—Smyrna—dream of Alexander), A.D. 244-249.
3. *Aes* (Antoninus Pius—Aboniteichus—sacred snake), A.D. 138-161.
4. *Aes* (Claudius I—Philippi—Julius Caesar and Augustus), A.D. 42-54.
5. *Aes* (Trajan—Ephesus—" Parthia capta "), A.D. 98-117.
6. *Aes* (Gordian III—Edessa—Gordian III and Abgar X), A.D. 244-249.
7. *Aes* (Julia Domna—Tomi—shrine of legionary eagle), A.D. 193-211.
8. *Aes* (Commodus—Nicaea—group of athletes), A.D. 186-192.

PLATE LIII (pp. 210 ff.).

1. *Aes* (Gallienus—Synnada—wild-beast fight in arena), A.D. 253-268.
2. *Aes* (Augustus—Cnossus—labyrinth), 27 B.C.-A.D. 14.
3. *Aes* (Macrinus—Neapolis Samariae—Mt. Gerizim), A.D. 217-218.
4. *Aes* (Septimius Severus—Nicopolis Moesiae—city-gates), A.D. 193-211.
5. *Aes* (Athens—theatre of Dionysus), 1st century A.D.
6. *Aes* (Septimius Severus—Corinth—temple of Aphrodite on Acropolis), A.D. 193-211.
7. *Aes* (Augustus—Italica—" Genius populi Romani "), *c.* 20 B.C.
8. *Aes* (Tiberius—Bilbilis—wreath and magistrates' names), A.D. 14-37.
9. *Aes* (Tiberius—Romula—" Divus Augustus—Iulia Augusta genetrix orbis "), *c.* A.D. 20.
10. *Aes* (Tiberius—Tarraco—temple of " deus Augustus "), *c.* A.D. 20.

PLATE LIV (pp. 222 ff.).

1. Aureus (60 to lb.) (Diocletian—Thessalonica), *c.* A.D. 296.
2. Aureus (60 to lb.) (Galerius—Nicomedia), *c.* A.D. 308.
3. Tremissis (⅓rd aureus) (Licinius I—Treveri), *c.* A.D. 315.
4. Double solidus (Constantine I—Ticinum), *c.* A.D. 320.
5. Solidus (Constantine I—Treveri), *c.* A.D. 320.
6. Semissis (half-solidus) (Crispus—Treveri), *c.* A.D. 320.
7. Solidus (Constantius II—Antioch), *c.* A.D. 353.
8. Five-solidus piece (Honorius—Rome), *c.* A.D. 400.
9. Double solidus (Eugenius—Treveri), *c.* A.D. 393.
10. Semissis (Honoria—Rome), *c.* A.D. 430.
11. Tremissis (Julius Nepos—Rome), *c.* A.D. 473.
12. Solidus (Valentinian III—Rome), *c.* A.D. 450.

PLATE LV (pp. 222 ff.).

1. Argenteus (96 to lb.) (Diocletian—Rome), c. A.D. 296.
2. Half-argenteus (Constantine I—Treveri), c. A.D. 308.
3. Argenteus (Constantius II—Treveri), c. A.D. 340.
4. Miliarense (Constantius II—Sirmium), c. A.D. 340.
5. Miliarense (Valentinian I—Treveri), A.D. 364-375.
6. Four-argenteus piece (Constantine II—Siscia), c. A.D. 337.
7. Siliqua (Theodosius I—Treveri), A.D. 378-395.
8. Follis (Double sestertius) of 20 denarii (Constantius I—Siscia), A.D. 305-306.
9. Follis (Double sestertius) of 20 denarii (Diocletian—Treveri), A.D. 296-305.
10. Follis (Double sestertius) of 20 denarii (Galerius—Nicomedia), c. A.D. 308.
11. Follis (Double sestertius) of 20 denarii (Maximinus II—Treveri), c. A.D. 308.
12. Half-sestertius of 5 denarii (Maximian—Alexandria), A.D. 296-305.

PLATE LVI (pp. 222 ff.).

1. Follis (Double sestertius) of 20 denarii (Constantine I—Lugdunum), c. A.D. 308.
2. Two-denarius piece (Diocletian—Rome), A.D. 296-305.
3. Half-sestertius of 5 denarii (Maximian (after death)—Rome), c. A.D. 312.
4. Half-sestertius of 5 denarii (Maxentius—Rome), c. A.D. 308.
5. Half-sestertius of 5 denarii (Constantius I. Chlorus (after death)—Rome), c. A.D. 324.
6. Half-sestertius of 5 denarii (Constantine I.—Rome), c. A.D. 320.
7. Follis (Double sestertius) of 20 denarii (Constantine I—Treveri), c. A.D. 312.
8. Follis (Double sestertius) of 20 denarii (Constantine I—Treveri), c. A.D. 315.
9. Sestertius of 10 denarii (Licinius I—Nicomedia), c. A.D. 317.
10. Sestertius of 10 denarii (Constantine I—Treveri), c. A.D. 317.
11. Sestertius of 10 denarii (Constantine I—Treveri), c. A.D. 330.
12. Sestertius of 10 denarii (Constantine I—Treveri), c. A.D. 335.
13. Centenionalis (Constantius II—Treveri), c. A.D. 345.
14. Pecunia Maiorina (Magnentius—Ambianum), A.D. 350-353.

PLATE LVII (pp. 217 ff., 229 ff.).

1. Centenionalis (Constantius Gallus—Aquileia), A.D. 351-354.
2. Centenionalis (reduced) (Constantius Gallus—Aquileia), A.D. 351-354.
3. Pecunia Maiorina (Jovian—Antioch), A.D. 363-364.
4. Pecunia Maiorina (Julian II—Antioch), c. A.D. 361.

5. Centenionalis (Gratian—Antioch), *c.* A.D. 378.
6. Ten-denarius piece (?) (Valens—Rome), A.D. 364-378.
7. Ten-denarius piece (?) (Theodosius I—Antioch), A.D. 378-395.
8. Four-denarius piece (?) (Theodosius I—Antioch), A.D. 378-395.
9. Solidus (Magnus Maximus—Londinium—-Augusta), A.D. 383-388.
10. Aureus (Galerius—Treveri), *c.* A.D. 308.
11. Centenionalis (Magnentius—Ambianum), A.D. 350-353.
12. Follis (Double sestertius) of 20 denarii (Constantine I—Arles), *c.*
A.D. 312.

PLATE LVIII (pp. 219 ff.).

1. Follis (Double sestertius) of 20 denarii (Maxentius—Ostia), *c.* A.D.
308.
2. Solidus (Petronius Maximus—Ravenna), *c.* A.D. 456.
3. Solidus (Priscus Attalus—Rome), *c.* A.D. 410.
4. Solidus (Anthemius—Mediolanum), *c.* A.D. 468.
5. Sestertius of 10 denarii (Licinius I—Aquileia), *c.* A.D. 320.
6. Miliarense (Julian II—Sirmium), *c.* A.D. 361.
7. Argenteus (Maximian—Serdica), A.D. 296-305.
8. Ten-denarius piece (?) (Theodosius I—Thessalonica), A.D. 378-395.
9. Sestertius of 10 denarii (Constantine I—Constantinopolis), *c.* A.D.
330.
10. Aureus (Licinius I—Nicomedia), *c.* A.D. 312.
11. Follis (Double sestertius) of 20 denarii (Alexander—Carthage), *c.*
A.D. 308.
12. Follis (Double sestertius) of 20 denarii (Domitius Domitianus—
Alexandria), A.D. 296.
13. Sestertius of 10 denarii (?) (Anonymous—Antioch), *c.* A.D. 317 (?).

PLATE LIX (pp. 242 ff.).

1. Aureus (Severus—Serdica—" princeps iuventutis "), A.D. 305-306.
2. Follis (Double sestertius) of 20 denarii (Maxentius—Rome—" Con-
servatores urbis suae "), *c.* A.D. 308.
3. Follis (Double sestertius) of 20 denarii (Maxentius—Rome—" Fel.
process. cons. III Aug."), *c.* A.D. 308.
4. Follis (Double sestertius) of 20 denarii (Constantine I—Lugdunum
—" bono reipublicae natus "), *c.* A.D. 307.
5. Solidus and a half (Constantine I—Nicomedia—" Eques Romanus ")
c. A.D. 320.
6. Follis (Double sestertius) of 20 denarii (Constantine I—Rome—
" Liberator orbis "), *c.* A.D. 313.
7. Solidus (Constantine I—Treveri—" Felicitas reipublicae "), *c.* A.D.
320.
8. Solidus (Constantine I—Treveri—" Restitutor libertatis "), *c.* A.D.
320.

9. Sestertius of 10 denarii (Fausta—Alexandria—" Spes reipublicae "), *c.* A.D. 324.
10. Solidus (Crispus—Aquileia—" Princeps iuventutis "), *c.* A.D. 320.
11. Centenionalis (Constans—Treveri—" Fel. temp. reparatio "), *c.* A.D. 345.
12. Centenionalis (Constans—Lugdunum—" Fel. temp. reparatio "), *c.* A.D. 345.
13. Centenionalis (Constantius II—Rome—" Fel. temp. reparatio "), *c.* A.D. 345.
14. Solidus (Constantius II—Antioch—largesse), *c.* A.D. 350.
15. Miliarense (Constantius II—Sirmium—" Felicitas Romanorum "), *c.* A.D. 340.

PLATE LX (pp. 242 ff.).

1. Argenteus (Constantius II—Treveri—" pax Augustorum "), *c.* A.D. 340.
2. Sestertius of 10 denarii (Constantius II—Thessalonica—" Spes reipublicae "), *c.* A.D. 340.
3. Solidus (Vetranio—Siscia—" Salvator reipublicae "), A.D. 350.
4. Solidus (Procopius—Constantinople—" Securitas reipub."), A.D. 365.
5. Siliqua (Valentinian I—Arelate—" Restitutor orbis "), A.D. 364-375.
6. Solidus (Valentinian I—Thessalonica—" Restitutor reipublicae "), A.D. 364-375.
7. Miliarense (Valens—Siscia—" Gloria Romanorum "), A.D. 364-378.
8. Solidus (Valens—Antioch—" Salus reip."), A.D. 364-375.
9. Solidus (Gratian—Antioch—" Spes r.p."), *c.* A.D. 368.
10. Solidus (Theodosius I—Antioch—" Victoria Augg."), A.D. 378-395.
11. Centenionalis (Theodosius I—Sirmium—" Gloria Romanorum ") A.D. 378-395.
12. Ten-denarius piece (?) (Theodosius I—Cyzicus—" Gloria Romanorum "), A.D. 378-395.
13. Solidus (Honorius—Ravenna—" Victoria Augg."), *c.* A.D. 405.
14. Four-denarius piece (?) (Honorius—Constantinople—" Gloria Romanorum "), *c.* A.D. 406.
15. Centenionalis (Honorius—Nicomedia—" Gloria Romanorum "), *c.* A.D. 405.
16. Four-denarius piece (?) (Honorius—Antioch—" Gloria Romanorum "), *c.* A.D. 405.
17. Solidus (Eudoxia—Rome—" Salus reipublicae "), *c.* A.D. 437.
18. Aureus (Constantine I—Antioch—" Votis V. Multis X "), *c.* A.D. 311.

PLATE LXI (pp. 243 ff.).

1. Sestertius of 10 denarii (Crispus—Arelate—" Vot. X."), *c.* A.D. 325.
2. Siliqua (Constantius II—Arelate—" Votis XXX Multis XXXX "), *c.* A.D. 353.

19 *

3. Solidus (Honorius—Mediolanum—" Vota publica "), *c.* A.D. 400.
4. Solidus (Galla Placidia—Ravenna—" Vot. XX mult. XXX "), *c.* A.D. 427.
5. Solidus (Valentinian III—Rome—" Vot. XXX Mult. XXXX "), *c.* A.D. 455.
6. Follis (Double sestertius) of 20 denarii (Maximian—Carthage— " salvis Augg. et Caess. fel. Kart."), A.D. 296-305.
7. Argenteus (Constantius I—Carthage—Africa), *c.* A.D. 305.
8. Solidus (Constantine I—Treveri—Alamannia), *c.* A.D. 324.
9. Sestertius of 10 denarii (Hannibalianus—Constantinople—Bosphorus), *c.* A.D. 337.
10. Aureus (Maximian—Rome—" comitatus Augg."), A.D. 296-305.
11. Sestertius of 10 denarii (Constantine I—Constantinople—" Constantiniana Dafne "), *c.* A.D. 330.
12. Follis (Double sestertius) of 20 denarii (Galerius—Aquileia—" Virtus Augg. et Caess. nn."), A.D. 296-305.
13. Sestertius of 10 denarii (Constantine I—Thessalonica—" Virt. exerc."), *c.* A.D. 330.
14. Sestertius of 10 denarii (Constantine I—Siscia—" Virtus exercit."), *c.* A.D. 324.
15. Solidus (Julian II—Antioch—" Virtus exercitus Romanorum "), *c.* A.D. 363.
16. Miliarense (Constantius II—Arelate—standards), *c.* A.D. 340.

PLATE LXII (pp. 246 ff.).

1. Aureus (Constantine I—Aquileia—Dioscuri), *c.* A.D. 308.
2. Follis (Double sestertius) of 20 denarii (Maxentius—Ostia—Dioscuri, she-wolf and twins), *c.* A.D. 308.
3. Aureus (Maximian—Treveri—Hercules and hydra), A.D. 296-305.
4. Follis (Double sestertius) of 20 denarii (Constantius I—Siscia—Hercules), *c.* A.D. 305.
5. Sestertius of 10 denarii (Licinius I—Treveri—Jupiter on eagle's back), *c.* A.D. 320.
6. Aureus (Galerius—Siscia—Mars propugnator), *c.* A.D. 308.
7. Solidus (Constantine II—Treveri—Virtus exercitus Gall.), *c.* A.D. 337.
8. Follis (Double sestertius) of 20 denarii (Constantine I—Treveri—Mars Conservator), *c.* A.D. 312.
9. Follis (Double sestertius) of 20 denarii (Constantine I—Rome—Roma Aeterna), *c.* A.D. 312.
10. Siliqua (Valentinian II—Treveri—Urbs Roma), *c.* A.D. 380.
11. Pecunia Maior. (Valentinian II—Rome—Urbs Roma), *c.* A.D. 380.
12. Siliqua (Constantine III—Arles—Urbs Roma), *c.* A.D. 411.
13. Sestertius of 10 denarii (?) (Maximin II—Treveri—Sol Invictus Comes), *c.* A.D. 312.
14. Follis of 20 denarii (Double sestertius) (Maximin II—Alexandria—Sol Invictus), *c.* A.D. 310.

15. Follis of 20 denarii (Double sestertius) (Valeria—Alexandria—Venus Victrix), *c.* A.D. 308.
16. Ten-denarius piece ?) (Julian II (?)—Alexandria—Isis Faria-Anubis), *c.* A.D. 361.
17. Ten-denarius piece (?) (Julian II (?)—Alexandria—Deus Sarapis-Isis), *c.* A.D. 361.

PLATE LXIII (pp. 248 ff.).

1. Follis (Double sestertius) of 20 denarii (Constantius I—posthumous—Ticinum—altar), *c.* A.D. 306.
2. Follis (Double sestertius) of 20 denarii (Romulus, posthumous—Rome—temple), *c.* A.D. 310.
3. Half-sestertius of 5 denarii (?) (Maximian, posthumous—Rome—lion), *c.* A.D. 312.
4. Half-sestertius of 5 denarii (?) (Maximian, posthumous—Rome—eagle), *c.* A.D. 312.
5. Sestertius of 10 denarii (Constantine I, posthumous—Antioch—veiled figure), *c.* A.D. 337.
6. Sestertius of 10 denarii (Constantine I, posthumous—Constantinople—chariot), *c.* A.D. 337.
7. Sestertius of 10 denarii (Constantine I—Constantinople—labarum on serpent), *c.* A.D. 333.
8. Siliqua (Julian II—Arelate—star in wreath), *c.* A.D. 361.
9. Semissis (Valentinian III—Roma—⚹, Salus reipublicae), A.D. 425-455.
10. Half-siliqua (Anthemius—Mediolanum—⚹ in wreath), A.D. 467-472.
11. Four-denarius piece (Honorius—Cyzicus—+, Concordia Augg.), *c.* A.D. 400.
12. Solidus (Olybrius—Rome—Cross, SALVS MVNDI), A.D. 472.
13. Solidus (Valentinian II—Mediolanum—Roma), *c.* A.D. 390.
14. Follis (Double sestertius) of 20 denarii (Maximin II—Alexandria—Concordia), *c.* A.D. 308.
15. Aureus (Diocletian—Rome—Fata Victricia), A.D. 296-305.
16. Follis (Double sestertius) of 20 denarii (Galerius—Ticinum—Fides militum), A.D. 296-305.
17. Miliarense (Constantius II—Thessalonica—Gloria Exercitus), *c.* A.D. 340.
18. Follis (Double sestertius) of 20 denarii (Maximian—Treveri—Fortuna Redux), *c.* A.D. 296-305.

PLATE LXIV (pp. 250 ff.).

1. Sestertius of 10 denarii (Constantine I (?)—Constantinople—Populus Romanus), *c.* A.D. 335.
2. Solidus (Constantine I—Ticinum—Liberalitas XI), *c.* A.D. 324.
3. Aureus (Diocletian—Treveri—Pietas), A.D. 296-305.

4. Follis (Double sestertius) of 20 denarii (Diocletian—Ticinum—Sacra Moneta), A.D. 296-305.
5. Follis (Double sestertius) of 20 denarii (Diocletian—Ticinum—Providentia Deorum), A.D. 296-305.
6. Solidus (Helena—Ticinum—Securitas Reipublicae), c. A.D. 324.
7. Solidus (Constantine I—Treveri—Victory), c. A.D. 315.
8. Sestertius of 10 denarii (Constantine I—Londinium—two Victories), c. A.D. 324.
9. Sestertius of 10 denarii (Constantine I—Constantinople—Libertas Publica), c. A.D. 330.
10. Solidus (Constantius II—Thessalonica—two Victories), c. A.D. 340.
11. Solidus (Magnentius—Arelate—Victory and Libertas), A.D. 350-353.
12. Centenionalis (Magnentius—Lugdunum—two Victories), A.D. 350-353.
13. Solidus (Aelia Flaccilla — Constantinople — Salus Reipublicae), c. A.D. 390.
14. Solidus (Romulus Augustulus—Rome—Victory), A.D. 475-476.
15. Aureus (Maxentius—Ostia—she-wolf and twins), c. A.D. 308.
16. Centenionalis (Constantius II—Siscia—phoenix), c. A.D. 345.
17. Four-denarius piece (?) (Magnus Maximus — Arelate — gateway), A.D. 383-388.
18. Ten-denarius piece (?) (Theodosius I — Thessalonica — gateway), A.D. 378-395.
19. Four-denarius piece (?) (Valentinian III—Rome—gateway), A.D. 425-455.

PRINTED IN GREAT BRITAIN AT THE UNIVERSITY PRESS, ABERDEEN

PLATE I

DENOMINATIONS · ROMANO · CAMPANIAN · COINAGE

PLATE II

DENOMINATIONS - ROMANO - CAMPANIAN - COINAGE (1, 2),
EARLY REPUBLICAN
A/, AR, Æ (3-15)

PLATE III

1

DENOMINATIONS - LIBRAL

PLATE IV

DENOMINATIONS - SEMIS, TRIENS, QUADRANS

PLATE V

1

2

DENOMINATIONS - DUPONDIUS, SEMIS

PLATE VI

DENOMINATIONS - Æ (1-8, 14), DEXTANS, etc.,
Æ (9-11, 15), A/ (12, 13)

PLATE VII

MINT-OFFICIÀLS

PLATE VIII

MARKS OF CONTROL, etc. (1-10), FABRIC (11-15), ART (16-20)

PLATE IX

MINTS - c. 268-180 B. C.

PLATE X

MINTS - c. 130-31 B. C

PLATE XI

TYPES - SILVER - c. 242-123 B.C.

PLATE XII

TYPES - VARIATIONS OF TYPES ON AES

PLATE XIII

TYPES · RELIGIOUS · APOLLO · JUPITER

PLATE XIV

TYPES - RELIGIOUS - MARS - VESTA

PLATE XV

VIRTUES - BONUS EVENTUS - VICTORY

PLATE XVI

PORTRAITURE (1-10), FAMILY HISTORY (11-20)

PLATE XVII

TRADITIONAL HISTORY OF ROME (1-17)
PROVOCATIO (18), VOTING (19), VESTAL VIRGIN (20)

PLATE XVIII

CONTEMPORARY HISTORY - c. 133-75 B. C.

PLATE XIX

CONTEMPORARY HISTORY - c. 66-40 B. C.

PLATE XX

CONTEMPORARY HISTORY - c. 42-31 B. C.

PLATE XXI

INANIMATE OBJECTS (1-14), BUILDINGS (15-20)

PLATE XXII

CURRENCIES OF THE WEST IN RELATION TO THE EARLY ROMAN

PLATE XXV

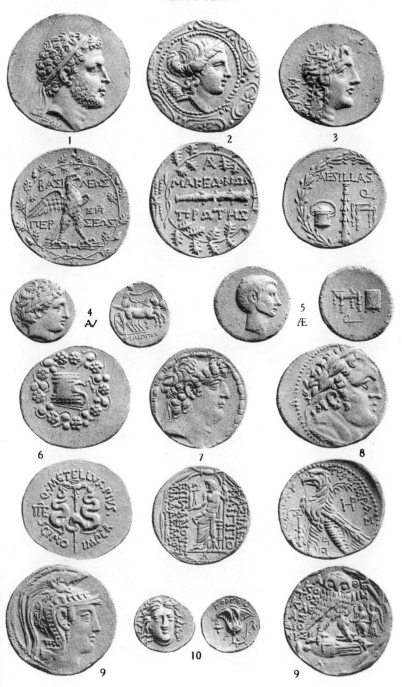

EASTERN CURRENCIES - 2ᴺᴰ TO 1ˢᵗ CENTURIES B.C.

PLATE XXVI

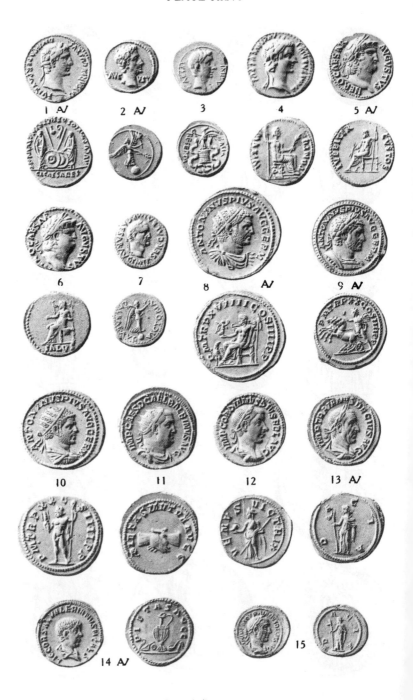

1 A/   2 A/   3   4   5 A/

6   7   8   A/   9 A/

10   11   12   13 A/

14 A/   15

DENOMINATIONS - A/ , AR

PLATE XXVII

DENOMINATIONS - A/, AR

PLATE XXVIII

DENOMINATIONS · AES

PLATE XXIX

DENOMINATIONS - AES. etc.

PLATE XXX

MINTS - AUGUSTUS TO VITELLIUS

PLATE XXXI

MINTS - VESPASIAN - PHILIP I

PLATE XXXII

MINTS · PHILIP I · CLAUDIUS II

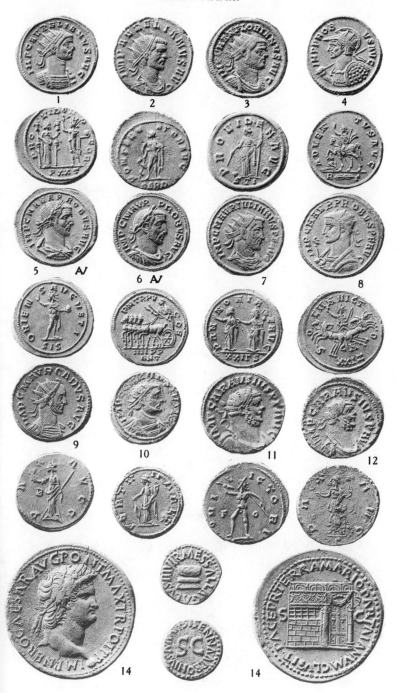

PLATE XXXIII

INTS - AURELIAN - CARAUSIUS (N, R) - AUGUSTUS - NERO (AES)

PLATE XXXIV

MINTS · AUGUSTUS · DOMITIAN (AES)

PLATE XXXV

TYPES - EMPEROR AND FAMILY

PLATE XXXVI

TYPES - EMPERORS - CONSECRATION, TRIUMPH, TRAVELS

PLATE XXXVII

TYPES - EMPERORS - LIBERALITIES, THE STATE, VOWS

PLATE XXXVIII

TYPES - PROVINCES, etc·

PLATE XXXIX

TYPES - EMPEROR AND ARMY

PLATE XL

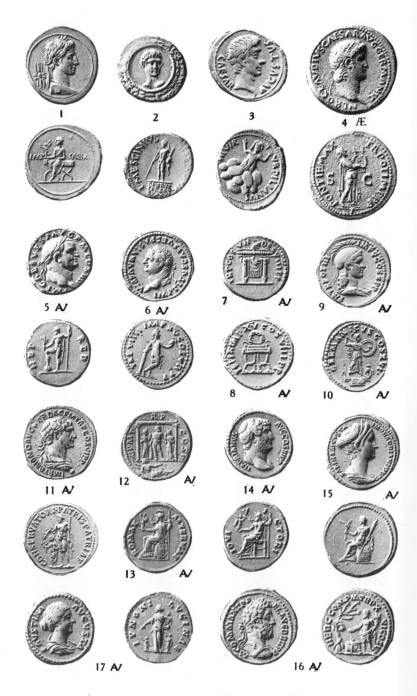

TYPES - RELIGIOUS - AUGUSTUS - COMMODUS

PLATE XLI

TYPES - RELIGIOUS - ALBINUS - PROBUS
PERSONIFICATIONS - AEQUITAS - FELICITAS

PLATE XLII

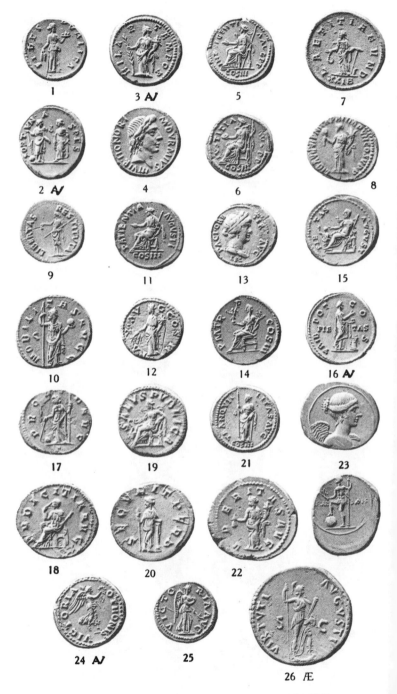

PLATE XLIII

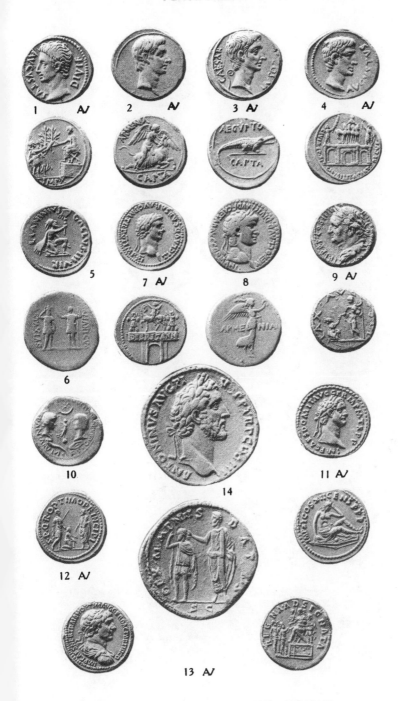

TYPES - HISTORICAL - AUGUSTUS - TRAJAN

PLATE XLIV

TYPES - HISTORICAL - L. VERUS - CARAUSIUS

PLATE XLV

HISTORY OF ROME AND ITALY

PLATE XLVI

TYPES - ANIMATE & INANIMATE

PLATE XLVII

TYPES - BUILDINGS

PLATE XLVIII

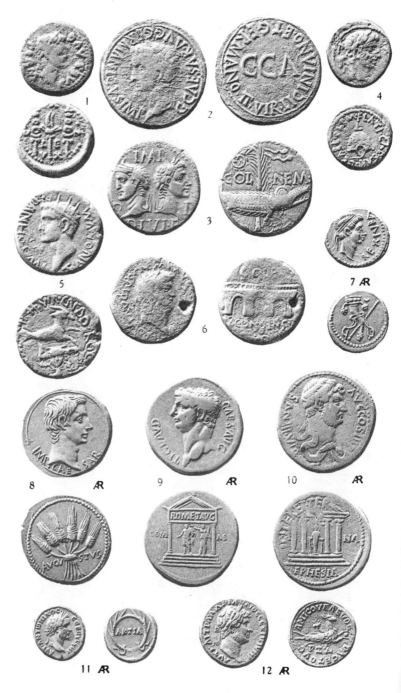

LOCAL AND PROVINCIAL COINAGE

PLATE XLIX

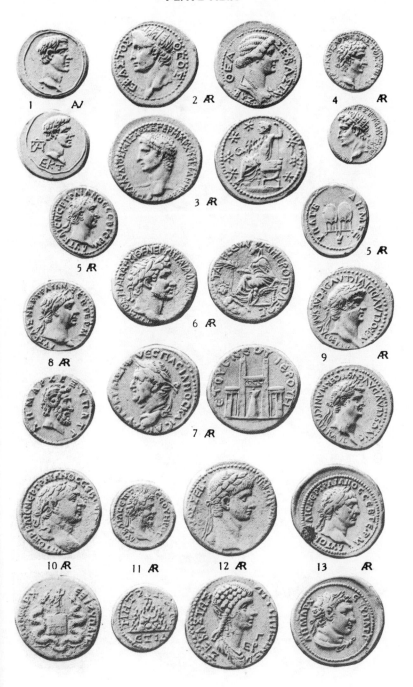

LOCAL AND PROVINCIAL COINAGE

PLATE L

PLATE LI

LOCAL AND PROVINCIAL COINAGE - TYPES

PLATE LII

LOCAL AND PROVINCIAL COINAGE - TYPES

PLATE LIII

LOCAL AND PROVINCIAL COINAGE - TYPES

PLATE LIV

DENOMINATIONS - A/

PLATE LV

DENOMINATIONS

PLATE LVI

1

2

3

4

5

6

7

8

9

10

11

12

13

14

DENOMINATIONS - SILVERED BRONZE

PLATE LVII

DENOMINATIONS - SILVERED BRONZE - MINTS

PLATE LVIII

PLATE LIX

TYPES RELATING TO EMPEROR

PLATE LX

TYPES RELATING TO EMPEROR

PLATE LXI

TYPES RELATING TO EMPEROR, PROVINCES, ARMY

PLATE LXII

RELIGIOUS TYPES

PLATE LXIII

RELIGIOUS TYPES, PERSONIFICATIONS

PLATE LXIV

TYPES   PERSONIFICATIONS, VARIOUS